PENGUIN BOOKS

# THE GREAT RAILWAY BAZAAR

Paul Theroux was born and educated in the United States. After graduating from university in 1963, he travelled to Italy and then Africa, where he worked as a teacher in Malawi and as a lecturer at Makerere University in Uganda. In 1968 he joined the University of Singapore and taught in the Department of English for three years. Throughout this time he was also publishing short stories and journalism, and wrote a large number of novels. In the early 1970s he moved with his wife and two children to Dorset, and then later to London. During his seventeen years' residence in Britain he wrote a number of successful travel books as well as a great deal of highly praised fiction.

Paul Theroux's acclaimed books include *Dark Star Safari*, *Riding the Iron Rooster*, *The Great Railway Bazaar*, *The Old Patagonian Express*, *Fresh Air Fiend* and *The Elephanta Suite*. *The Mosquito Coast* and *Dr Slaughter* have both been made into successful films. Paul Theroux is also a frequent contributor to magazines, and divides his time between Cape Cod and the Hawaiian islands.

D0177173

# The Great Railway Bazaar

*By Train Through Asia*

PAUL THEROUX

PENGUIN BOOKS

PENGUIN BOOKS

Published by the Penguin Group
Penguin Books Ltd, 80 Strand, London WC2R ORL, England
Penguin Group (USA) Inc., 375 Hudson Street, New York, New York 10014, USA
Penguin Group (Canada), 90 Eglinton Avenue East, Suite 700, Toronto, Ontario, Canada M4P 2Y3
(a division of Pearson Penguin Canada Inc.)
Penguin Ireland, 25 St Stephen's Green, Dublin 2, Ireland (a division of Penguin Books Ltd)
Penguin Group (Australia), 250 Camberwell Road,
Camberwell, Victoria 3124, Australia (a division of Pearson Australia Group Pty Ltd)
Penguin Books India Pvt Ltd, 11 Community Centre,
Panchsheel Park, New Delhi – 110 017, India
Penguin Group (NZ), 67 Apollo Drive, Rosedale, North Shore 0632, New Zealand
(a division of Pearson New Zealand Ltd)
Penguin Books (South Africa) (Pty) Ltd, 24 Sturdee Avenue,
Rosebank, Johannesburg 2196, South Africa

Penguin Books Ltd, Registered Offices: 80 Strand, London WC2R ORL, England

www.penguin.com

First published by Hamish Hamilton 1975
Published in Penguin Books 1977
Reissued in 2008

007

Copyright © Paul Theroux, 1975
All rights reserved

Portions of this book have appeared in the *Atlantic* and *Oui*

The moral right of the author has been asserted

Set in 11/13 pt Monotype Bembo
Typeset by Rowland Phototypesetting Ltd, Bury St Edmunds, Suffolk
Printed in England by Clays Ltd, St Ives plc

ISBN 978-0-141-03884-1

www.greenpenguin.co.uk

MIX
Paper from
responsible sources
FSC
www.fsc.org    FSC™ C018179

Penguin Books is committed to a sustainable
future for our business, our readers and our planet.
This book is made from Forest Stewardship
Council™ certified paper.

'To the legion of the lost ones, to the cohort of the damned,
To my brethren in their sorrow overseas . . .'

And to my brothers and sisters,
namely Eugene, Alexander, Ann-Marie,
Mary, Joseph, and Peter,
with love

# Contents

Marian had just caught the far-off sound of the train. She looked eagerly, and in a few moments saw it approaching. The front of the engine blackened nearer and nearer, coming on with a dread force and speed. A blinding rush, and there burst against the bridge a great volley of sunlit steam. Milvain and his companion ran to the opposite parapet, but already the whole train had emerged, and in a few seconds it had disappeared round a sharp curve. The leafy branches that grew out over the line swayed violently backwards and forwards in the perturbed air.

'If I were ten years younger,' said Jasper, laughing, 'I should say that was jolly! It inspirits me. It makes me eager to go back and plunge into the fight again.'

– George Gissing, *New Grub Street*

frseeeeeeeefronnnng train somewhere whistling the strength those engines have in them like big giants and the water rolling all over and out of them all sides like the end of Loves old sweet sonnnng the poor men that have to be out all the night from their wives and families in those roasting engines

– James Joyce, *Ulysses*

. . . the first condition of right thought is right sensation – the first condition of understanding a foreign country is to smell it . . .

– T. S. Eliot, 'Rudyard Kipling'

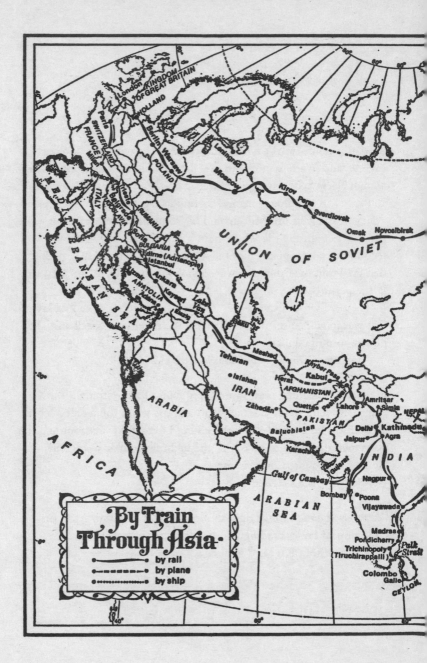

By Train Through Asia

• — • — • by rail
- - - - - - by plane
• • • • • • • by ship

ARCTIC CIRCLE

SOCIALIST REPUBLICS

Sea of
Okhotsk

Irkutsk
Chita
Ingoda
Khabarovsk

Sapporo
HOKKAIDO
Hakodate
Aomori

MANCHURIA

Vladivostok
Hakodate
Tsugaru Str.

MONGOLIA

Sea of
Japan

J A P A N
HONSHU
Tokyo
Yokohama
Kyoto
Osaka

Peking

PACIFIC

OCEAN

Shanghai

30°

C H I N A

BANGLADESH
Bhamo
Lashio
Maymyo
Calcutta
Mandalay
BURMA

Naung-Peng

NORTH
VIET
NAM
Hanoi

Hong Kong

PHILIPPINES

Bay of
Bengal

Vientiane

THAILAND
Bangkok

Hue
Danang

CAMBODIA
Phnom
Penh
Can Tho

Bien Hoa
Saigon
SOUTH
VIET NAM

South

China Sea

Rangoon

Penang
MALAYSIA
Kuala Lumpur
Singapore

0  100    400      750   1000 STATUTE
                              MILES
0   250  500  750        1500
                         KILOMETRES

EQUATOR

100°

120°

140°

Sam H. Bryant

# 1. The 15.30 – London to Paris

EVER since childhood, when I lived within earshot of the Boston and Maine, I have seldom heard a train go by and not wished I was on it. Those whistles sing bewitchment: railways are irresistible bazaars, snaking along perfectly level no matter what the landscape, improving your mood with speed, and never upsetting your drink. The train can reassure you in awful places – a far cry from the anxious sweats of doom aeroplanes inspire, or the nauseating gas-sickness of the long-distance bus, or the paralysis that afflicts the car passenger. If a train is large and comfortable you don't even need a destination; a corner seat is enough, and you can be one of those travellers who stay in motion, straddling the tracks, and never arrive or feel they ought to – like that lucky man who lives on Italian Railways because he is retired and has a free pass. Better to go first class than to arrive, or, as the English novelist Michael Frayn once rephrased McLuhan: 'the journey is the goal'. But I had chosen Asia, and when I remembered it was half a world away I was only glad.

Then Asia was out the window, and I was carried through it on these eastbound expresses marvelling as much at the bazaar within the train as the ones we whistled past. Anything is possible on a train: a great meal, a binge, a visit from card players, an intrigue, a good night's sleep, and strangers' monologues framed like Russian short stories. It was my intention to board every train that chugged into view from Victoria Station in London to Tokyo Central; to take the branch line to Simla, the spur through the Khyber Pass, and the chord line that links Indian Railways with those in Ceylon; the Mandalay Express, the Malaysian Golden Arrow, the locals in Vietnam, and the trains with bewitching names, the Orient Express, the North Star, the Trans-Siberian.

I sought trains; I found passengers.

The first was Duffill. I remember him because his name later became a verb – Molesworth's, then mine. He was just ahead of me in the line at Platform 7 at Victoria, 'Continental Departures'. He was old and his clothes were far too big for him, so he might have left in a hurry and grabbed the wrong clothes, or perhaps he'd just come out of the hospital. He walked treading his trouser cuffs to rags and carried many oddly shaped parcels wrapped in string and brown paper – more the luggage of an incautiously busy bomber than of an intrepid traveller. The tags were fluttering in the draught from the track, and each gave his name as *R. Duffill* and his address as *Splendid Palas Hotel, Istanbul*. We would be travelling together. A satirical widow in a severe veil might have been more welcome, and if her satchel was full of gin and an inheritance, so much the better. But there was no widow; there were hikers, returning Continentals with Harrods shopping bags, salesmen, French girls with sour friends, and grey-haired English couples who appeared to be embarking, with armloads of novels, on expensive literary adulteries. None would get farther than Ljubljana. Duffill was for Istanbul – I wondered what his excuse was. I was doing a bunk, myself. I hadn't nailed my colours to the mast; I had no job – no one would notice me falling silent, kissing my wife, and boarding the 15.30 alone.

The train was rumbling through Clapham. I decided that travel was flight and pursuit in equal parts, but by the time we had left the brick terraces and coal yards and the narrow back gardens of the South London suburbs and were passing Dulwich College's playing fields – children lazily exercising in neckties – I was tuned to the motion of the train and had forgotten the newspaper billboards I had been reading all morning: BABY KRISTEN: WOMAN TO BE CHARGED and PLAN TO FREE STAB

GIRL AGED NINE – none lettered NOVELIST VANISHES, and just as well. Then, past a row of semi-detached houses, we entered a tunnel, and after travelling a minute in complete darkness we were shot wonderfully into a new setting, open meadows, cows cropping grass, farmers haying in blue jackets. We had surfaced from London, a grey sodden city that lay underground. At Sevenoaks there was another tunnel, another glimpse of the pastoral, fields of pawing horses, some kneeling sheep, crows on an oasthouse, and a swift sight of a settlement of prefab houses out one window. Out the other window, a Jacobean farmhouse and more cows. That is England: the suburbs overlap the farms. At several level crossings the country lanes were choked with cars, backed up for a hundred yards. The train passengers were gloating vindictively at the traffic and seemed to be murmuring, 'Stop, you bitches!'

The sky was old. Schoolboys in dark blue blazers, carrying cricket bats and school bags, their socks falling down, were smirking on the platform at Tonbridge. We raced by them, taking their smirks away. We didn't stop, not even at the larger stations. These I contemplated from the dining car over a sloshing carton of tea, while Mr Duffill, similarly hunched, kept an eye on his parcels and stirred his tea with a doctor's tongue depressor. Past the hopfields that give Kent a Mediterranean tangle in September; past a gypsy camp, fourteen battered caravans, each one with its own indestructible pile of rubbish just outside the front door; past a farm and, forty feet away, the perimeter of a housing estate with lots of interesting clothes on the line: plus fours, long johns, snapping black brassieres, the pennants of bonnets and socks, all forming an elaborate message, like signal flags on the distressed convoy of those houses.

The fact that we didn't stop gave this English train an air of hurrying purpose. We sped to the coast for the Channel crossing. But it was a false drama. Duffill, at his pitching table, ordered a second cup of tea. The black train yards of Ashford loomed and tumbled past, and we were crossing the hummocky grass of

Romney Marsh, headed towards Folkestone. By then I had left England behind. So had the other passengers. I returned to my compartment to hear Italians raising their voices, perhaps deriving courage from the assurance that we were at the edge of England. Some Nigerians, who until that moment had been only a quartet of bobbing headgear – two Homburgs, a turban, and a beehive wig – became vocal in Yoruba, seeming to spell out each word they used, smacking their lips when they completed a syllable. Each passenger migrated to his own language, leaving the British muttering and averting their eyes.

'Oh, look,' said a woman, unfolding a handkerchief on her lap.

'It's so neat and orderly,' said the man at the window.

'Fresh flowers.' The woman gently bandaged her nose with the handkerchief and snorted on one side, then the other.

The man said, 'War Graves Commission takes care of them.'

'They do a lovely job.'

A small figure carrying paper parcels bound with string walked down the passage, his elbows thumping the corridor window. Duffill.

The Nigerian lady leaned over and read the station sign: 'Frockystoon.' Her mispronunciation was like sarcasm and she looked as unimpressed as Trollope's Lady Glencora ('there was nothing she wanted so much as to see Folkestone').

The wind, rising from the harbour, which was lead grey and pimpled with drizzle, blew into my eyes. I was squinting with the cold I had caught when the first September chill hit London and roused in me visions of palm trees and the rosy heat of Ceylon. That cold made leaving all the easier; leaving was a cure: 'Have you tried aspirin?' 'No, I think I'll go to India.' I carried my bags into the ferry and made for the bar. Two elderly men stood there. One was tapping a florin on the counter, trying to get the barman's attention.

'Reggie's got awfully small,' said the first man.

'Do you think so?' said the second.

'I'm afraid I do. Awfully small. His clothes don't fit him.'

'He was never a big man.'

'I know that. But have you seen him?'

'No. Godfrey said he'd been sick.'

'I'd say *very* sick.'

'Getting old, poor chap.'

'And awfully small.'

Duffill came over. He might have been the person under discussion. But he wasn't: the elderly gentlemen ignored him. Duffill had that uneasy look of a man who has left his parcels elsewhere, which is also the look of a man who thinks he's being followed. His oversized clothes made him seem frail. A mouse grey gaberdine coat slumped in folds from his shoulders, the cuffs so long, they reached to his fingertips and answered the length of his trampled trousers. He smelled of bread crusts. He still wore his tweed cap, and he too was fighting a cold. His shoes were interesting, the all-purpose brogans country people wear. Although I could not place his accent – he was asking the barman for cider – there was something else of the provinces about him, a stubborn frugality in his serviceable clothes, which is shabbiness in a Londoner's. He could tell you where he bought that cap and coat, and for how much, and how long those shoes had lasted. A few minutes later I passed by him in a corner of the lounge and saw that he had opened one of his parcels. A knife, a length of French bread, a tube of mustard, and discs of bright red salami were spread before him. Lost in thought, he slowly chewed his sandwich.

The station at Calais was dark, but the Paris Express was floodlit. I was comforted. Lady Glencora says to her friend, 'We can get to the Kurds, Alice, without getting into a packet again. That, to my way of thinking, is the great comfort of the Continent.' Well, then, to Paris, and the Orient Express, and the Kurds. I boarded and, finding my compartment oppressively full, went to the dining car for a drink. A waiter showed me to a table where a man and woman were tearing their bread rolls apart but not eating them. I tried to order wine. The waiters, hurrying back and forth with trays, ignored my pleading face. The train started up; I looked out the window, and when I turned back to the table I saw that I had been served with a piece of burned fish. The roll-shredding couple explained that I'd have to ask the wine waiter. I looked for him, was served the second course, then saw him and ordered.

'Angus was saying in *The Times* that he did research,' the man said. 'It just doesn't make sense.'

'I suppose Angus has to do research,' said the woman.

'Angus Wilson?' I said.

The man and woman looked at me. The woman was smiling, but the man gave me a rather unfriendly stare. He said, 'Graham Greene wouldn't have to do research.'

'Why not?' I said.

The man sighed. He said, 'He'd know it already.'

'I wish I could agree with you,' I said. 'But I read *As If By Magic* and I say to myself, "Now there's a real agronomist!" Then I read *The Honorary Consul* and the thirty-year-old doctor sounds an awful lot like a seventy-year-old novelist. Mind you, I think it's a good novel. I think you should read it. Wine?'

'No, thank you,' said the woman.

'Graham sent me a copy,' said the man. He spoke to the woman. '*Affectionately, Graham*. That's what he wrote. It's in my bag.'

'He's a lovely man,' said the woman. 'I always like seeing Graham.'

There was a long silence. The dining car rocked the cruets and sauce bottles, the dessert was served with coffee. I had finished my half-bottle of wine and was anxious for another, but the waiters were again busy, reeling past the tables with trays, collecting dirty plates.

'I love trains,' said the woman. 'Did you know the next carriage on is going to be attached to the Orient Express?'

'Yes,' I said. 'As a matter of fact – '

'Ridiculous,' said the man, addressing the small pencilled square of paper the waiter had given him. He loaded the saucer with money and led the woman away without another glance at me.

My own meal came to forty-five francs, which I estimated to be about ten dollars. I was horrified, but I had my small revenge. Back in my compartment I realized I had left my newspaper on the table in the dining car. I went back for it, but just as I put my hand on it, the waiter said, '*Qu'est-ce que vous faîtes?*'

'This is my paper,' I snapped.

'*C'est votre place, cela?*'

'Of course.'

'*Eh bien alors, qu'est-ce que vous avez mangé?*' He seemed to be enjoying the subtlety of his cross-examination.

I said, 'Burned fish. A tiny portion of roast beef. *Courgettes*, burned and soggy, cold potatoes, stale bread, and for this I was charged forty-five, I repeat, *forty-five* –'

He let me have my paper.

At the Gare du Nord my car was shunted on to a different engine. Duffill and I watched this being done from the platform and then we boarded. It took him a long time to heave himself up, and he panted with effort on the landing. He was still standing there, gasping, as we pulled out of the station for our twenty-minute trip to the Gare de Lyons to meet the rest of the Direct-Orient Express. It was after eleven, and most of the apartment blocks were in darkness. But in one bright window there was a dinner party ending, like a painting of a city interior, hung and illuminated in the shadowy gallery of rooftops and balconies. The train passed and printed the window on my eye: two men and two women around a table on which there were three wine bottles, the remains of a large meal, coffee cups, a raided bowl of fruit. All the props, and the men in shirt sleeves, spoke of amiable intimacy, the sad comedy of a reunion of friends. Jean and Marie had been away. Jean was smiling, preparing to clown, and had pulled one of those confounded French faces. He waved his hand back and forth and said, 'She got up on the table like a mad-woman and began shaking it at me like this. Incredible! I said to Marie, "The Picards will never believe this!" This is the truth. And then she —'

The train made its slow circuit of Paris, weaving among the dark buildings and shrieking *frseeeeeeeefronnnng* into the ears of sleeping women. The Gare de Lyons was alive, with that midnight glamour of bright lights and smoking engines, and across the gleaming tracks the ribbed canvas over one particular train turned it into a caterpillar about to set off and chew a path through France. On the platform arriving passengers were yawning, shambling with fatigue. The porters leaned on luggage carriers and watched people struggling with suitcases. Our car met, and coupled with, the rest of the Direct-Orient Express; that bump slid the compartment doors open and threw me forward into the lap of the lady opposite, surprising her from sleep.

## 2. The Direct-Orient Express

DUFFILL had put on a pair of glasses, wire-framed and with enough Scotch tape on the lenses to prevent his seeing the Blue Mosque. He assembled his parcels and, grunting, produced a suitcase, bound with a selection of leather and canvas belts as an added guarantee against it bursting open. A few cars down we met again to read the sign on the side of the wagon-lit: DIRECT—ORIENT and its itinerary, PARIS—LAUSANNE—MILANO — TRIESTE — ZAGREB — BEOGRAD — SOFIYA — ISTANBUL. We stood there, staring at this sign; Duffill worked his glasses like binoculars. Finally he said, 'I took this train in nineteen twenty-nine.'

It seemed to call for a reply, but by the time a reply occurred to me ('Judging from its condition, it was probably this very train!') Duffill had gathered up his parcels and his strapped suit-case and moved down the platform. It was a great train in 1929, and it goes without saying that the Orient Express is the most famous train in the world. Like the Trans-Siberian, it links Europe with Asia, which accounts for some of its romance. But it has also been hallowed by fiction: restless Lady Chatterley took it; so did Hercule Poirot and James Bond; Graham Greene sent some of his prowling unbelievers on it, even before he took it himself ('As I couldn't take a train to Istanbul the best I could do was buy a record of Honegger's Pacific 231,' Greene writes in the Introduction to *Stamboul Train*). The fictional source of the romance is *La Madone des Sleepings* (1925) by Maurice Dekobra. Dekobra's heroine, Lady Diana ('the type of woman who would have brought tears to the eyes of John Ruskin'), is completely sold on the Orient Express: 'I have a ticket for Constantinople. But I may step off at Vienna or Budapest. That depends

absolutely on chance or on the colour of the eyes of my neighbour in the compartment.' In the end I stopped wondering why
so many writers had used this train as a setting for criminal
intrigues, since in most respects the Orient Express really is
murder.

My compartment was a cramped two-berth closet with an
intruding ladder. I swung my suitcase in and, when I had done
this, there was no room for me. The conductor showed me how
to kick my suitcase under the lower berth. He hesitated, hoping
to be tipped.

'Anybody else in here?' It had not occurred to me that I
would have company; the conceit of the long-distance traveller
is the belief that he is going so far, he will be alone – inconceiv-
able that another person has the same good idea.

The conductor shrugged, perhaps yes, perhaps no. His vagueness made me withhold my tip. I took a stroll down the car: a
Japanese couple in a double couchette – and it was the first and
last time I saw them; an elderly American couple next to them;
a fat French mother breathing suspicion on her lovely daughter;
a Belgian girl of extraordinary size – well over six feet tall,
wearing enormous shoes – travelling with a chic French woman;
and (the door was shutting) either a nun or a plump diabolist.
At the far end of the car a man wearing a turtleneck, a seaman's
cap, and a monocle was setting up bottles on the windowsill;
three wine bottles, Perrier water, a broad-shouldered bottle of
gin – he was obviously going some distance.

Duffill was standing outside my compartment. He was out of
breath; he had had trouble finding the right car, he said, because
his French was rusty. He took a deep breath and slid off his
gabardine coat and hung that and his cap on the hook next to
mine.

'I'm up here,' he said, patting the upper berth. He was a
small man, but I noticed that as soon as he stepped into the
compartment he filled it.

'How far are you going?' I asked gamely, and even though

I knew his reply, when I heard it I cringed. I had planned on studying him from a little distance; I was counting on having the compartment to myself. This was unwelcome news. He saw I was taking it badly.

He said, 'I won't get in your way.' His parcels were on the floor. 'I just have to find a home for these.'

'I'll leave you to it,' I said. The others were in the corridor waiting for the train to start. The Americans rubbed the window until they realized the dirt was on the outside; the man with the monocle peered and drank; the French woman was saying '– Switzerland.'

'Istanbul,' said the Belgian girl. She had a broad face, which a large pair of glasses only complicated, and she was a head taller than I. 'My first time.'

'I am in Istanbul two years before,' said the French woman, wincing the way the French do before lapsing into their own language.

'What is it like?' asked the Belgian girl. She waited. I waited. She helped the woman. 'Very nice?'

The French woman smiled at each of us. She shook her head, and said, '*Très sale.*'

'But pretty? Old? Churches?' The Belgian girl was trying hard.

'*Sale.*' Why was she smiling?

'I am going to Izmir, Cappadocia, and –'

The French woman clucked and said, '*Sale, sale, sale.*' She went into her compartment. The Belgian girl made a face and winked at me.

The train had started to move, and at the end of the car the man in the seaman's cap was braced at his door, drinking and watching our progress. After several minutes the rest of the passengers went into their compartments – from my own I heard the smashing of paper parcels being stuffed into corners. This left the drinker, whom I had started to think of as the Captain, and me alone in the passage. He looked my way and said, 'Istanbul?'

'Yes.'

'Have a drink.'

'I've been drinking all day,' I said. 'Do you have any mineral water?'

'I do,' he said. 'But I keep it for my teeth. I never touch water on trains. Have a real drink. Go on. What will it be?'

'A beer would be nice.'

'I never drink beer,' he said. 'Have some of this.' He showed me his glass and then went to his shelf and poured me some, saying, 'It's a very drinkable Chablis, not at all chalky – the ones they export often are, you know.'

We clinked glasses. The train was now moving fast.

'Istanbul.'

'Istanbul! Right you are.'

His name was Molesworth, but he said it so distinctly that the first time I heard it I thought it was a double-barrelled name. There was something military in his posture and the promptness of his speech, and at the same time this flair could have been an actor's. He was in his indignant late fifties, and I could see him cutting a junior officer at the club – either at Aldershot or in the third act of a Rattigan play. The small glass disc he wore around his neck on a chain was not, I saw, a monocle, but rather a magnifying glass. He had used it to find the bottle of Chablis.

'I'm an actors' agent,' he said. 'I've got my own firm in London. It's a smallish firm, but we do all right. We always have more than we can handle.'

'Any actors I might know?'

He named several famous actors.

I said, 'I thought you might be army.'

'*Did* you?' He said that he had been in the Indian army – Poona, Simla, Madras – and his duties there were of a theatrical nature, organizing shows for the troops. He had arranged Noël Coward's tour of India in 1946. He had loved the army and he said that there were many Indians who were so well bred you could treat them as absolute equals – indeed, talking to them you would hardly know you were talking to Indians.

'I knew a British officer who was in Simla in the forties,' I said. 'I met him in Kenya. His nickname was "Bunny".'

Molesworth thought a moment, then said, 'Well, I knew several Bunnys.'

We talked about Indian trains. Molesworth said they were magnificent. 'They have showers, and there's always a little man who brings you what you need. At mealtime they telegraph ahead to the next station for hampers. Oh, you'll like it.'

Duffill put his head out the door and said, 'I think I'll go to bed now.'

'He's your chap, is he?' said Molesworth. He surveyed the car. 'This train isn't what it was. Pity. It used to be one of the best, a *train de luxe* – royalty took it. Now, I'm not sure about this, but I don't think we have a dining car, which is going to be a terrible bore if it's true. Have you got a hamper?'

I said I hadn't, though I had been advised to bring one.

'That was good advice,' Molesworth said. 'I don't have a hamper myself, but then I don't eat much. I like the *thought* of food, but I much prefer drinking. How do you like your Chablis? Will you have more?' He inserted his eyeglass and found the bottle and, pouring, said, 'These French wines take an awful lot of beating.'

A half hour later I went into the compartment. The lights were blazing, and in his upper berth Duffill was sleeping; his face turned up to the overhead light gave him a grey corpselike look, and his pyjamas were buttoned to his neck. The expression on his face was one of agony; his features were fixed and his head moved as the train did. I turned out the lights and crawled into my berth. But I couldn't sleep, at first; my cold and all that I'd drunk – the fatigue itself – kept me awake. And then something else alarmed me: it was a glowing circle, the luminous dial of Duffill's watch, for his arm had slipped down and was swinging back and forth as the train rocked, moving this glowing green dial past my face like a pendulum.

Then the dial disappeared. I heard Duffill climbing down the ladder, groaning on each rung. The dial moved sideways to the sink, and then the light came on. I rolled over against the wall and heard the clunk of Duffill dislodging the chamber pot from the cupboard under the sink; I waited, and after a long moment a warbling burble began, changing in pitch as the pot filled. There was a splash, like a sigh, and the light went out and the ladder creaked. Duffill groaned one last time and I slept.

In the morning Duffill was gone. I lay in bed and worked the window curtain up with my foot; after a few inches it shot up on its roller, revealing a sunny mountainside, the Alps dappled with light and moving past the window. It was the first time I had seen the sun for days, this first morning on the train, and I think this is the place to say that it continued to shine for the next two months. I travelled under clear skies all the way to southern India, and only then, two months later, did I see rain again, the late monsoon of Madras.

At Vevey, I thought of Daisy and restored myself with a glass of fruit salts, and at Montreux felt well enough to shave. Duffill came back in time to admire my rechargeable electric razor. He said he used a blade and on trains always cut himself to pieces. He showed me a nick on his throat, then told me his name. He'd be spending two months in Turkey, but he didn't say what he'd be doing. In the bright sunlight he looked much older than he had in the greyness of Victoria. I guessed he was about seventy. But he was not in the least spry, and I could not imagine why anyone except a fleeing embezzler would spend two months in Turkey.

He looked out at the Alps. He said. 'They say if the Swiss had designed these mountains, um, they'd be rather flatter.'

I decided to have breakfast, but I walked to both ends of the Direct-Orient and saw no dining car — nothing except more sleeping cars and people dozing in their second-class seats. On my way back to Car 99 I was followed by three Swiss boys who, at each compartment door, tried the handle; if it responded they slid the door open and looked in, presumably at people dressing or lounging in bed. Then the boys called out, '*Pardon, Madame!*' '*Pardon, Monsieur!*' as the occupants hastily covered themselves. As these ingenious voyeurs reached my sleeping car they were in high spirits, hooting and shrieking, but it was always with the greatest politeness that they said, '*Pardon, Madame!*' once they got a door open. They gave a final yell and disappeared.

The door to the Americans' compartment opened. The man was out first, swinging the knot of his tie, and then the woman, feebly balancing on a cane, tottered out and followed after, bumping the windows as she went. The Alps were rising, and in the sheerest places wide-roofed chalets were planted, as close to the ground as mushrooms and clustered in the same way at various distances from gravity-defying churches. Many of the valleys were dark, the sun showing only farther up on cliff faces and at the summits. At ground level the train passed fruit farms and clean villages and Swiss cycling in kerchiefs, calendar scenes that you admire for a moment before feeling an urge to move on to a new month.

The American couple returned. The man looked in my direction and said, 'I can't find it.'

The woman said, 'I don't think we went far enough.'

'Don't be silly. That was the engine.' He looked at me. 'Did you find it?'

'What?'

'The dining car.'

'There isn't one,' I said. 'I looked.'

'Then why the hell,' the man said, only now releasing his anger, 'why the hell did they call us for breakfast?'

'Did they call you?'

'Yes. "Last call." Didn't you hear them? "Last call for breakfast," they said. That's why we hurried.'

The Swiss boys, yelling and sliding the compartment doors open, had preceded the Americans' appearance. This commotion had been interpreted as a summons to breakfast; hunger's ear is not finely tuned.

The man said, 'I hate France.'

His wife looked out the window. 'I think we're out of it. That's not France.'

'Whatever it is,' said the man. He said he wasn't too happy, and he didn't want to sound like a complainer, but he had paid twenty dollars for a taxi from 'the Lazarus to the Lions'. Then a porter had carried their two suitcases from the taxi to the platform and demanded ten dollars. He didn't want French money; he wanted ten dollars.

I said that seemed excessive and added, 'Did you pay?'

'Of course I paid,' said the man.

'I wanted him to make a fuss,' said the woman.

The man said, 'I never get into arguments with people in foreign countries.'

'We thought we were going to miss the train,' said the woman. She cackled loudly. 'I almost had a haemorrhage!'

On an empty stomach, I found this disconcerting. I was glad when the man said, 'Well, come along, mother; if we're not going to get any breakfast we might just as well head back,' and led her away.

Duffill was eating the last of his salami. He offered me some, but I said I was planning to buy my breakfast at an Italian station. Duffill lifted the piece of salami and brought it to his mouth, but just as he bit into it we entered a tunnel and everything went black.

'Try the lights,' he said. 'I can't eat in the dark. I can't taste it.'

I groped for the light switch and flicked it, but we stayed in darkness.

Duffill said, 'Maybe they're trying to save electricity.'

His voice in the darkness sounded very near to my face. I moved to the window and tried to see the tunnel walls, but I saw only blackness. The sound of the wheels' drumming seemed louder in the dark and the train itself was gathering speed, the motion and the dark producing in me a suffocating feeling of claustrophobia and an acute awareness of the smell of the room, the salami, Duffill's woollens, and bread crusts. Minutes had passed and we were still in the tunnel; we might be dropping down a well, a great sink-hole in the Alps that would land us in the clockwork interior of Switzerland, glacial cogs and ratchets and frostbitten cuckoos.

Duffill said, 'This must be the Simplon.'

I said, 'I wish they'd turn the lights on.'

I heard Duffill wrapping his uneaten salami and punching the parcel into a corner.

I said, 'What do you aim to do in Turkey?'

'Me?' Duffill said, as if the compartment was crammed with old men bound for Turkey, each waiting to state a reason. He paused, then said, 'I'll be in Istanbul for a while. After that I'll be travelling around the country.'

'Business or pleasure?' I was dying to know and in the confessional darkness did not feel so bad about badgering him; he could not see the eagerness on my face. On the other hand, I could hear the tremulous hesitation in his replies.

'A little of both,' he said.

This was not helpful. I waited for him to say more, but when he added nothing further, I said, 'What exactly do you do, Mr Duffill?'

'Me?' he said again, but before I could reply with the sarcasm he was pleading for, the train left the tunnel, and the compartment filled with sunlight and Duffill said, 'This must be Italy.'

Duffill put on his tweed cap. He saw me staring at it and said, 'I've had this cap for years – eleven years. You dry clean it. Bought it in Barrow-on-Humber.' And he dug out his parcel of salami and resumed the meal the Simplon tunnel had interrupted.

At 9.35 we stopped at the Italian station of Domodossola, where a man poured cups of coffee from a jug and sold food from a heavily laden pushcart. He had fruit, loaves of bread and rolls, various kinds of salami, and lunch bags that, he said,

contained '*tante belle cose*'. He also had a stock of wine. Molesworth bought a Bardolino and ('just in case') three bottles of
Chianti; I bought an Orvieto and a Chianti; and Duffill had his
hand on a bottle of claret.

Molesworth said, 'I'll take these back to the compartment.
Get me a lunch bag, will you?'

I bought two lunch bags and some apples.

Duffill said, 'English money, I only have English money.'

The Italian snatched a pound from the old man and gave him
change in lire.

Molesworth came back and said, 'Those apples want washing.
There's cholera here.' He looked again at the pushcart and said,
'I think *two* lunch bags, just to be safe.'

While Molesworth bought more food and another bottle of
Bardolino, Duffill said, 'I took this train in nineteen twenty-nine.'

'It was worth taking then,' said Molesworth. 'Yes, she used
to be quite a train.'

'How long are we staying here?' I asked.

No one knew. Molesworth called out to the train guard,
'I say, George, how long are we stopping for?'

The guard shrugged, and as he did so the train began to
back up.

'Do you think we should board?' I asked.

'It's going backwards,' said Molesworth. 'I expect they're
shunting.'

The train guard said, '*Andiamo.*'

'The Italians love wearing uniforms,' said Molesworth. 'Look
at him, will you? And the uniforms are always so wretched.
They really are like overgrown schoolboys. Are you talking to
us, George?'

'I think he wants us to board,' I said. The train stopped going
backwards. I hopped aboard and looked down. Molesworth and
Duffill were at the bottom of the stairs.

'You've got parcels,' said Duffill. 'You go first.'

'I'm quite all right,' said Molesworth. 'Up you go.'

'But you've got parcels,' said Duffill. He produced a pipe from his coat and began sucking on the stem. 'Carry on.' He moved back and gave Molesworth room.

Molesworth said, 'Are you sure?'

Duffill said, 'I didn't go all the way, then, in nineteen twenty-nine. I didn't do that until after the second war.' He put his pipe in his mouth and smiled.

Molesworth stepped aboard and climbed up – slowly, because he was carrying a bottle of wine and his second lunch bag. Duffill grasped the rails beside the door and as he did so the train began to move and he let go. He dropped his arms. Two train guards rushed behind him and held his arms and hustled him along the platform to the moving stairs of Car 99. Duffill, feeling the Italians' hands, resisted the embrace, went feeble, and stepped back; he made a half-turn to smile wanly at the fugitive door. He looked a hundred years old. The train was moving swiftly past his face.

'George!' cried Molesworth. 'Stop the train!'

I was leaning out the door. I said, 'He's still on the platform.'

There were two Italians beside us, the conductor and a bed-maker. Their shoulders were poised, preparing to shrug.

'Pull the emergency cord!' said Molesworth.

'No, no, no, no,' said the conductor. 'If I pull that I must pay five thousand lire. Don't touch!'

'Is there another train?' I asked.

'*Si*,' said the bed-maker in a tone of irritation. 'He can catch us in Milano.'

'What time does the next train get to Milano?' I asked.

'Two o'clock.'

'When do we get to Milano?'

'One o'clock,' said the conductor. 'We leave at two.'

'Well, how the hell –'

'The old man can take a car,' explained the bed-maker. 'Don't worry. He hires a taxi at Domodossola; the taxi goes *varoom*! He's in Milano before us!'

Molesworth said, 'These chaps could use a few lessons in how to run a railroad.'

The meal that followed the abandoning of Duffill only made that point plainer. It was a picnic in Molesworth's compartment; we were joined by the Belgian girl, Monique, who brought her own cheese. She asked for mineral water and got Molesworth's reprimand: 'Sorry, I keep that for my teeth.' We sat shoulder to shoulder on Molesworth's bed, gloomily picking through our lunch bags.

'I wasn't quite prepared for this,' said Molesworth. 'I think each country should have its own dining car. Shunt it on at the frontier and serve slap-up meals.' He nibbled a hard-boiled egg and said, 'Perhaps we should get together and write a letter to Cook's.'

The Orient Express, once unique for its service, is now unique among trains for its lack of it. The Indian Rajdhani Express serves curries in its dining car, and so does the Pakistani Khyber Mail; the Meshed Express serves Iranian chicken kebab, and the train to Sapporo in Northern Japan smoked fish and glutinous rice. Box lunches are sold at the station in Rangoon, and Malaysian Railways always include a dining car that resembles a noodle stall, where you can buy *mee-hoon* soup; and Amtrak, which I had always thought to be the worst railway in the world, serves hamburgers on the James Whitcomb Riley (Washington–Chicago). Starvation takes the fun out of travel, and from this point of view the Orient Express is more inadequate than the poorest Madrasi train, where you exchange stained lunch coupons for a tin tray of vegetables and a quart of rice.

Monique said, 'I hope he takes a taxi.'

'Poor old chap,' said Molesworth. 'He panicked, you see. Started going backwards. "You've got parcels," he said, "you go first." He might have got on if he hadn't panicked. Well, we'll see if he gets to Milan. He should do. What worries me is that he might have had a heart attack. He didn't look well, did he? Did you get his name?'

'Duffill,' I said.

'Duffill,' said Molesworth. 'If he's got any sense at all, he'll sit down and have a drink. Then he'll get a taxi to Milan. It's not far, but if he panics again he's lost.'

We went on eating and drinking. If there had been a dining car we would have had a simple meal and left it at that. Because there was no dining car we ate all the way to Milan, the fear of hunger producing a hunger of its own. Monique said we were like Belgians, who ate constantly.

It was after one o'clock when we arrived at Milan. There was no sign of Duffill either on the platform or in the crowded waiting room. The station, modelled on a cathedral, had high vaulted ceilings, and simple signs like USCITA gained the metaphorical quality of religious mottoes from their size and dramatic position on the walls; balconies served no further purpose than to provide roosts for brooding stone eagles that looked too fat to fly. We bought more lunch bags, another bottle of wine, and the *Herald Tribune*.

'Poor old chap,' said Molesworth, looking around for Duffill. 'Doesn't look as if he's going to make it.'

'They warn you about that, don't they? Missing the train. You think it's shunting, but really it's on its way. The Orient Express especially. There was something in the *Observer* about it. Everyone misses it. It's famous for that.'

At Car 99, Molesworth said, 'I think we'd better get aboard. I know *I* don't want to be duffilled.'

Now, as we travelled to Venice, there was no hope for Duffill. There wasn't the slightest chance of his catching up with us. We finished another bottle of wine and I went to my compartment. Duffill's suitcase, shopping bag, and paper parcels were piled in a corner. I sat down and looked out the window, resisting the urge to rummage through Duffill's effects for a clue to his going to Turkey. It had grown hotter; the corn fields were baked yellow and strewn with shocks and stubble. Beyond Brescia, the shattered windows in a row of houses gave me a headache. Moments later, drugged by the Italian heat, I was asleep.

Venice, like a drawing room in a gas station, is approached through a vast apron of infertile industrial flatlands, crisscrossed with black sewer troughs and stinking of oil, the gigantic sinks and stoves of refineries and factories, all intimidating the delicate dwarfed city beyond. The graffiti along the way are as professionally executed as the names of the firms: MOTTA GELATI, LOTTA COMMUNISTA, AGIP, NOI SIAMO TUTTI ASSASSINI, RENAULT, UNITA. The lagoon with its luminous patches of oil slick, as if hopelessly retouched by Canaletto, has a yard-wide tidewrack of rubble, plastic bottles, broken toilet seats, raw sewage, and that bone white factory froth the wind beats into drifts of foam. The edges of the city have succumbed to industry's erosion, and what shows are the cracked back windows and derelict posterns of water-logged villas, a few brittle Venetian steeples, and farther in, but low and almost visibly sinking, walls of spaghetti-coloured stucco and red roofs over which flocks of soaring swallows are teaching pigeons to fly.

'Here we are, mother.' The elderly American man was helping his wife down the stairs, and a porter half-carried her the rest of the way to the platform. Oddly appropriate, this couple who had seen Venice in better days: now the city and its visitors were enfeebled, suffering the fatal poisoning of the age. But Mrs Ketchum (for that was her name: it was the very last thing she told me) looked wounded; she walked with pain, using joints that had turned to stone, leaning on her stick. The Ketchums would be going to Istanbul in a few days, though it struck me as foolhardy, to say the least, for them to carry their feebleness from one remote country to another.

I handed over Duffill's violated belongings to the Venetian *Controllare* and asked him to contact Milan and reassure Duffill. He said he would, but spoke with the kind of Italianate careless-ness that mocks trust. I demanded a receipt. This he provided, showing me his sour resignation as he slowly and distastefully itemized Duffill's parcels on the chit. As soon as we left Venice I clawed it to pieces and threw it out the window. I had asked for it only to chasten him.

At Trieste, Molesworth discovered that the Italian conductor had mistakenly torn out all the tickets from his Cook's wallet. The Italian conductor was in Venice, leaving Molesworth no ticket for Istanbul, or, for that matter, Yugoslavia. But Molesworth stayed calm. He said his strategy in such a situation was to say he had no money and knew only English. 'That puts the ball in their court.'

But the new conductor was persistent. He hung by the door of Molesworth's compartment. He said, 'You no ticket.' Molesworth didn't reply. He poured himself a glass of wine and sipped it. 'You no ticket.'

'Your mistake, George.'

'You,' said the conductor. He waved a ticket at Molesworth. 'You *no* ticket.'

'Sorry, George,' said Molesworth, still drinking. 'You'll have to phone Cook's.'

'You no ticket. You pay.'

'I no pay. No money.' Molesworth frowned and said to me, 'I do wish he'd go away.'

'You cannot go.'

'I go.'

'No ticket! No go!'

'Good God,' said Molesworth. This argument went on for some time. Molesworth was persuaded to go into Trieste Station. The conductor began to perspire. He explained the situation to the stationmaster, who stood up and left his office; he did not return. Another official was found. 'Look at the uniform,' said Molesworth. 'Absolutely wretched.' That official tried to phone Venice. He rattled the pins with a stumpy finger and said, '*Pronto! Pronto!*' But the phone was out of order.

Finally Molesworth said, 'I give up. Here – here's some

money.' He flourished a handful of 10,000 lire notes. 'I buy a new ticket.'

The conductor reached for the money. Molesworth withdrew it as the conductor snatched.

'Now look, George,' said Molesworth. 'You get me a ticket, but before you do that, you sit down and write me an endorsement so I can get money back. Is that clear?'

But all Molesworth said when we were again underway was, 'I think they're all very naughty.'

At Sežana, on the Yugoslav border, they were very naughty, too. Yugoslav policemen with puffy faces and black belts crossed on their chests crowded the train corridor and examined passports. I showed mine. The policeman pawed it, licked his thumb, and wiped at pages, leaving damp smudges, until he found my visa. He passed it back to me. I tried to step by him to retrieve my wine glass from Molesworth's compartment. The policeman spread his fingers on my chest and gave me a shove; seeing me stumble backwards he smiled, lifting his lips over his terrible teeth.

'You can imagine how these Jug policemen behave in third class,' said Molesworth, in a rare display of social conscience.

'"And still she cried and still the world pursues,"' I said, '"'Jug Jug' to dirty ears." Who says *The Waste Land*'s irrelevant?'

'Jug' seemed uncannily exact, for outside the train little Jugs frolicked on the tracks, big parental Jugs crouched in rows, balanced on suitcases, and uniformed Jugs with leather pouches and truncheons strolled, smoking evil-smelling cigarettes with the apt brand name, 'Stop!'

More passengers had installed themselves in Car 99 at Venice: an Armenian lady from Turkey (with a sister in Watertown, Massachusetts), who was travelling with her son – each time I talked to this pretty woman the boy burst into tears, until I got the message and went away; an Italian nun with the face of a Roman emperor and traces of a moustache; Enrico, the nun's brother, who was now in Duffill's berth; three Turkish men, who somehow managed to sleep in two berths; and a doctor from Verona.

The doctor, a cancer specialist on his way to a cancer conference in Belgrade, made a play for Monique, who, in an effort to divert the man, brought him to Molesworth's compartment for a drink. The man sulked until the conversation turned to cancer; then like William Burroughs' Doctor Benway ('Cancer! My first love!'), he became quite companionable as he summarized the paper he was going to read at the conference. All of us tried as well as we could to be intelligent about cancer, but I noticed the doctor pinching Monique's arm and, feeling that he might have located a symptom and was planning a more thorough examination, I said good night and went to bed to read *Little Dorrit*. I found some inspiration in Mr Meagles' saying, 'One always begins to forgive a place as soon as it's left behind,' and, with that thought repeating in my brain, fell into that deep slumber familiar to infants in old-fashioned rocker cradles and railway travellers in sleeping cars.

I was shaving the next morning, amazing Enrico with my portable electric razor as I had Duffill, when we pulled level with a train that bore an enamelled plate on its side inscribed MOSKVA-BEOGRAD. The Direct-Orient halted, making its couplings grunt, and Enrico dashed out of the door. This was Belgrade, calling attention to the fact with acronyms, CENTROCOOP, ATEKS, RAD, and one I loved, TRANSJUG. It was here, at Belgrade Station, that I thought I would try out my camera. I found a group of Yugoslav peasants, Mama Jug, Papa Jug, Granny Jug, and a lot of little Jugs; the men had Halloween moustaches, and one of the women wore a green satin dress over a pair of men's trousers; the granny, wearing a shawl that hid everything but her enormous nose, carried a battered Gladstone bag. The rest of their luggage, an unmanageable assortment of cardboard boxes and neatly sewn bales, was in the process of being transferred across the track, from one platform to the other. Any one of the bundles would have caused a derailment. *Migrants in Belgrade*: a poignant portrait of futility. I focused and prepared to snap, but in my view finder I saw the granny muttering to the man, who whipped around and made a threatening gesture at me.

Farther down the platform I had another excellent chance. A man in the uniform of a railway inspector, with a correct peaked cap, epaulettes, and neatly pressed trousers was walking towards me. But the interesting and photogenic feature was that he carried a shoe in each hand and was in his bare feet. They were big splayed feet, as blunt and white as turnips. I waited until he passed, and then clicked. But he heard the click and turned to yell a meaningful insult. After that I took my pictures with more stealth.

Molesworth saw me idling on the platform and said, 'I think I shall board. I don't trust this train any more.'

But everyone was on the platform; indeed, all the platforms at Belgrade Station were filled with travellers, leaving with me the unforgettable image of Belgrade as a terminal where people wait for trains that will never arrive, watching locomotives endlessly shunting. I pointed this out to Molesworth.

He said, 'I think of it now as getting duffilled. I don't want to get duffilled.' He hoisted himself into Car 99 and called out, 'Don't you get duffilled!'

We had left the Italian conductor at Venice; at Belgrade our Yugoslav conductor was replaced by a Bulgarian conductor.

'American?' said the Bulgarian as he collected my passport.

I told him I was.

'Agnew,' he said; he nodded.

'You know Agnew?'

He grinned. 'He is in bad situation.'

Molesworth, all business, said, 'You're the conductor, are you?'

The Bulgarian clicked his heels and made a little bow.

'Wonderful,' said Molesworth. 'Now what I want you to do is clean out those bottles.' He motioned to the floor of his compartment, where there was an impressive heap of wine bottles.

'The empty ones?' The Bulgarian smirked.

'Quite right. Good point. Carry on,' said Molesworth, and joined me at the window.

The Belgrade outskirts were leafy and pleasant, and as it was noon by the time we had left the station, the labourers we passed had downed their tools and were sitting cross-legged in shady spots by the railway line having lunch. The train was going so slowly, one could see the plates of sodden cabbage and could count the black olives in the chipped bowls. These groups of eaters passed loaves of bread the size of footballs, reducing them by hunks and scrubbing their plates with the pieces.

Much later on my trip, in the bar of a Russian ship in the Sea of Japan, on my way from the Japanese railway bazaar to the Soviet one beginning in Nakhodka, I met a jolly Yugoslav named Nikola who told me, 'In Yugoslavia we have three things – freedom, women, and drinking.'

'But not all three at the same time, surely?' I said, hoping he wouldn't take offence. I was seasick at the time, and I had forgotten Yugoslavia, the long September afternoon I had spent on the train from Belgrade to Dimitrovgrad, sitting in my corner seat with a full bottle of wine and my pipe drawing nicely.

There were women, but they were old, shawled against the sun and yoked to green watering cans in trampled corn fields. The landscape was low and uneven, barely supporting in its dust a few farm animals, maybe five motionless cows, and a herdsman leaning on a stick watching them starve in the same way the scarecrows – two plastic bags on a bony cross-piece – watched the devastated fields of cabbages and peppers. And beyond the rows of blue cabbage, a pink pig butted the splintery fence of his small pen and a cow lay under a goal of saplings in an unused football field. Red peppers, as crimson and pointed as clusters of poinsettias, dried in the sun outside farm cottages in districts where farming consisted of men stumbling after oxen dragging wooden ploughs and harrows, or occasionally wobbling on bicycles loaded with hay bales. Herdsmen were not simply herdsmen; they were sentries, guarding little flocks from marauders: four cows watched by a woman, three grey pigs driven by a man with a truncheon, scrawny chickens watched by scrawny children. Freedom, women, and drinking was Nikola's definition; and there was a woman in a field pausing to tip a water bottle to her mouth; she swallowed and bent from the waist to continue tying up cornstalks. Large ochre squashes sat plumply in fields of withering vines; people priming pumps and swinging buckets out of wells on long poles; tall narrow hay-stacks, and pepper fields in so many stages of ripeness I first took them for flower gardens. It is a feeling of utter quietness, deep rural isolation the train briefly penetrates. It goes on without a change for hours, this afternoon in Yugoslavia, and then all people disappear and the effect is eerie: roads without cars or bicycles, cottages with empty windows at the fringes of empty fields, trees heavy with apples and no one picking them. Perhaps it's the wrong time – 3.30; perhaps it's too hot. But where are the people who stacked that hay and set those peppers so carefully to dry? The train passes on – that's the beauty of a train, this heedless movement – but it passes on to more of the same. Six neat beehives, a derelict steam engine with wild flowers garlanding its smokestack, a stalled ox at a level crossing. In the heat haze of the afternoon my compartment grows dusty, and down at the front of the train Turks lie all over their seats, sleeping with their mouths open and children wakeful on their stomachs. At each river and bridge there were square brick emplacements, like Croatian copies of Martello towers, pocked by bombs. Then I saw a man, headless, bent over in a field, camouflaged by cornstalks that were taller than he; I wondered if I had missed all the others because they were made so tiny by their crops.

There was a drama outside Niš. At a road near the track a crowd of people fought to look at a horse, still in its traces and hitched to an overloaded wagon, lying dead on its side in a mud puddle in which the wagon was obviously stuck. I imagined its heart had burst when it tried to free the wagon. And it had just happened: children were calling to their friends, a man was dropping his bike and running back for a look, and farther along a man pissing against a fence was straining to see the horse. The scene was composed like a Flemish painting in which the pissing man was a vivid detail. The train, the window frame holding the scene for moments, made it a picture. The man at the fence flicks the last droplets from his penis and, tucking it in his baggy pants, begins to sprint; the picture is complete.

'I hate sightseeing,' said Molesworth. We were at the corridor window and I had just been reprimanded by a Yugoslav policeman for snapping a picture of a steam locomotive that, in the late afternoon sun, and the whirling dust the thousands of homeward-bound commuters had raised crossing the railway lines, stood amidst a magnificent exhalation of blue vapours mingling with clouds of gold gnats. Now we were in a rocky gorge outside Niš, on the way to Dimitrovgrad, the cliffs rising as we moved and holding occasional symmetries, like remainders of intelligent brickwork in the battlements of a ruined castle. The sight of this seemed to tire Molesworth, and I think he felt called upon to explain his fatigue. 'All that tramping around with guidebooks,' he said after a moment. 'In those horrible crocodiles of tourists, in and out of churches, museums, and mosques. No, no, no. I just like to be still, find a comfortable chair. Do you see what I mean? I like to *absorb* a country.'

He was drinking. We were both drinking, but drink made him reflective and it made me hungry. All I had had to eat during the day was a cheese bun in Belgrade, an envelope of pretzels, and a sour apple. The sight of Bulgaria, with its decrepit houses and skinny goats, did not make me hopeful of a good meal at Sofia Station, and at the fearfully named town of Dragoman a number of people, including several from Car 99, were taken off the train because they hadn't had cholera shots. Italy, the Bulgarians said, was stricken.

I found the Bulgarian conductor and asked him to describe for me a typical Bulgarian meal. Then I wrote down the Bulgarian words for the delicacies he had mentioned: cheese, potatoes, bread, sausages, salad with beans, and so forth. He assured me that there would be food in Sofia.

'This is an awfully slow train,' said Molesworth as the Direct-Orient creaked through the darkness. Here and there was a yellow lantern, a fire far off, a light in a hut at a remote halt where, barely visible, the stationmaster could be seen five paces from his hut, presenting his flag to the dawdling express.

I showed Molesworth my list of Bulgarian foods, and said I planned to buy what was obtainable at Sofia; it would be our last night on the Direct-Orient – we deserved a good meal.

'That should be very useful,' said Molesworth. 'Now, what are you going to use for money?'

'I haven't the slightest idea,' I said.

'They use the lev here, you know. But the snag is, I couldn't find a quotation for it. My bank manager said it was one of those hopeless currencies – I suppose it's not really money at all, just pieces of paper.' From the way he talked I could tell he wasn't hungry. He went on, 'I always use plastic. Plastic's incredibly useful.'

'Plastic?'

'Well, these things.' He set his drink down and took out a wad of credit cards, shuffled them, and read their names.

'Do you think the Barclaycard has hit Bulgaria yet?'

'Let's hope so,' he said. 'But if not, I still have some lire left.'

It was after eleven at night when we pulled into Sofia, and, as Molesworth and I leaped off the train, the conductor told us to hurry: 'Fifteen minutes, maybe ten.'

'You said we'd have a half-hour!'

'But we are running late now. Don't talk – hurry!'

We quick-marched down the platform, searching for food. There was a cafeteria with a mob at the counter and then nothing more except, at the far end of the platform, a man with a steaming metal pushcart. He was bald. He held a small paper bag in one hand and with the other he flipped open the several tabernacles of his pushcart and stabbed at white buns and red, dripping sausages, the size of bananas, with pink meat showing in slightly burst seams. There were three customers ahead of us. He served them, taking his time, urging buns and sausages into the bags with his busy fork. When my turn came I showed him two fingers, changed my mind, three fingers. He bagged three of each.

'The same again,' said Molesworth and handed him a 1000-lire note.

'No, no,' said the man; he pushed my dollar away and at the same time took my bag from me and put it on the pushcart.

'He won't take our money,' said Molesworth.

'*Banka, banka,*' said the man.

'He wants us to get change.'

'This is a dollar,' I said. 'Take the whole thing.'

'He won't wear it,' said Molesworth. 'Where's your *banka*, eh?'

The bald man pointed to the station. We ran in the direction his finger was pointing and found a teller's cage where a long line of disconsolate people stood clutching pieces of paper and kicking their luggage as the line inched forward.

'I think we'll have to give this up as a bad job,' said Molesworth.

'I'm dying for one of those sausages.'

'Unless you want to get duffilled,' said Molesworth, 'you should get back on the train. I think I shall.'

We did and minutes later the whistle blew and the Bulgarian darkness swallowed Sofia. Enrico, seeing us empty-handed, got Italian crackers from his sister, the nun, and gave them to us; the Armenian lady presented a slab of cheese and even sat with us and had a drink, until her son wandered in wearing a pair of pyjamas. He saw his mother laughing; he burst into tears. 'Now I go,' she said, and went. Monique had gone to bed; so had

Enrico. Car 99 was asleep, but we were picking up speed. 'And we're not badly off,' said Molesworth, slicing the cheese. 'Two more bottles of wine – that's one apiece – and still some Orvieto to finish. Cheese and biscuits. We can call it a late supper.' We went on drinking, and Molesworth talked of India, how he had gone out for the first time on a P & O liner with thousands of enlisted men, tough mineworkers from the Durham coal fields. Molesworth and his fellow officers had plenty to drink, but the lower ranks were battened down. After a month they ran out of beer. There were fights, the men were mutinous, 'and by the time we reached Bombay most of them were in chains. But I got an extra pip on my shoulder for behaving myself.'

'This is the idea,' said Molesworth. The train was racing, and he was uncorking the last bottle. 'It's usually a good rule to drink the wine of the country you're passing through.' He glanced out the window into the blackness. 'I suppose that's still Bulgaria. What a great pity.'

Large grey dogs, a pack of seven, presumably wild, were chasing across the harsh steppes of northwestern Turkey, barking at the train. They woke me in Thrace, which Nagel calls 'rather unattractive', and when the wild dogs slackened their pace and fell behind the fleeing train there was little else to see but a dreary monotony of unambitious hills. The occasional army posts, the men shovelling sugar beets caked with dirt into steel hoppers, and the absence of trees made the dreariness emphatic. And I couldn't bear those hairless hills. Edirne (Adrianople) was to the north, Istanbul still four hours away; but we travelled over the steppes, stopping at only the smallest stations, an unremark-able journey across a barren landscape: featurelessness is the steppes' single attribute, and, having said that, and assigned it a shade of brown, there is nothing more to say.

And yet I hung by the window, hoping to be surprised. We passed another station. I searched it for a detail; it repeated fifty previous stations and this repetition kept it out of focus. But just past it was a garden plot and, next to that, three turkeys, moving with that clockwork bustle characteristic of fowl.

'Look!' Molesworth had seen them.

I nodded.

'Turkeys. In *Turkey*!' he exclaimed. 'I wonder if that's why they're called –'

But it isn't. These birds got their name from African guinea fowl which, imported through Istanbul, were called turkey cocks. We discussed this over our morning drink for the next hour or two, and it struck me that, for a man with a wife and children, I was embarked on a fairly aimless enterprise, the lazy indulgence of travel for its own sake.

The great express from Paris became a doubtful and irritating Turkish local once it got to Istanbul's outskirts, stopping at every station simply to give conductors a chance to fool with notebooks in the Turkish Clapham Junctions and Scarsdales.

On the right-hand side of the train was the Sea of Marmara, where freighters with rusty hulls and fishing boats with the contours of scimitars lay surrounded by caïques in the glittering water. On our left the suburbs were passing, altering every fifty yards: scattered tent settlements and fishing villages gave way to high-rise apartment houses, with shacks at their ankles; then a shantytown on an outcrop of rock, bungalows where it levelled out, and an uneven terrace of wooden houses toppling grandly from a cliff – a style of building (the falling, unpainted, three-decker house) favoured in Somerville, Massachusetts, as well as in Istanbul. It takes a while to realize that what are represented in these vastly different building styles are not social classes, but rather centuries, each style an example of its own age – Istanbul has been a city for twenty-seven centuries – and getting older and more solid (shingle to timber, timber to brick, brick to stone) as you get closer to the Seraglio.

Istanbul begins as the train passes the city wall at the Golden Gate, the Arch of Triumph of Theodosius – built in 380 but not appreciably more decrepit than the strings of Turkish laundry that flap at its base. Here, for no apparent reason, the train picked up speed and rushed east along Istanbul's snout, past the Blue Mosque and the Topkapi Sarayi, and then circled to the Golden Horn. Sirkeči Station is nothing compared to its sister station, Haydarpasa, just across the Bosporus, but its nearness to the busy Eminönu Square and one of the prettiest mosques in the city, Yeni Valide Camii, not to mention the Galata Bridge (which accommodates a whole community of hawkers, fish stalls, shops, restaurants, and pickpockets disguised as peddlers and touts), gives to one's arrival in Istanbul by the Direct-Orient Express the combined shock and exhilaration of being pitched headfirst into a bazaar.

'It all looks absolutely hideous,' said Molesworth. But he was smiling. 'I think I'm going to like it.' He was off to the high-priced fishing village of Tarabya. He gave me his telephone number and said I should ring if I got bored. We were still on the platform at Sirkeči. Molesworth turned to the train. 'I must say I'm not sad to see the back of that train, are you?' But he said it in a tone of fussy endearment, in the way a person who calls himself a fool really means the opposite.

To catch a glimpse of oneself in a gilt-framed ten-foot mirror at the Pera Palas Hotel in Istanbul is to know an instant of glory, the joy of seeing one's own face in a prince's portrait. The décor in the background is decayed sumptuousness, an acre of mellow carpet, black panelling, and rococo carving on the walls and ceilings, where cupids patiently smile and flake. Overhead are complicated chandeliers, like giant wind chimes in crystal, and past the ballroom's marble pillars and potted palms is the mahogany bar, hung with excellent copies of mediocre French paintings. This palace, which from the outside looks no more imposing than the Charlestown Savings Bank in Boston, is run by small dark men who look as if they belong to several generations of the same family, and each wears a courtly smirk under his moustache as he gives French replies to English questions.

Happily, the hotel is a charitable foundation, according to the wishes of the late owner, a Turkish philanthropist: the profits of your princely spending, every voluptuous excess, improve the lot of needy Turks.

My first day in the city I spent obsessively walking, like a man released on a sudden from the closeness of a long captivity. The single penalty of the train, for a rambler like me, is this deprivation of walking. As the days passed I slowed down and, with Nagel's *Turkey* in my hand, began sightseeing, an activity that delights the truly idle because it seems so much like scholarship, gawping and eavesdropping on antiquity, flattering oneself with the notion that one is discovering the past when really one is inventing it, using a guidebook as a scenario of swift notations. But how should one see Istanbul? Gwyn Williams in his *Turkey, A Traveller's Guide and History* recommends:

A day for walls and fortifications, a few days in pursuit of aqueducts and cisterns in and outside the city, a week for palaces, another for museums, a day for columns and towers, weeks for churches and mosques . . . Days may be spent on tombs and cemeteries and the décor of death will be found to be gayer than one thought . . .

After those exhausting forays death itself, never mind the décor, would seem fairly gay. In any case, I had a train to catch; so I poked in a few corners and satisfied myself that this was a city I would gladly return to. In the Topkapi harem I was shown the quarters of the black eunuchs. Outside each cell were various instruments of torture, thumbscrews, lashes, and so forth. But punishments, according to the guide, were not always elaborate. I pressed her for an example.

'They hang them up and beat them on their feet,' she said.

A Frenchman turned to me and asked, 'Is she talking in English?'

She was, and also in German, but she gave to both languages Turkish rhythms and fricatives. No one seemed to mind this, however, and most of the people simply shuffled back and forth, saying, 'How'd you like to have one of those?' In the jewel room the remark acquired a curious irony, since most of the jewels on the daggers and swords are fakes, the real ones having been pilfered years ago. The average air fare to Istanbul would undoubtedly buy the whole Topkapi treasury, though the Turks insist, for patriotic reasons, that those eggsized emeralds are genuine, just as they insist that the footprint of Mohammed in the sacred museum across the courtyard is really that of the Prophet. If so, he may have been the only Arab in history to wear a size 14 triple-E sandal.

Stranger than this, but manifestly true, is the story behind the mosaic in an upper gallery of Saint Sofia, which depicts the Empress Zoë (980–1050) and her third husband, Constantine Monomachus. Constantine's face has the masklike quality of Gertrude Stein's in the famous Picasso portrait. Indeed, the face of Constantine was put in this mosaic after Zoë's first husband, Romanus III, died or was exiled. But the best mosaics are not in the grand churches and mosques of central Istanbul. They are in a tiny crumbling dirt-coloured building called the Kariye Camii in the outskirts of the city. Here, the mosaics are wonderfully supple and human, and the millions of little tiles have the effect of brush strokes: Christ seems to breathe, and the Virgin in one fresco looks exactly like Virginia Woolf.

That afternoon, anxious to have a look at the Asian side of Istanbul and prepared to buy my train ticket to Teheran, I took the ferry across the Bosporus to Haydarpasa. The sea was unexpectedly calm. I had thought, having read *Don Juan*, that it would be rough:

> There's not a sea the passenger e'er pukes in,
> Turns up more dangerous breakers than the Euxine.

But that is farther up the Bosporus. Here the sea was mirror-smooth, and Haydarpasa Station, a heavy dark European building with a clock and two blunt spires, was reflected in it. The station is an incongruous gateway to Asia. It was built in 1909, from the designs of a German architect who apparently assumed that Turkey would soon be part of a German empire in which, in station like this, subject peoples would loyally be eating sausages. The intention seems to have been to put up a building in which the portrait of the Kaiser could be hung and not look out of place.

'*Teheran gitmek ichin bir bilet istiyorum,*' I said to the girl at the counter, glancing at my phrase book for courage.

'We do not sell tickets on Sunday,' she said in English. 'Come tomorrow.'

Because I was on the right side of the Bosporus, I walked from the station to the Selimiye Barracks, where Florence Nightingale tended gangrenous soldiers during the Crimean War. I asked the sentry if I could go in. He said, 'Nightingale?' I nodded. He said her room was closed on Sunday and directed me to the cemetery at Üsküdar, Istanbul's largest necropolis.

It was on the way to Üsküdar that I had an insight into what had, up to then, been bothering me about Turkey. The father of the Turks, which is what his surname means, was Mustafa Kemal Atatürk, and everywhere one goes in Turkey one sees photographs, portraits, and statues of him; he is on billboards, stamps, coins – always the same wincing banker's profile. His name is given to streets and plazas and it enters nearly every conversation one has in the country. The face has become emblematic, the shape of a softening star, with the suggestions of a nose and chin, and is ubiquitous as the simplified character the Chinese use to frighten devils away. Atatürk came to power in 1923, declared Turkey a republic, and, by way of moderniz-ation, closed down all religious schools, dissolved dervish orders, and introduced the Latin alphabet and the Swiss civil code. He died in 1938, and that was my insight: modernization stopped in Turkey with the death of Atatürk, at five minutes past nine on 10 November 1938. As if to demonstrate this, the room in which he died is as he left it, and all the clocks in the palace show the time as 9.05. This seemed to explain why the Turks typically dress the way people did in 1938, in hairy brown sweaters and argyle socks, in baggy pinstriped pants and blue serge suits with padded shoulders, flapping winglike lapels and a three-pointed hanky in the breast pocket. Their hair is wavy with brilliantine and their moustaches are waxed. The hemlines on the brown gabardine skirts the women habitually wear are below the knees, about two inches. It is prewar modernity, and you don't have to look far to see 1938 Packards, Dodges, and Pontiacs lumbering along streets that were last widened when those models appeared. The furniture stores of Istanbul show their latest designs in the window – boxy over-upholstered chairs and clawfoot sofas. All this leads one to the inescapable conclusion that, if the zenith of Ottoman elegance was the sixteenth-century reign of Suleiman the Magnificent, the high-water mark of the modern was in 1938, when Atatürk was still modelling Turkish stylishness on the timid designs of the West.

'Why, that's awfully clever of you,' said Molesworth, when I rang him up to explain this to him. Then he changed the subject. He was enjoying Tarabya; the weather was perfect. 'Come up for lunch. The taxi will cost the earth but I can promise you a very good wine. It's called either Cankia or Ankia. It's dry, white, with a slight *twinkle* – a pinky colour, but definitely not a rosé, because I hate rosé and this was very drinkable indeed.'

I could not meet Molesworth for lunch. I had a previous engagement, my single duty in Istanbul, a luncheon lecture arranged by a helpful American embassy man. I couldn't cancel it: I had a hotel bill to pay. So I went to the conference room where about twenty Turks were having a pre-lecture drink; I was told they were poets, playwrights, novelists, and academics. The first man I spoke to was the most pompous, the president of the Turkish Literary Union, a Mr Ercumena Behzat Lav, a name I found as hard to conjure with as to pronounce. He had a look of spurious eminence – white-haired, with tiny feet, and an unwilling gaze that was disdainful in an overpractised way. He smoked with the squinting disgust people affect when they are on the verge of giving up smoking. I asked him what he did.

'He says he does not speak English,' said Mrs Nur, my pretty translator. The president had spoken and looked away. 'He prefers to speak in Turkish, though he will speak to you in German or Italian.'

'*Va bene*,' I said. '*Allora, parliamo in Italiano. Ma dové imparava questa lingua?*'

The president addressed Mrs Nur in Turkish.

'He says, "Do you speak German?"'

'Not very well.'

The president said something more.

'He will speak Turkish.'

'Ask him what he does. Is he a writer?'

'This,' said the man through Mrs Nur, 'is a completely mean-ingless question. One cannot say in a few words what one does or is. That takes months, sometimes years. I can tell you my name. Beyond that you have to find out for yourself.'

'Tell him he's too much work,' I said, and walked away. I fell into conversation with the head of the English Department of Istanbul University, who introduced me to his colleague. Both wore tweeds and stood rocking on their heels, the way English academics size up new members of the Senior Common Room.

'He's another old Cantabrigian,' said the head, slapping his colleague on the back. 'Same college as me. Fitzbill.'

'Fitzwilliam College?'

'That's right, though I haven't been back there for donkey's years.'

'What do you teach?' I asked.

'Everything from *Beowulf* to Virginia Woolf!'

It seemed as if everyone had rehearsed his lines except me. As I was thinking of a reply, I was seized by the arm and dragged away in a very powerful grip. The man dragging me was tall and stoutly built, bull-necked, with a great jaw. His palely tinted glasses did not quite hide his right eye, which was dead and looked like a withered grape. He talked rapidly in Turkish as he hustled me into the corner of the room.

'He says,' Mrs Nur said, trying to keep up with us, 'he always captures beautiful girls and good writers. He wants to talk to you.'

This was Yashar Kemal, the author of *Mehmet My Hawk*, the only Turkish novel I could ever remember having read. It is thought that before long he will be awarded the Nobel Prize for literature. He had, he said, just returned from a visit to the Soviet Union where he had been lecturing with his friend, Aziz Nesin. He had addressed audiences in Moscow, Leningrad, Baku, and Alma-Ata.

'At my lectures I said many terrible things! They hated me and they were very upset. For example, I said that socialist realism was anti-Marxist. This I believe. I am a Marxist: I know. All the writers in the Soviet Union except Sholokhov are anti-Marxist. They did not want to hear this terrible thing. I told them, "Do you want to know the greatest Marxist writer?" Then I said, "William Faulkner!" They were very upset. Yes, Sholokhov is a great writer, but Faulkner was a much greater Marxist.'

I said I didn't think Faulkner would have agreed with him. He ignored me and pressed on.

'And the greatest comic writer, of course we all know – Mark Twain. But the next greatest is Aziz Nesin. And don't think I'm saying that simply because we're both Turkish or because he's my best friend.'

Aziz Nesin, who was across the room mournfully nibbling an American embassy *vol-au-vent*, has written fifty-eight books. Most are collections of short stories. They are said to be hilarious, but none has been translated into English.

'I have no doubt about it,' Yashar said. 'Aziz Nesin is a greater comic writer than Anton Chekhov!'

Aziz Nesin, hearing his name, looked up and smiled sadly.

'Come to my house,' said Yashar. 'We go swimming, eh? Eat some fish? I will tell you the whole story.'

'How will I find your house?' I had asked Yashar the previous day. He said, 'Ask any child. The old people don't know me, but all the little ones do. I make kites for them.'

I took him at his word, and when I arrived at the apartment block on a bluff above a Marmara fishing village called Menakse, I asked a fairly small child the way to Yashar's house. The child pointed to the top floor.

The disorder in Yashar's apartment was that comfortable littering and stacking that only another writer can recognize as order – the considered scatter of papers and books a writer builds around himself until it acquires the cosy solidity of a nest. On several of Yashar's shelves were editions of his own books in thirty languages; the English ones had been translated by his wife, Thilda, whose narrow desk held an open *Shorter Oxford English Dictionary*.

Yashar had just been interviewed by a Swedish newspaper. He showed me the article, and although I could not read it, the word *Nobelpreiskandidate* caught my eye. I commented on it.

'Yes,' said Thilda, who interpreted my questions and Yashar's replies, 'it's possible. But they feel it's Graham Greene's turn now.'

'My frint,' said Yashar, hearing Greene's name. He placed his hairy hand on his heart when he said it.

Graham Greene seemed to have a lot of friends on this route. But Yashar knew many other writers and he slapped his heart as he listed them. William Saroyan was his friend, and so were Erskine Caldwell, Angus Wilson, Robert Graves, and James Baldwin, whom he called 'Jimmy' – he reminded me that *Another Country* had been written in a luxurious Istanbul villa.

'I can't face going swimming,' said Thilda. She was a patient, intelligent woman who spoke English so well I didn't dare to compliment her on it for fear she might say, as Thurber did on a similar occasion, 'I ought to – I spent forty years in Columbus, Ohio, working on it like a dog.' Thilda sees to the practical side of his affairs, negotiating contracts, answering letters, explaining Yashar's harangues about the socialist paradise he envisions, that Soviet pastoral where the workers own the means of production and complete sets of Faulkner.

It was unfortunate that Thilda didn't come swimming with us because it meant three hours of talking pidgin English, an activity that Yashar must have found as fatiguing as I did. Carrying our bathing trunks, we walked down the dusty hill to the beach. Yashar pointed out the fishing village and said he was planning a series of stories based on the life there. On the way, we met a small quivering man with a shaven head and the regulation rumpled thirties suit. Yashar shouted a greeting at him. The man crept over and grabbed Yashar's hand and tried to kiss it, but Yashar, by jerking his own hand, turned this servility into a handshake. They spoke together for a while, then Yashar slapped the man on the back and sent him tottering away.

'His name Ahmet,' said Yashar. He put his thumb to his mouth and tilted his hand. 'He drunk.'

We changed at a swimming club where some men were sunning themselves. In the water I challenged him to a race. He won it easily and splashed water at me as I struggled in his wake. The previous day he had looked like a bull; but now, swimming, his bulk making the water foam at his arms, he had the movement of a mature sea monster, with hairy shoulders and a thick neck, and he surfaced roaring as his vast head dripped. The champion swimmers – he claimed to be one – all came, he said, from Adana, his birthplace in South Anatolia.

'I love my country,' he said, meaning Anatolia. 'I *love* it. Taurus Mountains. Plains. Old villages. Cotton. Eagles. Oranges. The best horses – very *long* horses.' He put his hand on his heart: 'I love.'

We talked about writers. He loved Chekhov; Whitman was

a good man; Poe was also great. Melville was good: every year Yashar read *Moby Dick*, and *Don Quixote*, 'and Homerus'. We were pacing up and down in the hot sun on the beach front, and Yashar cast a giant shadow over me that eliminated any danger of my getting sunburned. He didn't like Joyce, he said. '*Ulysses* – too simple. Joyce is a very simple man, not like Faulkner. Listen. I am interested in form. New form. I hate traditional form. Novelist who use traditional form is' – he fumbled for a word – 'is dirt.'

'I don't speak English,' he said after a moment. 'Kurdish I speak, and Turkish, and gypsy language. But I don't speak barbarian languages.'

'Barbarian languages?'

'English! German! Ya! French! All the barbarian –' As he spoke, there was a shout. One of the men sunning himself in a beach chair called Yashar over and showed him an item in a newspaper.

Returning, he said, 'Pablo Neruda is dead.'

Yashar insisted on stopping at the fishing village on the way back. About fifteen men sat outside a café. Seeing Yashar, they leaped to their feet and Yashar greeted each one with a bear hug. One was a man of eighty; he wore a ragged shirt and his trousers were tied with a piece of rope. He was deeply tanned, barefoot, and toothless. Yashar said he had no home. The man slept in his caïque every night, whatever the weather, and he had done so for forty years. 'So he has his caïque and sleeps in it too.' These men, and one we met later on the steep path (Yashar kissed him carefully on each cheek before introducing him to me), obviously looked upon Yashar as a celebrity and regarded him with some awe.

'These my friends,' said Yashar. 'I hate writers; I love fishermen.' But there was a distance. Yashar had attempted to overcome it with clowning intimacy, yet the distance remained. In the atmosphere of the café one would never take Yashar – twice as big as any of the others and dressed like a golf pro – for a fisherman; neither would one take him for a writer on the prowl. There, he looked like a local character, part of the scenery and yet in contrast to it.

It seemed to me that his restless generosity led him into contradictions. My conclusion did not make my understanding any easier. Over lunch of fried red mullet and white wine Yashar talked about prison, Turkey, his books, his plans. He had been to jail; Thilda had served an even longer jail sentence; their daughter-in-law was in jail at the moment. This girl's crime, according to Thilda, was that she had been found making soup in the house of a man who had once been wanted for questioning in connection with a political offence. It was no good expressing disbelief at the muddled story. Turkey, the Turks say, is not like other places, though, after describing in the dour Turkish way the most incredible horrors of torture and cruelty, they invite you to come and spend a year there, assuring you the whole time that you'll love the place.

Yashar's own characteristics were even stranger. A Kurd, he is devoted to Turkey and will not hear of secession; he is an ardent supporter of both the Soviet government and Solzhenitsyn, which is something like rooting for the devil as well as Daniel Webster; he is a Muslim Marxist, his wife is a Jew, and the only foreign country he likes better than Russia is Israel, 'my garden'. With the physique of a bull and the gentleness of a child, he maintains in the same breath that Yoknapatawpha County has an eternal glory and that the Kremlin's commissars are visionary archangels. His convictions defy reason, and at times they are as weirdly unexpected as the blond hair and freckles you see in Asia Minor. But Yashar's complexity is the Turkish character on a large scale.

I told Molesworth this at our farewell lunch. He was sceptical. 'I'm sure he's a marvellous chap,' he said. 'But you want to be careful with the Turks. They were neutral during the war, you know, and if they'd had any backbone at all they would have been on our side.'

## 3. The Van Gölü ('Lake Van') Express

'I BEG you to look at this scroll and look at me,' said the antique dealer in Istanbul's Covered Bazaar. He flapped the decaying silk scroll at his ears. 'You say the scroll is stained and dirty! Yes! It is stained and dirty! I am forty-two years old and bald on my head and many wrinkles. This scroll is *not* forty-two years old – it is two hundred years old, and you won't buy it because you say it is stained! What do you expect? Brand shiny new one? You are cheating me!'

He rolled it up and stuck it under my arm, and stepping behind the counter he sighed. 'Okay, cheat me. It is early in the morning. Take it for four hundred liras.'

'*Olmaz*,' I said, and handed it back. I had expressed only a polite curiosity in the scroll, but he had taken this for canny interest, and each time I tried to walk away he reduced his price by half, believing my lack of enthusiasm to be a wily bargaining ploy.

Finally I broke away. I had overslept. I was hungry, and I had provisions to buy for my trip on the Lake Van Express, which had a reputation for running out of food and arriving at the Iranian border as much as ten days late. Food was on my mind for another reason. I had intended to sample some dishes mentioned in Nagel. The names tempted me, and, as I would be leaving on the afternoon train, this was my last chance to try them. I had drawn up a menu for myself. This included 'The Imam Fainted' (*Imam Bayildi*, a kind of *ratatouille*), 'Vizier's Finger' (*Vezir Parmagi*), 'His Majesty Liked It' (*Hunkar Begendi*), and two irresistible ones, 'Lady's Thigh' (*Kadin Badu*) and 'Lady's Navel' (*Kadin Bobegi*).

There wasn't enough time for me to try more than the last

two. I stopped at a coffee shop on my way to the ferry and wondered if the Turks' taste in anatomy was revealed in their choice of names: the thigh was meaty, the navel sweet. At twenty cents each they were a good deal cheaper and probably a lot safer than their namesakes arrayed after midnight in the alleys off Istiklal Caddesi. To the braying of saxophones in the dimly lit taverns, these alley cats pluck at your sleeve as you pick your way along the steep cobbled footpath. But I was resolute. I never got closer to a lady's thigh in Istanbul than the pastry with the euphemistic name. Besides, I had been warned that most of the alley cats were transvestites who, during the day, worked as crew members on the Bosporus ferries.

I believed that when the epicene voice of a youth in a sailor suit, addressing me sweetly as *Effendi*, urged me to hurry as I boarded the ferry for my last trip to Haydarpasa. I found the upper deck and sorted out my provisions: I had cans of tuna fish, beans and stuffed grape leaves, several cucumbers and a lump of white goat's cheese, as well as crackers, pretzels, and three bottles of wine – one bottle for each day to Lake Van. I also took with me three cartons of whipped yogurt, which they call *ayran*, said to be the traditional drink of Turkish shepherds.

But I needn't have bothered, for while the Lake Van Express was standing at Haydarpasa Station I spotted the dining car. I found my compartment, then went to the dining car for lunch and watched the activity on the platform. Groups of hippies, like small clans of tribesmen setting out for a *baraza* or new pastures, fought past soberly dressed Turkish families. Minutes later, Turks and hippies found themselves in the same third-class compartments, quarrelling over window seats. The steam loco-motives, used by Turkish Railways for short runs, were being stoked at the platform; they poured soot over the boarding passengers and darkened the sky with smoke, giving the German station a German atmosphere.

It was pleasant to be eating, drinking, reading *Little Dorrit*, and moving east once again on a railway bazaar that would bring me to the shores of Turkey's largest lake. And I was reassured by what I saw of Turkish Railways: the train was long and solid, the sleeping car was newer than the wagon-lit on the Direct-Orient, the dining car had fresh flowers on the tables and was well stocked with wine and beer. It was three days to Lake Van, five to Teheran, and I was supremely comfortable. I went back to my compartment and propped myself at the window – a cool corner seat – and was lulled by the feel of Asia rumbling under the wheels.

We approached the coast and balanced there, on the eastern-most shore of the Sea of Marmara, stopping at the outlying towns of Kartal and Gebze (where Hannibal committed suicide) and then to the Gulf of Izmit, flecked with the last lighted eddies of sunset. It grew dark and we were inland, travelling towards Ankara. Our stops were briefer and less frequent, and at these stations little men in cloth caps, figures of discouragement, alighted from the train with roped bundles and, once clear of the stairs, dropped their bundles and looked for the next train. I watched them as we pulled out, taking the light with us, until the only visible thing about them were their cigarettes, bright from their impatient puffing. Most provincial stations had out-door cafés, full of white chairs and tables and green floodlit trees. The people drinking in them are not travellers; they are locals who have come down to the station after dinner to spend the evening watching the trains go by. The Lake Van Express is an event for the café: as soon as we leave, the hulking fellow shifts in his seat and, pointing over his coffee cup, calls to the waiter in the white jacket, who is momentarily fixed into a posture of concentration by the express. He hears the man's voice and comes alive, patting the small towel on his forearm and starting towards the table, preparing to bow.

'*Guten Abend.*' There was a Turk at the door to my compart-ment. He did not speak English, he said, but he knew some German. He had spent a year assembling cars in Munich. He was sorry to bother me, but his friend had a few questions. His friend, an old man who spoke no language but his own, stood just behind him. They entered the compartment timidly; then the German-speaker started in: Why was I alone in the compartment? Where was I going? Why did I leave my wife behind? Did I like Turkey? Why was my hair so long? Was everyone's hair that long at home? The questions ceased. The old man had picked up *Little Dorrit* and was turning the pages, marvelling at the tiny print and weighing the 900-page volume in his hand.

I felt I had earned a right to ask them the same questions they had asked me, but I hesitated. They were fresh from the meal they'd had in their compartment and carried an aroma of sour vegetables into mine. They were eyeing my gin. Their fly buttons were undone, and now I could understand why these buttons were called 'Turkish medals' by British soldiers in the First World War. The old man kept moistening his finger with spittle and smearing it on my book.

Children's faces appeared at the door; one youngster began to cry, and my annoyance was complete. I asked for my book back and evicted them. I bolted the door and slept. In my dream I was trying to fly, pumping my arms against a stiff wind that held me like a kite as I tried to rise from the ground. But I remained skimming horizontally the way a coot moves across the water, flapping wildly, but dragging my toes. I had this dream several times a week for three months, but it took a lungful of opium in Vientiane to get me airborne.

There were only Turks in the de luxe sleeping car. So much for the traveller's truism that natives don't go first class. As if fearing contamination from the rest of the train, these Turks seldom left their couchettes and they never left the car itself. Each couchette was fitted with two narrow berths, and I spent some time speculating on how these berths were allotted. For example, next to me a saffron-faced man travelled with two fat women and two children. I saw them seated in a row on the lower berth during the day, but God alone knows what happened at night. None of the couchettes held fewer than four people and this crowding gave to the sleeping car the air of squalor in third class these travellers seemed anxious to avoid.

The German-speaking Turk described the rest of the train as *schmoozy* and made a face. But it was only in the schmoozy part that English was spoken. There, one saw tall fellows with pigtails and braids, and short-haired girls who, lingering near their boy-friends, had the look of pouting catamites. Gaunt wild-haired boys with shoulder bags and sunburned noses stood rocking in the corridors, and everyone had dirty feet. They grew filthier and more fatigued-looking as I moved down the cars, and at the very front of the train they might have passed for the unfortunate distant relatives of the much cleaner Turks who shared their compartments, munching bread, combing food out of their moustaches, and burping their babies. On the whole, the hippies ignored the Turks; they played guitars and harmonicas, held hands, and organized card games. Some simply lay on their seats lengthwise, hogging half the compartment, and humped under the astonished eyes of Turkish women who sat staring in dark *yashmaks*, their hands clasped between their knees. Occasionally, I saw an amorous pair leave their compartment hand in hand to go copulate in a toilet.

Most were on their way to India and Nepal, because

the wildest dreams of Kew are the facts of Khatmandhu,
And the crimes of Clapham chaste in Martaban.

But the majority of them, going for the first time, had that look of frozen apprehension that is the mask on the face of an escapee. Indeed, I had no doubt that the teenaged girls who made up the bulk of these loose tribal groups would eventually appear on the notice boards of American consulates in Asia, in blurred snap-shots or retouched high-school graduation pictures: MISSING PERSON and HAVE YOU SEEN THIS GIRL? These initiates had leaders who were instantly recognizable by the way they dressed: the faded dervish outfit, the ragged shoulder bag, the jewellery – earrings, amulets, bracelets, necklaces. Status derived solely from experience, and it was possible to tell from the ornaments alone – that jangling in the corridor – whose experience had made him the leader of his particular group. All in all, a social order familiar to the average Masai tribesman.

I tried to find out where they were going. It was not easy. They seldom ate in the dining car; they often slept; they were not allowed in the fastness of the Turks' de luxe. Some stood by the windows in the corridor, in the trancelike state the Turkish landscape induces in travellers. I sidled up to them and asked them their plans. One did not even turn around. He was a man of about thirty-five, with dusty hair, a T-shirt that read 'Moto-Guzzi', and a small gold earring in the lobe of his ear. I surmised that he had sold his motorcycle for a ticket to India. He held the windowsill and stared at the empty reddish yellow flatlands. In reply to my question he said softly, 'Pondicherry.'

'The ashram?' Auroville, a kind of spiritual Levittown dedicated to the memory of Sri Aurobindo and at that time ruled over by his ninety-year-old French mistress (the 'Mother'), is located near Pondicherry, in South India.

'Yes. I want to stay there as long as possible.'

'How long?'

'Years.' He regarded a passing village and nodded. 'If they let me.'

It was the tone of a man who tells you, with a mixture of piety and arrogance, that he has a vocation. But Moto-Guzzi had a wife and children in California. Interesting: he had fled his children and some of the girls in his group had fled their parents.

Another fellow sat on the steps of the bogie, dangling his feet in the wind. He was eating an apple. I asked him where he was going. 'Maybe try Nepal,' he said. He took a bite of the apple. 'Maybe Ceylon, if it's happening there.' He took another bite.

The apple was like the globe he was calmly apportioning to himself, as small, bright, and accessible. He poised his very white teeth and bit again. 'Maybe Bali.' He was chewing. 'Maybe go to Australia.' He took a last bite and winged the apple into the dust. 'What are you, writing a book?'

It wasn't a challenge. He was contented – they all were, with one exception. This was the German marathon runner. He could be seen at any hour of the day doing isometric exercises in second class. His addiction was yogurt and oranges. He wore his track suit, a blue zippered outfit, and walked on the balls of his feet. 'I am going crazy,' he said. He was used to running twelve miles a day. 'And if this train takes very long I am going to get out of shape.' For a reason I did not grasp he was going to Thailand to run. He had been to Baluchistan. He told me the trains were running to Zarand. He smiled at the thought of it: 'You will be very dirty when you get to Zāhedān.'

A bump that night roused me to look out the window and see the disappearing station signboard of Eskisehir. At six in the morning we were at Ankara, where the marathon runner leaped from the train and jogged furiously up and down beside the shunting engines. At lunch, in Central Turkey, the marathon runner told me he had enough yogurt to see him to the Afghanistan border, where there would be more.

Then we stared out of the dining-car window in silence. There was little to remark upon. The landscape was changeless and harsh: long strings of treeless hills lay at the horizon; before us was an arid plain, streaming with the fulvous dust the Lake Van Express had raised. The desert glare hurt my eyes. The only variations I saw were uninteresting acts of God, evidence of floods, droughts, and sandstorms, dry riverbeds in eroded gullies and exposed outcrops of rock. The rest was a waterless immensity that continued for hours under a clear blue sky. The people I saw were like those pathetic figures in a Beckett play, made absurd by their worried movement in a landscape of unheeding devastation. From nowhere a little girl in a charming skirt hobbled with two pails of water, a futile example of the desert's emphasis; standing in a dry sluice, like a weed, was a Turkish man in his pinstripes, woollen golfer's cap, V-neck sweater, and tie, his big moustache framing his big grin. Miles from that spot we passed some houses, six of them, built like adobe huts with log butts sticking in a trim row from the roof. This was the Central Plateau, and descending it after lunch we saw signs of irrigation, some green oases, and, far off, the dusty outlines of high mountains. But it was a strain to look out the window, for the glare and the heat increased. By late afternoon the temperature was in the 90s and suffocating dust collected on every surface.

'It looks more or less like this all the way to Pakistan,' said the marathon runner. 'The same, very flat and brown, but of course much hotter and dustier.'

I went to my compartment and lay down, like a Hindu widow on a pyre, resigned to *suttee*. To cheer me up still further, a small spotty-faced Australian girl from one of the third-class cars wandered by my couchette and asked if she could have a drink. I offered her *raki*; she wanted water. There were six people in her compartment. The previous night one had crept away – she didn't know where – 'so it wasn't so bad with five. I mean, I slept for a couple of hours, but tonight there'll be six again, and I'm buggered if I know what I'm going to do.' She looked around my couchette and smiled. 'I'm Linda.'

'I'd ask you to stay here,' I said, 'but the thing is, Linda, it's so small we'd be on top of each other in no time.'

'Well, thanks for the drink.'

She was a student and, like the others, had a student card to prove it. Even the oldest, most ragged and drugged chieftain had a student card. And for good reason: a card got each one a 50 per cent reduction on the ticket. The spotty Australian girl was paying nine dollars to get from Istanbul to Teheran. My own ticket cost fifty dollars, which was ridiculously cheap for two thousand miles of travel in a private compartment with a fan, a sink, and enough pillows so that I could prop myself on my berth like a pasha and consult Nagel on the passing towns.

One was Kayseri, formerly Caesarea. It appeared at the window that hot afternoon. It had known a number of conquerors since the year A.D. 17, when Tiberius made it the capital of Cappadocia: the Sassanids in the sixth century, the Arabs in the seventh and eighth; it was Byzantine in the ninth, Armenian in the tenth, and the Seljuks captured it a year after the Battle of Hastings. Eventually it was taken by Bayezid, whom some English lecturers know as Bajazeth, Tamburlaine's crazed captive who brains himself against the bars of a cage in the first part of Marlowe's *Tamburlaine the Great*. It was after the historical Tamerlane defeated Bayezid at the Battle of Angora (1402) that Caesarea was annexed; then it was occupied by the Mamelukes and in the sixteenth century became part of the Ottoman Empire. But dust does not hold the footprints of conquerors, and not even the bright name of Tamerlane makes this monotonous-looking town interesting. The successive conquests only robbed it of its features, leaving it nothing marvellous except a mosque that might have been built by the architect Sinan, a genius who put up the greatest mosques of Istanbul and is best known for having repaired Saint Sofia's with ingenious and massive buttresses. The pencil-like minarets of the mosque in Kayseri are just visible between the grotesque tenements, and farther from the town, beyond rows of poplar trees with pale spinning leaves, there are straggling suburbs of doghouses with crooked windows and fatuous little bungalows where Tamerlane's inheritors are lounging in their gardens, dolefully scanning the horizon for another conqueror.

It is dusk, the serenest hour in Central Turkey: a few bright stars depend from a velvet blue sky, the mountains are suitably black, and the puddles near the spigots of village wells have the shimmering colour and uncertain shape of pools of mercury. Night falls quickly, and it is all black, and only the smell of the dust still settling reminds you of the exhausting day.

'Mister?' It is the green-eyed Turkish conductor on his way to lock the sleeping-car door against the marauders he imagines in the rest of the train.

'Yes?'

'Turkey good or bad?'

'Good,' I said.

'Thank you, Mister.'

From Malatya that third day we crossed the upper reaches of the Euphrates River, to Elazig and beyond, pushing slowly towards Lake Van, stopping often, and, as the whistle's echo dies, starting again. The houses were still square, but were made of round stones and appeared like cairns showing the way to a carefully irrigated oasis. Farther on there were sheep and goats on the humpy plain; if there had been any grass in evidence one would have said they were grazing. But there was no grass at all, and the battered features of these animals matched the battered ground they stood upon. At several halts children chased the train; they were blond and lively and might have been Swiss, except for their rags. The landscape repeated, becoming bigger, drier, emptier with repetition; the distant mountains had massive volcanic wrinkles, some very green, and the closer hills had these folds as well, but they were brown and scorched, like overbaked pie crust.

The door to my compartment flew open as I was looking at this desolation. It was the saffron-faced man from next door with the large family. He gestured, winced, closed the door, and sat down. He held his head. His children were crying; I could hear them through the window. The man had a narrow moustache and his expression was that of the comedian to whom everything bad happens, the sad figure who suits comedy. He made another helpless gesture, somewhat apologetic, and lit a cigarette. Then he sat back and smoked it. He did not speak. He sighed, finished his cigarette, stubbed it out, slapped his knee and pulled the door open, and, without looking back, marched in the direction of his screaming children.

It was lunchtime, and lunch on the Lake Van Express could be very pleasant if you got to the dining car early enough to be on the shady side and had sufficient elbow room to continue with *Little Dorrit*. I had just started to eat and read when one of the subchiefs sloped in and sat with me. He had long blond hair in the page-boy style affected by aspiring prophets. His shirt had been artistically cut from a flour sack and he wore a very faded pair of 'Washington Brand' bib overalls, an elephant-hair bracelet on one wrist, and an Indian bangle on the other. I had seen him sitting in a lotus posture in second class. He put a worn book by Idries Shah on the table; it had the chewed-over look Korans have in the hands of the languid fanatics I saw later in the holy city of Meshed. But he did not read it.

I asked him where he was going.

He shook his head; his hair danced. 'Just' – he raised his eyes and said with drama – '*travelling*.'

He looked rather pious, but it might have been the train. Second class in that part of Turkey lent to every dusty face a look of suffering piety.

His melon came. It was cut into cubes. He smiled at it in a pitying way and said, 'They *cut* it.'

I volunteered the information that the Turks at the next table had uncut melon. Whole slices, complete with rinds, rested on their plates.

The subchief considered this; then he leaned over and looked me in the eye. 'It's a strange world.'

I hoped for his state of mind that it wouldn't get any hotter. But it did, searing the air, and the shades were drawn in every compartment. Each time I began to read or write I dropped off to sleep, waking only when the train came to a complete stop. These were halts in the desert, a little hut, a man with a flag, a signboard reading MUSH or BUG. I wrote a few lines and was alarmed to see my handwriting assume the anxious irregularity of the lost explorer's, the desert diary script that is decoded and published posthumously by the man's widow. *The next time the whistle blows*, I would say to myself, *I will get up and walk to the engine*. But I was always asleep when the whistle blew.

We reached Lake Van at about ten at night, which was annoying. The darkness made it impossible for me to confirm the stories I had heard of the swimming cats, the high soda content of the water that bleaches clothes and turns the hair of Turks who swim in it a bright red. I had another regret: it was the end of the line for this express. The sleeping car was taken off and I had no idea what the arrangements were for the rest of the journey. The diesel engine was removed; a steam locomotive pulled us down to the ferry landing and for several hours shunted the cars two at a time on to the ferry itself. While this was going on I found the new conductor, an Iranian; I showed him my ticket.

He pushed it aside and said, 'No couchette.'

'This is a first–class ticket,' I said.

'No room,' he said. 'You go down dere.'

*Down there*. He was pointing to the cars just being loaded on to the ferry, the third–class coaches. After three days of passing through them on my way to the dining car, I thought of them with pure horror. I knew the occupants: there was a bandy-legged gang of dark Japanese with bristly hair who travelled with a dwarf squaw, also Japanese, whose camera on a thong around her neck bumped her knees. Their chief was a fierce-looking young man in military sunglasses who sucked an unlit pipe and wore rubber shower sandals. There was also a Germanic tribe: bearded boys and porcine girls with crew cuts. Their chief was a gorilla who loitered in the passage and sometimes refused to let anyone pass. There were Swiss and French and Australians who slept, waking only to complain or ask the time. And there were the Americans, some of whom I knew by name. The chiefs were having a powwow on the ferry; the others were watching from the rail.

'Go,' said the conductor.

But I didn't want to go, for besides the overcrowded compart-

ments of Europeans and Americans there were the compartments of Kurds, Turks, Iranians, and Afghans, who slept on
top of each other and cooked stews between their berths over
dangerously flaring kerosene stoves.

The ferry moved off, hooting into the black lake. I chased
the conductor from one deck to the other, trying to continue
my argument. It was past midnight, I said, cornering him down
below where the huge railway cars clanked against the chains that
held them to the tracks in the deck: where was my compartment?

He put me in second class with three Australians. It was a
situation I grew to recognize over the next three months. At
my lowest point, when things were at their most desperate
and uncomfortable, I always found myself in the company of
Australians, who were like a reminder that I'd touched bottom.
This trio on the Lake Van ferry considered me an intruder. They
looked up surprised in their meal: they were sharing a loaf of
bread, hunched over it like monkeys, two boys and a pop-eyed
girl. They grumbled when I asked them to move their knapsacks
from my berth. The engines of the ferry rattled the compartment
windows and I went to bed wondering how, if the ferry sank, I
could scramble to safety, out of the compartment and the car
and up the narrow stairs to the boat deck. I did not sleep well,
and once I was awakened by the harsh antipodean groans of the
girl, who, not two feet from me, lay beneath one of her snorting
companions.

At dawn, in the rapid light of early morning, we arrived at
the eastern shore of the lake. Here the train becomes the Teheran
Express. The Australians were breakfasting, pulling the remainder of their loaf to bits. I went into the corridor to count out
what I thought the conductor might accept as a bribe.

# 4. The Teheran Express

As the new Teheran Express pulls out of the modern supermarket-style frontier station at Qotūr on tracks that shriek with newness (Iranian National Railways are modernizing and expanding), the steward in the French-built dining car takes off his crisp white jacket, unrolls a lovely square of carpet, and gets down on his knees to pray. He does this five times a day in a little corner between the cash register and the kitchen, intoning, 'There is no God but God and Mohammed is his prophet,' while diners slurp lemony soup and pick at chicken kebab. The giant glass and concrete stations house three portraits – the Shah, his queen, and their son. They are fifteen times life-size and the vulgarity of the enlargement makes them look plump and greedy and monstrously regal. The smiling son might be one of those precocious child entertainers who tap-dance in talent shows, singing 'I've Got Rhythm'. It is an old country; everywhere in the gleaming modernity are reminders of the orthodox past – the praying steward, the portraits, the encampments of nomads, and, on what is otherwise one of the best-run railways in the world, the yearning for *baksheesh*.

Again I showed the conductor my ticket. 'First-class ticket,' I said. 'You give me first-class couchette.'

'No couchette,' he said. He pointed to my berth in the Australian compartment.

'No,' I said. I pointed to an empty compartment. 'I want this one.'

'No.' He gave me a fanatical grin.

He was grinning at my hand. I held thirty Turkish liras (about two dollars). His hand appeared near mine. I dropped my voice and whispered the word that is known all over the East, '*Baksheesh.*'

He took the money and pocketed it. He got my bag from the Australian compartment and carried it to another compartment in which there were a battered suitcase and a box of crackers. He slid the bag into the luggage rack and patted the berth. He asked if I wanted sheets and blankets. I said yes. He got them, and a pillow, too. He drew the curtains, shutting out the sun. He bowed and brought me a pitcher of ice water, and he smiled, as if to say, 'All this could have been yours yesterday.'

The suitcase and crackers belonged to a large bald Turk named Sadik, who wore baggy woollen trousers and a stretched sweater. He was from one of the wilder parts of Turkey, the Upper Valley of Greater Zap; he had boarded the train in Van; he was going to Australia.

He came in and drew his arm across his sweating face. He said, 'Are you in here?'

'Yes.'

'How much did you give him?'

I told him.

He said, 'I gave him fifteen rials. He is very dishonest, but now he is on our side. He will not put anyone else in here, so now we have this big room together.'

Sadik smiled; he had crooked teeth. It is not skinny people who look hungry, but rather fat ones, and Sadik looked famished.

'I think it's only fair to say,' I said, wondering how I was going to finish the sentence, 'that I'm not, um, queer. Well, you know, I don't like boys and –'

'And me, I don't like,' said Sadik, and with that he lay down and went to sleep. He had the gift of slumber; he needed only to be horizontal and he was sound asleep, and he always slept in the same sweater and trousers. He never took them off, and for the duration of the trip to Teheran he neither shaved nor washed.

He was an unlikely tycoon. He admitted he behaved like a pig, but he had lots of money and his career was a successful record of considerable ingenuity. He had started out exporting Turkish curios to France and he seems to have been in the vanguard of the movement, monopolizing the puzzle-ring and copper-pot trade in Europe long before anyone else thought of it. He paid no export duties in Turkey, no import duties in France. He managed this by shipping crates of worthless articles to the French border and warehousing them there. He went to French wholesalers with his samples, took orders, and left the wholesalers the headache of importing the goods. He did this for three years and banked the money in Switzerland.

'When I have enough money,' said Sadik, whose English was not perfect, 'I like to start a travel agency. Where you want to go? Budapesht? Prague? Rumania? Bulgaria? All nice places, oh boy! Turkish people like to travel. But they are very silly. They don't speak English. They say to me, "Mister Sadik, I want a coffee" – this is in Prague. I say, "Ask the waiter." They are afraid. They shout their eyes. But they have money in their packets. I say to the waiter, "Coffee" – he understand. Everyone understand coffee, but Turkish people don't speak any language, so all the time I am translator. This, I tell you, drive me crazy. The people they follow me. "Mister Sadik, take me to a night-club"; "Mister Sadik, find me a gairl." They follow me even to the lavabo and sometime I want to escape, so I am clever and I use the service elevator.

'I give up Budapesht, Belgrade. I decide to take pilgrims to Mecca. They pay me five thousand liras and I take care of everything. I get smallpox injections and stamp the book – sometimes I stamp the book and don't get smallpox injections! I have a friend in the medical. Ha! But I take good care of them. I buy them rubber mattresses, each person one mattress, blow them up so you don't have to sleep on the floor. I take them to Mecca, Medina, Jiddah, then I leave them. "I have business in Jiddah," I say. But I go to Beirut. You know Beirut? Nice place

– nightclubs, gairls, lots of fun. Then I come back to Jiddah, pick up the *hajis* and bring them back to Istanbul. Good profit.'

I asked Sadik why, if he was a Muslim and he was so close to Mecca, he never made the *haj* himself.

'Once you go to Mecca you have to make promises – no drinking, no swearing, no women, money to poor people.' He laughed. 'Is for old men. I'm not ready!'

He was headed now for Australia, which he pronounced 'Owstraalia'; he had another idea. It had come to him one day in Saudi Arabia when he was bored (he said as soon as he began making money in a project he lost interest in it). His new idea concerned the export of Turks to Australia. There was a shortage of workers there. He would go, and, much as he had sold puzzle rings to the French, visit Australian industrialists and find out what sort of skilled people they required. He would make a list. His partner in Istanbul would get up a large group of emigrants and deal with the paperwork, obtaining passports, health cards and references. Then the Turks would be sent on a charter flight that Sadik would arrange, and after collecting a fee from the Turks he would collect from the Australians. He winked. 'Good profit.'

It was Sadik who pointed out to me that the hippies were doomed. They dressed like wild Indians, he said, but basically they were middle-class Americans. They didn't understand *baksheesh*, and because they were always holding tight to their money and expecting to scrounge food and hospitality they would always lose. He resented the fact that the hippie chiefs were surrounded by such young pretty girls. 'These guys are ugly and I am ugly too, so why don't the gairls like me?'

He enjoyed telling stories against himself. The best one concerned a blonde he had picked up in an Istanbul bar. It was midnight; he was drunk and feeling lecherous. He took the blonde home and made love to her twice, then slept for a few hours, woke up and made love to her again. Late the next day as he was crawling out of bed he noticed the blonde needed a shave and then he saw the wig and the man's enormous penis. ' "Only Sadik," my friends say, "only Sadik can make love to a man three times and think it is a woman!" But I was very drunk.'

Sadik was good company on a dull stretch of the journey. We had taken on thirty freight cars and the train moved very slowly through northwestern Iran towards Teheran, across the most infertile soil I have ever seen. Here, in a baking desert, one is grateful for a good train, and the Teheran Express could not have been better. The dining car was a clean cheerful place, and there were vases of red gladioli on each starched tablecloth. The food was excellent, but unvarying; always the lemony soup, the kebab, and a stack of flat, square, blotterlike bread. The sleeping car was air-conditioned to such a degree that one needed two blankets at night. The farther one got from Europe, it seemed, the more sumptuous the trains became. At Qazvīn, another oversized supermarket station in the desert, I discovered that we were running ten hours late, but I had no deadline to meet and in any case have always preferred comfort to punctuality. So I sat and read and over lunch I listened to Sadik's plan to make a killing in Australia. Outside, the landscape had begun to acquire features – hills rose, a plateau appeared, then a blue-green range of mountains to the north; villages grew more frequent, and there were refineries spouting flames and shortly we were in Teheran.

Sadik bought a ticket for a train to Meshed that was leaving that same day. He hadn't planned to, but as he was standing in line he overheard two pretty girls buying third-class tickets and saw the clerk assign them a compartment. In third class on Iranian Railways no distinction is made as to sex. Sadik asked for third class and was put in the same compartment: 'So we see what can happen! Wish me luck.'

Teheran, a boom town grafted on to a village, is a place of no antiquity and little interest, unless one has a particular fascination for bad driving and a traffic situation twenty times worse than

New York's. There is talk of building a subway system, but the plumbing in Teheran is of the village variety; the sewage is pumped into the ground beneath each building, so the process of tunnelling would very likely produce a cholera epidemic of gigantic proportions. One man I met verified this by claiming that you had to dig down only ten feet anywhere in the city and you would strike sewage; in a few years it would be five.

In spite of its size and apparent newness it retains the most obnoxious features of a bazaar, as Dallas does, and Teheran has all the qualities of that oil-rich Texas city: the spurious glamour, the dust and heat, the taste for plastic, the evidence of cash. The women are lovely; they skitter around holding other women's hands — even the most chic — or else they are bent sideways, on the arm of a small shrouded granny. Wealth has allowed the Iranian little except the single excess of being overdressed; in-deed, the freezing air conditioning seems to be designed for no other purpose than permitting rich Iranians to wear fashionable English clothes, for which they have a special fondness. There is about this decadence a peculiar absence of the physical that begins to look uncivilized in the most limiting way. Women are seldom seen with men; there are few couples, no lovers, and at dusk Teheran becomes a city of males, prowling in groups or loitering. The bars are exclusively male; the men drink in expen-sive suits, continually searching the room with anxious eyes, as if in expectation of a woman. But there are no women, and the lugubrious alternatives to sex are apparent: the film posters showing fat Persian girls in shortie pyjamas; nightclubs with belly dancers, strippers, kick lines, and comedians in ridiculous hats whose every Farsi joke is a reference to the sex the patrons are denied. Money pulls the Iranian in one direction, religion drags him in another, and the result is a stupid starved creature for whom woman is only meat. Thus spake Zarathustra: an ugly monomaniac with a diamond tiara, who calls himself 'The King of Kings', is their answer to government, a firing squad their answer to law.

Less frightening, but no less disgusting, is the Iranian taste for jam made out of carrots.

Because of the oil, Teheran is very much a city of foreigners. There are two daily papers in English, a French daily, *Journal de Teheran*, and a German weekly, *Die Post*. Not surprisingly, the sports page of the English-language *Teheran Journal* is taken up with such non-Persian news as a profile of Hank Aaron ('A Great Player – A Great Person'), who was then about to break Babe Ruth's lifetime homer record of 714 before an uninterested Atlanta crowd ('Atlanta is the disgrace of baseball'); the rest of the sports news was similarly American, except for one small item about Iran's cycling team. You do not have to go far in Teheran to find out whom these newspapers are written for. There is no shortage of Americans in the city, and even the American oil-rig fitters in outlying areas of the country are allowed seven days in Teheran for every seven they spend on the site. Consequently, the bars have the atmosphere of Wild West saloons.

Take the Caspien Hotel Bar. There are tall Americans lounging on sofas drinking Tuborg straight from the bottle, a few hard-faced wives and girlfriends chain-smoking near them, and one man holding forth at the bar.

'I go up to the son of a bitch and say, "X-ray them welds," and he just looks at me kind of dumb. Ain't been no X-raying here for three weeks. Whole goddamned thang gonna fall down sure as anything. He says to me –'

'We saw the Albrights down in Qom. She had just the prettiest dress,' says the lady on the sofa. She had kicked off her shoes. 'Bought it right here, she said.'

'Well, shit, I didn't know what to do,' says the man at the bar. 'I told him I wouldn't leave the site if it didn't look okay to me. If he keeps it up he can have his damned job. I can go back to Saudi any old time I want.'

A big middle-aged man in blue jeans comes in. He staggers a bit, but he is smiling.

'Gene, you old son of a bitch, get in here,' calls the man from the bar.

'Hi, Russ,' says the big man, and as he says it a few Iranians move aside.

'Sit down afore you fall down.'

'Buy me a drink, ya dirty bastard.'

'Your ass I will,' says Russ. He pulls out a lumpy wallet and shows Gene. 'Only got a hundred rials to my name.'

'They're Texas,' says the lady on the sofa. 'We're Oklahoma.'

The voices in the bar grow louder. Russ is saying 'ole buddy' to a man at the bar, who is hunched over a bottle and from the back looks wholly crapulous. Gene is standing a few feet away, drinking beer and smiling between pulls on his bottle.

'Hey, Wayne,' says Russ to the hunched-over man, 'who we gonna fight tonight?'

Wayne shakes his head, Gene rubs his cheek with a hand so sunburned, the tattoos barely show.

'Have a drink, Wayne,' says Russ. 'Have a drink, Gene. And ask Billy what he wants.'

Russ slaps Wayne on the back and there is a great crash as Wayne tumbles to the floor between the bar stools. His gold jersey is hiked up to his armpits. Billy comes over (he has been drinking with the women) and helps Russ and Gene get Wayne to his feet and propped against a stool. Wayne's pink back is exposed. His head is shaven, his ears stick out, his elbows are braced on the bar, and he takes hold of his bottle the way a sailor might grip a mast in a high wind, squinting at his two hands and muttering.

The Iranians, who have been silent the whole time, begin to babble in Farsi to the waiter. They look as if they want to start a scene, and Billy, sensing this, says, 'What are you telling him?' to one of the Iranians.

'Come here, ole buddy,' says Russ to the other Iranian. He winks at Wayne, and Wayne, recovering, stands up. Russ jerks the Iranian's jacket sleeve. 'I wanna talk to you real quick.'

The ladies on the sofa begin to leave, hugging handbags, making for the door.

'Hey!' says Russ to them.

'You boys are getting kinda roughhouse.'

The ladies leave, and, seeing what was about to happen, I follow them into the noisy street, swearing that I will flee Teheran on the next available train.

My original route, the one I had marked out on my map before I left London, took me south from Teheran to Khalidabad for the spur to Isfahan, and from there southeast to Yazd, Bāfq, and Zarand, where the railway stops. I would then cross Baluchistan by bus and pick up Pakistan Western Railways at the Iranian station of Zāhedān, and head eastward on the main lines of Pakistan.

'Sure it's possible,' said an embassy officer, 'but it's not advisable. It'll take you the best part of a week to get to Quetta, and apart from anything else that's a hell of a long time to go without a shower.'

I said that I had just gone five days without a shower and it hadn't worried me. What I was concerned about were the Baluchi tribesmen: were they fighting in that area?

'You better believe it!'

'So you don't think it's a very good idea for me to go that way?'

'I'd say you'd be a damned fool to risk it.'

Another traveller might have taken up the challenge to go southeast. I was grateful for the chance to turn my back on it. I thanked him for his advice and bought a ticket for a train northeast to Meshed.

# 5. The Night Mail to Meshed

MESHED, in the northeast of Iran – about 100 miles from the Afghanistan border and even fewer to the Soviet one – is a holy city; consequently, the most fervent Muslims take the Night Mail, and everywhere on it are Persians in the postures of devotion, murmuring prayers to get to Heaven, though

> A Persian's Heav'n is easily made –
> 'Tis but black eyes and lemonade.

At the evening call to prayer it is as if the train has been stricken with some strange illness. The passengers fall to their knees and salaam. The Night Mail to Meshed is probably the only train in the world in which all the passengers ride facing in the opposite direction from the one they're travelling in: they bob along with their eyes turned to Mecca. During the trip, the pressure of prayer builds and the carriages vibrate with these devotions. On the Teheran Express the women wear skirts and blouses; on the Night Mail they are swathed in robes, and their veils reveal nothing of their faces.

It was undoubtedly the Muslim character of the train that had eliminated beer from the dining car. But it was a hot evening when we left Teheran and I was anxious for a drink. I was saving my full bottle of gin for Afghanistan.

'No beer, eh?' I said to the steward. 'What *do* you have?'

'Chichen chebub.'

'No, what other drinks do you have?'

'Biftek.'

'Any wine?'

He nodded.

'What kind?'

'Chichen pilaff, soup, *salade*.'

I abandoned the idea of drinking and decided to have a meal. I was eating and watching the passing moonscape – craters, stark mountains on the horizon, and sand as far as the eye could see – when a man in a bush jacket, carrying a newspaper and a shopping bag, approached and said, 'Mind if I join you?'

'Not at all.' His newspaper, the London *Daily Telegraph*, was five days old; his shopping bag contained many cans of disinfectant. He sat, his elbow on the paper, his chin resting in his hand, in an attitude of concentration.

'Look at that girl,' he said. A pretty girl went past, and as she was in a rather tight-fitting dress and not the heavy wimple and habit the other women were wearing, she drew stares from the diners. I started to remark on this, but he shushed me. 'Wait. I want to concentrate on this.' He regarded the girl's backside until she was out of the car and said, 'I'd love to meet a girl like that.'

'Why don't you introduce yourself? It shouldn't be too difficult.'

'Impossible. They won't talk to you. And if you want to take them out – say, for a meal or a show – they won't go unless you intend to marry them.'

'That *is* awkward,' I said.

'And that's not all. I live in the wilds – no women in Ezna.'

'I take it you come up on weekends.'

'You're joking! This is my second time in Teheran – the first was four months ago.'

'You've been in the desert for four months?'

'The mountains,' he said. 'But it comes to the same thing.'

I asked him why he had chosen to live in the mountains of Iran, on a station where there were no women, if he was so keen on meeting a nice girl.

'I was supposed to meet one here. I knew her in Riyadh – a secretary, very nice girl – and she said she was coming to

Teheran. Change of job. So when I got back to the U.K. I took this contract and wrote her a letter. But that was six months ago and she still hasn't answered.'

It was now dark outside, moonless, impenetrable, desert darkness; the tables of the dining car transmitted the click–click of the wheels to the knives and forks, and the stewards were removing the jackets of their neatly pressed uniforms for evening prayers. The engineer – he was an engineer, supervising the construction of an oil rig – continued his melancholy tale, about having signed a three-year contract in Iran on the slender possibility of meeting the secretary.

'What I'd really like to do is meet a wealthy girl, not Sophia Loren, but pretty and with some money. I used to know one – her father was in banking – but she was queer, always putting on a little-girl act. Couldn't see myself being married to that! Look.'

The girl who had passed through the dining car earlier had returned and was marching past once again. This time I had a good look at her, and I think one would have had to have been alone in the Iranian mountains for four months to find any charm in her. The engineer was absolutely ecstatic in a way I found touching and hopeless. 'God,' he said, 'the things I could do with her!'

Attempting to change the subject, I asked him what he did for amusement on the site.

'There's a snooker table and a darts board,' he said, 'but they're in such bad condition I don't use them. Anyway, even if they were usable I wouldn't go to the club. Can't stand the smell of the toilets. That's one of the reasons I went into Teheran – to buy some Harpic. I've got nine cans of it.

'What do I do? Well, let's see. Normally I read – I love reading. And I'm learning Farsi. Sometimes I work overtime. I listen to the radio a lot. Oh, it's a quiet sort of life. That's why I'd like to meet a girl.'

I suggested that the fact that he had spent, as he told me, the past seven years in Saudi Arabia, Abu Dhabi, and Iran might have something to do with his protracted bachelorhood. He readily agreed.

'What about brothels?'

'Not for me, mate. I want a nice steady girl – clean, pretty, with money, the works. My brother's had lots of them. It really annoys me. There was a ladies' hairdresser from Uxbridge, lovely she was, and she was mad about him. I was staying with him – I had home leave – in his flat in Hayes. But would he pay the slightest bit of attention to her? Not at all! She finally left him. Married someone else. I don't blame her. I'd love to have a chance with a girl like that. I'd take her to a show, buy her flowers, treat her to a slap-up meal. That's what I'd do. I'd be good to her. But my brother's selfish, always has been. Wants a big car and a colour telly, only interested in himself. Me, I'm interested in all kinds of people.

'I don't know why I'm running on like this, but my last home leave nearly finished me. I found a really sweet girl, a typist, from Chester, and just as things were going well I was rung up by her ex-boyfriend. Said he was going to kill me. I had to drop her.'

The dining car was now empty, the stewards had ended their prayers and were setting the tables for breakfast.

'I think they want us to leave,' I said.

'I've got great respect for these people,' said the engineer. 'You can laugh if you want, but I've often thought of becoming a Muslim.'

'I wouldn't laugh at that.'

'You have to know the Koran backwards and forwards. It's not easy. I've been reading it on the site – course, I keep it quiet. If my manager caught me reading the Koran he wouldn't understand. He'd think I was a nutter. But I think that might be the answer. Become a Muslim, renew my contract after three years, and meet a nice Persian girl. It should be dead easy to meet them if you're a Muslim.'

The conversation, like many others I had with people on

trains, derived an easy candour from the shared journey, the comfort of the dining car, and the certain knowledge that neither of us would see each other again. The railway was a fictor's bazaar, in which anyone with the patience could carry away a memory to pore over in privacy. The memories were inconclusive, but an ending, as in the best fiction, was always implied. The sad engineer would never go back to England; he would become one of these elderly expatriates who hide out in remote countries, with odd sympathies, a weakness for the local religion, an unreasonable anger, and the kind of total recall that drives curious strangers away.

There were three people in my compartment, a Canadian husband and wife and a grim hairy boy from an East London slum. They were all going to Australia – the Canadian couple because 'We didn't feel like learning French', the cockney because London 'is 'eaving with bloody Indians'. It must be a sociological fact that prejudice is a more common motive for emigration than poverty, but what interested me about these three was that they were, like so many others, going to Australia the cheapest way, via Afghanistan and India, living like the poorest they were among, eating vile food, and sleeping in bug-ridden hotel rooms, because they were rejecting a society they saw to be in decay.

Their dialogue was absolutely petrifying. I hired a blanket and pillow from the conductor, who demanded only a token bribe, had a gin anaesthetic, and went to sleep.

The hooting of the train woke me early the next morning for the sight of camels grazing among brown bushes and great herds of sheep bunched together on sandy hillsides. The villages were few, but their design was extraordinary; they were walled and low and resembled the kind of sand castles you see parents making for their children at the seashore, with a bucket and spade. They had tiny windows, crumbling ramparts, and inexact crenelations; impressive at a distance, up close they were visibly coming apart, the fortifications merely a feeble challenge to intruders. Women squatted in front of the walls in a stiff wind, keeping their veils against their faces by biting on a corner, holding the cloth in their teeth.

Meshed appeared abruptly from the desert, a city of gold-domed mosques and the white quills of minarets. At the station, pilgrims piled out of the train dragging carpetbags and bedrolls. This station, 4000 miles from London, is the end of the line: between this easternmost station of Iranian National Railways and the little Pakistani station at Landi Kotal in the Khyber Pass, lies Afghanistan, a country without a single inch of railway track.

After an hour in Meshed I was anxious to leave. It was Ramadhan, the Muslim period of fasting, and no food was being sold during the day. I ate my Iranian processed cheese and found two hippies, chiefs who seemed to have lost the rest of their tribe. They couldn't understand why I didn't want to stay in Meshed. 'It's good,' one said. 'It's funky, it's loose. You could hang out here.'

'I'm trying to get to Pakistan,' I said.

'First you have to cross Afghanistan,' the other said. He was little, bearded, and carried a guitar. 'It's in the way, like.'

'Come with us if you want. We're going to move out. We've been this way so many times we just get in that train, pull down the shades, and crash.' He was wearing Indian pyjamas, sandals, an embroidered waistcoat, a beaded necklace, and bangles, like a Turk in a Victorian etching, but without the scimitar or turban. 'Hurry up if you're coming, or we'll miss the bus.'

'I hate buses,' I said.

'Hear that, Bobby? He hates buses.'

But Bobby didn't reply. He was staring at a girl, probably American, who was leaving the station. She clomped unsteadily in a pair of high-soled wooden clogs.

'Those shoes really get me,' said Bobby. 'Chicks can't even walk in them. I'll bet the guy that invented them is some screamer who really hates chicks.'

*

Afghanistan is a nuisance. Formerly it was cheap and barbarous, and people went there to buy lumps of hashish – they would spend weeks in the filthy hotels of Herat and Kabul, staying high. But there was a military coup in 1973, and the king (who was sunning himself in Italy) was deposed. Now Afghanistan is expensive but just as barbarous as before. Even the hippies have begun to find it intolerable. The food smells of cholera, travel there is always uncomfortable and sometimes dangerous, and the Afghans are lazy, idle, and violent. I had not been there long before I regretted having changed my plans to take the southern route. True, there was a war in Baluchistan, but Baluchistan was small. I was determined to deal with Afghanistan swiftly and put that discomfort into parentheses. But it was a week before I boarded another train.

The Customs Office was closed for the night. We could not go back to the Iranian frontier; we could not proceed into Herat. So we remained on a strip of earth, neither Afghanistan nor Iran, in a hotel without a name. There was no electricity in this hotel, there was no toilet, and there was enough water for only one cup of tea apiece. Bobby and his friend, who went under the name Lopez (his real name was Morris), became frightfully happy when the Afghan in the candlelit foyer told us our beds would cost thirty-five cents each. Lopez asked for hashish. The Afghan said there was none. Lopez called him a 'scumbag'. The Afghan brought a piece the size of a dog's turd and we spent the rest of the evening smoking it. At about midnight a telephone rang in the darkness. Lopez said, 'If it's for me, tell them I'm not here!'

On our way into Herat the next day an Afghan passenger fired his shotgun through the roof of the bus and there was a fight to determine who would pay to have the hole mended. My ears were still ringing from the explosion a day later in Herat, as I watched groups of hippies standing in the thorn bushes complaining about the exchange rate. At three o'clock the next morning there was a parade down the main street of Herat, farting cornets and snare drums: it was the sort of bizarre nightmare old men have in German novels. I asked Lopez if he'd heard the parade, but he brushed my question aside. He was worried, he said; cawing like a broker, and waving his bangled wrists despairingly, he told his bad news: the dollar was quoted at fifty afghanis. 'It's a rip-off!'

I went, by bus and plane, to Kabul, via Mazar-i-Sharif. Two incidents in Kabul stay in my mind: a visit to the Kabul Insane Asylum, where I failed to gain the release of a Canadian who had been put there by mistake (he said he didn't mind staying there as long as he had a supply of chocolate bars; it was better than going back to Canada), and, later that week, passing a Pathan tent encampment and seeing a camel suddenly collapse under a great load of wood – a moment later the Pathans pounced, dismembering and skinning the poor beast. I had no wish to stay longer in Kabul. I took a bus east, to the top of the Khyber Pass. I had a train to catch there, at Landi Kotal, for Peshawar; and I dreaded missing it, because there is only one train a week, a Sunday local called the '132-Down'.

# 6. The Khyber Pass Local

THE Khyber Pass on the Afghanistan side of the frontier is rockier, higher, and more dramatic than on the Pakistan side, but at Tor Kham – the border – it turns green, and for this foliage one feels enormous gratitude. It was the first continuous greenery I had seen since leaving Istanbul. It begins as lichen on the rock faces, and pale clumps of weed sprouting from crevices; then bushes and low trees the wind has twisted into a mass of elbows, and finally grassy slopes, turning leafy as one nears Peshawar. It is like a seasonal change in the space of a day, this movement from the sharp-featured heights and gorges outside Jalalabad to the cliffs of Landi Khana, bearded with windblown bouquets of wild flowers. The change is abrupt; there cannot be many countries so close geographically and yet so distinctly different. The landscape softens where the border line on the map begins, and the grizzled faces of Afghans, whose heads are sloppily swathed in white turbans, are replaced by the angular beakiness of Pakistanis, who wear narrow slippers and have the thin scornful moustaches of magicians and movie villains.

And there is the Khyber Railway, a further pleasure. Built fifty years ago at great cost, it is an engineering marvel. It has thirty-four tunnels, ninety-two bridges and culverts, and climbs to 3600 feet. The train is well guarded: on bluffs above the track, in little garrisons and pillboxes, the Khyber Rifles stand sentry duty, staring blankly at the plummeting blue-black ravines on Afghanistan's inhospitable edge.

There is only one train a week on the Khyber Railway, and practically all the passengers are what the Pakistanis refer to as 'tribal people', the Kuki, Malikdin, Kambar, and Zakka Khel, indistinguishable in their rags. They use the train for their weekly visit to the bazaar in Peshawar. It is an outing for them, this day in town, so the platform at Landi Kotal station in the Khyber Pass is mobbed with excited tribesmen tramping up and down in their bare feet, waiting for the train to start. I found a seat in the last car and watched a tribesman, who was almost certainly insane, quarrelling on the platform with some beggars. A beggar would limp over to a waiting family and stick his hand out. The lunatic would then rush up to the beggar and scream at him. Some of the beggars ignored him; one hit back, rather lazily slapping him until a policeman intervened.

The lunatic was old. He had a long beard, an army surplus overcoat, and wore sandals cut from rubber tyres. He squawked at the policeman and boarded the train, choosing a seat very near me. He began to sing. This amused the passengers. He sang louder. Beggars had been passing through the car – lepers, blind men led by little boys, men on crutches – the usual parade of rural unfortunates. They shuffled from one end of the car to the other, moaning. The passengers watched them with some interest, but no one gave them anything. The beggars carried tin cans of dry bread crusts. The lunatic mocked them: he made faces at a blind man; he screamed at a leper. The passengers laughed; the beggars passed on. A one-armed man boarded. He stood flourishing his good arm, presenting his stump, a four-inch bone at his shoulder.

'Allah is great! Look, my arm is missing! Give something to my wounded self!'

'Go away, you stupid man!' shouted the lunatic.

'Please give,' said the one-armed man. He started down the car.

'Go away, stupid! We don't want you here!' The lunatic rose to torment the man, and as he did so the man pounced on him and gave him a terrific wallop on the side of his head, sending him reeling into his seat. When the one-armed man left, the lunatic resumed his singing. But now he had no listeners.

The translation of this dialogue was provided by two men

sitting near me, Mr Haq and Mr Hassan. Mr Haq, a man of about sixty-five, was a lawyer from Lahore. Mr Hassan, from Peshawar, was his friend. They had just come from the border where, Mr Haq said, 'We were making certain inquiries.'

'You will like Peshawar,' said Mr Hassan. 'It is a nice little town.'

'I would like to interrupt my learned friend to say that he does not know what he is talking,' said Mr Haq. 'I am an old man – I know what I am talking. Peshawar is *not* a nice town at all. It *was*, yes, but not now. The Afghanistan government and the Russians want to capture it. It was the Russians and Indians who took a piece of Pakistan away, what they are calling Bangladesh. Well. Peshawar was once great some time back. It is full of history, but I don't know what is going to happen to us.'

The train had started, the lunatic was now tormenting a small boy who appeared to be travelling alone, the tribesmen – all elbows – were at the windows. It was an odd trip: one moment the car would be filled with sunshine, and outside the head of the valley shifted to a view of a tumbling stone gorge; the next moment we would be in darkness. There are three miles of tunnels on the Khyber Railway, and as there were no lights on the train, we travelled those three miles in the dark.

'I would like very much to talk to you,' said Mr Haq. 'You have been to Kabul. You can tell me: is it safe there?'

I told him I had seen a lot of soldiers, but I supposed they were around because of the military coup. Afghanistan was ruled by decree.

'Well, I have a problem, and I am an old man, so I need some advice.'

The problem was this: a Pakistani boy, a distant relative of Mr Haq's, had been arrested in Kabul. What with difficulties in obtaining foreign currency and the impossibility of travelling to India, the only place holiday-minded Pakistanis go to is Afghanistan. Mr Haq thought the boy had been arrested for having hashish, and he had been asked whether he would go to

Kabul to see if he could get the boy released. He wasn't sure he wanted to go.

'You tell me. You make the decision.'

I told him he should put the matter in the hands of the Pakistani embassy in Kabul.

'Officially we have diplomatic relations, but everyone knows we have no diplomatic relations. I cannot do.'

'Then you have to go.'

'What if they arrest me?'

'Why would they do that?'

'They might think I'm a spy,' said Mr Haq. 'We are almost at war with Afghanistan over the Pakhtoonistan issue.'

The Pakhtoonistan issue was a few villages of armed Pathan tribesmen, supported by Russia and Afghanistan, who were threatening to secede from Pakistan, declare a new state, and, deriving their income from dried fruit, become a sovereign power; the liberated warriors would then compete in the world market of raisins and prunes.

'My advice is don't go,' I said.

'How can you say that! What about the boy? He is a relative – his family is very worried. I wish,' said Mr Haq, 'to ask you one further question. Do you know Kabul's jail?'

I said I didn't, but I had seen Kabul's insane asylum and did not find it encouraging.

'Kabul's jail. Listen, I will tell you. It was built in the year 1626 by King Babar. Well, they call it a jail, but it is a number of holes in the ground, like deep wells. They put the prisoners in. At night they cover them up with lids. That is the truth. They do not give food. The boy might be dead. I don't know what I should do.'

He fretted in Urdu with Mr Hassan, while I snapped pictures of the ravines. We ducked into tunnels, emerging through spurs to reversing stations; above us were fortified towers and stone emplacements, bright in the mid-afternoon sun. It seems an impossible journey for a train. The 132-Down teeters on the cliff sides, breathing heavily, and when there is nothing ahead but air and a vertical rock face the train swerves into the mountain. Plunging through a cave, it dislodges bats from the ceiling, which the tribesmen at the windows swat with their sticks. Then into the sunlight again, past the fort at Ali Masjid, balancing on a high peak, and an hour later, after twenty sharp reverses, moves on a gentler slope in the neighbourhood of Jamrud. Above Jamrud is its bulky fort, with walls ten feet thick and its hornworks facing Afghanistan.

Some tribesmen got out at Jamrud, moving Mr Haq to the observation: 'We do what we can with them, and they are coming right up.'

He fell silent again and did not speak until we were travelling through the outskirts of Peshawar, beside a road of clopping *tongas* and beeping jalopies. Here, it was flat and green, the palms were high; it was probably hotter than Kabul had been, but so much green shade made it seem cool. Behind us the sun had dropped low, and the peaks of the Khyber Pass were mauve in a lilac haze so lovely it looked scented. Mr Haq said he had business here – 'I have to solve my great worry.'

'But let us meet later,' he said at Peshawar Cantonment Station. 'I will not trouble you with my problems. We will have tea and talk about matters of world interest.'

Peshawar is a pretty town. I would gladly move there, settle down on a verandah, and grow old watching sunsets in the Khyber Pass. Peshawar's widely spaced mansions, all excellent examples of Anglo-Muslim Gothic, are spread along broad sleepy roads under cool trees: just the place to recover from the hideous experience of Kabul. You hail a *tonga* at the station and ride to the hotel, where on the verandah the chairs have swing-out extensions for you to prop up your legs and get the blood circulating. A nimble waiter brings a large bottle of Murree Export Lager. The hotel is empty; the other guests have risked a punishing journey to Swat in hopes of being received by His

Highness the Wali. You sleep soundly under a tent of mosquito net and are awakened by the fluting of birds for an English breakfast that begins with porridge and ends with a kidney. Afterwards a *tonga* to the museum.

How was Buddha conceived, you may wonder. There is a Graeco-Buddhist frieze in the Peshawar Museum showing Buddha's mother lying on her side and being impregnated through her ribs by what looks like the nozzle of a hot-air balloon suspended over her. In another panel the infant Buddha is leaping from a slit in her side – a birth with all the energy of a broad jump. Farther on is a nativity scene, Buddha lying at the centre of attending figures, who kneel at prayer: the usual Christmas card arrangement done delicately in stone with classical faces. The most striking piece is a three-foot stone sculpture of an old man in a lotus posture. The man is fasting: his eyes are sunken, his rib cage is prominent, his knees are knobbly, his belly hollow. He looks near death, but his expression is beatific. It is the most accurate representation in granite of an emaciated body that I've ever seen, and again and again, throughout India and Pakistan, I was to see that same body, in doorways and outside huts and leaning against the pillars of railway stations, starvation lending a special quality of saintliness to the bony face.

A little distance from the museum, when I was buying some matches at a shop, I was offered morphine. I wondered if I heard right and asked to see it. The man took out a matchbox (perhaps 'matches' was a code word?) and slipped it open. Inside was a small phial marked *Morphine Sulphate*, ten white tablets. The man said they were to be taken in the arm and told me that I could have the whole lot for twenty dollars. I offered him five dollars and laughed, but he saw he was being mocked. He turned surly and told me to go away.

I would have liked to stay longer in Peshawar. I liked lazing on the verandah, shaking out my newspaper, and watching the *tongas* go by, and I enjoyed hearing Pakistanis discussing the coming war with Afghanistan. They were worried and aggrieved, but I gave them encouragement and said they would find an enthusiastic well-wisher in me if they ever cared to invade that barbarous country. My prompt reassurance surprised them, but they saw I was sincere. 'I hope you will help us,' one said. I explained that I was not a very able soldier. He said, 'Not you in person, but America in general.' I said I couldn't promise national support, but that I would be glad to put a word in for them.

Everything is easy in Peshawar except buying a train ticket. This is a morning's work and leaves you exhausted. First you consult the timetable, *Pakistan Western Railways*, and find that the Khyber Mail leaves at four o'clock. Then you go to the Information window and are told it leaves at 9.50 p.m. The Information man sends you to Reservations. The man in Reservations is not there, but a sweeper says he'll be right back. He returns in an hour and helps you decide on a class. He writes your name in a book and gives you a chit. You take the chit to Bookings, where, for 108 rupees (about ten dollars), you are handed two tickets and an initialled chit. You go back to Reservations, and wait for the man to return once again. He returns, initials the tickets, examines the chit, and writes the details in a ledger about six feet square.

Nor was this the only difficulty. The man in Reservations told me no bedding was available on the Khyber Mail. I suspected he was angling for *baksheesh* and gave him six rupees to find bedding. After twenty minutes he said it had all been booked. He was very sorry. I asked for my bribe back. He said, 'As you wish.'

Later in the day I worked out the perfect solution. I was staying in Dean's Hotel, one in a chain of hotels that includes Faletti's in Lahore. I had to pester the clerk a good deal, but he finally agreed to give me what bedding I needed. I would give him sixty rupees and he would give me a chit. In Lahore I would give the bedding and chit to Faletti's and get my sixty rupees back. This was the chit:

Please refund this man Rs 60/ – (RS. SIXTY ONLY) if he produce you this receipt and One Blanket and One Sheet One Pillow and Credit it in Dean's Hotel Peshawar Account.

# 7. The Khyber Mail to Lahore Junction

RASHID, the conductor on the sleeping car, helped me find my compartment, and after a moment's hesitation he asked me to have a look at his tooth. It was giving him aches, he said. The request was not impertinent. I had told him I was a dentist. I was getting tired of the Asiatic inquistion: Where do you come from? What do you do? Married or single? Any children? This nagging made me evasive, secretive, foolish, an inventor of cock-and-bull stories. Rashid made the bed and then opened up, tugging his lip down to show me a canine gnawed with decay.

'You'd better see a dentist in Karachi,' I said. 'In the meantime chew your food on the other side.'

Satisfied with my advice (and I also gave him two aspirins), he said, 'You will be very comfortable here. German carriage, about fifteen years old. Heavy, you see, so no shaking.'

It had not taken long to find my compartment. Only three were occupied – the other two by army officers – and my name was on the door, printed large on a label. Now I could tell on entering a train what sort of a journey it would be. The feeling I had on the Khyber Mail was slight disappointment that the trip would be so short – only twelve hours to Lahore. I wished it were longer: I had everything I needed. The compartment was large, well lighted, and comfortable, with a toilet and sink in an adjoining room; I had a drop-leaf table, well-upholstered seat, mirror, ashtray, chrome gin-bottle holder, the works. I was alone. But if I wished to have company I could stroll to the dining car or idle in the passage with the army officers. Nothing is expected of the train passenger. In planes the traveller is condemned to hours in a tight seat; ships require high spirits and sociability; cars and buses are unspeakable. The sleeping car is the most painless form of travel. In *Ordered South*, Robert Louis Stevenson writes,

Herein, I think, is the chief attraction of railway travel. The speed is so easy, and the train disturbs so little the scenes through which it takes us, that our heart becomes full of the placidity and stillness of the country; and while the body is being borne forward in the flying chain of carriages, the thoughts alight, as the humour moves them, at unfrequented stations . . .

The romance associated with the sleeping car derives from its extreme privacy, combining the best features of a cupboard with forward movement. Whatever drama is being enacted in this moving bedroom is heightened by the landscape passing the window: a swell of hills, the surprise of mountains, the loud metal bridge, or the melancholy sight of people standing under yellow lamps. And the notion of travel as a continuous vision, a grand tour's succession of memorable images across a curved earth – with none of the distorting emptiness of air or sea – is possible only on a train. A train is a vehicle that allows residence: dinner in the diner, nothing could be finer.

'What time does the Khyber Mail get to Karachi?'

'Timetable says seven-fifteen in the night,' said Rashid. 'But we will be five and a half hours late.'

'Why?' I asked.

'We are always five and a half hours late. It is the case.'

I slept well on my Dean's Hotel bedding and was awakened at six the following morning by a Sikh with a steel badge pinned to his turban that read *Pakistan Western Railways*. His right eye was milky with trachoma.

'You wanting breakfast?'

I said yes.

'I coming seven o'clock.'

He brought an omelette, tea, and toast, and for the next

half-hour I sprawled, reading Chekhov's wonderful story 'Ariadne' and finishing my tea. Then I snapped up the shade and flooded the compartment with light. In brilliant sunshine we were passing rice fields and stagnant pools full of white lotuses and standing herons. Farther on, at a small tree, we startled a pair of pistachio-green parrots; they flew up, getting greener as they rose. Looking out a train window in Asia is like watching an unedited travelogue without the obnoxious soundtrack: I had to guess at the purpose of activities – people patting pie-shaped turds and slapping them on to the side of a mud hut to dry; men with bullocks and submerged ploughs, preparing a rice field for planting; and at Badami Bagh, just outside Lahore, a town of grass huts, cardboard shelters, pup tents, and hovels of papers, twigs, and cloth, everyone was in motion – sorting fruit, folding clothes, fanning the fire, shooing a dog away, mending a roof. It is the industry of the poor in the morning, so busy they look hopeful, but it is deceptive. The position of their settlement gives them away; this is the extreme of poverty, the shantytown by the railway tracks.

The shantytown had another witness: a tall thin Indian of about twenty, with long hair, stood at the corridor window. He asked me the time; his London accent was unmistakable. I asked him where he was headed.

'India. I was born in Bombay, but I left when I was three or four. Still, I'm an Indian right the way through.'

'But you were brought up in England.'

'Yeah. I've got a British passport too. I didn't want to get one, after all they did to me. But an Indian passport is too much trouble. See, I want to go to Germany eventually – they're in the Common Market. It's easy with a British passport.'

'Why not stay in London?'

'You can stay in London if you like. They're all racialists. It starts when you're about ten years old, and that's all you hear – wog, nigger, blackie. There's nothing you can do about it. At school it's really terrible – ever hear about Paki-bashing? And

I'm not even a Pakistani. They don't know the difference. But they're cowards. When I'm with me mate no one comes up and says nothing, but lots of times about ten blokes would start trouble with me. I hate them. I'm glad to be here.'

'This is Pakistan.'

'Same thing. Everyone's the same colour.'

'Not really,' I said.

'More or less,' he said. 'I can relax here – I'm free.'

'Won't you feel rather anonymous?'

'The first thing I'm going to do in India is get a haircut; then no one will know.'

It seemed a cruel fate. He spoke no Indian language, his parents were dead, and he was not quite sure how to get to Bombay, where he had some distant relatives who seldom replied to letters unless he enclosed money. He was one of those colonial anomalies, more English than he cared to admit, but uneasy in the only country he understood.

'In England they were always staring at me. I hated it.'

'I get stared at here,' I said.

'How do *you* like it?' I could see he was reproaching me with my colour; after all, he was almost home.

I said, 'I rather enjoy it.'

'Sahib.' It was Rashid, with my suitcase. 'We are approaching.'

'He calls you sahib,' said the Indian. He looked disgusted. 'He's afraid of you, that's why.'

'Sahib,' said Rashid. But he was speaking to the Indian. 'Now, please show me your ticket.'

The Indian was travelling second class. Rashid evicted him from first as the train drew in.

At Lahore Junction I stepped out (Rashid was at my side apologizing for the train's being late) into a city that was familiar: it matched a stereotype in my memory. My image of the Indian city derives from Kipling, and it was in Lahore that Kipling came of age as a writer. Exaggerating the mobs, the vicious bazaar, the colour and confusion, the Kipling of the early stories and *Kim* is really describing Lahore today, that side of it beyond the Mall where processions of rickshaws, pony carts, hawkers, and veiled women fill the narrow lanes and sweep you in their direction. The Anarkali Bazaar and the walled city, with its fort and mosques, have retained the distracted exoticism Kipling mentions, though now, with a hundred years of repetition, it is touched with horror.

'Bad girls here,' said the *tonga* driver when he dropped me in a seedy district of the old city; but I saw none, and nothing resembling a Lahore house. The absence of women in Pakistan, all those cruising males, had an odd effect on me. I found myself staring, with other similarly idle men, at garish pictures of film stars, and I began to think that the strictures of Islam would quickly make me a fancier of the margins of anatomy, thrilling at especially trim ankles, seeking a wink behind a veil, or watching for a response in the shoulders of one of those shrouded forms. Islam's denials seemed capable of turning the most normal soul into a foot fetishist, and as if to combat this the movie posters lampooned the erotic: fat girls in boots struggling helplessly with hairy, leering men; tormented women clutching their breasts, Anglo-Indians (regarded as 'fast') swinging their bums and crooning into microphones. The men in Lahore stroll with their eyes upturned to these cartoon fantasies.

'They invite you out to eat,' an American told me. This was at the spectacular fort, and we were both admiring the small marble pavilion, called *Naulakha* (Kipling named his house outside Brattleboro, Vermont, after it, because it was so expensive to build: 'naulakha' means 900,000). The American was agitated. He said, 'You finish eating and they start eyeballing your chick. It's always your chick they're after. The chick's strung out. "Gee, Mohammed, why don't you have any pockets in your dhoti?" "We are not having any pockets, miss" – that kind of crap. One guy – this really pissed me off – he takes me aside and says, "*Five minutes! Five minutes!* That's all I want with her!" But would he let me have *his* chick for five minutes? You've gotta be joking.'

The order in Lahore is in the architecture, the moghul and colonial splendour. All around it are crowds of people and vehicles, and their dereliction makes the grandeur emphatic, as the cooking fat and cow-dung makes the smells of perfume and joss-sticks keener. To get to the Shalimar Gardens I had to pass through miles of congested streets of jostling people with the starved look of predators. I shouldered my way through the venereal township of Begampura; but inside the gardens it is peaceful, and though it has been stripped of its marble, and the reflecting pools are dark brown, the gardens have the order and shade – a sense of delicious refuge – that could not be very different from that imagined by Shah Jahan, when he laid them out in 1637. The pleasures of Lahore are old, and though one sees attempts everywhere, the Pakistanis have not yet succeeded in turning this beautiful city into a ruin.

Ramadhan continued, and the restaurants were either closed or on emergency rations, eggs and tea. So I was forced into an unwilling fast too, hoping it wouldn't drive me crazy as it manifestly did the Afghan and Pakistani. Instead of somnolence, hunger produced excitable, glassy-eyed individuals, some of whom quick-marched from alleyways to clutch my sleeve.

'Pot – hashish – LSD.'

'LSD?' I said. 'You sell LSD?'

'Yes, why not? You come to my place. Also nice copper, silver, handicraft.'

'I don't want handicraft.'

'You want hashish? One kilo twenty dollar.'

It was tempting, but I preferred bottled mango juice, which was sweet and thick, and the curry puffs known as *samosas*. The *samosas* were always wrapped in pages from old school copybooks. I sat down, drank my juice, ate my *samosa*, and read the wrapper: '. . . the shearing force at any [grease mark] on the

Beam is represented by the Vertical Distance between that Line and the Line CD.'

There were forty-seven tables in the dining room of Faletti's Hotel. I found them easy to count because I was the only diner present on the two evenings I ate there. The five waiters stood at various distances from me, and when I cleared my throat two would rush forward. Not wanting to disappoint them I asked them questions about Lahore, and in one of these conversations I learned that the Punjab Club was not far away. I thought it would be a good idea to have a postprandial snooker game, so on the second evening I was given directions by one of the waiters and set off for the club.

I lost my way almost immediately in a district adjacent to the hotel where there were no street lights. My footsteps roused the watchdogs and as I walked these barking hounds leaped at fences and hedges. I have not conquered a childhood fear of strange dogs, and, although the trees smelled sweet and the night was cool, I had no idea where I was going. It was ten minutes before a car approached. I flagged it down.

'You are coming from?'

'Faletti's Hotel.'

'I mean your country.'

'United States.'

'You are most welcome,' said the driver. 'My name is Anwar. May I give you a lift?'

'I'm trying to find the Punjab Club.'

'Get in please,' he said, and when I did, he said, 'How are you please?' This is precisely the way the posturing Ivan Turkin greets people in Chekhov's story 'Ionych'.

Mr Anwar drove for another mile, telling me how fortunate it was that we should meet – there were a lot of thieves around at night, he said – and at the Punjab Club he gave me his card and invited me to his daughter's wedding, which was one week away. I said I would be in India then.

'Well, India is another story altogether,' he said, and drove off.

The Punjab Club, a bungalow behind a high hedge, was lighted and looked cosy, but it was completely deserted. I had imagined a crowded bar, a lot of cheerful drinkers, a snooker game in progress, a pair in the corner plotting adultery, waiters with trays of drinks, and chits flying back and forth. This could have been a clinic of some kind; there was not a soul in sight, but it had the atmosphere – and even the magazines – of a dentist's waiting room. I saw what I wanted a few doors along a corridor: large red letters on the window read WAIT FOR THE STROKE, and in the shadows were two tables, the balls in position, ready for play under a gleaming rack of cues.

'Yes?' It was an elderly Pakistani, and he had the forlorn abstraction of a man interrupted in his reading. He wore a black bow tie, and the pocket of his shirt sagged with pens. 'What can I do for you?'

'I just happened to be passing,' I said. 'I thought I might stop in. Do you have reciprocal privileges with any clubs in London?'

'No, not that I know of.'

'Perhaps the manager would know.'

'I am the manager,' he said. 'We used to have an arrangement with a club in London – many years ago.'

'What was the name of it?'

'I'm sorry, I've forgotten, but I know the club is no longer in existence. What was it you wanted?'

'A game of snooker.'

'Who would you play with?' He smiled. 'There is no one here.'

He showed me around, but the lighted empty rooms depressed me. The place was abandoned, like Faletti's dining room with its forty-seven empty tables, like the district where there were only watchdogs. I said I had to go, and at the front door he said, 'You might find a taxi over there, in the next road but one. Good night.'

It was hopeless. I had walked about a hundred yards from the club and could not find the road, though I was going in the direction he had indicated. I could hear a dog growling behind a near-by hedge. Then I heard a car. It moved swiftly towards me and screeched to a halt. The driver got out and opened the back door for me. He said the manager had sent him to take me back to my hotel; he was afraid I'd get lost.

I set off in search of a drink as soon as I got back to the hotel. It was still early, about ten o'clock, but I had not gone fifty yards when a thin man in striped pyjamas stepped from behind a tree. His eyes were prominent and lighted in the dusky triangle of his face.

'What are you looking for?'

'A drink.'

'I get you a nice girl. Two hundred rupees. Good fucking.' He said this with no more emotion than a man hawking razor blades.

'No thanks.'

'Very young. You come with me. Good fucking.'

'And good fucking to you,' I said. 'I'm looking for a drink.'

He tagged along behind me, mumbling his refrain, and then at an intersection, by a park, he said. 'Come with me – in here.'

'In there?'

'Yes, she is waiting.'

'In those trees?' It was black, unlighted and humming with crickets.

'It is a park.'

'You mean I'm supposed to do it there, under a tree?'

'It is a *good* park, sahib!'

A little farther on I was accosted again, this time by a young man who was smoking nervously. He caught my eye. 'Anything you want?'

'No.'

'A girl?'

'No.'

'Boy?'

'No, go away.'

He hesitated, but kept after me. At last he said softly, '*Take me.*'

A twenty-minute walk did not take me any closer to a bar. I turned, and, giving the pimps a wide berth, went back to the hotel. Under a tree in front three old men were hunched around a pressure lamp, playing cards. One saw me pass and called out, 'Wait, sahib!' He turned his cards face down and trotted over to me.

'No,' I said before he opened his mouth.

'She's very nice,' he said.

I kept walking.

'All right, only two hundred and fifty rupees.'

'I know where I can get one for two hundred.'

'But this is in your room! I will bring her. She will stay until morning.'

'Too much money. Sorry.'

'Sahib! There are expenses! Ten rupees for your sweeper, ten also for your *chowkidar*, ten for your bearer, *baksheesh* here and there. If not, they will make trouble. Take her! She will be very nice. My girls are experienced in every way.'

'Thin or fat?'

'As you like. I have one, neither thin nor fat, but like this.' He sketched a torso in the air with his fingers, suggesting plumpness. 'About twenty-two or twenty-three. Speaks very good English. You will like her so much. Sahib, she is a trained nurse!'

He was still calling out to me as I mounted the steps to the hotel's verandah. It turned out that the only bar in Lahore was the Polo Room in my hotel. I had an expensive beer and fell into conversation with a young Englishman. He had been in Lahore for two months. I asked him what he did for amusement. He said there wasn't very much to do, but he was planning to visit Peshawar. I told him Peshawar was quieter than Lahore. He said he was sorry to hear that because he found Lahore intolerable. He was bored, he said, but there was hope. 'I've got an application pending at the club,' he said. He was a tall plain fellow, who blew his nose at the end of every sentence. 'If they let me in I think I'll be all right. I can go there in the evenings – it's a pretty lively place.'

'What club are you talking about?'

'The Punjab Club,' he said.

# 8. The Frontier Mail

AMRITSAR, two taxi rides from Lahore (the connecting train hasn't run since 1947), is on the Indian side of the frontier. It is to the Sikh what Benares is to the Hindu, a religious capital, a holy city. The object of the Sikh's pilgrimage is the Golden Temple, a copper-gilt gazebo in the centre of a tank. The tank's sanctity has not kept it from stagnation. You can smell it a mile away. It is the dearest wish of every Sikh to see this temple before he dies and to bring a souvenir back from Amritsar. One of the favourite souvenirs is a large multicoloured poster of a headless man. Blood spurts from the stump of his neck; he wears the uniform of a warrior. In one hand he carries a sword, in the other he holds his dripping head. I asked nine Sikhs what this man's name was. None could tell me, but all knew his story. In one of the Punjab wars he was decapitated. But he was very determined. He picked up his head, and, holding it in his hand so that he could see what he was doing (the eyes of the severed head blaze with resolution), he continued to fight. He did this so that he could get back to Amritsar and have a proper cremation. This story exemplifies the Sikh virtues of piety, ferocity, and strength. But Sikhs are also very kind and friendly, and an enormous number are members of Lions Club International. This is partly a cultural misunderstanding, since all Sikhs bear the surname Singh, which means lion; they feel obliged to join.

Special underpants are required by the Sikh religion, along with uncut hair, a silver bangle, a wooden comb, and an iron dagger. And as shoes are prohibited at the Golden Temple, I hopped down the hot marble causeway, doing a kind of fire-walker's tango, watching these leonine figures stripped to their holy drawers bathing themselves in the tank and gulping the green water, swallowing grace and dysentery in the same mouth-ful. The Sikhs are great soldiers and throughout the temple enclosure there are marble tablets stating the fact that the Poona Horse Regiment and the Bengal Sappers contributed so many thousand rupees. For the rest of the Indians, Gujaratis in particu-lar, Sikhs are yokels, and jokes are told to illustrate the simplicity of the Sikh mind. There is the one about the Sikh who, on emigrating to Canada, is told that he must prove himself a true Canadian by going into the forest and wrestling a bear and raping a squaw. He sets out and returns a month later, with his turban in tatters and his face covered with scratches, saying, 'Now I must wrestle the squaw.' Another concerns a Sikh who misses his bus. He chases the bus, trying to board, and soon realizes he has run all the way home. 'I've just chased my bus and saved fifty paisas,' he tells his wife, who replies, 'If you had chased a taxi you could have saved a rupee.'

I had a meal at a Sikh restaurant after wandering around the city and then went to the railway station to buy my ticket on the Frontier Mail to Delhi. The man at Reservations put me on the waiting list and told me there was 'a 98 per cent chance' that I would get a berth, but that I would have to wait until half-past four for a confirmation. Indian railway stations are wonderful places for killing time in, and they are like scale models of Indian society, with its divisions of caste, class, and sex: SECOND-CLASS LADIES' WAITING ROOM, BEARERS' ENTRANCE, THIRD-CLASS EXIT, FIRST-CLASS TOILET, VEGETARIAN RESTAURANT, NON-VEGETARIAN RESTAURANT, RETIRING ROOMS, CLOAKROOM, and the whole range of occupations on office signboards, from the tiny one saying SWEEPER, to the neatest of all, STATION-MASTER.

A steam locomotive was belching smoke at one of the plat-forms. I crossed over and as I snapped a picture a Sikh appeared on the footplate and asked me to send him a print. I said I would. He asked me where I was going, and when I told him I was taking the Frontier Mail he said, 'You have so many hours to wait. Come with me. Get in this bogie' – he pointed to the first car – 'and at the first station you can come in here and ride with me.'

'I'm afraid I'll miss my train.'

'You will not,' he said. 'Without fail.' He said this precisely, as if remembering an English lesson.

'I don't have a ticket.'

'No one is having a ticket. They are all cheating!'

So I climbed aboard and at the first station joined him in the cab. The train was going to Atari, on the Pakistan border, sixteen miles away. I had always wanted to ride in the engine of a steam locomotive, but this trip was badly timed. We left just at sunset and as I was wearing my prescription sunglasses – my other pair was in my suitcase in the station cloakroom – I could not see a thing. I held on, blind as a bat, sweating in the heat from the firebox. The Sikh shouted explanations of what he was doing, pulling levers, bringing up the pressure, spinning knobs, and dodging the coal shoveller. The noise and the heat prevented me from taking any pleasure in this two-hour jaunt, and I suppose I must have looked dispirited because the Sikh was anxious to amuse me by blowing the whistle. Every time he did it the train seemed to slow down.

My face and arms were flecked with soot from the ride to Atari. On the Frontier Mail this was no problem, and I had the enjoyable experience that humid evening of taking a cold shower, squatting on my heels under the burbling pipe, as the train tore through the Punjab to Delhi.

I returned to my compartment to find a young man sitting on my berth. He greeted me in an accent I could not quite place, partly because he lisped and also because his appearance was somewhat bizarre. His hair, parted in the middle, reached below his shoulders; his thin arms were sheathed in tight sleeves and he wore three rings with large orange stones on each hand, bracelets of various kinds and a necklace of white shells. His face frightened me: it was that corpselike face of lunacy or a fatal illness, with sunken eyes and cheeks, deeply lined, bloodless, narrow, and white. He had a cowering stare, and as he watched me – I was still dripping from my shower – he played with a small leather purse. He said his name was Hermann; he was going to Delhi. He had bribed the conductor so that he could travel with a European. He didn't want to be in a compartment with an Indian – there might be trouble. He hoped I understood.

'Of course,' I said. 'But do you feel all right?'

'I have been sick – four days in Amritsar I have been in the hospital, and in Quetta also. I was so nervous. The doctors take tests and they give me this medicine, but it does no good. I don't sleep, I don't eat – just maybe glass of milk and piece of bread. I fly to Amritsar from Lahore. I was so sick in Lahore – three days in hospital and in Quetta two days. I cross Baluchistan. Yazd, you know Yazd? It is a terrible place. Two nights I am there and I am on the bus two days from Teheran. I cannot sleep. Every five hours the bus stops and I take some tea and a little melon. I am sick. The people say, "Why you don't talk – are you angry?" But I say, "No, not angry, but sick –"'

This was the way he spoke, in long lisped passages, interrupting himself, repeating that he was sick in a voice that was monotonously apologetic. He was German and had been a sailor, a deck hand on a German ship, then a steward on a Finnish one. He had sailed for seven years and had been to the States – 'Yes, to every country,' he said, 'but only for a few hours.' He loved ships, but he couldn't sail anymore. I asked why. 'Hepatitis,' he said, giving it a German pronunciation. He caught it in Indonesia and was in the hospital for weeks. He had never managed to shake it off: he still needed tests. He'd had one in Amritsar. 'People say to me, "Your face is sick." I know my face is sick, but I cannot eat.'

His face was ghastly, and he was trembling. 'Are you taking any medicine?'

'No.' He shook his head. 'I take this.' He opened the leather purse he had been smoothing with his scrawny fingers and took out a cellophane envelope. He peeled the cellophane away and showed me a wad of brown sticky stuff, like a flattened plug of English toffee.

'What is it?'

'Opium,' he said. 'I take it in little balls.'

His lisp made 'balls' moistly vicious.

'I am a yunk.' He broke off a piece of opium and rolled it between his fingers, slowly making it a pellet.

'A junkie?'

'Yes, I take needle. See my arms.'

He locked the compartment door and pulled the curtain across the window. He rolled up his left sleeve. His arm appalled me: each vein was clearly defined by dark bruised scars of needle marks, thick welts that made the veins into black cords. He touched his arm shyly, as if it didn't belong to him and said, 'I cannot get heroin. In Lahore I am not feeling so well. I stay in hospital but still I am weak and nervous. The people are making noise and it is so hot. I don't know what I can do. So I escape and I walk down the street. A Pakistani says to me he has some morphine. I go with him and he shows me. It is good – German morphine. He asks me for one hundred and fifty rupees. I give him and take an injection. That is how I get to Amritsar. But in Amritsar I get very sick and I cannot get any more of morphine. So I take this –' He patted his right pocket and took out a cake of hashish, roughly the size of the opium blob, but dry and cracked. 'Or I smoke this –' He withdrew a little sack of marijuana.

I told him that with his budget of drugs he was lucky to have got into India. At the border post I had seen an Indian customs official ask a boy to drop his jeans.

'Yes,' said Hermann. 'I am so nervous! The man asks me do I have pot and I say no. Do I smoke it? I say, yes, sometimes; but he doesn't look at my luggages. If I am nervous I can hide it in secret places.'

'Then I suppose you don't have anything to worry about.'

'No, I am hot and nervous always.'

'But you can hide your drugs.'

'I can even throw them away and buy more,' he said. 'But my arms! If they see my arms they know. I have to hide my arms always.' He pushed his sleeves up and looked again at the long dark scars.

He told me how it was that he had come to India. In Hanover, he decided to cure himself of his heroin habit. He registered as an addict and entered a rehabilitation centre – he called it 'The Release' – where he was given 700 Deutsche marks a month and a daily glass of methadone. In return for this he helped clean the centre. He never went out; he was afraid that if he did he would meet someone who'd sell him heroin. But an odd thing happened: by staying in he rarely spent his monthly allowance, and he found that at the end of a year he had saved quite a lot of money – enough to live on in India for six months or more. So he picked up and left, just like that, on a charter flight to Teheran, where his withdrawal symptoms began.

He had carried his dereliction to a derelict land. He was doomed, he stank of death, and his condition was not so different from that of the unfortunates who appeared at the railway stations we passed, gathering for the light and water. There are foreigners who, knowing they are wrecked, go to India to be anonymous in her decrepitude, to age and sicken in the *bustees* of the East. They are people, V. S. Naipaul wrote recently, 'who wish themselves on societies more fragile than their own . . . who in the end do no more than celebrate their own security.'

'I take this now.' He popped the pellet of opium into his mouth and closed his eyes. 'Then I take some water.' He drank a glass of water. He had already drunk two, and I realized that the Indian water would kill him if the drugs didn't. 'Now I sleep. If I don't sleep I take another opium.'

Twice during the night a match flared in the upper berth, lighting the fan on the ceiling. I heard the crackle of cellophane, the snap of the gummy opium in his fingers, and Hermann gulping water.

The signs in Amritsar Station (THIRD-CLASS EXIT, SECOND-CLASS LADIES' WAITING ROOM, FIRST-CLASS TOILET, SWEEPERS ONLY) had given me a formal idea of Indian society. The less formal reality I saw at seven in the morning in the Northern Railways Terminal in Old Delhi. To understand the real India, the Indians say, you must go to the villages. But that is not strictly true, because the Indians have carried their villages to the railway stations. In the daytime it is not apparent – you might mistake any of these people for beggars, ticketless travellers (sign: TICKETLESS TRAVEL IS A SOCIAL EVIL), or unlicensed hawkers. At night and in the early morning the station village is complete, a community so preoccupied that the thousands of passengers arriving and departing leave it undisturbed: they detour around it. The railway dwellers possess the station, but only the new arrival notices this. He feels something is wrong because he has not learned the Indian habit of ignoring the obvious, making a detour to preserve his calm. The newcomer cannot believe he has been plunged into such intimacy so soon. In another country this would all be hidden from him, and not even a trip to a village would reveal with this clarity the pattern of life. The village in rural India tells the visitor very little except that he is required to keep his distance and limit his experience of the place to tea or a meal in a stuffy parlour. The life of the village, its interior, is denied to him.

But the station village is all interior, and the shock of this exposure made me hurry away. I didn't feel I had any right to watch people bathing under a low faucet – naked among the incoming tide of office workers; men sleeping late on their *charpoys* or tucking up their turbans; women with nose rings and cracked yellow feet cooking stews of begged vegetables over smoky fires, suckling infants, folding bedrolls; children pissing on their toes; little girls, in oversized frocks falling from their shoulders, fetching water in tin cans from the third-class toilet; and, near a newspaper vendor, a man lying on his back, holding a baby up to admire and tickling it. Hard work, poor pleasures, and the scrimmage of appetite. This village has no walls. I distracted myself with the signs, GWALIOR SUITINGS, RASHMI SUPERB COATINGS, and the film poster of plump faces that was never out of view, BOBBY ('A Story of Modern Love'). I was moving so quickly I lost Hermann. He had drugged himself for the arrival: crowds made him nervous. He floated down the platform and then sank from view.

I wondered whether I would find any of this Indian candour familiar enough to ignore. I was told that I should not draw any conclusions from Delhi: Delhi wasn't India – not the real India. Well, I said, I had no intention of staying in Delhi. I wanted to go to Simla, Nagpur, Ceylon – to wherever there was a train.

'There is no train to Ceylon.'

'There's one on the map.' I unrolled my map and traced the black line from Madras to Colombo.

'*Acha*,' said the man. He wore a colourful hand-loomed shirt and he waggled his head from side to side, the Indian gesture – like a man trying to shake water out of his ears – that means he is listening with approval. But the man, of course, was an American. Americans in India practise these affectations to endear themselves to Indians, who seem so embarrassed by these easily parodied mannerisms that (at the American embassy at least) the liaison men say 'We're locking you into that programme,' while the American looking on says '*Acha*' and giggles mirthlessly.

I was being locked into a programme: lectures in Jaipur, Bombay, Calcutta, Colombo. Wherever, I said, there was a train.

'There is no train to Colombo.'

'We'll see,' I said, and then listened to one of those strange conversations I later found so common as to be the mainstay of American small talk in India: The American on His Bowels. After the usual greetings and pauses these people would report on the vagaries of their digestive tracts. Their passion was grace-less and they were as hard to silence as whoopee cushions.

'I had a bad night,' one embassy man said. 'The German ambassador gave a party. Delicious meal – it always is. All kinds of wine, umpteen courses, the works. But, God, I was up at five this morning, sick as a dog. Tummy upset.'

'It's a funny thing,' said another man. 'You have a good meal at some dirty little place and you know you're going to pay for it. I just came back from Madras. I was fine – and I had some pretty risky meals. Then I go to some diplomatic thing and I'm doubled up for days. So there's no telling where you'll get it.'

'Tell Paul about Harris.'

'Harris! Listen,' said the man, 'there was a fella here. Harris. Press Section. Went to the doctor. Guess why? He was consti-pated. *Constipated*! In *India*! It got around the embassy. People used to see him and laugh like hell.'

'I've been fine lately,' said a junior officer, holding his end up, as it were. 'Knock on wood. I've had some severe – I mean, really bad times. But I figured it out. What I usually do is have yogurt. I drink tons of the stuff. I figure the bacteria in yogurt keeps down the bacteria in lousy food. Kind of an equalizing thing.'

There was another man. He looked pale, but he said he was bearing up. Kind of a bowel thing. Up all night. Cramps. Delhi belly. Food goes right through you. He said, 'I had it in spades. Bacillary. Ever have bacillary? No? It knocked me flat. For six days I couldn't do a thing. Running back and forth, practically living in the john.'

Each time the subject came up, I wanted to take the speaker by his hand-loomed shirt, and, shaking him, say, 'Now listen to me! There is absolutely nothing wrong with your bowels!'

# 9. The Kalka Mail for Simla

In spite of my dishevelled appearance, it was thought by some in Delhi to be beneath my dignity to stand in line for my ticket north to Simla, though perhaps this was a tactful way of suggesting that if I did stand in line I might be mistaken for an Untouchable and set alight (these Harijan combustions are reported daily in Indian newspapers). The American official who claimed his stomach was collapsing with dysentery introduced me to Mr Nath, who said, 'Don't sweat. We'll take care of everything.' I had heard that one before. Mr Nath rang his deputy, Mr Sheth, who told his secretary to ring a travel agent. At four o'clock there was no sign of the ticket. I saw Mr Sheth. He offered me tea. I refused his tea and went to the travel agent. This was Mr Sud. He had delegated the ticket-buying to one of his clerks. The clerk was summoned. He didn't have the ticket; he had sent a messenger, a low-caste Tamil whose role in life, it seemed, was to lengthen lines at ticket windows. An Indian story: and still no ticket. Mr Nath and Mr Sud accompanied me to the ticket office, and there we stood ('Are you sure you don't want a nice cup of tea?') watching this damned messenger, ten feet from the window, holding my application. Bustling Indians began cutting in front of him.

'Now you see,' said Mr Nath, 'with your own eyes why things are so backwards over here. But don't worry. There are always seats for VIPs.' He explained that compartments for VIPs and senior government officials were reserved on every train until two hours before departure time, in case someone of importance might wish to travel at the last minute. Apparently a waiting list was drawn up every day for each of India's 10,000 trains.

'Mr Nath,' I said, 'I'm not a VIP.'

'Don't be silly,' he said. He puffed his pipe and moved his eyes from the messenger to me. I think he saw my point because his next words were, 'Also we could try money.'

'*Baksheesh*,' I said. Mr Nath made a face.

Mr Sud said, 'Why don't you fly?'

'Planes make me throw up.'

'I think we've waited long enough,' said Mr Nath. 'We'll see the man in charge and explain the situation. Let me do the talking.'

We walked around the barrier to where the ticket manager sat, squinting irritably at a ledger. He did not look up. He said, 'Yes, what is it?' Mr Nath pointed his pipe stem at me and, with the pomposity Indians assume when they speak to each other in English, introduced me as a distinguished American writer who was getting a bad impression of Indian Railways.

'Wait a minute,' I said.

'It is imperative that we do our utmost to ensure –'

'Tourist?' said the ticket manager.

I said yes.

He snapped his fingers. 'Passport.'

I handed it over. He wrote a new application and dismissed us. The application went back to the messenger, who had wormed his way to the window.

'It's a priority matter,' said Mr Nath crossly. 'You are a tourist. You have come all this way, so you have priority. We want to give favourable impression. If I want to travel with my family – wife, small children, maybe my mother too – they say, "Oh, no, there is a *tourist* here. Priority matter!"' He grinned without pleasure. 'That is the situation. But you have your ticket – that's the important thing, isn't it?'

The elderly Indian in the compartment was sitting cross-legged on his berth reading a copy of *Filmfare*. Seeing me enter, he took off his glasses, smiled, then returned to his magazine. I went to

a large wooden cupboard and smacked it with my hand, trying
to open it. I wanted to hang up my jacket. I got my fingers into
the louvred front and tugged. The Indian took off his glasses
again, and this time he closed the magazine.

'Please,' he said, 'you will break the air conditioner.'

'This is an air conditioner?' It was a tall box the height of the
room, four feet wide, varnished, silent, and warm.

He nodded. 'It has been modernized. This carriage is fifty
years old.'

'Nineteen twenty?'

'About that,' he said. 'The cooling system was very interesting
then. Every compartment had its own unit. That is a unit. It
worked very well.'

'I didn't realize there were air conditioners in the twenties,'
I said.

'They used ice,' he said. He explained that blocks of ice were
slipped into lockers under the floor – it was done from the
outside so that the passengers' sleep would not be disturbed.
Fans in the cupboard I had tried to open blew air over the ice
and into the compartment. Every three hours or so the ice was
renewed. (I imagined an Englishman snoring in his berth while
at the platform of some outlying station Indians with bright eyes
pushed cakes of ice into the lockers.) But the system had been
converted: a refrigerating device had been installed under the
blowers. Just as he finished speaking there was a whirr from
behind the louvres and a loud and prolonged *whoosh*!

'When did they stop using ice?'

'About four years ago,' he said. He yawned. 'You will excuse
me if I go to bed?'

The train started up, and the wood panelling of this old
sleeping car groaned and creaked; the floor shuddered, the metal
marauder-proof windows clattered in their frames, and the
*whooshing* from the tall cupboard went on all night. The Kalka
Mail was full of Bengalis, on their way to Simla for a festival,
the Kali *puja*. Bengalis, whose complexion resembles that of the

black goddess of destruction they worship, and who have the same sharp hook to their noses, have the misfortune to live at the opposite end of the country from the most favoured Kali temple. Kali is usually depicted wearing a necklace of human skulls, sticking her maroon tongue out, and trampling a human corpse. But the Bengalis were smiling sweetly all along the train, with their baskets of food and neatly woven garlands of flowers.

I was asleep when the train reached Kalka at dawn, but the elderly Indian obligingly woke me up. He was dressed and seated at the drop-leaf table, having a cup of tea and reading the *Chandigarh Tribune*. He poured his tea into the cup, blew on it, poured half a cup into the saucer, blew on it, and then, making a pedestal of his fingers, drank the tea from the saucer, lapping it like a cat.

'You will want to read this,' he said. 'Your vice president has resigned.'

He showed me the paper, and there was the glad news, sharing the front page with an item about a Mr Dikshit. It seemed a happy combination, Dikshit and Agnew, though I am sure Mr Dikshit's political life had been blameless. As for Agnew's, the Indian laughed derisively when I translated the amount he had extorted into rupees. Even the black-market rate turned him into a cut-price punk. The Indian was in stitches.

In Kalka two landscapes meet. There is nothing gradual in the change from plains to mountains: the Himalayas stand at the upper edge of the Indo-Gangetic plain; the rise is sudden and dramatic. The trains must conform to the severity of the change; two are required – one large roomy one for the ride to Kalka, and a small tough beast for the ascent to Simla. Kalka itself is a well-organized station at the end of the broad-gauge line. Between the Himalayas and Kalka is the cool hill station of Simla on a bright balding ridge. I had my choice of trains for the sixty-mile journey on the narrow gauge: the toy train or the rail car. The blue wooden carriages of the train were already packed with pilgrims – the Bengalis, nimble at boarding trains, had performed the Calcutta trick of diving headfirst through the train windows and had got the best seats. It was an urban skill, this somersault – a fire drill in reverse – and it left the more patient hill people a bit glassy-eyed. I decided to take the rail car. This was a white squarish machine, with the face of a Model-T Ford and the body of an old bus. It was mounted low on the narrow-gauge tracks and had the look of a battered limousine. But considering that it was built in 1925 (so the driver assured me), it was in wonderful shape.

I found the conductor. He wore a stained white uniform and a brown peaked cap that did not fit him. He was sorry to hear I wanted to take the rail car. He ran his thumb down his clipboard to mystify me and said, 'I am expecting another party.'

There were only three people in the rail car. I felt he was angling for *baksheesh*. I said, 'How many people can you fit in?'

'Twelve,' he said.

'How many seats have been booked?'

He hid his clipboard and turned away. He said, 'I am very sorry.'

'You are very helpful.'

'I am expecting another party.'

'If they show up, you let me know,' I said. 'In the meantime, I'm putting my bag inside.'

'It might get stolen,' he said brightly.

'Nothing could please me more.'

'Wanting breakfast, sahib?' said a little man with a pushbroom.

I said yes, and within five minutes my breakfast was laid out on an unused ticket counter in the middle of the platform: tea, toast, jam, a cube of butter, and an omelette. The morning sunlight struck through the platform, warming me as I stood eating my breakfast. It was an unusual station for India: it was not crowded, there were no sleepers, no encampment of naked squatters, no cows. It was filled that early hour with the smell of damp grass and wildflowers. I buttered a thick slice of toast and ate it, but I couldn't finish all the breakfast. I left two slices of toast, the jam, and half the omelette uneaten, and I walked over to the rail car. When I looked back, I saw two ragged children reaching up to the counter and stuffing the remainder of my breakfast into their mouths.

At seven-fifteen, the driver of the rail car inserted a long-handled crank into the engine and gave it a jerk. The engine shook and coughed and, still juddering and smoking, began to whine. Within minutes we were on the slope, looking down at the top of Kalka Station, where in the train yard two men were winching a huge steam locomotive around in a circle. The rail car's speed was a steady ten miles an hour, zigzagging in and out of the steeply pitched hill, reversing on switchbacks through the terraced gardens and the white flocks of butterflies. We passed through several tunnels before I noticed they were numbered; a large number 4 was painted over the entrance of the next one. The man seated beside me, who had told me he was a civil servant in Simla, said there were 103 tunnels altogether. I tried not to notice the numbers after that. Outside the car, there was a sheer drop, hundreds of feet down, for the railway, which was opened in 1904, is cut directly into the hillside, and the line above is notched like the skidway on a toboggan run, circling the hills.

After thirty minutes everyone in the rail car was asleep except the civil servant and me. At the little stations along the way, the postman in the rear seat awoke from his doze to throw a mailbag out the window to a waiting porter on the platform. I tried to take pictures, but the landscape eluded me: one vista shifted into another, lasting only seconds, a dizzying displacement of hill and air, of haze and all the morning shades of green. The meat-grinder cogs working against the rack under the rail car ticked like an ageing clock and made me drowsy. I took out my inflatable pillow, blew it up, put it under my head, and slept peacefully in the sunshine until I was awakened by the thud of the rail car's brakes and the banging of doors.

'Ten minutes,' said the driver.

We were just below a wooden structure, a doll's house, its window boxes overflowing with red blossoms, and moss trimming its wide eaves. This was Bangu Station. It had a wide complicated verandah on which a waiter stood with a menu under his arm. The rail-car passengers scrambled up the stairs. My Kalka breakfast had been premature; I smelled eggs and coffee and heard the Bengalis quarrelling with the waiters in English.

I walked down the gravel paths to admire the well-tended flower beds and the carefully mown lengths of turf beside the track; below the station a rushing stream gurgled, and signs there, and near the flower beds, read NO PLUCKING. A waiter chased me down to the stream and called out, 'We have juices! You like fresh mango juice? A little porridge? Coffee-tea?'

We resumed the ride, and the time passed quickly as I dozed again and woke to higher mountains, with fewer trees, stonier slopes, and huts perched more precariously. The haze had disappeared and the hillsides were bright, but the air was cool and a fresh breeze blew through the open windows of the rail car. In every tunnel the driver switched on orange lamps, and the racket of the clattering wheels increased and echoed. After Solon the only people in the rail car were a family of Bengali pilgrims (all of them sound asleep, snoring, their faces turned up), the civil servant, the postman, and me. The next stop was Solon Brewery, where the air was pungent with yeast and hops, and after that we passed through pine forests and cedar groves. On one stretch a baboon the size of a six-year-old crept off the tracks to let us go by. I remarked on the largeness of the creature.

The civil servant said, 'There was once a *saddhu* – a holy man – who lived near Simla. He could speak to monkeys. A certain Englishman had a garden, and all the time the monkeys were causing him trouble. Monkeys can be very destructive. The Englishman told this *saddhu* his problem. The *saddhu* said, "I will see what I can do." Then the *saddhu* went into the forest and assembled all the monkeys. He said, "I hear you are troubling the Englishman. That is bad. You must stop; leave his garden alone. If I hear that you are causing damage I will treat you very harshly." And from that time onwards the monkeys never went into the Englishman's garden.'

'Do you believe that story?'

'Oh, yes. But the man is now dead – the *saddhu*. I don't know what happened to the Englishman. Perhaps he went away, like the rest of them.'

A little farther on, he said, 'What do you think of India?'

'It's a hard question,' I said. I wanted to tell him about the children I had seen that morning pathetically raiding the leftovers of my breakfast, and ask him if he thought there was any truth in Mark Twain's comment on Indians: 'It is a curious people. With them, all life seems to be sacred except human life.' But I added instead, 'I haven't been here very long.'

'I will tell you what I think,' he said. 'If all the people who are talking about honesty, fair play, socialism, and so forth – if they began to practise it themselves, India will do well. Otherwise there will be a revolution.'

He was an unsmiling man in his early fifties and had the stern features of a Brahmin. He neither drank nor smoked, and before he joined the civil service he had been a Sanskrit scholar in an Indian university. He got up at five every morning, had an apple, a glass of milk, and some almonds; he washed and said his prayers and after that took a long walk. Then he went to his office. To set an example for his junior officers he always walked to work, he furnished his office sparsely, and he did not require his bearer to wear a khaki uniform. He admitted that his example was unpersuasive. His junior officers had parking permits, sumptuous furnishings, and uniformed bearers.

'I ask them why all this money is spent for nothing. They tell me to make a good first impression is very important. I say to the blighters, "What about *second* impression?"'

'Blighters' was a word that occurred often in his speech. Lord Clive was a blighter and so were most of the other viceroys.

Blighters ask for bribes; blighters try to cheat the Accounts Department; blighters are living in luxury and talking about socialism. It was a point of honour with this civil servant that he had never in his life given or received *baksheesh*: 'Not even a single paisa.' Some of his clerks had, and in eighteen years in the civil service he had personally fired thirty-two people. He thought it might be a record. I asked him what they had done wrong.

'Gross incompetence,' he said, 'pinching money, hanky-panky. But I never fire anyone without first having a good talk with his parents. There was a blighter in the Audit Department, always pinching girls' bottoms. Indian girls from good families! I warned him about this, but he couldn't stop. So I told him I wanted to see his parents. The blighter said his parents lived fifty miles away. I gave him money for their bus fare. They were poor, and they were quite worried about the blighter. I said to them, "Now I want you to understand that your son is in deep trouble. He is causing annoyance to the lady members of this department. Please talk to him and make him understand that if this continues I will have no choice but to sack him." Parents go away, blighter goes back to work, and ten days later he is at it again. I suspended him on the spot, then I charge-sheeted him.'

I wondered whether any of these people had tried to take revenge on him.

'Yes, there was one. He got himself drunk one night and came to my house with a knife. "Come outside and I will kill you!" That sort of thing. My wife was upset. But I was angry. I couldn't control myself. I dashed outside and fetched the blighter a blooming kick. He dropped his knife and began to cry. "Don't call the police," he said. "I have a wife and children." He was a complete coward, you see. I let him go and everyone criticized me – they said I should have brought charges. But I told them he'll never bother anyone again.

'And there was another time. I was working for Heavy Electricals, doing an audit for some cheaters in Bengal. Faulty construction, double entries, and estimates that were five times what they should have been. There was also immorality. One bloke – son of the contractor, very wealthy – kept four harlots. He gave them whisky and made them take their clothes off and run naked into a group of women and children doing *puja*. Disgraceful! Well, they didn't like me at all and the day I left there were four *dacoits* with knives waiting for me on the station road. But I expected that, so I took a different road, and the blighters never caught me. A month later two auditors were murdered by *dacoits*.'

The rail car tottered around a cliffside, and on the opposite slope, across a deep valley, was Simla. Most of the town fits the ridge like a saddle made entirely of rusty roofs, but as we drew closer the fringes seemed to be sliding into the valley. Simla is unmistakable, for as *Murray's Handbook* indicates, 'its skyline is incongruously dominated by a Gothic Church, a baronial castle and a Victorian country mansion'. Above these brick piles is the sharply pointed peak of Jakhu (8000 feet); below are the clinging house fronts. The southerly aspect of Simla is so steep that flights of cement stairs take the place of roads. From the rail car it looked an attractive place, a town of rusting splendour with snowy mountains in the background.

'My office is in that castle,' said the civil servant.

'Gorton Castle,' I said, referring to my handbook. 'Do you work for the Accountant General of the Punjab?'

'Well, I *am* the A.G.,' he said. But he was giving information, not boasting. At Simla Station the porter strapped my suitcase to his back (he was a Kashmiri, up for the season). The civil servant introduced himself as Vishnu Bhardwaj and invited me for tea that afternoon.

The Mall was filled with Indian vacationers taking their morning stroll, warmly dressed children, women with cardigans over their saris, and men in tweed suits, clasping the green Simla guidebook in one hand and a cane in the other. The promenading has strict hours, nine to twelve in the morning and four to eight in the evening, determined by mealtimes and shop openings. These hours were fixed a hundred years ago, when Simla was the summer capital of the Indian empire, and they have not varied. The architecture is similarly unchanged – it is all high Victorian, with the vulgarly grandiose touches colonial labour allowed, extravagant gutters and porticoes, buttressed by pillars and steelwork to prevent its slipping down the hill. The Gaiety Theatre (1887) is still the Gaiety Theatre (though when I was there it was the venue of a 'Spiritual Exhibition' I was not privileged to see); pettifogging continues in Gorton Castle, as praying does in Christ Church (1857), the Anglican cathedral; the viceroy's lodge (Rastrapati Nivas), a baronial mansion, is now the Indian Institute of Advanced Studies, but the visiting scholars creep about with the diffidence of caretakers maintaining the sepulchral stateliness of the place. Scattered among these large Simla buildings are the bungalows – Holly Lodge, Romney Castle, The Bricks, Forest View, Sevenoaks, Fernside – but the inhabitants now are Indians, or rather that inherited breed of Indian that insists on the guidebook, the walking stick, the cravat, tea at four, and an evening stroll to Scandal Point. It is the Empire with a dark complexion, an imperial outpost that the mimicking vacationers have preserved from change, though not the place of highly coloured intrigues described in *Kim*, and certainly tamer than it was a century ago. After all, Lola Montez, the *grande horizontale*, began her whoring in Simla, and the only single women I saw were short red-cheeked Tibetan labourers in quilted coats, who walked along the Mall with heavy stones in slings on their backs.

I had tea with the Bhardwaj family. It was not the simple meal I had expected. There were eight or nine dishes: *pakora*, vegetables fried in batter; *poha*, a rice mixture with peas, coriander, and turmeric; *khira*, a creamy pudding of rice, milk, and sugar; a kind of fruit salad, with cucumber and lemon added to it, called *chaat; murak*, a Tamil savoury, like large nutty pretzels; *tikkiya*, potato cakes; *malai* chops, sweet sugary balls topped with cream; and almond-scented *pinnis*. I ate what I could, and the next day I saw Mr Bhardwaj's office in Gorton Castle. It was as sparely furnished as he had said on the rail car, and over his desk was this sign:

> I am not interested in excuses for delay;
> I am interested only in a thing done.
> — Jawaharlal Nehru

The day I left I found an ashram on one of Simla's slopes. I had been interested in visiting an ashram ever since the hippies on the Teheran Express had told me what marvellous places they were. But I was disappointed. The ashram was a ramshackle bungalow run by a talkative old man named Gupta, who claimed he had cured many people of advanced paralysis by running his hands over their legs. There were no hippies in this ashram, though Mr Gupta was anxious to recruit me. I said I had a train to catch. He said that if I was a believer in yoga I wouldn't worry about catching trains. I said that was why I wasn't a believer in yoga.

Mr Gupta said, 'I will tell you a story. A yogi was approached by a certain man who said he wanted to be a student. Yogi said he was very busy and had no time for man. Man said he was desperate. Yogi did not believe him. Man said he would commit suicide by jumping from roof if yogi would not take him on. Yogi said nothing. Man jumped.

'"Bring his body to me," said yogi. Body was brought. Yogi passed his hands over body and after a few minutes man regained his life.

'"Now you are ready to be my student," said yogi. "I believe you can act on proper impulses and you have shown me great sincerity." So man who had been restored to the living became student.'

'Have you ever brought anyone to life?' I asked.

'Not as yet,' said Mr Gupta.

*Not as yet!* His guru was Paramahansa Yogananda, whose sleek saintly face was displayed all over the bungalow. In Ranchi, Paramahansa Y. had a vision. This was his vision: a gathering of millions of Americans who needed his advice. He described them in his *Autobiography* as 'a vast multitude, gazing at me intently' that 'swept actorlike across the stage of consciousness . . . the Lord is calling me to America . . . Yes! I am going forth to discover America, like Columbus. He thought he had found India; surely there is a karmic link between these two lands!' He could see the people so clearly, he recognized their faces when he arrived in California a few years later. He stayed in Los Angeles for thirty years, and, unlike Columbus, died rich, happy and fulfilled. Mr Gupta told me this hilarious story in a tone of great reverence, and then he took me on a tour of the bungalow, drawing my attention to the many portraits of Jesus (painted to look like a yogi) he had tacked to the walls.

'Where do you live?' asked a small friendly ashramite, who was eating an apple. (Simla apples are delicious, but, because of a trade agreement, the whole crop goes to Poland.)

'South London at the moment.'

'But it is so noisy and dirty there!'

I found this an astonishing observation from a man who said he was from Kathmandu; but I let it pass.

'I used to live in Kensington Palace Gardens,' he said. 'The rent was high, but my government paid. I was the Nepalese ambassador at the time.'

'Did you ever meet the queen?'

'Many times! The queen liked to talk about the plays that were on in London. She talked about the actors and the plot and so on. She would say, "Did you like *this* part of the play or that one?" If you hadn't seen the play it was very difficult to reply. But usually she talked about horses, and I'm sorry to say I have no interest at all in horses.'

I left the ashram and paid a last visit to Mr Bhardwaj. He gave me various practical warnings about travelling and advised me to visit Madras, where I would see the real India. He was off to have the carburettor in his car checked and to finish up some accounts at his office. He hoped I had enjoyed Simla and said it was a shame I hadn't seen any snow. He was formal, almost severe in his farewell, but, walking down to Cart Road, he said, 'I will see you in England or America.'

'That would be nice. I hope we do meet again.'

'We will,' he said, with such certainty I challenged it.

'How do you know?'

'I am about to be transferred from Simla. Maybe going to England, maybe to the States. That is what my horoscope says.'

# 10. The Rajdhani ('Capital') Express to Bombay

MR RADIA (his name was on a label beside the door, with mine) was sitting on his berth, intoning a Hindi song through his nose. He saw me and sang louder. I took out my electric shaver and began to run it over my face; he drowned the whine of the motor with his lugubrious song. When he sang his expression was rapturous, in repose his face was sour. He looked at my gin bottle with distaste and told me that spirits were not allowed on Indian Railways, and to my owlish reply ('But I thought Indians believed in spirits') he only grunted. Moments later he pleaded with me to put my pipe out. He said he had once vomited in a compartment where an Englishman was smoking.

'I'm not English,' I said.

He grunted. I saw he was trying to read the cover of the book I had opened. It was *The Autobiography of a Yogi*, by Paramahansa Yogananda, a parting gift from Mr Gupta of the Simla ashram.

'Are you interested in yoga?' asked Mr Radia.

'No,' I said, studying the book closely. I wet my finger and turned a page.

'I am,' said Mr Radia. 'Not the physical side, but the mental side. The benefit is there.'

'The physical side is the best part.'

'Not for me. For me it is all mental. I like to exercise my mind with debates and discussions of all kinds.'

I snapped the book shut and left the compartment.

It was late afternoon, but already the orange sun was submerged in the dust haze at the far end of a perfectly flat landscape. Delhi is a city of three million, but a half an hour out of the station and you are in a countryside devoid of people, a green plain as flat as those areas of Turkey and Iran, which were so sunlit and empty they made my eyes ache. I made my way through the classes to the dining car: first class air-conditioned had carpets and cold door handles and fogged windows, and there was a shower in the Indian-style toilet but none in the awful booth designated (and this was an intemperate libel) 'Western-style'; the first-class sleeper had bare cells and plastic-covered berths, the chair car had seats arranged like those on a plane, and people were already tucked in for the night, with blankets over their heads to shut out the air conditioning and the bright overhead lights; there were card games in the wooden second-class compartments, and in the third-class sleeper the bookshelf berths were fixed to the wall in tiers like those on trains in old Russian movies. People reclined on the boards with their bony knees sticking out, and others queued in puddles at the toilet doors.

The dining car, at the bottom rung of this Indian social ladder, was a narrow room of broken chairs and slopped-over tables. Meal coupons were being sold. At this point in my trip I had turned vegetarian. The meat I saw in India was foul in any case, so I never had the cravings sometimes referred to as 'meat-fits'. And though I had no side effects (impotence, geniality, gas) I sometimes had second thoughts when I saw, as I did that evening, a fat sweating Indian cook in filthy pyjamas preparing vegetables for the pot by gathering them with his forearms and then slapping and squeezing them into a pulpous mass.

After dark we made a stop at Mathura Junction. I got out, and in the glare of the station platform was the now familiar (but no less horrifying) sight of the railway villagers. They were not locals: they were very black, thin, with small sharp teeth and narrow noses and thick glossy hair; they wore sarongs and camped on the platform with that air of proprietary completeness that suggested permanence. There were rows of *charpoys*, and at the unsheltered end of the platform greasy tarpaulins had been pitched like tents. They were spitting, eating, pissing, and strolling with such self-possession that they might have been in a remote village in the deepest Madrasi jungle (I took them to be Tamils) instead of under the gaze of the travellers on the Bombay express. One woman snatched up a child and helped him comb for lice in her scalp, and another woman, who I thought was crouching in despair, I saw after a moment to be playing peekaboo with an infant half-hidden in an orange crate.

I had passed these encampments too many times without looking closely at them. I found a man on the train and asked him if he would translate my questions. He agreed, and we found a willing interviewee. This was a fox-faced man with glittering white eyes and buck teeth, wearing a white sarong. He stood with his arms folded and stroked his biceps with slender fingers.

'He says they come from Kerala.'

'But why have they come so far? Are they looking for work?'

'Not looking for work. This is a *yatra*.'

So it was another pilgrimage.

'Where are they headed?'

'Here, Mathura,' the translator said, pronouncing it *Muttra*. The fox-faced man spoke again. The translator continued, 'He is asking that do you know this is a holy place?'

'The railway station?'

'The town. Lord Krishna was born here.'

And not only that, I read later. It was in Mathura that the Divine Cowherd was exchanged with the infant daughter of Jasoda in order to save him from being murdered by the giant Kans, a parallel of the Herod story. The town is also the scene of Krishna's youth, where he sported with the milkmaids and played his flute. The legends were pretty; the place itself seemed a grim contradiction.

'How long will the *yatris* stay?'

'For some days.'

'Why are they at the station instead of in town?'

'There is water and light here, and it is safe. There are robbers in town and some people get chased by rogues.'

'What do they do for food?'

'He says they have brought some, and some they get in town. The people on the train also give some.' The translator added, 'He is asking where are you from?'

I told him. In a corner of the platform, I saw the silhouette of a pot-bellied child with spindly legs, naked and clinging to a waterspout. It was alone, holding on, waiting for nothing; the sight of this futile patience cracked my heart.

'He is asking for money.'

'I will give him one rupee if he says a prayer for me at the Mathura temple.'

This was translated. The man from Kerala laughed and said something.

'He would have said a prayer for you even if you had given him nothing.'

The whistle blew and I boarded. Mr Radia had stopped singing. He was sitting in the compartment reading *Blitz*. *Blitz* is a noisy, irresponsible weekly paper in English that retails scandals in a semiliterate but bouncy style of which the following, from the film page, is a fair example:

Star-producer-director of JUHU, one of four bhais, hotted up his birthday like nobody's business.

The guest control order was out of bounds there! There were booze and broads and brawls by the host himself! He was high and headstrong, lording it over all. Hurled abuse at some and then fisted a guest. That's the time few walked out. Some hospitality that! What does he think himself to be? GOD-FATHER?

Mr Radia continued to read, scowling with appreciation. Then our dinner trays were brought, and I noticed his was non-vegetarian. His hamburger came apart under his knife and he poked at it disgustedly. But he ate it. 'The first time I took meat I was violently sick,' he said. 'But that happens when you do anything for the first time, isn't it?'

With this bewildering epigraph he told me about his work. He had worked for Shell for twenty years, but discovered he loathed the English so much that he finally quit. His sense of grievance was strong and his memory for the humiliations he had been subjected to amounted to total recall. The English were domineering and exclusive, he said, but he was quick to add, 'Mind you, we Indians can be the same. But the English had their chance. If only,' he said, and prodded his hamburger, 'if only the English had become Indians.'

'Was that ever on the cards?'

'Yes, they could have done it. No trouble at all. I went to a T-group session in Darjeeling. Debates and discussions. Very interesting. The wife of the director had just arrived from the States, and the second day she was there *that lady was wearing a sari.*'

I was sceptical about this proving anything and asked him how long the lady would stay in her sari.

'That's a point,' said Mr Radia.

Now he was the Deputy General Manager for a joint Japanese–Indian effort, making dry-cell batteries in Gujarat. He had had several run-ins with the Japanese – 'Head-on collisions – I had no choice!' I asked him how he found the Japanese. He said, 'Loyal, yes! Clean and hard-working, yes! But intelligent, *not at all!*' It turned out that they were getting under his skin, though he preferred them to the English. The company was run on Japanese lines: uniforms, no sweepers or bearers, morning assembly, a joint staff–worker canteen, and common toilets ('That was a shock'). What nettled Mr Radia was that the Japanese insisted on dating the factory girls.

'That's the best way I know to demoralize the others,' he said, 'but when I asked them about it they said it would make the workers friendlier if the bosses took the girls out on dates. And they smiled at me. Have you ever seen a Japanese smile? I wasn't going to have it. "*Nothing doing!*" I said. "You want to argue? Okay, we'll argue. Let's take it to the manager!" Now

I will be quite frank with you. I think these Japanese were going in twos and threes and having group sex.'

'Especially in twos,' I said. But Mr Radia was too worked up to hear me.

'I told them it was just *not on*! Prostitutes – okay, it happens all over the world! Girls from town – all right! Clean, healthy fun – fine! Picnics – count me in! I'll bring my wife, I'll bring my children, we'll all have a good time. But workers? *Never!*'

Mr. Radia grew increasingly peevish about the Japanese. I complained of a headache and went to bed.

The conductor brought tea at half-past six and said we were in Gujarat. Bullocks and cows cropped grass at the edge of the line, and at one station a goat skittered on the platform. Gujarat, Gandhi's birthplace, is a hot, flat, but apparently very fertile state. There were guava orchards and fields of lentils, cotton, papaya, and tobacco stretching to the tilted palm trees at the horizon, and the irrigation ditches were cut like chevrons in these sleeves of landscape. Occasionally, a marquee of trees identified a village and dusty people could be seen washing in brown streams where the mud banks were covered with footprints like the tracks of stray birds.

'And here we are at Baroda,' said Mr Radia, turning to the window.

In the foreground a migration of ragged people carried bundles on their heads, following a bullock cart mounded with bruised furniture. The white hairless patches on the children's heads spoke of overcrowding, malnutrition, and disease, and they were all grinning in the glare of the sun.

'That, I believe, is the new petrochemical plant. It's already in operation,' said Mr Radia.

We were passing a shantytown made entirely of flattened cardboard boxes and bits of hammered tin. Women squatted, slapping cow turds into pies, and inside the terrifying huts I could see people lying with their arms crossed over their faces.

A man screamed at a running child; another howled at the train.

'Everything's coming up. Patel's factory. It's completely industrial here. Jyoti Industries. Worth *crores*, I tell you. *Crores!*'

Mr Radia was looking past the muddy ditch, over the heads of the skinny cows, the children with streaming noses, the crones in tattered headdresses, the many squatters who were making puzzled faces and shitting, the leathery old men leaning on broken umbrellas.

'Another new factory, already famous – Baroda furniture. I know the director. We've had him around for drinks.'

Then heartily, Mr Radia the Anglophobe said, 'Well, cheerio!'

At Broach, fifty miles south of Baroda, we crossed the wide Narmada River. I was standing by the door. A man tapped me on the shoulder.

'Excuse me.' He was a dark bespectacled Indian in a flowered shirt, holding two coconuts and a garland of flowers. He moved to the door and, bracing himself on the handrail, pitched the garland, then the coconuts, into the river.

'Offerings,' he explained. 'I live in Singapore. I am so happy to be home.'

Late in the afternoon we were in the lowland of Maharashtra, gleaming swamps, the green inlets of the Gulf of Cambray, and just at the horizon the Arabian Sea. It had been cool in the morning, and pleasant at Baroda, but the afternoon ride to Bombay from Broach was stifling: the air was dense with humidity, and the feathery fronds on the tall palms drooped in the heat. At every siding I saw the feet of napping Indians sticking out from under packing cases and makeshift shelters. And then Bombay began. We were still quite far from the city centre – twenty miles or more – but the sight of a single sway-backed hut swelled to a hamlet of shacks, and then to an unbroken parade of low dwellings, their roofs littered with plastic sheets, bits of wood and paper, a rubber tyre, shingles held down with stones, and thatch tied with vines, as if this accumulated rubbish would keep the shacks from blowing away. The hovels became bungalows the colour of rotten cheese, then three-storey houses bandaged with laundry, and eight-storey apartment blocks with rusty fire escapes, getting larger and larger as we neared Bombay.

On the outskirts of the city the Rajdhani Express came to several alarming stops – so sudden, one of them toppled my water pitcher on to the floor and the next smashed a glass. We did not appear to be at stations for these stops, although there were people leaving the train. I saw them throwing their suitcases on to the tracks and leaping out themselves with the speed of deserters, picking up their baggage and racing across the line. I discovered they had pulled the emergency alarm cord (PENALTY FOR IMPROPER USE RUPEES 250) because they were passing their houses. This was an express train, but by pulling the alarm the Indian could turn it into a local.

There was a fat boy, a recent graduate from the Dehra Dun School of Engineering. He was on his way to Poona for a job interview. He told me why the train was stopping with such force, and he described how the alarm worked.

He said, 'Person who wishes to leave train pulls cord and dewice inside releases wacuum causing brakes to seize in that particular bogie. Conductor is sure which bogie alarm is pulled, but there are so many people he does not know who has pulled chain. Conductor must reconnect dewice and create wacuum in order for train to move.'

He spoke so slowly and methodically that by the time he finished this explanation we were in Bombay.

It was at a railway station in Bombay that V. S. Naipaul panicked and fled, fearing that he 'might sink without a trace into that Indian crowd.' The story is told in *An Area of Darkness*. But I did not find Bombay Central especially scarifying; a closer acquaintance with it made me think of it as a place of refugees and fortune hunters, smelling of dirt and money, in a neighbourhood that had the look of the neglected half of Chicago. The hurrying daytime crowds might have frightened me more if they had been idly prowling, but in their mass there was no sense of aimlessness. The direction of those speeding white shirts gave to these thousands of marchers the aspect of a dignified parade of clerks and their wives and cattle, preparing to riot according to some long-held custom, among the most distinguished architecture the British Empire produced (cover your good eye, squint at Victoria Station in Bombay, and you see the grey majesty of St Paul's Cathedral). Bombay fulfills the big-city requirements of age, depth, and frenzy, inspiring a chauvinism in its inhabitants, a threadbare metropolitan hauteur rivalled only by Calcutta. My one disappointment came at the Towers of Silence, where the Parsis place their dead to be eaten by vultures. This may strike a casual visitor as solemn barbarity, but it is based on an ecologically sound proposition. The Zoroastrian at the gate would not let me in to verify it. I had been brought there by Mushtaq, my driver, and, leaving, I said perhaps the stories were not true – I couldn't see any vultures. Mushtaq said they were all down at the towers feeding on a corpse. He looked at his watch: 'Lunchtime.' But he meant mine.

After my lecture that evening I met several writers. One was Mr V. G. Deshmukh, a jolly novelist who said that he could not make a living by his pen. He had written thirty novels. Writing is the single activity in India that doesn't pay, and anyway this man wrote about the poor: no one was interested in reading about poor people. He knew, because the poor were his business.

'Famine relief, resettlement, drought prevention, underprivileged, anything you can name. It is a headache sometimes. But my books don't sell, so I have no choice. You could call me an organizer.'

'How do you prevent droughts?'

'We have programmes.'

I saw committees, position papers, conferences – and dusty fields.

'Have you prevented any lately?'

'We are making steady progress,' he said. 'But I would rather write novels.'

'If you've written thirty, surely it's time to stop.'

'No, no! I must write one hundred and eight!'

'How did you arrive at that figure?'

'It is a magic number in Hindu philosophy. Vishnu has one hundred and eight names. I must write one hundred and eight novels! It is not easy – especially now, with this damned paper shortage.'

The paper shortage was also affecting Kushwant Singh's *Illustrated Weekly of India*. His circulation was 300,000 but he was about to cut it down to save paper. It was an Indian story: Indian enterprises seemed to work so well they produced disasters; success made them burst at the seams and the disruption of unprecedented orders led to shortages and finally failure. India, the largest rice-grower in the world, imports rice. 'Hunger is the handmaid of genius,' says the Pudd'nhead Wilson epigraph above one of the Bombay chapters in Mark Twain's *Following the Equator*, and truly India's hunger-inspired genius threatens to sink her. Every success I heard of convinced me that India, swamped by invention, was hopeless and must fail unless what I saw later that night ceases to exist. It is the simplest fact of Indian life: there are too many Indians.

Unable to sleep, I went for a walk. I turned left out of my hotel and walked a hundred yards past the brothels to the sea wall, counting the sleeping figures as I went along. They were stretched out on the sidewalk, lying side by side; some were on pieces of cardboard but most slept flat on the cement, with no bedding and few clothes, their arms crooked under their heads. The children slept on their sides, the others on their backs. There was no sign anywhere of their possessions. I reached seventy-three and turned the corner, where down the road that ran next to the sea wall there were hundreds more – just bodies, no bundles or carts, nothing to distinguish one from another, no evidence of life. It is sometimes thought that these sleepers in the Bombay streets are a recent phenomenon; but Mark Twain saw them. He was on his way to a midnight betrothal ceremony:

We seemed to move through a city of the dead. There was hardly a suggestion of life in those still and vacant streets. Even the crows were silent. But everywhere on the ground lay sleeping natives – hundreds and hundreds. They lay stretched at full length and tightly wrapped in blankets, heads and all. Their attitude and rigidity counterfeited death.

That was in 1896. They are more numerous today, and there is another difference. The ones I saw had no blankets. Hunger – *pace* Pudd'nhead Wilson – is also the handmaid of death.

## 11. The Delhi Mail from Jaipur

'WHAT's this?' I asked Mr Gopal, the embassy liaison man, pointing to a kind of fortress.

'That's a kind of fortress.'

He had ridiculed the handbook I had been carrying around: 'You have this big book, but I tell you to close it and leave it at hotel because Jaipur is like open book to me.' Unwisely, I had taken his advice. We were now six miles outside Jaipur, wading ankle-deep through sand drifts towards the wrecked settlement of Galta. Earlier we had passed through a jamboree of some two hundred baboons: 'Act normal,' said Mr Gopal, as they hopped and chattered and showed their teeth, clustering on the road with a curiosity that bordered on menace. The landscape was rocky and very dry, and each rugged hill was capped with a cracked fortress.

'Whose is it?'

'The Maharajah's.'

'No, who built it?'

'You would not know his name.'

'Do *you*?'

Mr Gopal walked on. It was dusk, and the buildings crammed into the Galta gorge were darkening. A monkey chattered and leaped to a branch in a banyan tree above Mr Gopal's head, yanking the branch down and making a punkah's *whoosh*. We entered the gate and crossed a courtyard to some ruined buildings, with coloured frescoes of trees and people on their façades. Some had been raked with indecipherable graffiti and painted over; whole panels had been chiselled away.

'What's this?' I asked. I hated him for making me leave my handbook behind.

'Ah,' said Mr Gopal. It was a temple enclosure. Some men dozed in the archways, others squatted on their haunches, and just outside the enclosure were some tea and vegetable stalls whose owners leaned against more frescoes, rubbing them away with their backs. I was struck by the solitude of the place – a few people at sundown, no one speaking, and it was so quiet I could hear the hooves of the goats clattering on the cobblestones, the murmuring of the distant monkeys.

'A temple?'

Mr Gopal thought a moment. 'Yes,' he said finally, 'a kind of temple.'

On the ornate temple walls, stuck with posters, defaced with chisels, pissed on, and scrawled over with huge Devanagri script advertising Jaipur businesses, there was a blue enamel sign, warning visitors in Hindi and English that it was 'forbidden to desecrate, deface, mark, or otherwise abuse the walls'. The sign itself had been defaced: the enamel was chipped – it looked partly eaten.

Farther along, the cobblestone road became a narrow path and then a steep staircase cut into the rock walls of the gorge. At the top of this was a temple facing a still, black pool. Insects swimming in circles on the pool's surface made minuscule ripples, and small clouds of vibrant gnats hovered over the water. The temple was an unambitious niche in the rock face, a shallow cave, lighted with oil lamps and tapers. On either side of its portals were seven-foot marble slabs, the shape of those handed down from Sinai but with a weight that would give the most muscular prophet a hernia. These tablets had numbered instructions cut into them in two languages. In the failing light I copied down the English.

1. The use of soap in the temple and washing clothes is strictly prohibited
2. Please do not bring shoes near the tank
3. It does not suit for women to take bath among male members

4. Spitting while swimming is quite a bad habit
5. Do not spoil others clothes by splitting water while swimming
6. Do not enter the temple with wet clothes
7. Do not spit improperly to make the places dirty

'*Splitting?*' I said to Mr Gopal. 'What is splitting?'
   'That does not say splitting.'
   'Take a look at number five.'
   'It says splashing.'
   'It says splitting.'
   'It says – '
We walked over to the tablet. The letters, two inches high, were cut deep into the marble.
   ' – splitting,' said Mr Gopal. 'I've never run across that one before. I think it's a kind of splashing.'
   Mr Gopal was doing his best, but he was a hard man to escape from. So far I had been travelling alone with my handbook and my Western Railway timetable; I was happiest finding my own way and did not require a liaison man. It had been my intention to stay on the train, without bothering about arriving anywhere; sightseeing was a way of passing the time, but, as I had concluded in Istanbul, it was activity very largely based on imaginative invention, like rehearsing your own play in stage sets from which all the actors had fled.
   Jaipur was a pink princely city of marvels, but the vandalism and ignorance of those people who herded their goats into the frail ruins, painted over frescoes, and used the palace as a back-drop for filming diminished its attraction. A shouting film crew had occupied the City Palace, and its presence made the place seem a construction of exorbitant fakery. I gave my lecture; I was anxious to catch the train, but the timetable said there would not be a train to Delhi until 12.34 the following morning. It was an awkward time to leave: a day and an entire evening lay before me, and I did not relish the prospect of standing at Jaipur Junction at midnight.

'Today we go to the museum,' said Mr Gopal, the day after Galta.

'Let's give the museum a miss.'

'Very interesting place, and you said you wanted to see Moghul paintings. This is *home* of Moghul paintings!'

Outside the museum I said, 'When was this built?'

'About 1550.'

He hadn't hesitated. But today I had my handbook. The building he had placed in the mid-sixteenth century was the Albert Hall, started in 1878 and finished in 1887. In 1550 Jaipur did not exist, though I didn't have the heart to tell that to Mr Gopal, who had sulked when I contradicted him the previous day. Anyway, a weakness for exaggeration seemed a chronic affliction of some Indians. Inside the museum, another guide was showing a tentlike red robe to a group of tourists. He said, 'This belong to famous Maharajah Madho Singh. A big fat man. Seven feet tall, four feet wide, and weighing five hundred pounds.'

At Jai Singh's observatory, a garden of astronomer's marble instruments that looks at first glance like a children's playground, with slides and ladders and fifty-foot chutes splayed out symmetrically against the sun, Mr Gopal said he had visited the place many times. He showed me a great bronze disk that looked as if it might be a map of the night sky. I asked him if that was so. No, he said, it was to tell the time. He showed me a beacon, a submerged truncated hemisphere, a tower with eighty steps, a series of radiating benches: these were also for telling time. All this delicate apparatus, used by Prince Jai Singh (I read in my handbook) for finding altitudes and azimuths and celestial longitudes, Mr Gopal saw as a collection of oversized clocks.

While Mr Gopal was having lunch I sneaked off and bought my ticket to Delhi. The station at Jaipur Junction is modelled after the lovely buildings in the walled city. It is red sandstone, with cupolas, great arches, and substantial pillars that approach the palatial; inside are murals of lemon-faced women and turbaned men, enlargements of the traditional paintings, with borders of posies.

'I take it I won't be able to catch the train until after midnight,' I said.

'No, no,' said the clerk. 'Sooner than that.'

And he explained. The first-class sleeping car was already on the siding, being cleaned up to join the Delhi Mail. I could board in the early evening, and after midnight the Mail would pull in from Ahmadabad and this sleeping car would be hitched to it. He said I should not be alarmed if I boarded a sleeping car detached from a train: the train would arrive on time.

'Come down here tonight,' he said, 'and ask for two-up first-class A.C.C. bogie. We will show you.'

Later in the day I had a long meal with Mr Gopal in a Jaipur restaurant and afterwards announced that I would be going to the station. Mr Gopal said there was no train: 'You will have hours to wait.' I said I didn't mind. I went to the station and climbed aboard the cosily lighted sleeping car that was parked at the far end of the platform. My compartment was large. The conductor showed me the desk, the shower, the lights. I took a shower, and then in my bathrobe wrote a letter to my wife and copied out the commandments from the temple at Galta into my notebook. It was still early. I sent the conductor out for beer and had a talk with the Indian in the next compartment.

He was a professor at Rajasthan University, and he was interested to learn that I had given a lecture for the English Department. He said he rather disliked university students; they littered the grounds with election posters and hired people to clean up after the election. They were silly, short-sighted, and disorderly; they were always posturing. 'Sometimes,' he said, 'it makes my blood boil.'

I told him about Mr Gopal.

'You see?' he said. 'I'll tell you something. The average Indian knows very little about his religion, or India, or anything else. Some are ignorant of the most simple things, such as Hindu concepts or history. I agree with Naipaul one hundred per cent. They don't like to appear ignorant before a Westerner, but most Indians don't know any more about their temples and writing and what-not than the tourists – many know a lot less.'

'Aren't you exaggerating?'

'I am saying what I know. Of course, when a man gets older he begins to take an interest. So some old men know about Hinduism. They get a bit worried about what is going to happen to them.'

I offered the professor a beer, but he said he had some paper-work to do. He said good night and went into his compartment, and I withdrew into mine. We were still at the siding at Jaipur Junction. I poured myself a beer and lay in my berth reading Forster's *The Longest Journey*. I had been misled: this was no travel book; it was the story of a bad short-story writer and his callow wife and sniping friends. I threw it aside and read a few pages of *The Autobiography of a Yogi*, then fell asleep. I was awakened at half-past twelve by a bump: my bogie's being coupled to the Delhi Mail. All night the train rocked and clicked towards Delhi, while I slumbered in my cool room, and I was so refreshed on arriving that I decided to leave that same evening for Madras to see if, as my map said – though everyone claimed it was impossible – I could take a train to Ceylon.

# 12. The Grand Trunk Express

THE lumbering express that bisects India, a 1400-mile slash from Delhi south to Madras, gets its name from the route. It might easily have derived it from the kind of luggage the porters were heaving on board. There were grand trunks all over the platform. I had never seen such heaps of belongings in my life, or so many laden people: they were like evacuees who had been given time to pack, lazily fleeing an ambiguous catastrophe. In the best of times there is nothing simple about an Indian boarding a train, but these people climbing into the Grand Trunk Express looked as if they were setting up house – they had the air, and the merchandise, of people moving in. Within minutes the compartments were colonized, the trunks were emptied, the hampers, food baskets, water bottles, bed-rolls, and Gladstones put in place; and before the train started up its character changed, for while we were still standing at Delhi Station the men stripped off their baggy trousers and twill jackets and got into traditional South Indian dress: the sleeveless gym-class undershirt and the sarong they call a *lungi*. These were scored with packing creases. It was as if, at once – in expectation of the train whistle – they all dropped the disguise they had adopted for Delhi, the Madras-bound express allowing them to assume their true identity. The train was Tamil; and they had moved in so completely, I felt like a stranger among residents, which was odd, since I had arrived earlier than anyone else.

Tamils are black and bony; they have thick straight hair and their teeth are prominent and glisten from repeated scrubbings with peeled green twigs. Watch a Tamil going over his teeth with an eight-inch twig and you begin to wonder if he isn't trying to yank a branch out of his stomach. One of the attractions of the Grand Trunk Express is that its route takes in the forests of Madhya Pradesh, where the best toothbrush twigs are found; they are sold in bundles, bound like cheroots, at the stations in the province. Tamils are also modest. Before they change their clothes each makes a toga of his bedsheet, and, hopping up and down and working his elbows, he kicks his shoes and trousers off, all the while babbling in that rippling speech that resembles the sputtering of a man singing in the shower. Tamils seem to talk constantly – only toothbrushing silences them. Pleasure for a Tamil is discussing a large matter (life, truth, beauty, 'walues') over a large meal (very wet vegetables studded with chillies and capsicums, and served with damp *puris* and two mounds of glutinous rice). The Tamils were happy on the Grand Trunk Express: their language was spoken; their food was served; their belongings were dumped helter-skelter, giving the train the customary clutter of a Tamil home.

I started out with three Tamils in my compartment. After they changed, unstrapped their suitcases, unbuckled bedrolls, and had a meal (one gently scoffed at my spoon: 'Food taken with hand tastes different from food taken with spoon – sort of metal taste') they spent an immense amount of time introducing themselves to each other. In bursts of Tamil speech were English words like 'reposting', 'casual leave', 'annual audit'. As soon as I joined the conversation they began, with what I thought was a high degree of tact and courage, to speak to one another in English. They were in agreement on one point: Delhi was barbarous.

'I am staying at Lodi Hotel. I am booked months ahead. Everyone in Trich tells me it is a good hotel. Hah! I cannot use telephone. You have used telephone?'

'I cannot use telephone at all.'

'It is not Lodi Hotel,' said the third Tamil. 'It is Delhi.'

'Yes, my friend, you are right,' said the second.

'I say to receptionist, "Kindly stop speaking to me in Hindi. Does no one speak English around this place? Speak to me in English if you please!"'

'It is really atrocious situation.'

'Hindi, Hindi, Hindi. *Tcha!*'

I said I'd had similar experiences. They shook their heads and added more stories of distress. We sat like four fugitives from savagery, bemoaning the general ignorance of English, and it was one of the Tamils – not I – who pointed out that the Hindi-speaker would be lost in London.

I said, 'Would he be lost in Madras?'

'English is widely spoken in Madras. We also use Tamil, but seldom Hindi. It is not our language.'

'In the south everyone has matric.' They had a knowing ease with abbreviations, 'matric' for matriculation, 'Trich' for the town of Tiruchirappalli.

The conductor put his head into the compartment. He was a harassed man with the badges and equipment of Indian authority, a gunmetal puncher, a vindictive pencil, a clipboard thick with damp passenger lists, a bronze conductor's pin, and a khaki pith helmet. He tapped my shoulder.

'Bring your case.'

Earlier I had asked for the two-berth compartment I had paid for. He had said they were overbooked. I demanded a refund. He said I'd have to file an application at the place of issue. I accused him of inefficiency. He withdrew. Now he had found a coupé in the next carriage.

'Does this cost extra?' I asked, sliding my suitcase in. I didn't like the extortionate overtones of the word *baksheesh*.

'What you want,' he said.

'Then it doesn't.'

'I am not saying it does or doesn't. I am not asking.'

I liked the approach. I said, 'What should I do?'

'To give or not to give.' He frowned at his passenger lists. 'That is entirely your lookout.'

I gave him five rupees.

The compartment was gritty. There was no sink; the dropleaf table was unhinged; and the rattling at the window, rising to a scream when another train passed, jarred my ears. Sometimes it was an old locomotive that sped by in the night, its kettle boiling, its whistle going, and its pistons leaking a hiss with the warning pitch of a blown valve that precedes an explosion. At about 6 a.m., near Bhopal, there was a rap on the door – not morning tea, but a candidate for the upper berth. He said, 'Excuse me,' and crept in.

The forests of Madhya Pradesh, where all the toothbrushes grow, looked like the woods of New Hampshire with the last faint blue range of mountains removed. It was green, uncultivated, and full of leafy bluffs and shady brooks, but as the second day wore on it grew dustier, and New Hampshire gave way to Indian heat and Indian air. Dust collected at the window and sifted in, covering my map, my pipe, my glasses and notebook, my new stock of paperbacks (Joyce's *Exiles*, Browning's poems, *The Narrow Corner* by Somerset Maugham). I had a fine layer of dust on my face; dust furred the mirror, made the plastic seat abrasive and the floor crunchy. The window had to be kept open a crack because of the heat, but the penalty for this breeze was a stream of choking dust from the Central Indian plains.

At Nagpur in the afternoon, my travelling companion (an engineer with an extraordinary scar on his chest), said, 'There are primitive people here called Gondis. They are quite strange. One woman may have four to five husbands and vicey-versy.'

I bought four oranges at the station, made a note of a sign advertising horoscopes that read MARRY YOUR DAUGHTERS FOR ONLY RUPEES 12.50, shouted at a little man who was bullying a beggar, and read my handbook's entry for Nagpur (so-called because it is on the River Nag):

Among the inhabitants are many aborigines known as Gonds. Of these the hill-tribes have black skins, flat noses and thick lips. A cloth round the waist is their chief garment. The religious belief varies from village to village. Nearly all worship the cholera and smallpox deities, and there are traces of serpent worship.

To my relief, the whistle blew and we were on our way. The engineer read the Nagpur paper, I ate my Nagpur oranges and then had a siesta. I awoke to an odd sight, the first rain clouds I'd seen since leaving England. At dusk, near the border of the South Indian province of Andhra Pradesh, broad blue-grey clouds, dark at the edges, hung on the horizon. We were headed for them in a landscape where it had recently rained: now the little stations were splashed with mud, brown puddles had collected at level crossings, and the earth was reddened by the late monsoon. But we were not under the clouds until we reached Chandrapur, a station so small and sooty it is not on the map. There, the rain fell in torrents, and signalmen skipped along the line waving their sodden flags. The people on the platform stood watching from under large black umbrellas that shone with wetness. Some hawkers rushed into the downpour to sell bananas to the train passengers.

A woman crawled into the rain from the shelter of the platform. She appeared to be injured: she was on all fours, moving slowly towards the train – towards me. Her spine, I saw, was twisted with meningitis; she had rags tied to her knees and woodblocks in her hands. She toiled across the tracks with painful slowness, and when she was near the door she looked up. She had a lovely smile – a girl's beaming face on that broken body. She propped herself up and lifted her free hand at me, and waited, her face streaming with rain, her clothes soaked. While I was fishing in my pockets for money the train started up, and my futile gesture was to throw a handful of rupees on to the flooded line.

At the next station I was accosted by another beggar. This was a boy of about ten, wearing a clean shirt and shorts. He implored with his eyes and said rapidly, 'Please, sir, give me money. My father and mother have been at station platform for two days. They are stranded. They have no food. My father has no job, my mother's clothes are torn. We must get to Delhi soon and if you give me one or two rupees we will be able.'

'The train's going to leave. You'd better hop off.'

He said, 'Please, sir, give me money. My father and mother –'

He went on mechanically reciting. I urged him to get off the train, but it was clear that apart from his spiel he did not speak English. I walked away.

It had grown dark, the rain was letting up, and I sat reading the engineer's newspaper. The news was of conferences, an incredible number of gatherings in the very titles of which I heard the clack of voices, the rattle of mimeographed sheets, the squeak of folding chairs, and the eternal Indian prologue: 'There is one question we all have to ask ourselves –' One Nagpur conference was spending a week discussing 'Is the Future of Zoroastrianism in Peril?' On the same page 200 Indians were reported attending a 'Congress of Peace-Loving Countries', 'Hinduism: Are We at a Crossroads?' occupied another group, and on the back page there was an advertisement for Raymond's Suitings (slogan: 'You'll have something to say in Raymond's Suitings . . .'). The man wearing a Raymond suit was shown addressing a conference audience. He was squinting, making a beckoning gesture; he had something to say. His words were, 'Communication is perception. Communication is expectations. Communication is involvement.'

A beggar's skinny hand appeared at my compartment door, a bruised forearm, a ragged sleeve. Then the doomed cry, '*Sahib!*'

At Sirpur, just over the border of Andhra Pradesh, the train ground to a halt. Twenty minutes later we were still there. Sirpur is insignificant: the platform is uncovered, the station has two rooms, and there are cows on the verandah. Grass tufts grow out of the ledge of the booking-office window. It smelled of rain and wood smoke and cow dung; it was little more than a hut, dignified with the usual railway signs, of which the most hopeful was TRAINS RUNNING LATE ARE LIKELY TO MAKE UP TIME. Passengers on the Grand Trunk Express began to get out. They promenaded, belching in little groups, grateful for the exercise.

'The engine has packed up,' one man told me. 'They are sending for new one. Delay of two hours.'

Another man said, 'If there was a cabinet minister on this train they would have an engine in ten minutes' time.'

The Tamils were raving on the platform. A native of Sirpur wandered out of the darkness with a sack of roasted chickpeas. He was set upon by the Tamils, who bought all the chickpeas and demanded more. A mob of Tamils gathered at the stationmaster's window to howl at a man tapping out Morse code with a little key.

I decided to look for a beer, but just outside the station I was in darkness so complete I had second thoughts. The smell of rain on the vegetation gave a humid richness to the air that was almost sweet. There were cows lying on the road: they were white; I could see them clearly. Using the cows as road markers I walked along until I saw a small orange light about fifty yards away. I headed towards it and came to a little hut, a low poky shack with mud walls and a canvas roof. There was a kerosene lantern on the doorway and another inside lighting the surprised faces of a half a dozen tea-drinkers, two of whom recognized me from the train.

'What do you want?' one said. 'I will ask for it.'

'Can I buy a bottle of beer here?'

This was translated. There was laughter. I knew the answer.

'About two kilometres down the road' – the man pointed into the blackness – 'there is a bar. You can get beer there.'

'How will I find it?'

'A car,' he said. He spoke again to the man serving tea. 'But there is no car here. Have some tea.'

We stood in the hut, drinking milky tea out of cracked glasses. A joss stick was lit. No one said a word. The train passengers looked at the villagers; the villagers averted their eyes. The canvas ceiling drooped; the tables were worn shiny; the joss stick filled the room with stinking perfume. The train passengers grew uncomfortable and, in their discomfort, took an exaggerated interest in the calendar, the faded colour prints of Shiva and Ganpati. The lanterns flickered in the dead silence as our shadows leaped on the walls.

The Indian who had translated my question said under his breath, 'This is the real India!'

We did not go far that night. The relief engine was late, there were more delays, the Tamils were cursing: damn, blast, ruddy, bloody. The train broke down throughout the night; it slowed, it stopped, the engine died and then I could hear, among the curses, loud crickets. We arrived at Vijayawada five hours behind time in a dark rainy dawn. I bought an apple at a stall, but before I could take a bite out of it a boy limped over to me, stuck his hand out and began to cry. I gave him that apple and bought another, which I hid until I got into the train.

The south was unexpectedly cool and lush: the greenness of the countryside matched the green on the map, the sea-level colour of this area. Because it was still early, and because Indian villagers seem to think of railway tracks as the margin of their world, there were people crouched all along the line, shitting. At first I thought they were simply squatting comfortably to watch the train go by, then I noticed the bright yellow hanks under them. I saw one man; he portended a hundred more, all facing the train for the diversion it offered, unhurriedly fouling the track. They were shitting when the train pulled in; they were still at it when the train pulled out. One curious group – a man, a boy, and a pig – were in a row, each shitting in his own way. A dignified man with his *dhoti* drawn up squatted a little distance from the tracks. He watched the train go by and he looked as if he would be there for some time: he held a large black umbrella over his head and a newspaper on his knees. Indeed, he seemed the perfect symbol for what a man in Delhi had called 'The Turd World'.

For the last leg of the journey the train veered to the coast and followed the low-lying shore along the Bay of Bengal. The fields were flooded, but men ploughed the water – teams of black buffaloes dragged them through the paddy fields. The rivers were swollen with fast red currents that brimmed to the lip of the banks. This southeastern part of Andhra Pradesh was the most fertile I had seen in India; and it was striking in another way, the people so black, the earth such a deep red brown, the green so green. Still the rain came down, more heavily as we neared Madras.

I asked my travelling companion about his scar. He said he had been stabbed in Assam by some *dacoits* who took him for a Bengali. He had gone to the door and three men jumped him and began ripping at his heart with daggers. He fell back, and they fled. 'The blood came out – I was on my back, but spouts of it shot up from my heart, high over my face, and splashed over me.' He called to his five-year-old son to get cloths to stanch the flow. The child did as he was told, but his hands were so small and he was so eager that his hand sank into the wound. The father was brought to the hospital at Siliguri, but it took a year for the wound to heal, and by the time he was released he had no money and no job. He described himself as 'a fairly typical Indian engineer'.

We had a conversation about his job. He had something to do with hydraulics. It was not a long conversation. Most Indians I met had jobs that defied analysis or even comment. They were salesmen canvassing for firms that made seamless tubes, plastic washers, or bleaching agents; they marketed bench marks or hasps for manila folders. Once I met a Sikh who made rubber goods, but nothing simple like tyres or contraceptives; he made rubber bushings and casings. I said I didn't understand. He explained: 'Casings – rubber ones – for lugged sprockets.'

It was my inability to understand these occupations that led these Indian railway conversations into anecdotes of the oddest sort. The engineer, seeing that my grasp of hydraulics was slender, told me a story about a yogi who neither ate nor drank a thing in his life. 'What did he live on?' I asked. It seemed a fair question. 'Air only,' he said, 'because he did not want to contaminate the body with food and drink.' The yogi lived to a ripe old age – over seventy. Mr Gopal, the liaison man, had been stumped by my ignorance of liaising. His story concerned a monkey and a tiger who always travelled together. No one could understand why the tiger didn't gobble up the monkey, but a man watched them closely (from behind a tree, unseen) and realized that the tiger was blind: the monkey guided the tiger from place to place. I had heard a story about a man in Bombay who walked on water, and another about a man who taught himself to fly using wings from palm leaves; the canvasser for seamless tubes told me about a bridge of monkeys from Ceylon to Dhanushkodi, across the Palk Strait. I saw these tall stories as a flight from the concrete, the Indian imagination requiring something more than the prosy details of the ledger. So Mr Bhardwaj, the accountant, believed in astrology; Mr Radia, maker of dry-cell batteries, improvised (he said) philosophical songs; and an otherwise completely rational man I met in Bombay claimed that many Indians were addicted to the bite of a cobra: 'You stick out your tongue, cobra bites tongue, and venom makes you wonderful.'

A few miles out of Madras, an English missionary found me clutching the window, gasping in the heat that had just descended on the train. He ignored my condition. He said he was absolutely livid. He was glad to hear that I was (as I told him) a journalist: he had a story for me.

'Some Americans,' he said, 'who call themselves Christians are paying four rupees a head – and that's a lot of money in Madras – to people they baptize. Why? I'll tell you. To put up their conversion figures, so they can get more money from their parishes back home. They do more harm than good. When you go back to the States I hope you mention it.'

'Gladly,' I said. Will whoever is responsible for these corrupt missionaries who offer baptismal bribes please persuade them that they are doing more harm than good?

Then we were at Madras Central and rickshaw-*wallahs* were flying at me like bats, repeating, 'Where you going? Where you going?'

They laughed when I told them Ceylon.

This was what I imagined: somewhere past the brick and plaster mansions of Madras, arrayed along Mount Road like so many yellowing wedding cakes, was the Bay of Bengal, on which I would find a breezy sea-front restaurant, palm trees, flapping tableclothes. I would sit facing the water, have a fish dinner and five beers and watch the dancing lights of the little Tamil fishing smacks. Then I would go to bed and be up early for the train to Rameswaram, that village on the tip of India's nose.

'Take me to the beach,' I said to the taxi driver. He was an unshaven, wild-haired Tamil with his shirt torn open. He had the look of the feral child in the psychology textbook: feral children, mangled demented Mowglis, abound in South India. It is said they are suckled by wolves.

'Beach Road?'

'That sounds like the place.' I explained that I wanted to eat a fish.

'Twenty rupees.'

'I'll give you five.'

'Okay, fifteen. Get in.'

We drove about two hundred yards and I realized that I was very hungry: turning vegetarian had confused my stomach with what seemed an imperfect substitute for real food. Vegetables subdued my appetite, but a craving – a carnivorous emotion – remained.

'You like English girls?' The taxi driver was turning the steering wheel with his wrists, as a wolf might, given the opportunity to drive a taxi.

'Very much,' I said.

'I find you English girl.'

'Really?' It seemed an unlikely place to find an English whore – Madras, a city without any apparent prosperity. In Bombay I might have believed it: the sleek Indian businessmen, running in and out of the Taj Mahal Hotel, oozing wealth, and driving at top speed past the sleepers on the sidewalk – they were certainly whore fodder. And in Delhi, city of conferees and delegates, I was told there were lots of European hookers cruising through the lobbies of the plush hotels, promising pleasure with a cheery swing of their hips. But in Madras?

The driver spun in his seat and crossed his heart, two slashes with his long nails. '*English* girl.'

'Keep your eyes on the road!'

'Twenty-five rupees.'

Three dollars and twenty-five cents.

'Pretty girl?'

'*English* girl,' he said. 'You want?'

I thought this over. It wasn't the girl but the situation that attracted me. An English girl in Madras, whoring for peanuts. I wondered where she lived, and how, and for how long; what had brought her to the godforsaken place? I saw her as a cast-away, a fugitive, like Lena in Conrad's *Victory* fleeing a tuneless travelling orchestra in Surabaya. I had once met an English whore in Singapore. She said she was making a fortune. But it wasn't just the money: she preferred Chinese and Indian men to the English, who were not so quick and, worse, usually wanted to spank her.

The driver noticed my silence and slowed down. In the heavy traffic he turned around once again. His cracked teeth, stained with betel juice, were red and gleaming in the lights from the car behind us. He said, 'Beach or girl?'

'Beach,' I said.

He drove for a few minutes more. Surely she was Anglo-Indian – 'English' was a euphemism.

'Girl,' I said.

'Beach or girl?'

'Girl, *girl*, for Heaven's sake.' It was as if he were trying to make me confess to an especially vicious impulse.

He swung the car around dangerously and sped in the opposite direction, babbling, 'Good – nice girls – you like – little house – about two miles – five girls –'

'English girls?'

'*English* girls.'

The luminous certitude had gone out of his voice, but still he nodded, perhaps trying to calm me.

We drove for twenty minutes. We went through streets where kerosene lamps burned at stalls, and past brightly lit textile shops in which clerks in striped pyjamas shook out bolts of yellow cloth and sequined saris. I sat back and watched Madras go by, teeth and eyes in dark alleys, night-time shoppers with full baskets, and endless doorways distinguished by memorable sign-boards, SANGADA LUNCH HOME, VISHNU SHOE CLINIC, and the dark funereal THOUSAND LIGHTS RESTAURANT.

He turned corners, choosing the narrowest unlighted lanes, and then we stayed on dirt roads. I suspected he was going to rob me, and when we came to the darkest part of a bumpy track – we were in the country now – and he pulled over and switched off the lights, I was certain he was a con man: his next move would be to stick a knife in my ribs. How stupid I'd been to believe his fatuous story about the twenty-five-rupee English girl! We were far from Madras, on a deserted road, beside a faintly gleaming swamp where frogs whistled and gulped. The taxi driver jerked his head. I jumped. He blew his nose into his fingers and flung the result out the window.

I started to get out of the car.

'You sit down.'

I sat down.

He thumped his chest with his hand. 'I'm coming.' He slid out and banged the door, and I saw him disappear down a path to the left.

I waited until he was gone, until the *shush* of his legs in the tall grass had died out, and then I carefully worked the door open. In the open air it was cool, and there was a mingled smell of swamp water and jasmine. I heard voices on the road, men chattering; like me they were in darkness. I could see the road around me, but a few feet away it vanished. I estimated that I was about a mile from the main road. I would head for that and find a bus.

There were puddles in the road. I blundered into one, and, trying to get out, plopped through the deepest part. I had been running; the puddle slowed me to a ponderous shamble.

'Mister! Sahib!'

I kept going, but he saw me and came closer. I was caught. 'Sit *down*, mister!' he said. I saw he was alone. 'Where you going?'

'Where *you* going?'

'Checking up.'

'English girl?'

'No English girl.'

'What do you mean, no English girl?' I was frightened, and now it all seemed a transparent preparation for ambush.

He thought I was angry. He said, 'English girl – forty, fifty. Like this.' He stepped close to me so that in the darkness I could see he was blowing out his cheeks; he clenched his fists and hunched his shoulders. I got the message: a fat English girl. '*Indian* girl – small, nice. Sit down, we go.'

I had no other choice. A mad dash down the road would have taken me nowhere – and he would have chased me. We walked back to the taxi. He started the engine angrily and we bumped along the grassy path he had taken earlier on foot. The taxi rolled from side to side in the potholes and strained up a grade. This was indeed the country. In all that darkness there was one lighted hut. A little boy crouched in the doorway with a sparkler, an anticipation of *Diwali*, the festival of lights: it illuminated his face, his skinny arm, and made his eyes shine. Ahead of us there was another hut, slightly larger, with a flat roof and two square windows. It was on its own, like a shop in a jungle clearing. Dark heads moved at the windows.

'You come,' said the taxi driver, parking in front of the door. I heard giggling and saw at the windows round black faces and gleaming hair. A man in a white turban leaned against the wall, just out of the light.

We went inside the dirty room. I found a chair and sat down. A dim electric bulb burned on a cord in the centre of the low ceiling. I was sitting in the good chair – the others were broken or had burst cushions. Some girls were sitting on a long wooden bench. They watched me, while the rest gathered around me, pinching my arm and laughing. They were very small, and they looked awkward and a bit comic, too young to be wearing lipstick, nose jewels, earrings, and slipping bracelets. Sprigs of white jasmine plaited into their hair made them look appropriately girlish, but the smudged lipstick and large jewellery also exaggerated their youth. One stout sulky girl held a buzzing transistor radio to the side of her head and looked me over. They gave the impression of schoolgirls in their mothers' clothes. None could have been older than fifteen.

'Which one you like?' This was the man in the turban. He was stocky and looked tough in a rather grizzled way. His turban was a bath towel knotted on his head.

'Sorry,' I said.

A thin man walked in through the door. He had a sly, bony face and his hands were stuck into the top of his *lungi*. He nodded at one. 'Take her – she good.'

'One hundred rupees all night,' said the man with the turban. 'Fifty for one jig.'

'He said it costs twenty-five.'

The taxi driver wrung his hands.

'Fifty,' said the grizzled man, standing firm.

'Anyway, forget it,' I said. 'I just came for a drink.'

'No drink,' said the thin man.

'He said he had an English girl.'

'What English girl?' said the thin man, now twisting the knot on his *lungi*. 'These Kerala girls – young, small, from Malabar Coast.'

The man in the turban caught one by the arm and shoved her against me. She shrieked delightedly and hopped away.

'You look at room,' said the man in the turban.

The room was right through the door. He switched on the light. This was the bedroom; it was the same size as the outside one, but dirtier and more cluttered. And it smelled horrible. In the centre of the room was a wooden bed with a stained bamboo mat on it, and on the wall six shelves, each holding a small tin padlocked suitcase. In a corner of the room a battered table held some medicine bottles, big and small, and a basin of water. There were scorch marks on the beaverboard ceiling, newspapers on the floor, and on the wall over the bed charcoal sketches of dismembered bodies, breasts, and genitals.

'Look!'

The man grinned wildly, rushed to the far wall and threw a switch.

'Fan!'

It began to groan slowly over the filthy bed, stirring the air with its cracked paddles and making the room even smellier.

Two girls came into the room and sat on the bed. Laughing, they began to unwind their saris. I hurried out, into the parlour, through the front door, and found the taxi driver. 'Come on, let's go.'

'You not liking Indian girl? *Nice* Indian girl?' Skinny was starting to shout. He shouted something in Tamil to the taxi driver, who was in as great a hurry as I to leave the place: he had produced a dud customer. The fault was his, not mine. The girls were still giggling and calling out, and Skinny was still shouting as we swung away from the hut and through the tall grass on to the bumpy back road.

I had a late dinner, served on a banana leaf in a dingy restaurant near my hotel. The windows of my hotel room were open; I could smell sweet flowers. The odour sang as I read *Exiles*: 'I am sure that no law made by man is sacred before the impulse of passion . . . There is no law before impulse.' The perfume was familiar; it was jasmine. I thought of the girls, laughing there in that hut, wearing the white flowers with such narrow petals.

# 13. The Local to Rameswaram

I HAD two ambitions in India: one was to find a train to Ceylon, the other was to have a sleeping car to myself. At Egmore Station in Madras both ambitions were fulfilled. My little cardboard ticket read *Madras – Colombo Fort*, and when the train pulled out the conductor told me I would be the only passenger in the car for the twenty-two-hour journey to Rameswaram. If I wished, he said, I could move to the second compartment – the fans worked there. It was a local train, and, since no one was going very far, everyone chose third class. Very few people went to Rameswaram, he said, and these days nobody wanted to go to Ceylon: it was a troublesome country, there was no food in the markets, and the prime minister, Mrs Bandaranaike, didn't like Indians. He wondered why I was going there.

'For the ride,' I said.

'It is the slowest train.' He showed me the timetable. I borrowed it and took it into my compartment to study. I had been on slow trains before, but this was perverse. It seemed to stop every five or ten minutes. I held the timetable to the window to verify it in the light.

| | |
|---|---|
| Madras Egmore | 11.00 |
| Mambalam | 11.11 |
| Tambaran | 11.33 |
| Perungalattur Halt | 11.41 |
| Vandalur | 11.47 |
| Guduvanchari | 11.57 |
| Kattargulattur | 12.06 |
| Singaperumalkoil | 12.15 |
| Chingleput | 12.35 |

And so forth. I counted. It stopped ninety-four times in all. I had got my wish, but I wondered whether it was worth the penalties.

The train gathered speed; the brakes squeaked; it lurched and stopped. It started again, and no sooner had it begun to roll easily than the brakes gave this metal wail. I dozed in my compartment, and each time the train stopped I heard laughter and the stamping of feet past my door, a muted galloping up and down the passage, doors banging and the ring of metal on metal. The voices ceased when the train was underway and did not start again until the next station, a commotion at the doors, shrieks, and clangs. I looked out the window and saw the strangest sight – children, girls and boys of anywhere from seven to twelve, the younger ones naked, the older ones wearing loincloths, were leaping off the train carrying cans of water. They were wild children, with long lank hair faded brown by the sun, with black shoulders and dusty faces and snub noses – like Australian aborigines – and at every station that morning they dashed into the sleeping car and got water from the sink in the toilet compartment. They raced with their cans to camps by the side of the track where thin older people waited, aged men with yellowing curly hair, women kneeling over cooking pots in front of crude lean-tos. They weren't Tamils. I assumed they were aborigines, like the Gonds. They had few belongings and they lived in this dry zone the monsoon had not yet reached. All morning they raided the sleeping car for water, skipping in and out, shouting and laughing, making their scavenging into a noisy game. I locked the inner door, preventing them from dancing down the corridor, but allowing them access to the water.

I had made no arrangements to eat and had no food with me. In the early afternoon I walked the length of the train but could not find a dining car. I was having a snooze at about two o'clock when there was a rap at the window. It was the conductor. Without a word he passed a tray of food through the bars. I ate

Tamil-fashion, squelching the rice into a ball with my right hand, mopping the ball into the soupy vegetables, and stuffing the whole business into my mouth. At the next station the conductor reappeared. He took the empty tray and gave me a drowsy salute.

We were travelling parallel to the coast, a few miles inland, and the fans in the compartment gave very little relief from the pressure of humidity. The sky was overcast with clouds that seemed to add weight to the suffocating heat, and the train was going so slowly there was no breeze at the windows. To shake off my feeling of sluggishness, I borrowed a broom and some rags from the conductor; I swept out my compartment and washed all the windows and woodwork. Then I did my laundry and hung it on hooks in the corridor. I plugged the sink and sluiced myself with water, then shaved and put on my slippers and pyjamas. It was my own sleeping car, after all. At Villupuram the electric engine was replaced by a steam locomotive, and at that same station I bought three large bottles of warm beer. I plumped the pillows in my compartment and, while my laundry dried, drank beer and watched the state of Tamil Nadu grow simpler: each station was smaller than the last and the people grew increasingly naked – after Chingleput there were no shirts, undershirts disappeared at Villupuram, and further on *lungis* were scarce and people were running around in drooping loincloths. The land was flat, featureless except for an occasional storklike Tamil poised in a distant paddy field. The huts were as poorly made as those temporary ones thrown up in the African interior, where it is considered unlucky to live in the same hut two years in a row. They were of mud and had palm-leaf roofs; the mud had cracked in the heat and the first of the monsoon would sweep those roofs away. In contrast to this haphazard building, the rice fields were cleverly irrigated by complex pumping systems and long canals.

The greatest annoyance that afternoon was the smoke from the steam engine. It poured through the windows, coating every surface with a fine film of soot, and the smell of burned coal – which is the smell of every Indian railway station – lingered in the compartment. It took much longer for the engine to build up speed, and the trip-hammer sound and the rhythmic puffing was transmitted through the carriages. But there was a gentleness in this power, and the sounds of the thrusting wheels gave a motion to the train that was not only different from the amplified lawnmower of the electric engine, but made the steam engine seem animal in the muscular way it moved and stopped.

After dark the compartment lights went out and the fan died. I went to bed; an hour later – it was 9.30 – they came on again. I found my place in the book I was reading, but before I finished a paragraph the lights failed a second time. I cursed, switched everything off, smeared myself with insect repellent (the mosquitoes were ferocious, nimble with their budget of malaria), and slept with the sheets over my head, waking only at Trichinopoly (Tiruchirappalli) to buy a box of cigars.

The next morning I was visited by a Buddhist monk. His head was shaved, he wore saffron robes, and he was barefoot. He was the very picture of piety, the mendicant monk with his sweaty head, going third class on the branch line to Nirvana. He was, of course, so right for the part that I guessed immediately he was an American, and it turned out he was from Baltimore. He was on his way to Kandy in Central Ceylon. He didn't like my questions.

'What do your folks think about you becoming a Buddhist?'

'I am looking for water,' he said obstinately.

'Are you in a monastery or what?'

'Look, if there's no water here, just tell me and I'll go away.'

'I've got some good friends in Baltimore,' I said. 'Ever get back there?'

'You're bothering me,' said the monk.

'Is that any way for a monk to talk?'

He was really angry then. He said, 'I get asked these questions a hundred times a day!'

'I'm just curious.'

'There are no answers,' he said, with mystifying glibness 'I'm looking for water.'

'Keep looking.'

'I'm dirty! I haven't slept all night; I want to wash!'

'I'll show you where the water is if you answer one more question,' I said.

'You're a nosy bastard, just like the rest of them,' said the Buddhist monk.

'Second door on your right,' I said. 'Don't drown.'

I think the next ten miles were the most exciting I have ever travelled in a train. We were on the coast, moving fast along a spit of land, and on either side of the train – its whistle screaming, its chimney full of smoke – white sand had drifted into magnificent dunes; beyond these dunes were slices of green sea. Sand whipped up by the engine pattered against the carriages behind, and spray from the breakers, whose regular wash dramatized the chugging of the locomotive, was flung up to speckle the windows with crystal bubbles. It was all light and water and sand, flying about the train speeding towards the Rameswaram causeway in a high wind. The palms under the scudding clouds bowed and flashed like fans made of feathers, and here and there, up to their stupas in sand, were temples flying red flags on their crooked masts. The sand covered the track in places; it had drifted into temple doorways and wrecked the frail palm-frond huts. The wind was terrific, beating on the windows, carrying sand and spray and the whistle's *hooeeee*, and nearly toppling the dhows in full sail at the hump of the spangled horizon where Ceylon lay.

'Few minutes more,' said the conductor. 'I think you are sorry you took this train.'

'No,' I said. 'But I was under the impression it went to Dhanushkodi – that's what my map says.'

'Indo-Ceylon Express formerly went to Dhanushkodi.'

'Why doesn't it go there now?'

'No Indo-Ceylon Express,' he said. 'And Dhanushkodi blew away.'

He explained that in 1965 a cyclone – the area is plagued with them – derailed a train, drowning forty passengers and covering Dhanushkodi with sand. He showed me what remained, sand dunes at the tip of the peninsula and the fragments of black roofs. The town had disappeared so thoroughly that not even fishermen lived there any more.

'Rameswaram is more interesting,' said the conductor. 'Nice temple, holy places, and tombs of Cain and Abel.'

I thought I had misheard him. I asked him to repeat the names. I had not misheard.

The story is that when Adam and Eve were driven from the Garden of Eden they went to Ceylon (Dhanushkodi is the beginning of the seven islands across the Palk Strait known as 'Adam's Bridge'). Christ went there; so did Buddha and Rama, and so, probably, did Father Divine, Joseph Smith, and Mary Baker Eddy. Cain and Abel ended up in Rameswaram, which might be the true Land of Nod, east of Eden. Their tombs are not signposted. They are in the care of the local Muslims, and in this town of Hindus, the majority of whom are high-caste Brahmins, I had some difficulty locating a Muslim. The driver of the horse-drawn cab (there are no cars in Rameswaram) thought there might be a Muslim at the ferry landing. I said that was too far to go: the tombs were somewhere near the railway station. The driver said the Hindu temple was the holiest in India. I said I wanted to see the tombs of Cain and Abel. We found a ruminant Muslim in a dusty shop on a side street. He said he would show me the tombs if I promised not to defile them with my camera. I promised.

The tombs were identical: parallel blocks of crumbling stone on which lizards darted and the green twine of tropical weeds had knotted. I tried to appear reverential, but could not suppress my disappointment at seeing what looked like the incomplete foundations of some folly concocted by a treasonous clerk in the

Public Works Department of the local mosque. And the tombs were indistinguishable.

'Cain?' I said, pointing to the right one. I pointed to the left. 'Abel?'

The Muslim didn't know.

The Hindu temple, founded by Rama (on his way to Lanka, Ceylon, to rescue Sita), was an impressive labyrinth, nearly a mile of subterranean corridors, garishly lit and painted. The traveller J. J. Aubertin, who visited the Rameswaram temple (but not the tombs of Cain and Abel: maybe they weren't there in 1890?) mentions the 'blasphemous' and 'ugly' dances of the *nautch* girls in his book, *Wanderings and Wonderings* (1892). I looked. I saw no *nautch* girls. Five aged women were gravely laundering their shrouds in the sacred pool at the centre of the temple. In India, I had decided, one could determine the sacredness of water by its degree of stagnation. The holiest was bright green, like this.

It was a three-hour trip across the Palk Strait on the old Scottish steamer, the T. S. S. *Ramanujam* (formerly the *Irwin*), from Rameswaram to Talaimannar at the top of Ceylon. Like everyone else I had met in India, the ship's second mate told me I was a fool to go to Ceylon. But his reason was better than others I'd heard: there was a cholera epidemic in Jaffna and it appeared to be spreading to Colombo. 'It's your funeral,' he said cheerfully. He held the Ceylonese in complete contempt, nor was he very happy with Indians. I pointed out that this must have been rather inconvenient for him since he was an Indian himself.

'Yes, but I'm a Catholic,' he said. He was from Mangalore on the Malabar Coast and his name was Llewellyn. We smoked my Trichinopoly cigars on the deck, until Talaimannar appeared, a row of lights dimmed to faint sequins by what Llewellyn said was the first rain of the monsoon.

## 14. The Talaimannar Mail

IT was raining so hard on the roof of the ticket office at Talai-mannar Station that the clerk was shouting, an operatic request for excess charges, uncharacteristically loud for a Singhalese. It was not a country where people raised their voices. They argued in whispers; catastrophe put them to sleep. They were not an excitable people – it had something to do with starvation. But these were unusual circumstances. It was like one of those pioneering talkies, the documentary in which curtains of brown rain slant into a railway platform, filling the sound track with a deafening crackle. The carriages of the Talaimannar Mail, made of thin wooden slats, amplified the rain; and the drumming on those bogie roofs, orchestrated by the wind, drowned the whin-nying barks of the emaciated pariah dogs, which had been driven out of the storm. The station was rusting, the signboard had peeled into illegibility, the train was greasy, and the feeble lights above the black verandah pillars gave the streaming rain the yellow opacity of molten plastic. It was a small tropical station in the north of Ceylon, smelling of soaked jungle and erupting drains, and with that decay that passes for charm in equatorial outposts.

I asked the ticket clerk in Bookings what time the train was leaving.

'Maybe midnight!' The rain still gushed on his dingy shed, making him squint.

'What do you mean *maybe*?'

'Maybe *later*!'

With the pariah dogs snapping at my heels, I hurried down the platform to the carriage with SLEEPING CAR lettered neatly in fading gilt script on its side. My two-berth compartment, a good example of colonial carpentry, was wood-panelled in the most complicated way to accommodate a system of hinged shelves, built-in cupboards, and a collapsible fold-out chair fitting to one wall. The rain beat against the wooden shutters and a fine mist found its way through the louvres. I went to sleep but was awakened at one in the morning by a Singhalese who dragged in three heavy crates and parked them next to my berth.

'This *mine*,' he said, pointing to the lower berth where I lay.

I smiled; it was the smile of placid incomprehension I had been taught by any number of Afghan stall-holders in Kabul.

'English?'

I shook my head, still smiling.

The Singhalese hooked the stepladder to the upper berth. But he did not climb it. He turned on the fan, sat on one of his crates, and began eating a stinking meal out of a piece of newspaper – the smell of his rotten onions and mildewed rice was to stay in the compartment for the remainder of the journey. At 3.15 the train pulled out of Talaimannar. I know this because when it started up I was jolted out of my berth on to the crates.

The wooden sleeping car was very light; it bounced and swayed on the uneven roadbed and all night made a constant creaking – that twisting and straining of wood that enlivens the nights of passengers on old storm-driven ships. I had a panicky nightmare of the sleeping car catching fire, burning furiously as the flames were fed by the draught from its travelling. I was trapped in the compartment, unable to open the doors, which the rain had warped in their jambs. The doors *were* warped, and waking from the nightmare I smelled the powerful smoke from the Singhalese's cheroot. The compartment lights were on, the fan was going, and this man – I could see him in the mirror – was lying in his berth, puffing the stogie and reading the wrapping of his aromatic dinner.

At dawn, the northwest of Ceylon was a neglected garden: the rice fields had dried out and were overgrown with grass; the foliage was dense in the yards of tumbledown huts; there was evidence of former cultivation. Everywhere I looked, I saw great idleness, people in all the attitudes of repose. I had come from South India, the land of leaping Tamils. Here, the Singhalese had the ponderous stumbling and negligent attention of sleepwalkers looking for a place to drop. The food shortage was obviously acute: the proof was in the disorderly plots of cassava, the most primitive vegetable on earth, a root that grows easily but exhausts the soil in a year. It was a new crop to Ceylon; they had begun to grow it in desperation.

In second class, the Singhalese were sleeping against their children. The children were wide awake, pinned to the benches by their snoring parents. One man I met in the corridor was frankly disgusted. He was Singhalese, a teacher of English language, and said he didn't often take the train because 'I don't like these travelling companions.'

'The Singhalese?'

'The cockroaches.' He said the train was full of them, but I saw them only in the carriage marked BUFFET, among the peanuts, stale bread, and tea that was sold as breakfast.

I asked the teacher if there was any future for the English language in Ceylon. (I should add that although the official name for the island is now Sri Lanka no one I met there called it anything but Ceylon: it had been changed too recently for people to overcome the habit of giving it the former name.)

'Funny you should ask,' he said. 'As a matter of fact we're being investigated.'

I asked him why.

'Our lessons are subversive.' He smoked and smiled coyly; he was clearly dying for me to pump him.

'Give me an example.'

'Oh, we have drill sentences. Five thousand of them. The government says they're subversive.'

'Drill sentences for English lessons?'

'Yes. We wrote them. One was "Mrs Bandaranaike has three children."'

'How many children *does* she have?'

'Three.'

'So what's the difficulty?'

'I'm giving you an example,' he said. 'There was another one: "Mrs B. is a woman." '

'She is, isn't she?'

'Yes. But they objected. Maybe you could call it harmful to her personality cult.'

'I see.'

'Also, "Mrs B. had an operation on nineteen September nineteen sixty-one." '

'They didn't like that?'

'Oh no! An inquiry is in the pipeline. As for me, I find the whole matter very amusing.'

I said he would probably lose his job. He said that was all right as long as he didn't go to jail. As a university teacher he earned $25 a week, before taxes.

At Kurunegala, about fifty miles north of Colombo, I bought a papaya and the Ceylon *Daily Mirror*. Starvation, which had turned the Indians into makers of the foolproof rubber-lugged sprocket and vendors of the fishmeal cutlet and vegetable chop, had made the Singhalese religious fanatics. According to the *Mirror* there was a renewed interest in St Jude, who is popularly known as 'the patron saint of hopeless cases'. A shrine to him in Colombo was beseiged by pilgrims, even Buddhists and Hindus. 'It is truly remarkable,' the article ran, 'how people of all faiths and communities continue to flock to this hallowed shrine.' On the feast day of St Jude, 28 October, hundreds of thousands of Singhalese were expected to go to the shrine and pray.

The devotees are multiplying. Letters pour in to the Parish Priest testifying to the wonderful favours granted by invocation to the Saint. Many of them have been those who, tangled in a seemingly hopeless web of bureaucratic red tape, and who invoked St Jude who has helped them find a solution. The Parish Priest receives regular remittances from abroad from those who, prior to leaving the island on some business visit or scholarship, were tied down by regulations and unsympathetic officialdom and who overcame these after prayer to St Jude.

In the same edition of the paper, food riots were reported in several towns after the rice ration had been cut (for the third time, said the teacher – it was now a quarter of what it had been five months previous). The current harvest was a failure, chillies were unobtainable, and from the train I could see bread lines – hundreds of listless people in misshapen queues, waiting with empty baskets. At the stations, children stood champing on sticks of raw cassava, and pariah dogs fought over the discarded peels, tearing with narrow fishlike jaws that were all teeth. The teacher said there were hunger marchers in Colombo, and a story was circulating that a military coup was imminent. The government had vigorously denied the coup story. There was no food shortage, really, said the minister of agriculture – many people were successfully growing yams and cassava in their gardens. There was plenty of food in Ceylon, he said, but some people didn't want to eat it: all these people had to do was to change their diet from the loaves of bread they craved. This American-style bread, introduced as an emergency measure during the war, had become a staple of the Singhalese diet. The catch is that not a single grain of wheat is grown in Ceylon, which makes bread as inconvenient a staple on that lovely island as water chestnuts would be in Nevada. The minister heaped scorn on Singapore's *Straits Times*, which had printed a story about the Singhalese army's being so starved it was eating grass. But the outraged denials only seemed to confirm that the food situation was desperate. At Colombo Fort I was approached separately by three piratical Singhalese. 'Anything to sell?' said the first; 'Chinese girl?' said the second; 'Give me a shirt,' said the third, not mincing his words – though he offered to carry my suitcase in exchange for it. Saint Jude seemed to have his work cut out for him, and the preparations for his feast day were perfectly understandable in the land no longer known as Serendip.

# 15. The 16.25 from Galle

IT struck me as practically insane in a country that was starving to death that thirty people should choose to attend a three-day seminar on American literature, at which I would be the principal speaker. American literature is fine, but I feel it to be an irrelevance in a disaster area. I had not counted on the resourcefulness of the American embassy; when the seminar got underway I saw my alarm was pointless. The clever man who supervised the seminar had assured me there would be 100 per cent attendance, and his method was not very different from that of the family planner in India who gives a new transistor radio to every male who agrees to a vasectomy. Here, on the hungry island of Ceylon, the American literature seminar included three huge meals, high tea, a free room in the New Orient Hotel in Galle, and all the whisky you could drink. Little wonder it was well attended. After a mammoth four-course breakfast, the bloated delegates met in an upstairs room and dozed through my inoffensive lecture, waking at noon to rush downstairs to a spectacular lunch. The afternoon meeting was short, truncated by tea, and the main event of the day was dinner, a leisurely good-humoured affair, followed by a movie that put everyone to sleep. The first day's meals were frenzied sessions of gourmandizing, but after that things settled down; the delegates padded back and forth from dining room to seminar room, to meals and their justification. In between they stoked themselves with cookies, occasionally finding it necessary to absent themselves with indigestion, and they were often so stupefied with food, they began to look like victims of some dropsical illness, the chief symptom of which was prolonged slumber interrupted by attacks of furious belching. Some of the delegates gave me books they had written. The gravy stains on the covers will continue to remind me of that weekend, and I shall always remember the unanimous hoot that went up at the end of the seminar when the American organizer said, 'Shall we leave at ten o'clock, or after lunch?'

One night I left the eructating delegates at the hotel and went in search of a snooker game. I found the Gymkhana Club, but several members had locked themselves in the snooker room where they were secretly listening to a fizzling short-wave radio. It was the latest racing news on the BBC Overseas Service, and the men, who were bookies, scribbled on tote-sheets as the plummy voice said, 'At Doncaster today, in a seven-furlong race on a slow track, Bertha's Pill came in at twenty to one, and Gallant Falcon, Safety Match, and Sub Rosa —' Racing is banned in Ceylon, so the Singhalese bet on races in Epsom, Doncaster, and Kempton Park. The bookies said I could use the table as soon as the broadcast was over.

The Public Services Club was right across the road. The snooker table was free, and the members said they had no objection to my playing, but added that it might be difficult because the billiard boy had to catch his bus. I was a bit puzzled by this explanation, but after a while I saw in the billiard boy a clue to the unspeakable idleness in Ceylon.

I began to play one of the gasconading Singhalese, and after a few balls were potted there was some muttering.

'Billiard boy will get later bus.'

The billiard boy, a shiny clerical Buddhist named Fernando, carried the bridge with the confident authority of a bishop with crook. The game depended on him. He kept score; he passed the bridge when it was needed; he spotted the balls; he chalked the cues; he reminded the players of the rules; once when I was in doubt about a shot he told me the best one to take, sucking his teeth when I missed. None of his tasks was especially strenuous, but they had the effect of ruining my concentration. The singular virtue of snooker and pool is that they are played in complete silence. Fernando's panting attentions violated this silence. I was glad to hear my opponent say – after about forty minutes – 'Billiard boy must go.'

'Good,' I said. 'Let him go.'

Fernando racked his bridge and sped out of the room.

'I beat you by one point.'

'No you didn't,' I said. 'The game's not over.'

'Game is over.'

I pointed out that there were still four balls on the table.

'But no billiard boy,' said the Singhalese. 'So the game is over. I win.'

Was it any wonder that in this fertile country – so fertile the fence posts and telephone poles had taken root and sprouted branches (and what a shame they didn't bear fruit) – people were faint with hunger? They had driven out the Tamils, who had done all the planting; they had forgotten how to scatter seeds on the ground – this scattering would have given them a harvest. Galle was a beautiful place, garlanded with red hibiscus and smelling of the palm-scented ocean, possessing cool Dutch interiors and ringed by forests of bamboo. The sunset's luminous curtains patterned the sky in rufous gold for an hour and a half every evening, and all night the waves crashed on the ramparts of the fort. But the famished faces of the sleepwalkers and the deprivation in that idyllic port made its beauty almost unbearable.

The train from Galle winds along the coast north towards Colombo, so close to the shoreline that the spray flung by the heavy rollers from Africa reaches the broken windows of the battered wooden carriages. I was going third class, and for the early part of the trip sat in a dark overcrowded compartment with people who, as soon as I became friendly, asked me for money. They were not begging with any urgency; indeed, they didn't look as if they needed money, but rather seemed to be taking the position that whatever they succeeded in wheedling out of me might come in handy at some future date. It happened fairly often. In the middle of a conversation a man would gently ask me if I had any appliance I could give him. 'What sort of appliance?' 'Razor blades.' I would say no and the conversation would continue.

After nearly an hour of this I crawled out of the compartment to stand by the door and watch the rain dropping out of a dark layer of high clouds just off the coast – the distant rain like majestic pillars of granite. To the right the sun was setting, and in the foreground were children, purpling in the sunset and skipping along the sand. That was on the ocean side of the train. On the jungle side it had already begun to pour heavily, and at each station the signalman covered himself with his flags, making the red one into a kerchief, the green one into a skirt, flapping the green when the train approached and quickly using it to keep the rain off when the train had passed.

A Chinese man and his Singhalese wife had boarded the train in Galle with their fat dark baby. They were the Wongs, off to Colombo for a little holiday. Mr Wong said he was a dentist; he had learned the trade from his father, who had come to Ceylon from Shanghai in 1937. Mr Wong didn't like the train and said he usually went to Colombo on his motorcycle except during the monsoon. He also had a helmet and goggles. If I ever went back to Galle he would show them to me. He told me how much they cost.

'Can you speak Chinese?'

'*Humbwa* – go, *mingwa* – come. That's all. I speak Singhalese and English. Chinese very hard.' He pressed his temples with his knuckles.

Simla had been full of Chinese dentists, with signboards showing horrible cross-sections of the human mouth and trays of white toothcaps in the window. I asked him why so many Chinese I had seen were dentists.

'Chinese are very good dentists!' he said. His breath was spiced with coconut. 'I'm good!'

'Can you give me a filling?'

'No, no stoppings.'

'Do you clean teeth?'

'No.'

'Can you pull them?'

'You want estraction? I give you name of a good estractionist.'

'What kind of dentist are you, Mr Wong?'

'Tooth mechanics,' he said. 'Chinese are the best ones for tooth mechanics.'

Tooth mechanics is this: you have a shop with a shelf of English putty, a pink semiliquid; you also have drawers filled with teeth in various sizes. A person comes in who has had two front teeth knocked out in a food riot or a quarrel over a coconut. You fill his mouth with pink putty and make a mould of his gums. A plate is made from this, and when it is trimmed, two Japanese fangs are stuck to it. Unfortunately, these plastic dentures are valueless for chewing food with and must be removed at mealtime. Mr Wong said business was excellent and he was taking in between 1000 and 1400 rupees a month, which is more than a professor gets at Colombo University.

Inside the train the passengers were banging the windows shut to keep the rain out. The sunset's fire was tangled in leaden clouds, and the pillars of rain supporting the toppling thunderheads were very close; the fishermen were fighting their catamarans ashore through high surf. The train had begun to smell awful; Mr Wong apologized for the stink. People were jammed in the compartments and pressed in the corridors. I was at the door and could see the more nimble ones clinging to the steel ladders, balanced on the coupling. When the rain increased – and now it was really coming down – they fought their way into the carriages and slammed the doors and stood in the darkness while the rain hit the metal doors like hail.

My door was still open, and I was against the wall, while blurred gusts of rain beat past me.

'At least you can breathe here.'

The man who had spoken knotted a handkerchief on his head and stood with me. He had a briefcase. He whispered that he was a jeweller, down from Calcutta to take advantage of the market. Previously Indians were smuggling gems out of Ceylon to sell in India. Now the price in Ceylon was five times what it had been a few months ago, so the Indians were smuggling the gems back into Ceylon to sell at inflated prices.

'It's a funny situation,' he said.

'It's a pretty desperate country.'

'How many people in Ceylon – you know?'

I said I thought it was about twelve million.

'That's right,' he said, 'twelve million or so. And they can't feed them. You know how many people we have in Calcutta, *in Calcutta alone*? Eight million!'

'Can you feed them?'

'Of course not. But we don't talk all the rubbish they talk. You hear the rubbish? Grow More Food Campaign, plant some yams, revolutionary rubbish, political rubbish, this and that.'

'The bread queues are the worst I've ever seen.'

'You call those bread queues? In Calcutta we have bread queues twice as long as that. Bread queues, rice queues, even milk queues. You name it, we've got a queue for it. This is nothing.'

The rain let up, and in the villages of grass huts with steeply pitched roofs the lime kilns were sending clouds of smoke into the palm groves. It was another example of Singhalese improvidence. They dynamite coral from reefs and burn it to make lime. But the broken reef lets in the sea to erode the shore. The government had begun a programme to cement the reefs, but the paradox is that cement is made with lime, and, as no cement can be imported, the reefs that are dynamited for the lime to mend others must themselves be replaced. They call it the cement-industry; it is an industry that is entirely self-consuming: nothing is achieved.

Normally in such a train – in India, for example – the people would be eating or reading to pass the time. But there was little food and the shortage of newsprint had drastically reduced the newspapers. So the passengers on the 16.25 from Galle to Colombo were sitting; in the early part of the trip they were sitting in the light from the glorious sunset, and now they were sitting in the storm's darkness. The train rattled; the waves crashed on the shore. Nearer Colombo, the monks in the last carriage (FOR CLERGY, said the sign over the door) serenely watched the sun go down; second class held a school outing, gaping in starched uniforms; in third, where I was, nearly everyone sat silently in the dark shuttered compartments. By six it was much lighter outside – the storm had let up and the sun cut through the haze – but no one bothered to open the shutters. At Mount Lavinia, when someone did unlatch a shutter and fling it down, the sun had disappeared.

## 16. The Howrah Mail

I SAW him at Madras Central, near the Howrah Mail, and, from the hesitant way he was standing, he looked as if he were working up the courage to board. His long hair hung like rags in the heat; his clothes were much washed and faded to pastel colours. His suitcase, a canvas affair, repeated his worn appearance and was bursting at the seams. He was a man, perhaps English, in his early thirties, for whom, I guessed, travel had become an exhausting routine: travel can be an addiction and can change the physique, like drugs, to stringy leanness. A beggar was bent beside him, coughing. The young man, paying no attention to the outstretched hand, continued to stare at the train. I avoided him. The trip to Calcutta was too long to begin making friends so soon. I noticed that when he picked up his bag to board he passed a coin to the beggar. He did it without looking at the coughing man, with embarrassed obedience, like handing over a small admission charge.

My taxi driver had been helpful. He had carried my bag, found me bedding, located my berth, and arranged for me to have a spoon included with my meals. He was about to go. I gave him five rupees – too much. He decided to stay, like an anxious bearer with nothing to bear.

'You have money?'

I told him I did.

'Be careful,' he said. 'Indians no good. They take from your pockets.'

He showed me how to lock the compartment. He glanced around, scowling at the Indians who passed down the corridor.

He told me repeatedly to be careful, and he continued warning me in this vein for so long that I began to believe that my trip up the neck of Andhra Pradesh and through Orissa to Bengal was fraught with danger. Perhaps those bandy-legged Madrasis, spitting betel juice through the windows, were waiting for this man to leave so that they could pounce. And when the driver did leave I felt peculiarly exposed, vulnerable to attack. Most of the time I remained happily alone in my corner seat, and only at moments like this, when a casually met person helped me and passed on, did I feel the absence of his attention. The assisting stranger in India served only to erode my competence: his presence made me a sahib; his presence turned me into a child.

But I was glad to be moving. It was the feeling I'd had on the Direct-Orient Express, on the Frontier Mail, on the Grand Trunk Express: the size, the great length of the train, was a comfort. The bigger the train, the longer the journey, the happier I was – none of the temporary suspense produced by the annoying awareness of the local train's spots of time. On the long trips I seldom watched the stations pass – the progress of the train didn't interest me very much. I had learned to become a resident of the express, and I preferred to travel for two or three days, reading, eating in the dining car, sleeping after lunch, and bringing my journal up to date in the early evening before having my first drink and deciding where we were on my map. Train travel animated my imagination and usually gave me the solitude to order and write my thoughts: I travelled easily in two directions, along the level rails while Asia flashed changes at the window, and at the interior rim of a private world of memory and language. I cannot imagine a luckier combination.

On my way to the dining car I saw the young man hunched at the window in the passage outside his compartment, breathing the hot dark air. 'You won't find much up there,' he said as I squeezed past. I nodded, and we exchanged the glance of tolerant recognition common to solitary travellers meeting on long-distance trains. I had dinner – the vegetarian special I'd accustomed myself to – and going back I saw the fellow again in the same place. This time, he appeared to be waiting for me. He made no immediate effort to move. He said, 'How was it?'

'The usual. I don't mind – I'm a vegetarian.'

'It's not that. It's the way they eat. It runs down their arms. Puts me off my food. Did you ever see them preparing it? They kick it around, step on it, cough on it. Still, maybe you'll be lucky.'

We talked about the food; he had brought his own. Then he said, 'I saw you in Madras, with that bearer. What a hole. Calcutta's worse. Ever been there?'

I said I hadn't.

'Maybe you like that sort of thing. I think it's a ghastly place.' He took a last puff of his cigarette and flipped it out the window, the sparks scattering in the dark. 'Everywhere you look. Horrible.'

An Indian girl was coming towards us. I could have used her approach as an opportunity to pass on, but I waited and we both stepped aside to let her go by. She lowered her eyes and glided along. She had delicate shoulders, dry dusted cheeks, and gleaming hair, and she smelled of some small sweetness like that of a single crushed flower.

'Pretty girl.'

'They turn me off,' he said. 'You don't believe me.'

'If you say so.'

'I had an Indian girlfriend – prettier than her. That's why I'm going to Calcutta.'

'Is she there?'

'She's in Bangalore. Ever been there? It's not too bad, but I'm glad to be away from it – I mean, from her. Am I keeping you?'

'It's still early.' So he was fleeing the girl. I wondered why, but I wanted a simple answer. He invited me into his compartment to tell me. Most men, alone, stay up late, lamenting the absence of women. He gave me a shot of Indian gin. It stung my lips but tasted like nothing at all.

He said: 'She was the daughter of a man I had to see. I don't know about you, but the first time I came to India I more or less ignored Indian girls. Yes, I found them pretty, but the funny thing about a woman's beauty is that if you're absolutely sure you can't go to bed with her you begin to notice something calculated in her prettiness. I mean, her beauty is completely ineffectual. So she looks plainer, and gets uninteresting until she's invisible. If she has a good figure you see her as sinister rather than just plain, waiting for you to make a move that'll land you in jail. You can really develop a hate for these Indian women with their good looks and their useless virtue. That's why I prefer Muslim countries. They cover up their women and they don't make any bones about it. No one would be silly enough to tamper with a woman wearing one of those veils. It's unthinkable. I mean, they don't even look like women – they look like furniture covered up to keep the dust off. Veils are supposed to be sexy. Veils aren't sexy – what's sexy about something four feet high with a sheet over it?

'That's how I felt about Indian girls. They were so unapproachable they might as well have had sheets over their heads. The prettier they were the farther away I stayed. I wasn't interested because I knew they weren't. You see what I mean? I stopped noticing them. I barely noticed the daughter of this man I had to see. She was padding back and forth, bringing food, tea, the family album, doing the Indian thing. Their name was Bapna, and when the old man left the room the girl spoke up for the first time, asked me where I was staying. I told her.

'It was about three-thirty in the afternoon. The old man came back. He seemed a bit nervous, but finally got to the point. He said if I was going back to the hotel would I be kind enough to give Primila and her friend a lift? They were going to a film, but it was a long bus ride and they might not get there in time.

'I said I'd be glad to. The houseboy went and found a taxi. While we were driving into the city, Primila and her friend were talking to the driver, giving him directions and sort of arguing with him about the best route. I said, "Are you school chums?" This made them giggle and pull their saris over their mouths. They were each twenty-two and embarrassed to be mistaken for schoolgirls.

'Then the taxi stopped. The friend got out and Primila and I drove away. "Where's this film of yours?" I said. She said it was near my hotel. I asked her what time it started. "It runs all day."

'I was just making conversation, and I found that after a few minutes I was talking about a painting I'd bought from a dealer the previous day, a fairly good one, Lakshmi and Vishnu inter-twined on a lotus blossom. Primila was so quiet, I became quite talkative. It happens – a person's reticence makes me talk an awful lot, kind of compensating.

'At the hotel I said, "I hope you don't have far to walk." She said the cinema was right around the corner. I asked her if she had ever been in the hotel before and when she said not I felt sorry for her, as if she'd been excluded from the place because she didn't have the money. I said, "Want to look it over?" She said yes. We went in. I showed her the restaurants and bars, the news-stand, the curio shop where I'd bought my painting. She was quite interested, walking beside me, taking it all in like a person in a museum.

'What I think I should have told you first is that about six months ago I was in Madras. I had some time to kill, so one afternoon I visited a palmist, Swami Sundram. He was a leathery old man and his house in Mylapore didn't have the usual charts and religious pictures and not even many cushions. He sat at a roll-top desk with a pencil and a piece of paper, in a kind of library stacked with mouldy books. He looked at my palm, line by line, then did a diagram on the paper and made notes, circling and underlining them as he went along. He didn't say a word for ten minutes or so, though he often paused as he was writing to press his forehead, like a person trying to remember something.

'Finally he said, "You have been very sick, pains in the

stomach, muscle pains, and trouble passing motion." I almost laughed – I mean, you don't have to be a palmist to tell someone in India he's had stomach trouble. He told me one or two other things, but I said, "Look, I know what's happened to me – what I want to know is what's *going* to happen."

'He said, "I see an Indian girl. Classical face, maybe a dancer. You are alone with her."

' "Is that all?" I said.

' "Not all," he said. "I see her dancing for you."

'Well, naturally, I thought of what Swami Sundram had said when I was with Primila at the hotel. I asked her if she was a dancer, and she said no. Then out on the verandah she said, "I used to do classical dancing when I was younger, if that's what you mean. But all Indian girls do that." I suggested tea. She said yes. I said we could have a drink instead. She said, "As you say." I ordered a gin and tonic. She said she wanted rum. I couldn't believe it. "Real rum?" I said. She giggled, like in the taxi, but didn't change her mind. When our drinks came we touched glasses and she went silent again.

'I was barely conscious of talking about my painting, but there wasn't very much to talk about, and I found I was having trouble describing the thing. Several times, I said, "You should see it." She said, "I'd like to," and that annoyed me because it meant I'd have to go upstairs, dig it out, and bring it down. It was in a sealed wrapper because of the dust. I was sorry I'd mentioned it – I'd only done it to keep the conversation going. I could have been having a nice drink alone – relaxing. I need to be alone after seeing people, sort of put myself back together. Lunch with old Bapna had tired me out. I didn't say anything more.

' "Do you have it with you?" she said. I told her it was upstairs and I felt as if I was getting into a corner because I couldn't refuse to show her. "Would you like to see it?" "Very much," she said. I said all right, but that it would be a lot easier if she came upstairs. She said fine. "When you finish your drink," I said. But she had finished her drink. I gulped mine down and we went upstairs. In the room she said, "I hate air conditioners." I gave the thing a kick and it shut off.

'We looked at the painting, sitting on the bed – it was the only place to sit – and as she pointed out what was good about it, how the figures were so well done, she reached over and picked it up from my lap. Has a girl ever lifted something from your lap? It gave me a thrill – I felt a surprising voltage in my groin from the light pressure of her hand.

'She showed me a detail of the picture, and when I looked closer I took her hand, and from the way she let me hold her hand I knew I could kiss her. They don't show kissing in Indian films. I know why. Because in India there is no such intimacy as a kiss that is not followed by a screw. A tiny particle of affection in India stands for passion, but what amazed me was that the whole thing was her idea, not mine. I had gone to the room with her against my will!

'I kissed her, and I was so surprised by her eagerness I practically fainted with excitement. I was really happy, and that sort of glee goes against the sex urge, but glee is more temporary than sex, and in a minute or so I was on her. She stayed for about two hours.

'The effect of this on me was incredible, like a conversion. Every woman I saw after that was attractive, and I saw each one as a possible lay. They really turned me on – I couldn't take my eyes off them. I saw them as coy, clever, geniuses of sexuality who had managed to disguise it all with that busy efficiency Indian women have. I was so assured by what I knew, I didn't bother to make a pass at any of them. But most of all I began to see some sense in what Swami Sundram had said: "She will dance for you." Obviously Primila was the girl he meant. I saw her a few more times and I really fell for her – I think even old Bapna suspected something was going on because he asked me a lot of questions about my family, and what sort of work did I do, and what were my plans? Primila talked a lot about leaving India and one day she turned up in a blouse and slacks. She looked insolent in Western clothes, but, as I say, I was beginning to love her and I imagined having one of those fantastic Indian weddings. Primila said she had always wanted to go to England – she had read so much about it, that sort of thing. I could see what was happening.

'Swami Sundram predicted it, I suppose, so the next chance I got I went to Madras, and to be absolutely sure he wouldn't recognize me I shaved off my beard and wore different clothes. This time I had to wait outside his house until he finished with another customer, and when I got inside he went through the same business of the diagrams and the notes. I didn't let on that I'd been there before. Then he said, "Head pains. I see many head pains, something like headache." I told him to go on. 'You are expecting an important letter," he said. He pressed his temples. "You will receive this letter soon." I asked him if that was all. "No," he said, "you have a large mole on your penis." "No, I don't," I said. But he stuck to his story. He said, "You most certainly do." It amazed me that he should keep telling me that I had a mole on my penis while I was denying it and could even prove how wrong he was. He seemed rather irritated that I should contradict him. I paid him and left.

'That was yesterday. I didn't go back to Bangalore. I bought a ticket to Calcutta. I'm leaving – flying to Bangkok. If I hadn't seen that Swami I might be married now, or at least betrothed – it's the same thing. She was a nice girl, but I must have bad *karma*, and I don't have a mole on my penis. I looked.

'Pass the bottle,' he said. He took a swig and said, 'Never go back to a palmist.'

Through Berhampur and Khurda to Cuttack where children splashed, diving around buffaloes submerged to their nostrils in the wide Mahanadi River. This was the northeast corner of Orissa, smallpox capital of the world – Balasore, the very name suggesting some itching illness. The station signboards were captions to images I saw from the train: Tuleswar, a woman carrying a red clay water jar on her head, bringing contagion to a far-off village; Duntan, a defecating Bengali posed like Rodin's *Thinker*; Kharagpur, a man twisting the tail of his buffalo to make him go faster; Panskura, a crowd of children in school uniforms running along the tracks to their shantytown for lunch; and then the impacted precincts of Budge-Budge, where what I first took to be the poignant sight of an old man leading a small boy through the detritus of a train yard was a blind man with a devilish face squeezing the arm of the frightened child who was his guide.

The travellers on the Howrah Mail had a look of fatigued solemnity. They paid no attention to the hawkers and vendors who became more frequent as we neared Calcutta, getting on at suburban stations to make a circuit of the open carriages. A man gets on with a teapot, balancing a row of nesting clay cups on his arm. He squawks, urging tea on the passengers, waving the teapot in each person's face, and gets off: no sale. He is followed by a man with a jar of candy and a spoon. The candy man bangs his jar with the spoon and begins a monotonous spiel. Everyone is shown the jar, and the man continues to pound his spoon all the way to the door, where another enters with a tray of fountain pens. The pen man babbles and, as he does so, he demonstrates how the cap is unscrewed, how the nib is poised, how the clip works; he twirls the pen and holds it for everyone to see; he does everything but write with it, and when he has finished he leaves, having sold nothing. More get on with things to sell: buns, roasted chickpeas, plastic combs, lengths of ribbon, soiled pamphlets; nothing is sold.

At some stations Indians dived through the windows for seats, but when the seats were filled they squashed themselves at the door, maintaining only an emotional contact with the railway car. They were suspended from the ceiling on straps, stacked against the wall like cordwood, heaped on the benches holding their knees together, and outside the Howrah Mail they clung to the fittings with such agility, they seemed magnetized.

Near Howrah Station throngs of Biharis were throwing themselves into the greasy Hooghly River from sanctified *ghats*. Their festival, *Chhat*, was enlivening Calcutta, and it offered a chance for the Biharis to make a show of strength against the Bengalis, whose own Kali festival had sealed many streets with the chamber of horrors that is a Kali shrine: the goggle-eyed goddess twice life-size, with her necklace of human heads, sticking out a tongue as bright as a raspberry popsicle and trampling the mortally wounded corpse of her husband. Behind Kali, plaster tableaux showed four doomed men, the first impaled on a bloody spear, the second having his neck wrung by a skeleton, the third flattened by a hag who is simultaneously severing the fourth's head. It was all a challenge to the Biharis, whose own processions involved tall mobile shrines draped in yellow cloth, carts loaded with women seated among heaps of banana offerings, looking deeply pious, and little troupes of transvestites dancing to bugle calls and drums.

'There go the Biharis, off to throw their bananas in the Hooghly,' said Mr Chatterjee, from the chair car. A Bengali, Mr Chatterjee wasn't sure of the purpose of the *Chhat* festival, but thought it might have something to do with the harvest. I said I didn't think the Calcutta harvest would be very large. He agreed, but said the Biharis enjoyed their annual chance to snarl Bengali traffic. At the head of every procession a black grinning boy, dressed as a girl, made the jerky movements of a dancer with his wrists and leaped in the air, his genitals whipping about in his crimson sari. From time to time, the young girls (who might have been boys) behind him dropped to the ground and prostrated themselves in the garbage-strewn streets.

The holy mob, the stink of sanctity, the legitimate noise: everything in Indian life seemed to sanction excess, and even politics had the *puja* flavour. While these religious festivals were going their bellowing way, the Socialist Unity Centre was organizing a *bundh* – a total work stoppage – and their preliminary rallies on the *maidan* with their flags and posters, processions and speeches, were practically indistinguishable from the displays of mass piety on Chowringhee's sidewalks and at the sloshing *ghats*. This aspect of Calcutta is the first that meets the traveller's eye, but the one that stays longest in the mind; it is an atmosphere of organized disturbance, everyone occupied in carrying out some programme or other, so much so that those stricken thousands one sees uniformly – uniformly, because space is scarce – lying or sitting on the sidewalk have the look of nonviolent protesters having a long afternoon of dedicated *satyagraha* ('clinging to truth'). I imagined another group in an ambiguous posture when I read, in a Calcutta newspaper, 'The leftist leaders also decided to resort to mass squatting . . .'

From the outside, Howrah Station looks like a secretariat, with its not quite square towers and many clocks – each showing a different time – and its impenetrable brickwork. The British buildings in India look as if they have been designed to withstand a siege – there are hornworks and cannon emplacements and watchtowers on the unlikeliest structures. So Howrah Station looked like a fortified version of a mammoth circumlocution office, an impression that buying a ticket there only confirms. But inside it is high and smoky from the fires of the people who occupy it; the ceiling is black, the floor is wet and filthy, and it is dark – the long shafts of sun streaming from the topmost windows lose their light in dust on the way down.

'It's much better than it was,' said Mr Chatterjee, seeing me craning my neck. 'You should have seen it *before* they cleaned it up.'

His remark was unanswerable. Yet at every pillar squatters huddled amid the rubbish they had created: broken glass, bits of wood and paper, straw, and tin cans. Some infants slept against their parents; others were curled up like changelings in dusty corners. Families sought refuge beside pillars, under counters and luggage carts: the hugeness of the station intimidated them with space and drove them to the walls. Their children prowled in the open spaces, combining their scavenging with play. They are the tiny children of tiny parents, and it's amazing how, in India, it is possible to see two kinds of people in the process of evolution, side by side, one fairly tall, quick, and responsive, the other, whose evolution is reduction, small, stricken, and cringing. They are two races whose common ground is the railway station, and though they come quite close (an urchin lies on his back near the ticket window watching the legs of the people in line) they do not meet.

I walked outside, into the midday chaos at the western end of the Howrah Bridge. In Simla, rickshaws were retained for their quaintness: people posed in them. In Calcutta, rickshaws, pulled by skinny running men in tattered clothes, are a necessary form of transport, cheap, and easy to steer in narrow back lanes. They are a crude symbol of Indian society, but in India all symbols are crude: the homeless people sleeping in the doorway of the mansion, the commuter running to his train accidentally trampling a station sleeper, the thin rickshaw-*wallah* hauling his plump passengers. Ponies harnessed to stagecoaches laboured over cobblestones; men pushed bicycles loaded with hay bales and firewood. I had never seen so many different forms of transport: wagons, scooters, old cars, carts and sledges, and odd, old-fashioned horse-drawn vehicles that might have been barouches. In one cart, their white flippers limp, dead sea turtles were stacked; on another cart was a dead buffalo, and in a third an entire family with their belongings – children, parrot cage, pots and pans. All these vehicles, and people surging among them. Then there was panic, and the people scattered as a tottering tram car marked TOLLYGUNGE swayed down the bridge. Mr Chatterjee said, 'Too much of people!'

Mr Chatterjee walked across the bridge with me. He was a Bengali, and Bengalis were the most alert people I had met in India. But they were also irritable, talkative, dogmatic, arrogant, and humourless, holding forth with malicious skill on virtually every subject except the future of Calcutta. Any mention of that brought them up short. But Mr Chatterjee had views. He had been reading an article about Calcutta's prospects. Calcutta had been very unlucky: Chicago had had a great fire, San Francisco an earthquake, and London a plague as well as a fire. But nothing had happened to Calcutta to give planners a chance to redesign it. You had to admit, he said, it had vitality. The problem of pavement dwellers (he put the figure at a quarter of a million) had been 'somewhat overdramatized', and when you considered that these pavement dwellers were almost exclusively engaged in ragpicking you could see how Calcutta's garbage was 'most intensively recycled'. It seemed an unusual choice of words, and it strayed close to claptrap: vitality in a place where people lay dead in the gutter ('But everyone dies eventually,' said Mr C.), the overdramatized quarter of a million, the recycling ragpickers. We passed a man who leaned at us and put his hand out. He was a monster. Half his face was missing; it looked as if it had been clumsily guillotined – he had no nose, no lips, no chin, and clamped in his teeth, which were perpetually exposed, was the bruised plug of his tongue. Mr Chatterjee saw my shock. 'Oh, *him*! He is always here!'

Before he left me at the Barabazar, Mr Chatterjee said, 'I *love* this city.' We exchanged addresses and we parted, I to a hotel, Mr Chatterjee to Strand Road, where the Hooghly was silting up so badly, soon all that would float on it would be the ashes of cremated Bengalis.

I stayed in Calcutta for four days, giving lectures, seeing the sights, and losing my lecture fees at the Royal Calcutta Turf Club on the Saturday I decided to leave. On the first day the city seemed like a corpse on which the Indians were feeding like flies; then I saw its features more clearly, the obelisks and pyramids in Park Street Cemetery, the decayed mansions with friezes and columns, and the fountains in the courtyards of these places: nymphs and sprites blowing on dry conches, who, like the people living under them in gunny sacks, are missing legs and arms; the gong of trams at night; and the flaring lamps lighting the wild cows pushing their snouts into rubbish piles, vying with the scrabbling Indians for something edible. The high mock-Moghul tenements

hustled it, and crushed it, and stuck brick-and-mortar elbows into it, and kept the air from it, and stood perpetually between it and the light . . .

You groped your way for an hour through lanes and bye-ways, and court-yards and passages; and you never once emerged upon anything that might be reasonably called a street. A kind of resigned distraction came over the stranger as he trod those devious mazes, and, giving himself up for lost, went in and out and round about and quietly turned back again when he came to a dead wall or was stopped by an iron railing, and felt that the means of escape might possibly present themselves in their own good time, but to anticipate them was hopeless . . .

Among the narrow thoroughfares at hand, there lingered, here and there, an ancient doorway of carved oak, from which, of old, the sounds of revelry and feasting often came; but now these mansions, only used for storehouses, were dark and dull, and, being filled with wool, and cotton, and the like – such heavy merchandise as stifles sound and stops the throat of echo – had an air of palpable deadness . . . In the throats and maws of dark no-thoroughfares . . . wholesale dealers in grocery-ware had perfect little towns of their own; and, deep among the foundations of these buildings, the ground was undermined and burrowed out into stables, where cart-horses, troubled by rats, might be heard on a quiet Sunday rattling their halters, as disturbed spirits in tales of haunted houses are said to clank their chains . . .

Then there were steeples, towers, belfries, shining vanes, and masts of ships: a very forest. Gables, housetops, garret-windows, wilderness upon wilderness. Smoke and noise enough for all the world at once.

There is more, and it is all good, but I think I have quoted enough to show that the best description of Calcutta is Todger's corner of London in Chapter IX of *Martin Chuzzlewit*. But having decided that Calcutta was Dickensian (perhaps more

Dickensian than London ever was), and knowing that I could not share either the excitement of the Bengalis, who agreed with the enormous billboard put up by the State Bank of India (CALCUTTA IS FOREVER), or, what is more curious, the chummy regard of the Americans I met there for this vast and yet incomplete city that I felt would someday undo them, I decided to leave it and so leave India.

I was on my way when I saw the hopping man in the crowd on Chowringhee. He was very strange: in a city of mutilated people only the truly monstrous looked odd. This man had one leg – the other was amputated at the thigh – but he did not carry a crutch. He had a greasy bundle in one hand. He hopped past me with his mouth open, pumping his shoulders. I went after him, and he turned into Middleton Street, hopping very fast on one muscular leg, like a man on a pogo stick, his head rising above the crowd, then descending into it. I couldn't run because of the other people, black darting clerks, swamis with umbrellas, armless beggars working their stumps at me, women proffering drugged babies, strolling families, men seeming to block the sidewalk with their wide flapping trousers and swinging arms. The hopping man was in the distance. I gained on him – I saw his head clearly – then lost him. On one leg he had outrun me, so I never found out how he did it. But afterwards, whenever I thought of India, I saw him – hop, hop, hop – moving nimbly through those millions.

# 17. The Mandalay Express

At sundown in Rangoon, the crows that have been blackening the sky all day soar to their roosts as the shrill bats waken and flap in hectic circles around the pagoda-style towers of the railway station. I arrived at this hour: the bats were tumbling past the crows, and the pale yellow sky was inked like Burmese silk with the brush marks of the black bodies. I had arrived by air in Rangoon on a Saturday night – there is no train from India – and the Burmese appetite for movies I had noticed on a previous visit was undiminished. Sule Pagoda Road, with its five theatres, was mobbed with people, dressed identically in shirt, sarong, and rubber sandals, men and women alike puffing thick green cheroots, and looking (as they waved away the smoke with slender dismissing fingers) like a royal breed, strikingly handsome in this collapsing city, a race of dispossessed princes.

I had only one objective in Burma: to take the northbound trains from Rangoon via Mandalay and Maymyo to the Gokteik Gorge in the Shan States, beyond which China sprawls. Across this gorge is a magnificent steel trestle bridge, the Gokteik Viaduct, built in 1899 by the Pennsylvania Steel Company for the British *Raj*. I had read about the bridge, but not in any recent book. Early in this century enthusiasm for railway travel produced a spate of optimistic books about railway travel: the French were building the *Transindochinois* line to Hanoi, the Russians had brought the Trans-Siberian almost to Vladivostok, the British had laid track to the very end of the Khyber Pass, and it was assumed that Burmese railways would extend in one direction to the Assam-Bengal line and in the other to the railways of China. The books had apocalyptic titles like *The*

*Railway Conquest of the World* (by Frederick Talbot, 1911) and described, country by country, how the globe was to be stitched by railway track. The judgements were occasionally disagreeable. Ernest Protheroe in *Railways of the World* (1914) wrote: 'John Chinaman – cunning, tenacious, and virile – for centuries kept the "foreign devil" at arm's length . . . But, however much the Chinese hated the white man, they commenced to recognize the value of railways . . .' The Gokteik Viaduct, much celebrated in these books, was an important link in a line that was projected beyond the northern border town of Lashio into China. But the line had stopped at Lashio (nor were Burmese railways ever to meet Indian ones), and I had heard many rumours about this American-built bridge: one was that it had been blown up during the Second World War; another that the line had been captured by Burmese rebel forces under the command of U Nu; and another that it was off-limits to foreigners.

To avoid startling the Burmese at the ticket window of Rangoon Station I asked about the train to Mandalay. There were two men at the window. The first said there was no printed timetable I could buy. The second said, 'Yes, we have no timetable.' It seemed to be the practice in Burma to have two men at each job, the second to confirm whatever the first said. Instead of a timetable, and like Ceylon, there was a blackboard at each station with the arrivals and departures chalked on it. But both men were certain about the Mandalay train.

'Departure, seven o'clock. Morning time.'

There was one class, they said. I was to find this to be the equivalent of Indian third class – wooden seats, broken windows, no berths, no bedrolls, no dining car, none of the complex comfort of Indian Railways, involving retiring rooms, dinner coupons, bedding chits, invoice for upper-class luggage, ticket vouchers, and morning tea.

'I'd like a ticket to Mandalay.'

'Sorry, the window is closed.'

But the window was open. I mentioned this.

'Yes, it is open so to say, but it is closed for selling.'

'You come at six o'clock, morning time,' said the second man.

'Are you sure I'll get a ticket?'

'Maybe. Even much better come at five-thirty.'

'How long does it take to get to Mandalay?'

'Twelve hours. But it breaks down. You might arrive Mandalay at eight.'

'Or nine?'

They both laughed.

'Or nine, but not later!'

I walked over the bridge to the city, and I was in a large crowd of Burmese when a hand reached out and grabbed my wrist in such a powerful clamp of fingers I couldn't shake it off. It was a Buddhist monk, holding on and yapping at me. Small, monkey-faced, with a shaven head, he was half my size and seemed angry as he repeated the phrase '*Blum chyap . . . blum chyap.*' I overcame my surprise and stopped struggling, assuming he was asking for money, and finally I fathomed that he was begging, saying, 'One kyat' (about twenty cents). This gripping seemed an extortionate way to beg, so I gave him half a kyat and when he released me to take the money I ducked into the crowd. There were other monks in the mob, looking sweet and benign as they cadged money from strangers.

Further on, a Burmese with a telescope urged me to have a look. I paid my fee of 25 pyas (five cents), but the star I saw through his instrument looked slightly smaller and less impressive than it did with the naked eye. I walked aimlessly, speeding up when a man sidled over to me and offered a Chinese girl ('Come!'), slowing down at temples where children – still awake at eleven at night – wove ropes of flowers and laughed before Buddhas. Older people knelt in veneration, or set up displays of fruit, balancing a melon in a hand of bananas on a temple shelf and sticking a red paper flag into the melon. Elderly women leaned against flower stalls, the smoking cheroots in their hands giving them a look of haughtiness and self-possession.

That night I dreamed I missed the Mandalay train. I woke up breathless at five-thirty and had breakfast, then ran to the station. Once before, on a morning like this, I had set off for Rangoon Station and a woman had jumped out of a bush, where she had been sleeping, and tried to tempt me by undoing her sarong and showing me her yellow thighs. It was before dawn; I hadn't seen her face, but her squawking echoed on the road. She had chased me all the way to the station, her feet slapping on the pavement. That was in 1970, and what I remembered of the station were the rats, hopping on the tracks to sniff and chew at wastepaper; the hawkers, selling fruit and paperbacks, putting the rats to flight and treading in the pools of excrement; the heat and flies at dawn; and Burmese boys jeering at their departing friends.

But Rangoon Station had changed. There were no rats or hawkers and the tracks were clean. There were two barbed-wire fences on the platform and barbed wire ran along each of the four tracks. The only food being sold was in lunch boxes, cardboard cartons filled with cold damp rice and pieces of sinewy chicken. The station was orderly, like the high-security prison it strongly resembled, and the barriers separated well-wishers from passengers.

I asked the conductor about the fences.

'To stop the smuggling,' he said. 'Also to stop people crossing the line. Also to stop incidents.'

'What sort of incidents?'

'Bombs. Last year some fellows threw a bomb. They threw it at the train. It was the "45-Up" – very many people. It stopped the train and there were three casualties. For these reasons the fences were put up. I think it is a good thing. Now we have no troubles.'

A Buddhist monk went by, smiling broadly. He was a fat man and he carried his umbrella like *fasces*, a Roman senator in an orange toga. I was glad it was not he who had twisted my arm the previous night. I bought a lunch box and two bottles of soda water and boarded. It is pleasant to leave Rangoon by rail: the train goes around the city and five minutes from the station you are in the country, a low swampy rice-growing area beside the Pazandaung Creek, where in the courtyards of the monasteries the monks are at prayer, and crossing the fields are processions of people – schoolchildren with satchels, office workers setting out in white shirts, farmers with mattocks – the early morning march in the tropics to the tune of temple bells.

There was music inside the train as well. This was new. It was piped through loudspeakers and never stopped once in thirteen hours. To a background of oriental music-hall melodies – gongs and saxophones vying with a wheezy harmonium – a reedy complaining voice gave a Burmese rendition of 'Deep Purple' and then 'Stars Fell on Alabama'. The music prevented me from reading, the cramped bench kept me from writing, and the rest of the passengers were asleep. I went to the door and watched Burmese pedalling their bikes along country roads, under giant peepul trees. The distant hills were blue with teak forests, but we were travelling along the flat plain known as the Dry Zone, moving north in a straight line through the heat that drugs the train passenger into thinking he is disappearing down Burma's gullet. At a well near the halt of Indian Fort a Burmese girl was combing her hair. She was bent forward, all her hair down – so long it nearly touched the ground – and she was drawing her comb through it and shaking it out. It was such a beautiful sight on this sunny morning – that cascade of black hair, swaying under the comb, and the posture of the girl, her feet planted apart, her arms caressing her lovely mane. Then she tossed it and looked up to see the train go past.

The whistle at the station at Toungoo is a dinner bell. Toungoo is halfway exactly, and until then no one in the train has touched his food. But when the whistle sounds, lunch boxes are thrown open and tiffin tins spread over the seats; rice tied up in palm leaves is passed through the windows with crawfish and prawns reddened with pepper, apples, pawpaws, oranges, and roasted bananas. The tea seller and water carrier appear, and the eating and drinking goes on until the whistle blows again. Then the bundles are retied, garbage is dropped on the floor, and scraps are thrown out the windows. Pariah dogs leap from nowhere to snarl over the leavings.

'Why don't they shoot those dogs?' I asked a man at Toungoo.

'Burmese think it is wrong to kill animals.'

'Why not feed them then?'

He was silent. I was questioning one of the cardinal precepts of Buddhism, the principle of neglect. Because no animals are killed all animals look as if they are starving to death, and so the rats, which are numerous in Burma, co-exist with the dogs, which have eliminated cats from the country. The Burmese – removing their shoes and socks for sacred temple floors where they will spit and flick cigar ashes – see no contradiction. How could they? Burma is a socialist country with a notorious bureaucracy. But it is a bureaucracy that is Buddhist in nature, for not only is it necessary to be a Buddhist in order to tolerate it, but the Burmese bureaucratic delays are a consistent encouragement to a kind of traditional piety – the commissar and the monk meeting as equals on the common ground of indolent and smiling unhelpfulness. Nothing happens in Burma, but then nothing is expected to happen.

Eight hours had passed since we left Rangoon, and the conductor, who on any other train would be seeing to the tickets or getting someone to sweep the littered coaches, remained seated in a little booth near the vile-smelling toilet, feeding cassettes into the tape recorder. There was no water on the train; the doors were loose and banging; the fans were broken; and the aisle was a trough of chicken bones, prawn shells, and sticky palm leaves. But the amplifying system worked with a vengeance, pouring out raucous music all the way to Mandalay.

Towards the end of the afternoon the engine kept breaking down. The man next to me, a policeman with exemplary patience, said, 'The oil is hot. They are waiting for it to cool.' He was obviously pained by my questions and assured me the train would arrive at seven: 'If not at seven, then definitely at eight.'

'It is a slow train,' he said at Thazi, where the train broke down for the fourth time. 'Dirty and old – old coaches, old engines. We have no foreign exchange.'

'But it doesn't take much foreign exchange to buy a broom.'

'That may be so.'

I wandered around the station and heard flutes, gongs, and the rattle of a snare drum, and there on the road next to the track a little procession appeared, weirdly lit by a sky layered red. It marched to the fence beside the track and made a semi-circle for a small girl, no more than ten years old. She had tucked up her sarong in a way that allowed her movement and she wore a delicate beaded cap on her head. The music stopped, then started, blaring and chiming, and, crooking her hands, the girl began to dance; she bent her knees, lifting one leg, then the other, in a jerky motion the swiftness made graceful.

The passengers turned to watch, puffing cheroots from the windows of the stalled train and strolling closer along the platform. The dance was for them; there was no talking – only this tinkling music and the dancing child in that empty place. It continued for perhaps ten minutes, then stopped abruptly, and the procession trailed off, the flute still warbling, the drum sounding. It was part of the Burmese sequence: the breakdown and delay softened by sweet music, a lovely sky, a dancing child, and then the unexpected resuming of the train.

We travelled the rest of the way to Mandalay in darkness, arriving at eight-thirty at a station enlivened by celebrants of the *Kathin* festival, frenzied drummers and pretty dancers jammed tight in a crowd of welcoming relatives leaping to embrace passengers. I fought my way to the stationmaster's office, to be greeted warmly by an old man in a peaked cap who seemed to be expecting me. He asked for my passport and laboriously copied out my name and asked me my destination.

'There is a train to Maymyo at seven tomorrow morning,' he

said. In a country where all trains leave at seven, a printed timetable was superfluous.

'I'd like to buy a ticket.'

'Ticket office is closed. Come at six. What is your final destination?'

'After Maymyo I want to go to Gokteik. To see the viaduct.'

'It is forbidden for foreign tourists to see the viaduct.'

He might have been cautioning me against defilement of a sacred shrine.

'Then I'll go to Lashio.'

'It is forbidden. Lashio is a security area. There are rebellions.'

'Then you mean I have to stay in Maymyo?'

'Maymyo is a nice place. All foreigners like Maymyo.'

'I wanted to go to Gokteik.'

'Too bad. Why don't you go to Pagan?'

'I've been to Pagan.'

'Or Inle Lake. They have a hotel.'

'I wanted to take a train.'

'Why not take the train back to Rangoon?' said the station-master.

He shook my hand and showed me to the door. Outside was Mandalay. It is a low city of immense size, so dusty at night the lanterns on the pony carts and the headlights of wooden buses shine as if through thick fog. The city is large but without interest; the fort is off-limits, the monasteries have burned down, and the temple at the top of Mandalay Hill is recent and unattractive. Mandalay is a magic name, but little more than that. What of Kipling's poem then? Well, the fact is Kipling never set foot in the place, and his experience of Burma was limited to a few days in 1889, when his ship stopped in Rangoon.

Mandalay has two hotels, one cheap, the other expensive. Both are uncomfortable, so I chose the cheap one. The manager said he had no rooms. He was frowning with fatigue and anxious for me to go. I said, 'But where will I sleep?' He considered the question and then showed me to a room, complaining as he did so about a leprosy conference meeting at his hotel ('They want this, they want that – '). I asked for food. He said he had none and proved it by showing me the empty kitchen. I ate a banana I had bought in Thazi, and thanked him for the room. He was a good Burmese. He could not turn me away, though he did not want me to stay. He allowed me a little shelter but no food, treating me, literally, the way he would a pariah, with a kind of grudging reverence.

# 18. The Local to Maymyo

ASIA washes with spirited soapy violence in the morning. The early train takes you past people discovered laundering like felons rehearsing – Pakistanis charging their sodden clothes with sticks, Indians trying to break rocks (this is Mark Twain's definition of a Hindu) by slapping them with wet *dhotis*, grimacing Singhalese wringing out their *lungis*. In Upper Burma, women squat in conspiratorial groups at bubbly streams, whacking their laundry flat with broad wooden paddles, children totter knee-deep in rock pools, and small-breasted girls, chastely covered by sarongs to their armpits, dump buckets of water over their heads. It was dull and cloudy, starting to mist, as we left Mandalay, and the old man next to me with a neat cloth bundle on his knees watched one of these bathing girls.

> Steeping tresses in the tank
> Blue-black, lustrous, thick like horsehairs,
> – Can't I see his dead eye glow
> Bright as 'twere a Barbary corsair's?
> (That is, if he'd let it show!)

Briefly, I thought of leaping from the train, proposing marriage, and throwing my life away on one of these nymphs. But I stayed in my seat.

The full streams, whitened by peaks of froth, told of heavy rains farther on; we had left the rancid heat and dusty palms of Mandalay and were climbing sideways through pine forests, where the gold-tipped pagodas, repeating the shape of pine tops, rose above the deep green trees. A dirigible of white cloud had settled against one station; we emerged from it to a view of hardier, muddier people carrying buckets on yokes. A light rain began to fall, and the train was moving so slowly I could hear the patter of raindrops on the leaves that grew beside the track.

At the early sloping stations, women with trays were selling breakfast to the passengers: oranges, sliced pawpaws, fried cakes, peanuts, and bananas. One had a dark shining assortment of beady objects on her tray. I beckoned her over and had a look. They were fat insects skewered on sticks – fried locusts. I asked the old man next to me if he'd like some. He said politely that he had had breakfast already, and anyway he never ate insects. 'But the local people are quite fond of them.'

The sight of the locusts took away my appetite, but an hour later, in a thunderstorm, my hunger came back. I was standing near the door and struck up a conversation with a Burmese man on his way to Lashio to see his family. He was hungry too. He said we would be arriving at a station soon where we could buy food.

'I'd like some tea,' I said.

'It is a short stop – a few minutes, not more.'

'Look, why don't you get the food and I'll get something to drink? It'll save time.'

He agreed, accepted my three kyats, and when the train stopped we leaped out – he to the food stall, I to an enclosure where there were bottles on display. The hawker explained with apologetic smiles that I couldn't remove his teacups, so I had a cup of tea there and bought two bottles of soda water. Back on the train I couldn't find the Burmese man, and it was not until after the train pulled away that he appeared, out of breath, with two palm-leaf parcels, bound with a knotted vine. We uncapped the bottles on the door hinge, and, elbow to elbow at the end of the coach, opened the palm leaves. There was something familiar in the contents, a wooden skewer with three blackened things on it – lumps of burned meat. It wasn't that they were irregularly shaped, but rather that they were irregular in exactly the same way. The skewers lay half-buried in beds of rice.

'In Burmese we call them –' He said the word.

I peered at them. 'Are those *wings*?'

'Yes, they are birds.'

Then I saw the little heads, the beaks and burned-out eyes, and dark singed claws on feeble feet.

'Maybe you call them sparrows,' he said.

Maybe we do. I thought, but they looked so tiny without their feathers. He slipped one off the skewer, put the whole thing into his mouth, and crunched it, head, feet, wings, the whole bird; he chewed it, smiling. I pinched a little meat from one of mine and ate it. It did not taste bad, but it is hard to eat a sparrow in Burma and not feel reproached by flights of darting birds. I risked the rice. I went back to my seat, so that the man would not see me throw the rest of the birds away.

The old man next to me said, 'How old do you think I am? Guess.'

I said sixty, thinking he was seventy.

He straightened up. 'Wrong! I am eighty. That is, I passed my seventy-ninth birthday, so I am in my eightieth year.'

The train switched back and forth on curves as sharp as those on the way to Simla and Landi Kotal. Occasionally, for no apparent reason, it ground to a halt, starting up without a warning whistle, and it was then that the Burmese who had jumped out to piss chased after the train, retying their sarongs as they ran along the track and being whooped at by their friends in the train. The mist, the rain, and cold low clouds gave the train a feel of early morning, a chill and predawn dimness that lasted until noon. I put a shirt over my jersey, then a sweater and a plastic raincoat, but I was still cold, the damp penetrating to my bones. It was the coldest I had been since leaving England.

'I was born in eighteen ninety-four in Rangoon,' said the old man suddenly. 'My father was an Indian, but a Catholic. That is why I am called Bernard. My father was a soldier in the Indian Army. He had been a soldier his whole life – I suppose he joined up in Madras in the eighteen seventies. He was in the

Twenty-sixth Madras Infantry and he came to Rangoon with his regiment in eighteen eighty-eight. I used to have his picture, but when the Japanese occupied Burma – I'm sure you have heard of the Japanese war – all our possessions were scattered, and we lost so many things.'

He was eager to talk, glad to have a listener, and he didn't need prompting questions. He spoke carefully, plucking at the cloth bundle, as he remembered a clause, and I hugged myself in the cold, grateful that all that was required of me was an occasional nod to show I was interested.

'I don't remember much about Rangoon, and we moved to Mandalay when I was very young. I can remember practically everything from nineteen hundred onwards. Mr MacDowell, Mr Owen, Mr Stewart, Captain Taylor – I worked for them all. I was head cook in the Royal Artillery officers' mess, but I did more than cook – I did everything. I went all over Burma, in the camps when they were in the field. I have a good memory, I think. For example, I remember the day Queen Victoria died. I was in the second standard at Saint Xavier's School in Mandalay. The teacher said to us, "The Queen is dead, so there is no school today." I was – what? – seven years old. I was a good student. I did my lessons, but when I finished with school there was nothing to do. In nineteen ten I was sixteen and I thought I should get a job on the railways. I wanted to be an engine driver. I wanted to be in a loco, travelling to Upper Burma. But I was disappointed. They made us carry coal in baskets on our heads. It was very hard work, you can't imagine – so hot – and the man in charge of us, one Mr Vander, was an Anglo-Indian. He shouted at us, of course, all the time; fifteen minutes for lunch and he still shouted. He was a fat man and not kind to us at all. There were a lot of Anglo-Indians on the railway then. I should say most of them were Anglo-Indians. I imagined I would be driving a loco and here I was carrying coal! The work was too much for me, so I ran away.

'I liked my next job very much. This was in the kitchen of

the officers' mess in the Royal Artillery. I still have some of the
certificates, with *RA* written on them. I helped the cook at first
and later became a cook myself. The cook's name was Stewart
and he showed me how to cut vegetables in various ways and
how to make salad, fruit cup, the trifle, and all the different
kinds of joints. It was nineteen twelve then, and that was the
best time in Burma. It will never be nice like that again. There
was plenty of food, things were cheap, and even after the First
World War started things were still fine. We never knew about the
First World War in Burma; we heard nothing – we didn't feel it. I
knew a little bit about it because of my brother. He was fighting
in Basra – I'm sure you know it – Basra, in Mesopotamia.

'At that time I was getting twenty-five rupees a month. It
doesn't sound so much, does it? But, do you know, it only cost
me ten rupees to live – I saved the rest and later I bought a farm.
When I went for my pay I collected one gold sovereign and a
ten-rupee bank note. A gold sovereign was worth fifteen rupees.
But to show you how cheap things were, a shirt cost four annas,
food was plentiful, and life was very good. I married and had
four children. I was at the officers' mess from nineteen twelve
until nineteen forty-one, when the Japanese came. I loved doing
the work. The officers all knew me and I believe they respected
me. They only got cross if something was late. Everything had
to be done on time, and of course if it wasn't – if there was a
delay – they were very angry. But not a single one was cruel to
me. After all, they were officers – British officers, you know –
and they had a good standard of behaviour. Throughout that
time, whenever they ate, they wore full-dress uniforms, and
there were sometimes guests or wives in evening dress, black
ties, and the ladies wore gowns. Beautiful as moths. I had a
uniform, too, white jacket, black tie, and soft shoes – you know
the kind of soft shoes. They make no noise. I could come into
a room and no one could hear me. They don't make those shoes
anymore, the kind that are noiseless.

'Things went on this way for some years. I remember one

night at the mess. General Slim was there. You know him. And Lady Slim. They came into the kitchen. General and Lady Slim and some others, officers and their wives.

'I stood to attention.

' "You are Bernard?" Lady Slim asked me.

'I said, "Yes, Madam."

'She said it was a good meal and very tasty. It was glazed chicken, vegetables, and trifle.

'I said, "I am glad you liked it."

' "That is Bernard," General Slim said, and they went out.

'Chiang Kai-shek and Madame Chiang came as well. He was very tall and did not speak. I served them. They stayed for two days – one night and two days. And the viceroy came – that was Lord Curzon. So many people came – the Duke of Kent, people from India, and another general – I will think of his name.

'Then the Japanese came. Oh, I remember that very well! It was like this. I was standing in the bush near my house – outside Maymyo, where the road forks. I wore a singlet and a *longyi*, as the Burmese do. The car was so huge, with a flag on the bonnet – the Japanese flag, rising sun, red and white. The car stopped at the fork. I didn't think they could see me. A man called me over. He said something to me in Burmese.

'I said, "I speak English."

' "You are Indian?" says this Japanese gentleman. I said yes. He put his hands together like this and said, "India–Japan. Friends!" I smiled at him. I had never been to India in my life.

'There was a very high official in the car. He said nothing, but the other man said, "Is this the road to Maymyo?"

'I said it was. They drove on, up the hill. That was how the Japanese entered Maymyo.

'My wife was dead. In nineteen forty-one I remarried and had three more sons, John Henry, Andrew Paul, and, in nineteen forty-five, Victor. Victor, you know, because the war was over. I tried to retire. I was getting old, but the Burmese government called me back whenever there was a dinner – to Mandalay.

I have not been to Rangoon since nineteen twenty-four or twenty-five, though I have been to Mandalay many times. I am coming from there now. There was a dinner two nights back, a large joint, two vegetables. Not as fancy as the Victory Dinner. I had full charge of the Victory Dinner in nineteen forty-five – for two hundred people. We started off with cream vegetable soup, then salmon mayonnaise, and roast chicken, vegetables, potatoes roast and boiled, and sauce. To finish there was sundae trifle and savory. Well, a savory might be anything, but on that occasion it was "Devils on Horseback". You wrap bacon and cheese around a piece of toast and fix it with a toothpick. They were all happy at the Victory Dinner. I worked hard and they all enjoyed it. Ah, this is Maymyo.'

There were houses upraised on poles, splashed with red, like festival ribbons fluttering from branches – these were poinsettia bushes, some eight feet high. Then, after a temple and monastery, whose wood was so weathered it had the look of tarnished bronze, more buildings appeared, a row of shop houses, a theatre, a mosque on a wide muddy street. The station had a wide unpaved platform, and, as it was still drizzling, parts of it were under water and the rest had been trampled into a porridge of muck.

Mr Bernard said, 'Where are you putting up?'

I said I didn't have the slightest idea.

'Then you should come to Candacraig,' he said. 'I am the manager – shall I book you in?'

'Yes,' I said. 'I'll be along later – I have to buy a ticket to Gokteik.'

Looking for the ticket office, I stumbled into the radio operator's room where a bearded Eurasian with a yellow cravat and slicked-down hair was seated, listening to Morse code and scribbling on a pad. He looked at me and jumped up, reaching for my hand. 'Is there anything I can do for you?'

The Morse code continued. I said perhaps he'd better listen to it.

'It's not very important,' he said.

I noticed the pad, pencilled with Burmese characters.

'Are they sending you Burmese Morse code?'

'Why not?' He explained that there were thirty-six letters in Burmese, but that occasionally they used English Morse code.

'How do you know whether they're sending Burmese or English?'

'Say you're getting Burmese. It goes on for a while. Then you get twelve dots. That means English is coming. Then you get English. Twelve more dots means they're going back into Burmese. See, there's no word for "piston-rod" and "crankshaft" in Burmese. It's interesting.'

He spoke rapidly, with nervous gestures. He was as dark as a Burmese, but had the beaky features and lined face of an Italian peasant.

'Your English is very good.'

'It's my mother tongue!' He said his name was Tony. 'Actually I'm going crazy in this joint. I'm up at Hsipaw, but I came here because the Maymyo chap packed it up. They didn't have a relief, so I'll be here until the nineteenth. My family's at Hsipaw, and I should have been back weeks ago – I've got six kids and they're wondering when I'm coming back. Where are you headed for?'

I told him I wanted to take the train to Gokteik, but I had heard it was forbidden.

'No problem. When do you want to go? Tomorrow? There's a train at seven. Sure, I can get you on it. I suppose you want to see the bridge – it's a nice one. Funny, not many people come up here. About a year ago there was a chap – he was English – heading for Lashio. The soldiers stopped him and put him off the train at Hsipaw. He was in a terrible shape – all disconnected. I told him not to worry. The police came and made a little trouble, but the next day I put him on the train to Lashio and when the police came at nine o'clock I said, "He's in Lashio," so there wasn't anything they could do.'

'Is it against the law to go to Gokteik?'

'Maybe yes, maybe no. No one knows – but I'll get you on the train. Don't worry.'

He walked me out to the forecourt of the station where, in the rain, on that muddy open space, there were about thirty stagecoaches – wooden carriages with faded paint and split shutters, and drivers in wide-brimmed hats and plastic capes flicking stiff whips at blinkered ponies. The ponies were stamping, and many were straining to pull loaded coaches out of the mud – they were overloaded, with boxes and trunks roped to the roof and six faces at the windows. With the steam engine shunting bogies just behind them, the sight of these *gharries* – and the rain and mud, and Burmese bandaged in scarves against the cold – completed the picture of a frontier town. A driver clomped towards me in mud-spattered boots (others wore rubber sandals, and some were barefoot, although all wore heavy overcoats), and Tony told him to take me to Candacraig.

The old man hoisted my bag on to the roof and covered it with a stiff piece of canvas before tying it down. I got into the wooden box and we were away, rocking; I was sitting bolt upright, peering through the rain at the broad streets of Maymyo lined with eucalyptus trees. The crooked wood and brick houses looked ancient and frail in the rain, and at a corner of the main street, before a two-storey wooden house with a covered verandah, a stagecoach was turning, the man whipping the pony as he cantered sideways in the broken road – not a car in sight – whinnying in the rain-darkened town, in the storm's dull gleam on the wet street, before the Chinese shops, SHANGHAI PINMEN and CHARLIE RESTAURANT. It was like a sepia photograph of the Klondike, brown and noiseless, a century old and nothing moving except the blurred black horse wheeling in the foreground.

Candacraig was above the town, on East Ridge, nearly three miles from the station. Here the houses were huge, the bricks reddened in the rain, with slate roofs and towers, the former homes of British civil servants who came to Maymyo when the capital moved there for the summer months. We passed *The Pines, Ridge House*, and *Forest View*; Candacraig was at the top of a little hill, like a mansion in Newport or Eastbourne, with porches and gables and over the door a neatly pruned trellis arch of ivy.

I paid the driver and went inside to a central hall as high as the house. The rooms were ranged along the upper sides of this hall, in a gallery broken by a lyre-shaped double staircase that rose to the gallery's walkway. Beyond a fireplace faced in teak was a bare counter, and the walls were bare, too, the floors gleaming with polish, the bannisters shining; in this large wooden hall there was no ornament. It was empty. It smelled of wax. I rapped on the counter.

A man appeared. I had expected Mr Bernard, but this was a man in thick glasses, neither Burmese nor Indian, with prominent teeth and large fretting hands. (I found out later he was Singhalese, but had been more or less marooned in Upper Burma for thirty years.) He said Mr Bernard had told him I was coming; I was wise to come to Candacraig – the other hotels in Maymyo had no facilities.

'What sort of facilities don't they have?'

'Soap, Uncle.'

'No soap?'

'None, Uncle. And blankets, sheets, towels, food sometimes. They have nothing. A place to lie down but nothing else. Uncle,' he said to Mr Bernard, who was just entering the room, 'I am putting this gentleman in Number Ten.'

Mr Bernard brought me to the room, and then got a shovelful of hot coals and started a fire in my fireplace, talking the whole time about Candacraig. The name was Scottish, the place was really a 'chummery' for unmarried officers of the Bombay–Burma Trading Company, to keep the lads out of trouble in the hot season after months in remote timber estates: here they could take cold showers and play rugby, cricket, and polo. The British

Empire operated on the theory that high altitudes improved morals. Mr Bernard went on talking. The rain hit the windows and I could hear it sweeping across the roof. But the fire was burning bright, and I was in an easy chair, toasting my feet, puffing on my pipe, opening my copy of Browning.

'Would you like a hot bath?' asked the gentle Mr Bernard. 'Very well then, I will send my son up with some buckets. What time would you like dinner? Eight o'clock. Thank you. Would you like a drink? I will find some beer. You see how warm the room is? It is a big room but the fire is nice. What a pity it is so rainy and cold outside. But tomorrow you will take the train to Gokteik. We used to camp there – the Royal Artillery. There will be nothing to eat at Gokteik, but I will make you a good breakfast, and tea will be ready when you come back. Here it is pleasant, but it is only jungle there.'

That night I dined alone, by candlelight, at an enormous table. Mr Bernard had laid my place near the hearth. He stood some distance away, saying nothing, gliding over from time to time to fill my glass or bring another course. I think I am as intrepid as the next man, but I have a side – and it may be the same side that is partial to trains – that enjoys the journey only because of the agreeable delays en route, a lazy vulgar sybarite searching Asia for comfort, justifying my pleasure by the distance travelled. So I had come 25,000 miles to be here, loafing in Maymyo, warming my bum at the fire, losing my place in 'Bishop Blougram's Apology' each time I was waited on: the only guest in the twenty-room Burmese mansion.

# 19. The Lashio Mail

In an early morning corner of Maymyo, a clearing beyond a pine grove, thirty people were standing at the fragrant teak pews of the Church of the Immaculate Conception and singing the 'Kyrie' from the *Missa di Angelis*. I had crept off the road and passed under the dripping trees towards the sweet imploring chant, the Gregorian High Mass I had learned twenty years before in a summer of idleness and devotion. It was my own youthful voice I heard there, brave with unrisked innocence, aged twelve, asking mercy for some clumsy sin. Out of respect for this little boy I stayed for the Consecration, standing behind a poor Burmese supplicant kneeling on the hard tiles in his bicycle clips. When I left, the priest's quavering 'Pater Noster' drifted with me all the way to the road, where novice monks, children in yellow robes, shaved and barefoot, hurried to their monastery hugging black lacquer bowls.

Travellers to Lashio were converging on the station: a rattling procession of *tongas* and stagecoaches down the avenue of eucalyptus trees; women running with shopping bags, clenching cigars in their teeth, and men dressed as frontiersmen, in boots and black hats, dodging the plodding oxen, who pulled wagonloads of firewood (split and bright, the colour of torn flesh) in the opposite direction. I had left my camera and passport behind; I felt the legality of the trip to Gokteik was questionable and I wanted to appear as unsuspicious a traveller as possible.

Tony, the Eurasian, was waiting for me. He took my three kyats and got me a ticket to Naung-Peng, the station after Gokteik. There was nothing but a bridge at Gokteik, he said, but there was a good canteen at Naung-Peng. We walked down the muddy platform to the last car. Three soldiers in mismatched uniforms – the poor fit indicating they might have been looted in the dark from some tiny enemies – stood outside the car, passing chopped betel nut across the barrels of the rifles they carried loosely at their shoulders. Tony spoke in Burmese to the tallest one, who nodded meaningfully at me. It struck me that their dented helmets and hand-me-down uniforms gave them the grizzled, courageous look you see in embattled legionnaires – a kind of sloppiness that seemed indistinguishable from hard-won experience.

'You will be safe here,' said Tony. 'Ride in this carriage.'

Ten years of guerrilla war in the outlying states of Upper Burma, as well as the persistent depredations of *dacoits* who hold up trains with homemade guns, have meant that the last car on the train is traditionally reserved for a group of armed escorts. They sit in this car, their vintage Enfields thrown higgledy-piggledy on the wooden benches, their woollen earflaps swinging; they lounge, eating bananas, slicing betel nut, reddening the floor with spittle; and they hope for a shot at a rebel or a thief. I was told they seldom have any luck. The rebels are demoralized and don't show their faces; but the thieves, wise to the escorts in the last car, have learned to raid the first few cars quickly, threatening passengers noisily with daggers, and can be safely back in the jungle before the soldiers can run up the line.

Our departure whistle put the crows to flight, and we were off, bowling along the single track. The early morning fog had become fine mist, the mist drizzle, but not even the considerable amount of rain that poured through the windows persuaded any of the soldiers (eating, reading, playfully fighting) to close the shutters. The windows that admitted light admitted rain: you had to choose between that and a dry darkness on upcountry trains. I sat on the edge of my bench, regretting that I hadn't brought anything to read, wondering if it really was illegal for me to be travelling to the Gokteik Viaduct, and feeling pity for the children I saw in soaked clothes splashing through the cold puddles in their bare feet.

Then the train pulled into a siding and stopped. Up ahead was a station, a wooden shed the size of a two-car garage. Its window boxes held the orange and red blossoms the Burmese call 'Maymyo flowers'. Some men in the forward coaches got out to piss. Two small girls ran from the jungle next to the line to sell bananas from enamel basins on their heads. Ten minutes passed, and a man appeared at the window waving a piece of paper, a leaf from the kind of pad on which Tony had scribbled his Morse code messages. This paper was passed to the tall soldier with the Sten gun, who read it out loud in an announcing voice. The other soldiers listened intently; one turned, and, with a swiftness I took to be embarrassment, glanced at me. I got up and walked to the back of the carriage, but before I reached the exit the soldier studying the message – a man who had only smiled apologetically earlier when I asked him if he could speak English – said, 'Sit down please.'

I sat down. A soldier muttered. The rain increased, making a boiling sputter on the roof.

The soldier put down his Sten gun and came over to me. He showed me the message. It was written in pencil, rows and rows of Burmese script that resembled the code in the Sherlock Holmes story 'The Adventure of the Dancing Men'. But in the middle of all the dancing men, those crooked heads and arms, those kicking legs, were two English words in capital letters: 'PASS BOOK'.

'You have pass book?'

'No pass book,' I said.

'Where you going?'

'Gokteik, Naung-Peng,' I said. 'Just for the ride. Who wants to know?'

He thought a moment; then folded the paper over and with the stub of a pencil wrote very carefully in a wobbly column, *Name, Number, Country*, and *Pass book*. He handed me the paper. I gave him the information, while the rest of the soldiers – there were six altogether – gathered around. One peered over my shoulder, sucked his teeth, and said 'American'. The others verified this, putting their heads close and breathing on to my hand.

The message was taken to the wooden shed. I stood up. One of the soldiers said, 'Sit down.'

Two hours passed, the coach dripped, the roof boiled in the downpour, and the soldiers who had been speaking in whispers, perhaps fearing that I knew Burmese, resumed their eating, shelling peanuts, peeling bananas, slicing betel nuts. I don't think time can pass more slowly than in a railway carriage parked in the rain between two low walls of jungle in Upper Burma. There was not even the diversion of hawkers, or the desperate antics of pariah dogs; there were no houses; the jungle was without texture or light; there was no landscape. I sat chilled to the bone watching raindrop rings widen in a pool of water next to the track, and I tried to imagine what had gone wrong. I had no doubt that I was the cause of the delay – there was an objection to my being on the train; I had been seen boarding in Maymyo. I would be sent back; or I might be arrested for violating security regulations, thrown into jail. The effort of getting so far seemed wasted; and, really, had I come all that way to find a jail, as people travel in the greatest discomfort to the farthest ends of the earth, through jungles and bad weather for weeks and weeks, to hurry into a doomed plane or step into the path of a bullet? It is ignominious when a person travels a great distance to die.

It wasn't death that worried me – they wouldn't be silly enough to kill me. But they could inconvenience me. Already they had. It was past ten o'clock, and I was on the point of resigning. If the sun had been out I would have volunteered to walk back to Maymyo, turning the whole fiasco into a hike. But it was raining too hard to do anything but sit and wait.

Finally the tall soldier with the Sten gun returned. He was accompanied by a small fellow, rather young, in a wet jacket and wet hat, who mopped his face with a handkerchief when he got inside the carriage. He said, 'You are Mister Paul?'

'Yes. Who are you?'

'Security Officer U Sit Aye,' he said, and went on to ask when I had entered Burma, and why, and for how long. Then he asked, 'You are a tourist?'

'Yes.'

He thought a moment, tilting his head, narrowing his hooded eyes, and said, 'Then where is your camera?'

'I left it behind,' I said. 'I ran out of film.'

'Yes, we have no film in Burma.' He sighed. 'No foreign exchange.'

As he spoke another train drew up beside the one we were in.

'We will get in that train.'

In the last armed coach of this second train, sitting with a new batch of soldiers, U Sit Aye said he was in charge of railway security; he had three children; he hated the rainy season. He said no more. I assumed he was my escort, and, though I had no idea why we had changed trains, we were on the move, travelling in the direction of Gokteik.

A haggard Burmese man in a woollen cap took a seat across from us and began emptying a filtertip cigarette on to a small square of paper. It was the sort of activity that occupied the foreign residents of Afghanistan hotels, a prelude to filling the empty tube with hashish grains and tobacco. But this man didn't have hashish. His drug, in a small phial, was white powder, which he tapped into the tube, alternating it with layers of tobacco. He stuffed the tube with great care, packing it tight, smoothing and tapping it.

'What's he doing?'

'I do not know,' said U Sit Aye.

The man peered into his cigarette. It was nearly full; he poked it down with a match.

'He's putting something inside.'

'I can see,' said U Sit Aye.

'But it's not *ganja*.'

'No.'

Now the man was finished. He emptied the last of the powder and threw the phial out of the window.

I said, 'I think it's opium.'

The man looked up and grinned. 'You are right!'

His English, clear as a bell, startled me. U Sit Aye said nothing, and as he was not wearing a uniform the man had no way of knowing he was making an opium cigarette under the nose of a security officer.

'Have a puff,' said the man. He twisted the top and licked the whole cigarette so that it would burn slowly. He offered it to me.

'No thanks.'

He looked surprised. 'Why not?'

'Opium gives me a headache.'

'No! *Very* good! I like it –' He winked at U Sit Aye. '– I like it for nice daydreamings!' He smoked the cigarette to the filter, rolled up his jacket, and put it behind his head. He stretched out on the seat and went to sleep with a smile on his face. He was perfectly composed, the happiest man on that cold rattling train.

U Sit Aye said, 'We don't arrest them unless they have a lot. It's so much trouble. We put the chap in jail. We then send a sample to Rangoon for tests – but his is number three; I can tell by the colour – and after two or three weeks they send the report back. You need a lot of opium for the tests – enough for lots of experiments.'

Towards noon we were in the environs of Gokteik. The mist was heavy and noisy waterfalls splashed down through pipe thickets of green bamboo. We crawled around the upper edges of hills, hooting at each curve, but out the windows there was only the whiteness of mist, shifted by a strong wind to reveal the more intense whiteness of cloud. It was like travelling in a slow plane with the windows open, and I envied the opium-smoker his repose.

'The views are clouded,' said U Sit Aye.

We climbed to nearly 4,000 feet and then began descending into the gorge where, below, boat-shaped wisps of cloud moved quickly across from hillside to hillside and other lengths of vapour depended in the gorge with only the barest motion, like veils of threadbare silk. The viaduct, a monster of silver geometry in all the ragged rock and jungle, came into view and then slipped behind an outcrop of rock. It appeared again at intervals, growing larger, less silver, more imposing. Its presence there was bizarre, this manmade thing in so remote a place, competing with the grandeur of the enormous gorge and yet seeming more grand than its surroundings, which were hardly negligible – the water rushing through the girder legs and falling on the tops of trees, the flights of birds through the swirling clouds and the blackness of the tunnels beyond the viaduct. We approached it slowly, stopping briefly at Gokteik Station, where hill people, tattooed Shans and straggling Chinese, had taken up residence in unused railway cars – freight cars and sheds. They came to the doors to watch the Lashio Mail go past.

There were wincing sentries at the entrance to the viaduct with rifles on their shoulders; the wind blew through their wall-less shelters and the drizzle continued. I asked U Sit Aye if I could hang out the window. He said it was all right with him, 'but don't fall.' The train wheels banged on the steel spans and the plunging water roared the birds out of their nests a thousand feet down. The long delay in the cold had depressed me, and the journey had been unremarkable, but this lifted my spirits, crossing the long bridge in the rain, from one steep hill to another, over a jungly deepness, bursting with a river to which the monsoon had given a hectoring voice, and the engine whistling again and again, the echo carrying down the gorge to China.

The tunnels began, and they were cavernous, smelling of bat shit and sodden plants, with just enough light to illuminate the water rushing down the walls and the odd night-blooming flowers growing amid fountains of creepers and leaves in the twisted stone. When we emerged from the last tunnel we were far from the Gokteik Viaduct, and Naung-Peng, an hour more of steady travelling, was the end of the line for me. This was a collection of wooden shacks and grass-roofed shelters. The 'canteen' Tony had told me about was one of these grass-roofed huts: inside was a long table with tureens of green and yellow stew, and Burmese, thinly clad for such a cold place, were warming themselves beside cauldrons of rice bubbling over braziers. It looked like the field kitchen of some Mongolian tribe retreating after a terrible battle: the cooks were old Chinese women with black teeth, and the eaters were that mixed breed of people with a salad of genes drawn from China and Burma, whose only racial clue is their dress, sarong or trousers, parasol coolie hat or woollen cap, damp and shapeless as a mitten. The cooks ladled the stews on to large palm leaves and plopped down a fistful of rice; this the travellers ate with cups of hot weak tea. The rain beat on the roof and crackled on the mud outside, and Burmese hurried to the train with chickens bound so tightly in feather bundles, they looked like a peculiar kind of native handicraft. I bought a two-cent cigar, found a stool near a brazier, and sat and smoked until the next train came.

The train I had taken to Naung-Peng didn't leave for Lashio until the 'down' train from Lashio arrived. Then the escort from Maymyo and the more heavily armed escort from Lashio changed trains in order to return to the places they had set out from that morning. Each train, I noticed, had an armoured van coupled just behind the engine; this was a steel box with gun slits, simplified almost to crudity, like a child's drawing of a tank, but it was empty because all the soldiers were at the end of the train, nine coaches away. How they would fight their way, under fire, eighty yards up the train during a raid, I do not know, nor did U Sit Aye supply an explanation. It was clear why the soldiers didn't travel in the iron armoured van: it was a cruelly uncomfortable thing, and very dark since the gun slits were so small.

The return to Maymyo, downhill most of the way, was quick,

and there was a continuous intake of food at small stations. U Sit Aye explained that the soldiers wired ahead for the food, and it was true, for at the smallest station a boy would rush up to the train as soon as it drew in, and with a bow this child with rain on his face would present a parcel of food at the door of the soldiers' coach. Nearer to Maymyo they wired ahead for flowers, so when we arrived each soldier stepped out with curry stains on his shirt, a plug of betel in his mouth, and a bouquet of flowers, which he clutched with greater care than his rifle.

'Can I go now?' I said to U Sit Aye. I still didn't know whether I was going to be arrested for going through forbidden territory.

'You can go,' he said, and smiled. 'But you must not take the train to Gokteik again. If you do there will be trouble.'

## 20. The Night Express from Nong Khai

THE fast train from Bangkok had taken me to Nong Khai, in the far north of Thailand. Nong Khai is unexceptional – five streets of neat houses; but a boat ride across the Mekong River takes you to Vientiane in Laos. Vientiane is exceptional, but inconvenient. The brothels are cleaner than the hotels, marijuana is cheaper than pipe tobacco, and opium easier to find than a cold glass of beer. Opium is a restful drug, the perfect thing for geriatrics, but the chromatic snooze it induces corrects fatigue; after an evening of it the last thing you want to do is sleep again. When you find the beer at midnight and are sitting quietly, wondering what sort of place this is, the waitress offers to fellate you on the spot, and you still don't know. Your eyes get accustomed to the dark and you see the waitress is naked. Without warning she jumps on to a chair, pokes a cigarette into her vagina and lights it, puffing it by contracting her uterine lungs. So many sexual knacks! You could teach these people anything. There are many bars in Vientiane; the décor and the beer are the same in all of them, but the unnatural practices vary.

The only English film I could find in Vientiane was a pornographic one, and the sombre reverence of the Japanese tourists, who watched like interns in an operating theatre, filled me with despair. I shopped for presents, imagining Laotian treasures, but discovered traditional handicrafts there to include aprons, memo pads, pot-holders, and neckties. Neckties! I tried to take a pleasure cruise on the Mekong, but was told the river was only used by smugglers. The food was unusual. One bowl of soup I had contained whiskers, feathers, gristle, and bits of intestine cut to look like macaroni. I told this to a prince I had been urged to visit. He took me to a restaurant where we had – I suppose it was his way of apologizing – a leg of lamb, mint sauce, and roasted potatoes. I asked him what it was like to be a prince in Laos. He said he couldn't answer that question because he didn't spend much time in Laos; he was mainly interested in skydiving and motor racing. His description of political life convinced me that Laos was really Ruritania, a slaphappy kingdom of warring half-brothers, heavily mortgaged to the United States. But there were enemies in Laos, he said that evening. Where were they? I asked. We were now at his house. He pointed out the window, and across the street, silhouetted in the top window of a three-storey building, was a man with a machine gun. The prince said, 'Him. He's a Pathet Lao.'

'So you're taking the train,' said the prince, when I told him about my trip. 'Do you know how fast that Bangkok train goes?'

I said I had no idea.

'Fifty kilometres an hour!' He made a face.

His wife wasn't listening. She looked up from a magazine and said, 'Don't forget we have to be in Paris on the twenty-sixth –'

Laos, a river bank, had been overrun and ransacked; it was one of America's expensive practical jokes, a motiveless place where nothing was made, everything imported; a kingdom with baffling pretensions to Frenchness. What was surprising was that it existed at all, and the more I thought of it, the more it seemed like a lower form of life, like the cross-eyed planarian or squashy amoeba, the sort of creature that can't die even when it is cut to ribbons.

Setting out from Nong Khai Station (the Thai children were flying kites along the tracks) I was headed south for Singapore. There is an unbroken railway system from this northerly station to Singapore, via Bangkok and Kuala Lumpur, roughly 1,400 miles of jungle, rice fields, and rubber estates. The State Railway of Thailand is comfortable and expertly run, and now I knew enough of rail travel in Southeast Asia to avoid the air-conditioned sleeping cars, which are freezing cold and have

216 The Great Railway Bazaar

none of the advantages of the wooden sleepers: wide berths and a shower room. There is not another train in the world that has a tall stone jar in the bath compartment, where, before dinner, one can stand naked, sluicing oneself with scoops of water. The trains in any country contain the essential paraphernalia of the culture: Thai trains have the shower jar with the glazed dragon on its side, Singhalese ones the car reserved for Buddhist monks, Indian ones a vegetarian kitchen and six classes, Iranian ones prayer mats, Malaysian ones a noodle stall, Vietnamese ones bulletproof glass on the locomotive, and on every carriage of a Russian train there is a samovar. The railway bazaar, with its gadgets and passengers, represented the society so completely that to board it was to be challenged by the national character. At times it was like a leisurely seminar, but I also felt on some occasions that it was like being jailed and then assaulted by the monstrously typical.

In the Night Express from Nong Khai were many Chinese and Filipino mechanics, deeply tanned from working on the American air fields, and wearing their baseball caps pulled down over their eyes. Thais gambled in the second-class sleeper, where American servicemen sat sheepishly with Thai girls, looking homesick but very proper as they held hands. I was in a compartment with an American civilian who said he was a salesman. He didn't look like a salesman. His hair was cut so short, I could see a white scar that ran along the top of his head from back to front like a part; he had a Thai charm around his neck and broken fingernails; on the back of his right hand was tattooed TIGER, and he talked continually of his 'hog', a Harley-Davidson Electraglide. He had been in Thailand for five years. He had no plans to go back to the States, and said it was his ambition to make $30,000 a year – or, as he put it, 'thirty K'.

'How close are you to that figure?'

'Pretty close,' he said. 'But I think I might have to go to Hong Kong.'

He had just spent a few days in Vientiane. I said I had found the place not exactly to my taste. He said, 'You should have gone to the White Rose.'

'I went to the White Rose,' I said.

'Did you see a tall girl there?'

'It was too dark to tell who was tall or short.'

'This one was wearing clothes. Most of them were bare-ass, right? But this one had long hair and slacks. The rest of them were putting cigarettes in their cats and puffing on them, but this one just comes over and sits down next to me. She wasn't wearing a bra and she had those nice tits models have. I offered her a beer, but she had a Pepsi and funnily enough I wasn't charged extra for it. I liked that!

'We sat there sort of fooling and I put my hand inside her blouse and gave her a honk. She laughs. "You want massage?" she says. I says forget it. They don't mean massage. Then she says, "Come upstairs – you give mama-san four dollars and she let me."

' "What happens when we go upstairs?"

'She leans over. She says, "Anything. Anything you want to do to me, you can do. Anything you want me to do, I do. I know how." Does this give me a hard-on or what?

'What if a beautiful girl – I mean, a real piece of ass – said that to you? "Do anything you want to me." It's like having a slave. I thought of two or three things – crazy things; I wouldn't even tell you. She's saying, "What? What?" I'm too embarrassed to tell her, but I'm thinking, She's making a bargain and she can't back out of it. I keep thinking these wild things and saying, "Anything?" and she says, "Sure, what you want?" But I didn't want to say.

'Then she says, "Tell me." I says, "I'll tell you upstairs," and I go over to the mama-san, a real hard-faced bitch, and give her four bucks. Then we go upstairs. Her name was Oy. She takes off her blouse, and she's got these fantastic knockers and this beautiful brown back. She says, "What you want?" I says, "Any-thing?" She says, "For five dollars – anything." '

'I gives her a fin and she takes my clothes off and starts washing my process and asking me if I've got the clap. The washing sort of turns me on and I tell her to hurry up. So she turns off the light and pushes me back on the bed, and God I've never been gobbled like that in my life. Her tongue's whirling around and I'm practically fainting. But I pulled it out before I came. *Now what?* I had these oddball ideas and I just said the first thing that came into my head. "Turn over," I says. "I want to piss on you."

' "Okay," she said. *Okay!* She gets down on the bed and I knelt over her. But I couldn't do it — I don't think I really wanted to — so I started screwing her ass for all it was worth. I came and rolled her over and that's when I slid my hand up her thigh and touched the biggest process I've ever — Look, I don't want to ruin your dinner.'

'I think I've heard that one before,' I said, as we passed down the train to the dining car.

'No, no,' said Tiger. 'You don't understand.'

We each had a Singha Beer. I ordered fried rice with prawns and mixed vegetables, and outside was the perfectly flat, unwrinkled Khorat Plateau. Tiger had been drinking whisky in the compartment and by the time the food came he looked a bit drunk; his face was flushed and even the scar on the top of his head was slightly rosy.

'You've heard the story, right? The girl that turns out to be a guy, right?' He began to eat. 'Well, this isn't the same story. Sure I panicked and she laughed — or *he* laughed. He says, "Don't you like girls?" and gives me a really horrible smile in the dark. I puts my clothes on — I'm dying to get out of there. But downstairs in the bar I decide to have another beer. I sit down and Oy comes over again. He says, "You don't like me." I buys him another Pepsi and by then I'm kind of calm. "I like you," I says and — believe it or not — I give him a kiss on the cheek. I mean, don't get me wrong. This wasn't really a man — it was a girl with a prick! It was fantastic. You probably think

I'm nuts – I know this sounds screwy – but if I go to Vientiane again I'll probably go over to the White Rose and if Oy is there I'll probably – yeah, I probably *will*!'

Sometime during the night, Tiger left the train. I woke to an empty compartment at six in the morning, and, snapping up the window shade, saw that we were moving quickly past black *klongs* to a city of temples and square buildings coloured pink by the sunrise. But the light was brief. It turned sickly, then dimmed to greyness, and we arrived shortly afterwards at Bangkok Station in a heavy rain.

WHEN the American troops left Vietnam and all the Rest and Recreation programmes ended it was thought that Bangkok would collapse. Bangkok, a hugely preposterous city of temples and brothels, required visitors. The heat, the traffic, the noise, the cost in this flattened anthill make it intolerable to live in; but Bangkok, whose discomfort seems a calculated discouragement to residents, is a city for transients. Bangkok has managed to maintain its massage-parlour economy without the soldiers, by advertising itself as a place where even the most diffident foreigner can get laid. So it prospers. After the early morning Floating Market Tour and the afternoon Temple Tour, comes the evening Casanova Tour. Patient couples, many of them very elderly, wearing yellow badges saying *Orient Escapade*, are herded off to sex shows, blue movies, or 'live shows' to put them in the mood for a visit later the same evening – if they're game – to a whorehouse or a massage parlour. As Calcutta smells of death and Bombay of money, Bangkok smells of sex, but this sexual aroma is mingled with the sharper whiffs of death and money.

Bangkok has an aspect of violation; you see it in the black jammed *klongs*, the impassable streets that are convulsed with traffic, and in the temples: every clumsy attempt to repair the latter seems to have been initiated by tourists rather than worshippers. There is a brisk trade in carvings and artifacts stolen from temples upcountry, and this rapacity – new to the once serene Thais – is encouraged by most of the resident foreigners. It is as if these expatriate *farangs* expect a kind of repayment for the misery of having to live in such an insufferable place. The Thais muddle along, as masseuses and marauders, but a month before I arrived several thousand Thai students (who described themselves rather curiously as 'revolutionary monarchists') marched on the police headquarters, brought down the government, and in the space of an afternoon managed to destroy seven fairly large buildings downtown. It was, like the patchy regilding of the recumbent Buddha, a popular violation, and now the street of gutted buildings is included in the Temple Tour: 'Over here you will see where our students burned –'

The railway station is not on any of the tours, which is a shame. It is one of the most carefully maintained buildings in Bangkok. A neat cool structure, with the shape and Ionic columns of a memorial gym at a wealthy American college, it was put up in 1916 by the Western-oriented King Rama V. The station is orderly and uncluttered, and, like the railway, it is run efficiently by men in khaki uniforms who are as fastidious as scoutmasters competing for good-conduct badges.

It was dark when the south-bound International Express (so called because it penetrated Malaysia to Butterworth) left the station. In the *klongs* Thai children were floating banana-leaf boats, with jasmine rigging and masts of flickering candles for the *Loy Krathong* festival. We rolled along under a full moon, which was the occasion for the festival, the lunar fluorescence mellowing the suburbs of Bangkok and giving to the Chao Phraya River a slippery sweetness that persisted until the wind changed. Fifteen minutes out of Thonburi, on the opposite bank – once the capital – the countryside and all its crickets rushed swiftly up to the train and we were swept with sighing grass.

Mr Thanoo, the aged traveller in my compartment, sat reading *Colonel Sun*, by Kingsley Amis. He said he had been saving it for the trip, and I didn't want to interrupt him in his reading. I went into the corridor. A Thai, about forty, with thinning hair and an engaging grin, said hello. He introduced himself: 'Call me Pensacola. It's not my name – my name is too hard for you to say. Are you a teacher?'

'Sort of,' I said. 'What about you?'

'You could call me a traveller,' he said. Out the window,

Thais wearing hats like inverted baskets were paddling canoes in the streams that ran next to the tracks. The lanterns on their narrow boats lighted the rippling water and clouds of gnats. 'I just travel here and there.'

'Where do you get your money?'

'Here and there. Out of the air; out of the ground.' He spoke playfully, with a laugh in his throat, in a tone of knowing vagueness.

'Out of the ground? So you're a farmer.'

'No! Farmers are silly.'

'Perhaps you don't have any money,' I said.

'Plenty!'

He laughed and turned, and now I noticed that he was holding a pouch under his arm. It was about the size of a squashed shoe box and he held it quite close to his side, almost in concealment.

'Where does your money come from, Mr Pensacola?'

'Someplace!'

'Is it a secret?'

'I don't know, but I always get it. I've been to your country three times. What state are you from?'

'Massachusetts.'

'Boston,' he said. 'I've been there. I thought it was so dull. Boston is a very sad place. The nightclubs! I went to all the nightclubs in Boston. They were awful. I had to leave. I even went to Negro nightclubs. I didn't care – I was prepared to fight, but they thought I was Puerto Rican, something like that. Negroes are supposed to be happy and smiling with teeth, but even the Negro nightclubs are awful. So I went to New York, Washington, Chicago, and, let's see, Texas and –'

'You've certainly been around.'

'They took me everywhere. I never paid anything – just enjoying, looking, and what and what.'

'Who took you?'

'Some people. I know so many people. Maybe I'm famous. The other day in Bangkok the head of USAID rang me up.

Someone must have told him about me. He said to me, "Come to lunch – I'll pay for everything." I said, "Okay, I don't care." So we went. It must have cost him a lot of money. I didn't care. I was talking about what and this and that. At the end of the lunch he said to me, "Pensacola, you're fantastic!"'

'Why did he say that?'

'I don't know; maybe he liked me.' He grinned and his hair was so sparse the grin and the movement of his malicious eyes caused his whole scalp to crawl with wrinkles. Each time he said 'I don't know', he smacked his lips, as if inviting another question. He said, 'The other day I took the train up to Bangkok. There was a suitcase on the seat of my compartment. I threw it on the floor.'

'Why did you do that?'

'I don't know. Maybe because it was on my seat. I didn't care. But I was going to say: the suitcase belonged to a police captain.'

'Did he see you throw it on the floor?'

'Why not? We Thais have good eyesight.'

'I'll bet he wasn't very happy.'

'Was cross! "Who are you?" he said to me. "A traveller," I said. "What do you do?" "Travel." He got very annoyed and asked me for my ID card, "*No ID Card!*" Later on he went to bed – I made him take the upper berth. But he couldn't sleep. All night he was tossing back and forth. Holding his head, and what and what.'

'I guess you upset him.'

'I don't know. Something like that. He was trying to think who I am.'

'I'm trying to think the same thing.'

'Go ahead,' said Mr Pensacola. 'I don't mind. I like Americans. They saved my life. I was up in the north, where they grow poppies for opium and heroin. So-called "golden triangle". I was stuck, and all the guys were shooting at me. They sent a plane for me, but it couldn't land in all the shooting, so they sent a helicopter. I looked up and saw three choppers circling around. I was shooting at the guys behind the tree – I was all alone; it wasn't easy. One chopper tried to land, but the guys shot at him. So I went across and shot one of the guys and the other chopper landed on the cliff. He was calling to me, "Pensacola, come on!" But I didn't want to go. I don't know why. Maybe I wanted to kill some more. So I kept still and moved closer and I killed – what? – maybe two more. Chinese. I was still shooting and I crawled over to the chopper –'

His extraordinary story, told in a mocking monotone, continued. He held off the gang of opium smugglers; he gunned down two more; and inside the helicopter he reloaded and murdered the rest of them from the air. When he finished I said, 'That's quite a story.'

'Maybe. If you think so.'

'I mean, you must be a pretty good shot.'

'Champion.' He shrugged.

But things had gone far enough. I said, 'Look, you don't expect me to believe all this, do you?'

'I don't know. Maybe.'

'I think you read it in a book, but not a very good book.'

'You Americans,' said Mr Pensacola. He beckoned me into his compartment and stood showing me the bulging pouch he had been carrying under his arm. He tapped it. 'It's a cheap one, right?'

'Maybe,' I said. 'I don't know.'

'Plastic,' he said and, before he pulled the flap open, he said, 'Don't be afraid. Peek inside.'

I leaned over and saw two pistols, a large black one and a smaller one in a holster, both nesting in a jumble of brass bullets. Pensacola gave me a wolfish grin, and, snapping the hasps of the pouch, said, 'A thirty-eight and a twenty-two. But don't tell anyone, will you?'

'What are you doing with two pistols?' I whispered.

'I don't know,' he said, and winked. He tucked the pouch

under his arm and walked down to the dining car, where I saw him later in the evening, drinking Mekong whisky, deep in conversation with two red-faced Chinese.

A rumour went through the train that we would be held up at Hua Hin, about 120 miles south of Bangkok, on the Gulf of Siam. It was said that the rains had swollen a river to a point where it was threatening a bridge on the line. But the train showed no signs of slowing down, and there was no rain yet. The moon lighted the flooded rice fields, making them depthless, and the water to the horizon made this stage of the journey like sailing across an unruffled sea.

Mr Thanoo said, 'Why are you reading a sad book?'

He had seen the cover: *Dead Souls*. I said, 'It's not sad at all. It's one of the funniest books I've ever read.'

He offered me a cigarette and lit it. 'I am sorry for this cigarette. It is of inferior quality. Do you say "inferior quality"? I don't talk English so well. My circle is all Thai people and they always want to talk in Thai. I say, "An incident happened to me today which was very surprising," and they say, "No English!" I need practice – I make too many mistakes, but I used to talk very well. That was in Penang. I am not a Malay, though. I am pure Thai, through and through.

'How old do you think I am? I am sixty-five. Not so old, but older than you, I think. I come from a well-educated family. My father, for example. He was educated in England – London. London. He was Lord Lieutenant of Penang – same as governor. So I received my schooling there. It was called the Anglo-Chinese School, but now it is the Methodist School. They have high standards.'

One thing I had regretted in my conversation with Mr Bernard on the train to Maymyo was that I hadn't asked him specific questions about his subjects at St Xavier's at the turn of the century in Mandalay. I did so with Mr Thanoo.

'English was my favourite subject,' said Mr Thanoo. 'I studied geography – Brazil, Ecuador, Canada. Also history – English history. James the First. Battle of Hastings. Also chemistry. Tin is Sn. Silver is Ag. Copper Cu. I used to know gold but I have forgotten. I liked English literature best of all. My masters were Mr Henderson, Mr B. L. Humphries, Mr Beach, Mr R. F. MacDonald. And others. The books I liked most? *Treasure Island*. And *Micah Clarke*, by Conan Doyle, author of Sherlock Holmes stories. *Tale of Two Cities* was very interesting, and *The Poison Island*, by Lord Tennyson – a kind of dream. And Wordsworth. I like Wordsworth still. And Shakespeare. The best Shakespeare play is *Like It or Not*. I hope you have read it. *David Copperfield* – about a poor boy who is mistreated by people – that was very sad. He worked hard and he fell in love. I can't remember the girl's name. *A Tale of Two Cities* is about France and England. Sidney Carton. He was a kind of genius, and he suffered. Who else? Let me see. I like Edgar Wallace, but best of all is Luke Short. Cowboy writer.

'I live on the island of Phuket, a very small place. People laugh at me when they see me reading English books on my island. What is that old man bluffing? Why is he pretending to read his English books? But I like to. You see this book, *Colonel Sun*? I thought it was a good one, but it is useless –'

As Mr Thanoo spoke the train came to a halt, nearly dumping us on the floor of the carriage. It had stopped with the suddenness that presages a long delay, but I looked out the window and saw that we were at Hua Hin: it was a scheduled stop. A breeze brought the sea air into the compartment, which became heavy with dampness and salt and the smell of fish. The station building at Hua Hin was a high wooden structure with a curved roof and wooden ornamentations in the Thai style – obsolete for Bangkok, but just the thing for this small resort town, empty in the monsoon season. The arrival of the International Express was something of an event: the stationmaster and signalmen approached us sombrely, and the rickshaw drivers left their vehicles parked in the palm-fringed forecourt of the station and stood on one leg, like cranes, to watch the passengers receive the news of the threatened bridge. Estimates for the delay, given in round figures, ranged from two to eight hours. If the bridge were washed away we might be at Hua Hin for a day or two. Then we could all go swimming in the gulf.

There was, on the International Express, a team of Chinese girl gymnasts and acrobats from Taiwan, who drove the other passengers wild by appearing in the dining car in flimsy flapping pyjamas. At Hua Hin they skipped on the platform, holding hands and laughing: they wore heavy make-up, including mascara and lipstick, with the pyjamas – an effective combination. They were eyed by little groups of passengers, who stopped grumbling when they danced past. I bought a quarter of a pound of cashews (for ten cents) and watched an old lady roasting squid over a brazier she had set up next to the train. Still chattering about the delay, people bought these and ate them gloomily, as if studying survival, tossing the burned tentacles on to the track.

One of the squid-eaters was Mr Lau, from Kuala Lumpur. He wasn't hungry, but he explained that he was eating the squid because they were so expensive in Kuala Lumpur. He was morose about the delay. He didn't have a berth. He asked how much I had paid for mine and seemed annoyed that my fare was so low; he behaved as if, by some devious stratagem, I had taken his bed from him. He hated his seat. The chair car was too cold; the passengers were rude; the girl gymnasts wouldn't talk to him. He said, 'In Malaysia I'm a second-class citizen, and in Thailand I'm a second-class passenger. Ha! Ha!'

Mr Lau was a purveyor of fluorescent tubes. He was also a civil servant ('Maybe you could say fluorescent tubes is my sideline'). He had been introduced to the business by his father-in-law, a clever man who had emigrated from Shanghai to Hong Kong, where he had learned how to make neon signs. Mr Lau said, 'You can make a fortune in neon signs in Hong Kong.'

I said I was sure of that.

'But there was heavy competition. So the old man came to K.L.' At first there were no competitors, then the fellow

Shanghainese he had trained to make the signs left him and set up shops of their own. They almost ran him out of business, until the old man began training Malays to do the work. He had chosen Malays and not the harder-working Indians or Chinese because he could depend on the Malays to be too lazy to quit and start establishments of their own.

'What brought you to Bangkok?' I asked.

'Fluorescent tubes.'

'Buying or selling?'

'Buying-*lah*. Cheaper.'

'How much cheaper?'

'I don't know. I got to work out the costing. It's all in my briefcase.'

'Give me a rough idea.'

'A hundred fifty models-*lah*! I haven't worked out the packing, transport, what-not. So many cost factors.'

I liked the lingo, but Mr Lau changed the subject, and, munching his squid, he told me how awful it was to be a Chinese in Malaysia. He had been passed over a dozen times and missed promotions and pay increments because 'the government wants to bring up the Malays. It's terrible. I don't like the light business but they're driving me further and further into fluorescent tubing.'

I went to bed while the train was still standing in the glare of the station lights, and at 3.10 the next morning (the whistle woke me) we began to move. Rain poured through the window, waking me again an hour later, and when I slammed down the shutter the room became suffocating and airless. We crossed the endangered bridge in the dark, and at dawn it was still raining. The line was so flooded all the next day we travelled at a crawl, sometimes stopping in the middle of nowhere, with flooded fields all around, like a becalmed boat. I sat and wrote: I read and went to sleep; I drank; and often I would look up and be incapable of remembering where I was, the concentration of writing or reading bringing on a trancelike state. Extensive

travelling induces a feeling of encapsulation; and travel, so broad-
ening at first, contracts the mind. It had happened briefly on
other trains, but on this one – it might have been prolonged by
the sameness of the landscape or the steady beating of the rain –
it lasted an entire day. I couldn't recall what day it was; I had
forgotten the country. Being on the train had suspended time;
the heat and dampness had slowed my memory. What day was
it anyway? Where were we? Outside there were only rice fields,
giving an alarming view of Maharashtra, in India. The station
signboards gave no clue: CHUMPHON and LANG SUAN moved
past the window, leaving me baffled. It was a long day in the
hot wet train with the sweating Thais, whom the heat had
moved to rapid speech. Pensacola had disappeared, and so had
Mr Thanoo. The conductor said we were ten hours late, but
this did not worry me as much as my failing memory and a kind
of squinting fear I took to be an intimation of paranoia. The
jungle was thick past Haadyai, perfect for an ambush (a month
later, on 10 December, five bandits with M16 rifles leaped out
of the second-class toilets where they had been hiding, robbed
seventy people, and vanished). After the passport control at
Padang Besar I locked the door of my compartment, and, though
it was only nine o'clock, went to bed.

A rattling of the door handle woke me. The train was not
moving. The room was hot. I slid the door open and saw a
Malay with a wet mop. He said, 'This is Butterworth.'

'I think I'll sleep here until the morning train comes.'

'Cannot,' he said. 'Have to wash the train.'

'Go ahead, wash it. I'll go back to sleep.'

'We don't wash it here. Have to take it to the shed.'

'What am I supposed to do in the meantime?'

'Mister,' said the little Malay, 'I want you to get out and
hurry up.'

I had slept through the arrival. It was two in the morning:
the train was empty; the station was deserted. I found a waiting
room, where two German men and two Australians, a boy and

girl, were sleeping in chairs. I sat down and opened *Dead Souls*. The Australian boy woke up and folded and refolded his legs, sighing. Then he said, 'Oh Christ!' and took his shirt off. He crumpled his shirt into a ball and got on to the cement floor, and, using the shirt as a pillow, curled up like a koala bear and began to snore. The Australian girl looked at me and shrugged, as if to say, 'He always does that!' She put her fists into her lap and crouched in her chair, the way people die in sparsely furnished rooms. The Germans woke and immediately started to argue over a map on which they were marking a route. It was then about four o'clock in the morning. When I couldn't bear it any longer I took a hooting ferry to Penang, returning to Butterworth as dawn broke; then everything was painted in simple colours, the ferry orange, the water pink, the island blue, the sky green. Minutes later the sun burned the vaporous colours away. I had breakfast at a Tamil coffee shop, milky tea and an egg scrambled with a doughy square of *paratha*. Strolling back to the station I saw a man and woman leaving a disreputable hotel. The unshaven man was European and wore a T-shirt; the rumpled woman, powdering her nose as she walked, was Chinese. They hurried into a very old car and drove away. The melancholy cliché of this tropical adultery – the scuttling pair in the Malaysian morning – had a comic aptness that put me in a good mood.

## 22. The Golden Arrow to Kuala Lumpur

THE two classes on Malaysian Railways include eight different varieties of carriage, from the simple cattle car with wooden benches to the teak-panelled sleeper with its wide berths, arm-chair, brass spittoon, and green curtains decorated with the railway motif (a tiger, rampant, savaging a dowsing rod). But the best place to ride on this ten-hour trip to Kuala Lumpur is on the wooden balcony between the coaches. This windy space, where the verandah of one car meets the verandah of the other, is about seven feet long: there are overhanging roofs at each end, and on either side are balusters and railings. A brass plate warns you in three languages of the dangers on this speeding porch – in fact, you are expressly forbidden to ride there – but it is quite safe, and that day it was certainly safer there than in the lounge car, where five Malay soldiers were getting drunk on Anchor beer and abusing the Chinese who passed by them. I had been in the lounge car reading, but when the soldiers had overcome their native shyness with drink and began singing 'Ten Green Bottles', I decided to move to the balcony. Just inside the car a Chinese man had crammed himself into a luggage rack, where he was sulking, and below me, on the verandah stairs, Malay boys clung, swinging their feet.

High world prices for rubber, tin, and palm oil have made Malaysia prosperous, and it seemed as relaxed and unaggressive a place as when I had first seen it, in 1969. But the Malay smile is misleading: it was shortly after I decided that it was one of the quietest countries in the world that Malays came howling out of mosques with white rags tied around their heads. When they were through, 2,000 Chinese lay dead and hundreds of shops had been burned to the ground. Mr Lau, who in Thailand had been strolling through the train complaining loudly about the ten-hour delay, was now seated uneasily in the Golden Arrow, hugging his briefcase, with his box of fragile samples between his knees. And the girl gymnasts from Taiwan were no longer limbering up in the corridors. The Chinese had fallen silent: it was a Malay train, and it would have been unthinkable for a group of Chinese to be in the lounge car, singing (as the Malay soldiers were) 'Roll Me Over in the Clover'. A Malay in third class was more privileged than a Chinese in first.

For lunch I had my old favourite, *mee-hoon* soup with a partly poached egg whisked in among the Chinese cabbage, meat scraps, prawn slices, bean sprouts, rice noodles, and a number of other atomized ingredients that thicken it to the point where it can be eaten with chopsticks. There were no tables in the dining car, which was a noodle stall; there were sticky counters and stools, and Chinese sitting elbow to elbow, shaking soy sauce over their noodles and calling out to the waiters, little boys in red clogs, carrying beer bottles on tin trays.

Ipoh, the first major stop on the Kuala Lumpur run, has a station hotel, a late Victorian Gormenghast with long windows covered by sombre curtains. The brown drapery hangs in thick folds, keeping out the breeze and preserving the heat, which is paddled around the dining room by ten slow fans. All the tables are set, and the waiter, who might be dead, is propped against the wall at the far end of the room. It is fairly certain there is a suicide upstairs waiting to be discovered, and the flies that soar through the high-ceilinged bar are making for the corpse of this ruined planter or disgraced *towkay*. It is the sort of hotel that has a skeleton in every closet and a register thick with the pseudo-nyms of adulterers. I once walked into the station hotel at Ipoh with my little boy, and as soon as we crossed the threshold he began to cry. His innocent nose had smelled what mine couldn't, and I rushed away with him, relieved, savouring the well-being of deliverance.

I remained on a balcony of the Golden Arrow, listening to

the excited talk of the passengers. English is spoken in Malaysia in a nasal bark, a continual elision of words; phrases are spat and every word-ending is bitten. It is a pared-down version of English and sounds for all the world like Chinese until one's ear is tuned to it by the din of jungle sounds next to the track, the squawks of locusts and macaws, and monkeys cleaning their teeth on twanging strips of bamboo. This brand of English is devoid of every emotion but whispered hysteria; it drones in excellent contrast to Malay, which to hear – the gliding dupli-cation for the plural and the constant gong of words like *pisang, kachang, sarong* – is almost to understand. The Malayanized Eng-lish, used in conversation and seen on station notice boards, is easily grasped: *feri-bot, jadual, setesyen, tiket, terafik*, and *nombor*.

Two Indians crept out to the balcony. Their size (very small) and their demeanor (fearful) said at once they were not of Malaysia. They had the slightly reptilian features of the hungriest people I'd seen in Calcutta. The other travellers on the balcony, mostly Malays, made way for them, and the Indians stood, the turbulence blowing the wrinkles out of their suit jackets, chatting softly in their own language. The stations raced by: Bidor, Trolak, Tapah, and Klang – names like science fiction planets – and more frequently rubber estates intruded on jungle, a sym-metry of scored trunks and trodden paths hemmed in by classic jungle, hanging lianas, palms like fountains, and a smothering undergrowth of noisy greenery all dripping in the rain. 'We mine tin in Thailand and Malaya, just like Cornwall in Great Britain,' Mr Thanoo had said on the International Express, and here were the battered huts, the rickety conveyor belts that looked like abandoned ski jumps, the smokestacks, and the little hills of washed soil.

'Industry,' said one of the Indians.

'But not vorking,' said the other.

'But not vorking,' said a Malay boy, mimicking the Indians for his friends. They all laughed. The Indians fell silent.

Towards the end of the afternoon the balcony emptied. The

sallow light just pierced the haze, and the air had gone stale; it was damp and hot. When the train stopped the air blanketed my shoulders. The Malays had gone inside to sleep, or perhaps to prowl for girls. It was the durian season, and this fruit, to which the Malays ascribe aphrodisiac properties, has inspired the Malay saying: 'When the durians come down the sarongs go up.'

Then there were only the two Indians and me on the balcony. They were taking a holiday – this was the end of it – having spent the previous week at a conference in Singapore. They were from Bangladesh; their names were Ghosh and Rahman; it was a family-planning conference.

'Are you family planners?'

'We are officers,' said Mr Rahman.

'Of course we have other jobs,' said Mr Ghosh, 'but we went to the conference as family-planning officers.'

'Did you read papers?'

'We were observers,' said Mr Ghosh. 'Others read papers.'

'Interesting?'

They waggled their heads; this meant yes.

'Many papers,' said Mr Rahman. ' "The Two-Child Family as a Social Norm", "Methods of Contraception", also sterilization, wasectomy, dewices, fitting IUD –'

'Some good discussion,' said Mr Ghosh. 'It was a seminar covering all aspects of family planning. Practical, very informative of course. But there are many problems.'

'What do you think is the greatest problem in family planning?'

'Without a doubt, communication,' said Mr Ghosh.

'In what way?'

'Rural areas,' said Mr Rahman. I thought he was going to add something to this observation, but he stroked his Vandyke beard and gazed off the balcony and said, 'So many girls on motor scooters in this country.'

I said, 'Now, you've been to the conference, right? And I suppose you're going back to Bangladesh –'

'Back to Singapore, then Bangkok by air, then Dacca,' said Mr Ghosh.

'Right. But when you get back there – I mean, you've heard all these papers about family planning – what are you going to do?'

'Ghosh?' said Rahman, inviting his colleague to reply.

Mr Ghosh cleared his throat. He said, 'There are many problems. I should say first we will start straightaway on curriculum. Curriculum is most important. We must build a model – work with a model of aims and objectives. What are we trying to do? What do we aim to achieve? And why? And costings must be considered. All those questions: answers must be found. Do you follow me?' He cleared his throat again. 'Then, next important, is areas of information' – he spread his hands to suggest the size of the areas – 'that is, we must create areas of information so that ordinary people can understand importance of our work.'

'Where are you going to do this?'

'In universities,' said Mr Ghosh.

'*Universities?*'

'We have many universities in Bangladesh,' said Mr Rahman.

'You mean you're going to get the universities to practise family planning?'

'No, to study the problem,' said Mr Ghosh.

'Hasn't it been studied before?'

'Not in these new ways,' said Mr Rahman. 'We haven't got areas of information, as Ghosh said. *And* we have no trained people. Ghosh and myself were the only delegates from Bangladesh at the conference. Now we must take all this knowledge back.'

'But why to the universities?'

'Explain,' said Mr Rahman to Mr Ghosh.

'He does not understand,' said Mr Ghosh. '*First* to the universities, *then*, when the trained people are there, to the rural areas.'

'What's the population of Bangladesh?'

'That is a difficult question,' said Mr Ghosh. 'There are many answers.'

'Give me a rough estimate.'

'Round about seventy-five million,' said Mr Ghosh.

'What's the growth rate?'

'Some say 3 per cent, some say 4,' said Mr Ghosh. 'You see, no work can begin until a proper census is taken. Do you know when the last census was taken in our country? Guess.'

'I can't guess.'

'It was years ago.'

'When?'

'So many, I don't know myself. Years and years. British time. Since then we have had cyclones, wars, floods, so many things to add and subtract. We cannot begin until we have a census.'

'But that could be years from now!'

'Well, that's the problem,' said Mr Rahman.

'In the meantime the population will get bigger and bigger – it'll be fantastic.'

'You see what I mean?' said Mr Ghosh. 'Our people don't know this. I can say at the moment they lack jeal.'

'Zeal?'

'Yes, and purpose.'

'May I ask you another question, Mr Ghosh?'

'Go right ahead. You ask so many!'

'How many children do you have?'

'I am having four.'

'Mr Rahman?'

'I am having five.'

'Is that a good size for Bangladesh?'

'Perhaps not. It is hard to say,' said Mr Rahman. 'We have no statistics.'

'Are there other family-planning people like yourselves in Bangladesh?'

'Many! We have had an ongoing programme for – what? Mr Ghosh – three years? Four years?'

'Do these other family planners have big families or small families?' I asked.

'Some family planners are having big and some are having small.'

'What do you call big?'

'More than five,' said Mr Rahman.

'Well, it's hard to say,' said Mr Ghosh.

'Do you mean more than five in the family?'

'More than five children,' said Mr Rahman.

'Okay, but if a family planner goes to a village and word gets out that he has five children of his own, how the hell is he going to convince people that –'

'It is so hot,' said Mr Rahman. 'I think I will go inside.'

'Wery interesting to talk to you,' said Mr Ghosh. 'I think you are a teacher. Your name?'

It was dark when we pulled into Kuala Lumpur Station, which is the grandest in southeast Asia, with onion-domed cupolas, minarets, and the general appearance of the Brighton Pavilion, but twenty times larger. As a monument to Islamic influence it is much more persuasive than the million-dollar National Mosque down the road, which gets all the tourists. I rushed off the train and ran to the Booking Hall to get a ticket for the next train to Singapore. It was leaving at eleven that night, so I had time to have a quiet beer with an old friend and a plate of chicken *satay* in one of those back lanes that made Cocteau call the city '*Kuala L'impure*'.

## 23. The North Star Night Express to Singapore

'I WOULDN'T go to Singapore if you paid me,' said the man at the end of the bar in the lounge car. He was an inspector in the Malaysian police, a Tamil Christian named Cedric. He was getting drunk in the lazy confident way people do when they are on a train and have a long journey ahead of them. It was overnight to Singapore, and the people in the lounge car (Chinese at mahjong, Indians at cards, a scrum of English planters and estate managers telling stories) had the relaxed look of members in the bar of a Malaysian club. Cedric said Singapore had lost its charm. It was expensive; people ignored you there. 'It's the fast life. I pity you.'

'Where are you headed for?' I asked.

'Kluang,' he said. 'On transfer.'

'Let's hear it for Kluang!' said one of the planters. 'Hip! Hip!'

The others, his friends, ignored him. A man near by, with his feet wide apart like a mate on a quarter deck – it is the stance of the railway drinker – said, 'Hugh got his fingers burned in Port Swettenham. Chap said to him –'

I moved over to Cedric and said, 'What's the attraction in Kluang?' Kluang, a small town in Johore State, is the typical Malaysian outstation, with its club, rest house, rubber estates, and its quota of planters going to pieces in their breezy bungalows.

'Trouble,' said Cedric. 'But that's why I like it. See, I'm a roughneck.' There were labour problems with the Tamil rubber-tappers, and I gathered Cedric had been chosen as much for his colour as for his size and intimidating voice.

'How do you deal with troublemakers?'

'I use this,' he said, and showed me a hairy fist. 'Or if we can get a conviction, the bloke gets the *rotan*.'

The *rotan* is a cane — a four-foot rod, about half a finger thick. Cedric said that most jail sentences included strokes of the *rotan*. The usual number was six strokes; one man in Singapore recently got twenty.

'Doesn't it leave a mark?'

'No,' said an Indian near Cedric.

'Yes,' said Cedric. He thought a moment and sipped his whisky. 'Well, it depends what colour you are. Some of the blokes are pretty dark, and *rotan* scars don't show up. But take you, for instance — it would leave a huge scar on you.'

'So you whip people,' I said.

'*I* don't,' he said. 'Anyway, it's much worse in Singapore, and they're supposed to be so civilized. Let's face it, it happens in every country.'

'It doesn't happen in the States,' I said.

'And it doesn't happen in U.K.,' said one of the planters, who was eavesdropping on the conversation. 'They did away with the birch years ago.'

'Maybe they should still have it,' said Cedric. It was a genial challenge.

The planter looked a bit nonplussed, as if he believed in corporal punishment but didn't want to admit his agreement with the views of a man he held in contempt. He said, 'It's against the law in U.K.'

I asked Cedric why, if it was such a marvellous solution, he was being sent to Kluang, where obviously they had been caning men for years?

'You don't know anything,' he said. 'It teaches them a good lesson. *Wham! Wham!* Then they're nice and quiet.'

As it grew late, some of the drinkers left the lounge car, and Cedric (shouting 'Boy!') told the Tamil barman to open the windows. He obeyed, and in the dark, just above the rumble of the train wheels, there was a continuous twitter, like amplified bubbles rapidly popping; and a whine, a vibrant warble that was nearly the crackle of a trunk call on a Malaysian telephone: the sound of locusts, frogs, and crickets, hidden in a pervading dampness that muffled their hubbub.

Cedric finished his drink and said, 'If you're ever in Kluang give me a tinkle. I'll see what I can fix up for you.' Then he staggered out.

'Peeraswamy,' said one of the planters to the barman, 'give each of these gentlemen a large Anchor and see if you can find a whisky for me.'

'There's someone missing here,' said one of the men, looking around the lounge car. 'Tell me who it is – no prizes.'

'Hench!' said another man. 'Used to stand right by that pillar. "Charming," he used to say. Christ, could that man drink!'

'Doesn't seem the same without Hench.'

'What do you hear from him?'

'Rafe was in touch with him.'

'No, I wasn't,' said Rafe. 'I just heard some stories. You know the ones.'

'Someone said he went blind,' said one man, who was pouring beer into a glass. 'Cheers, Boyce,' he said, and drank.

'All the best,' said Boyce.

'I never believed that story,' said Rafe.

'Then we heard he was dead,' said the third one.

'Didn't you say he went to Australia, Frank?'

'That's worse than being dead,' said Boyce.

'Cheers, Boyce,' said Frank. 'No, I never said that. In fact, I thought he was in the Federation somewhere.'

'Reminds me,' said Rafe. 'Used to be a bloke on the estate who thought he was going blind. Irish – complete hypochondriac, always pulling down his cheek and showing you his horrible eyeball. Bloody sickening it was, but everyone humoured him. Anyway, he goes and sees this specialist in Singapore. Comes back furious. "What's wrong, Paddy?" we ask. And he says, "That quack doesn't know a thing about glaucoma!"'

'Sounds like Frogget,' said Boyce.

'Thank you very much,' said Frank.

'Tell Rafe about your diabetes,' said Boyce.

'I never said I had it,' Frank complained. Then he spoke to Rafe. 'I just said it was possible. One symptom of diabetes – I was reading this somewhere – is that if you piss on your shoe and the spot turns white you're in trouble.'

'I think I'm in trouble,' said Boyce, lifting his foot to the bar.

'Very funny,' said Frank.

'Where are we?' said Rafe. He leaned towards the window. 'I can't see a thing. Peeraswamy, what's the next station? And while you're at it bring two more beers and a whisky for my father here.'

'This is my last one,' said Boyce. 'I've paid for a berth and I'm going to use it.'

'Coming up to Seremban,' said Peeraswamy, uncapping two bottles of beer and sliding over a glass of whisky.

'God, I miss Hench,' said Rafe. 'He was waiting for his chance to go. I never knew that. I hope he's not dead.'

'Well, I'm off,' said Frank, and, picking up his bottle of beer, he added, 'I'm taking this with me. Wish I had a woman.'

When he had gone, Boyce said, 'I'm worried about Frogget.'

'That caper about diabetes?'

'That's only part of it. He's beginning to behave like Hench did just before he disappeared. Secretive, you might say. Mention Australia sometimes – see what he says. He goes all queer.'

The whistle blew at Seremban, hushing the insects. Rafe turned to me. 'Saw you talking to that Indian chap. Don't let him worry you. In fact, if I were you I'd divide everything he said by ten. Good night.'

Then I was alone at the bar of the North Star Night Express. At the far end of the car the mahjong game was still in progress, and the curtains swayed as we left Seremban. Some insects had blown through the windows; they clustered at the lights and chased each other in dizzying spirals.

'Singapore?' said Peeraswamy.

I said yes, that's where I was going.

'Last year I myself in Singapore.' He had gone down for *Thaipusam*, he said. He had carried a *kavadi*. *Thaipusam*, a Tamil festival, has been banned in India. It is encouraged in Singapore, for the tourists, who photograph the frenzied Tamils parading to Tank Road with metal skewers through their cheeks and arms. The Tamils meet at a particular temple in the morning, and after being pierced by long skewers and having limes hung all over their bodies with fishhooks, carry enormous wooden shrines on their heads about two miles to another temple. I was interested that Peeraswamy had done it; I asked him about it.

'I have sixteen – one-six – what you call them, knives? – in body. Here, here, and here. One sticking through tongue. Also hooks in knees and up here, in my soldiers.

'I do this because wife getting pregnant ready, and I worried. I pray-pray for this matter, and son come out ready, so I give the thanks for my god Murugam, brother to Subramaniam. I make more prayers. We cannot sleep on the bed, cannot sleep on the pillow. Only can sleep on the floor until two weeks. Then, one week before, we cannot take the meat, just milk – banana and the fruits. I go to temple. Other people there, maybe one hundred or two. I pray ready, I take bath. The padre come and we make songs' – he showed me how he sang, clasping his hands under his chin, bulging his eyes, and jerking his head back and forth – 'and after songs is coming ready, we pray ready. The god comes inside! We hurry, cannot wait. The padre take the tongue and *pop*! Pop with the knives, pop with the hooks ready – no blood from knives, not hurting – can even kill me! I not care! The song come and the god come and we don't know anything. We want to go out, not want to stop. They put in knives, hooks, what, and we just walk ready.

'The crowd follow – lot of people. The traffic stop – all cars let us pass – and my wife and sister pray-pray and the god come inside them and they faint. I don't see anything. I go fast, almost running down Serangoon Road, Orchard Road, Tank Road, and three times around the temple. The padre is there. He pray and putting the powder on face and take out the pop. We don't know anything – just faint inside the temple.'

Peeraswamy was out of breath. He smiled. I bought him a bottle of Green-Spot and then set off for my compartment, banging my shoulders as I felt my way down the corridor of the speeding train.

I got up early to be on the balcony for the crossing of the causeway from Johore Bahru. But I was met in the corridor by two men, who blocked my way and demanded to see my passport. One said, 'Singapore immigration.'

'Your hair is radda rong,' said the other.

'And yours is rather short,' I said, feeling that one impertinence deserved another. But according to Singapore law the immigration officers were within their rights to refuse me entry if they thought my hair was untidy. Singapore police, who have virtually no effect on the extortionists and murderers in the Chinese secret societies, are in the habit of frog-marching long-haired youths into the Orchard Road police station to shave their heads.

'How much money you have?'

'Enough,' I said. Now the train was on the causeway, and I was eager to have a look at the Strait of Johore.

'Exact amount.'

'Six hundred dollars.'

'Singapore currency?'

'American.'

'Show.'

When every dollar had been counted they gave me an entry visa. By then I had missed the causeway. The North Star was rolling past the wooded marshland on the northern part of the island to the Jurong Road. I associated this road with debt: five years before, I drove down it in the mornings to take my wife to work. It was always cool when we left the house, but so quickly did the rising sun heat the island that it was nearly 80 by the time my small boy (carsick in his wicker seat) and I got back – he to his amah, I to my unfinished African novel. It was curious, travelling across the island, having one's memory jogged by the keen smells of the market near Bukit Timah Circus and the sight of the tropical plants I loved – the palms by the tracks called *pinang rajah*, which have feathery fronds gathered at the top and look like ceremonial umbrellas, and the plants that spray green plumes from the fissures and boles of every old tree in Singapore, the lush ornament called 'ghost leaf' that gives the deadest tree life. I felt kindly towards Singapore – how could I feel otherwise in a place where one of my children was born, where I wrote three books and freed myself from the monotonous routine of teaching? My life had begun there. Now we were passing Queenstown, where Anne had taught night-school classes in *Macbeth*; Outram Road General Hospital, where I'd been treated for dengue; and the island in the harbour – there, through the trees – where, on various Sunday outings, we had been caught in a terrifying storm, and seen a thick poisonous sea snake, and been passed ('Don't let the children see!') by a human corpse so old and buoyant it spun in the breeze like a beach toy.

Singapore Station is scheduled for demolition because its granite frieze of Anglo-Saxon muscle men posed as 'Agriculture', 'Commerce', 'Industry', and 'Transport' is thought to be as outmoded as the stone sign on the wall: FEDERATED MALAY STATES RAILWAY. Singapore thinks of itself as an island of modernity in a backward part of Asia, and many people who visit confirm this by snapping pictures of new hotels and apartment houses, which look like juke boxes and filing cabinets respectively. Politically, Singapore is as primitive as Burundi, with repressive laws, paid informers, a dictatorial government, and jails full of political prisoners. Socially, it is like rural India, with households dependent on washerwomen, amahs, gardeners, cooks, and lackeys. At the factory, workers – who, like everyone else in Singapore, are forbidden to strike – are paid low wages. The media are dull beyond belief because of the heavy censorship. Singapore is a small island, 227 square miles at low tide, and though the government refers to it grandly as 'the Republic', in Asian terms it is little more than a sand bank – but a sand bank that has been enriched by foreign investment (Singaporeans are great assemblers of appliances) and the Vietnam War. Its small size makes it easy to manage: immigration is strictly controlled, family planning is pervasive, no one is allowed to attend the university until he has a security clearance to show he is demonstrably meek, Chinese (from America, Hong Kong, and Taiwan) are encouraged to settle there, and everyone else is encouraged to leave. The police in Singapore are assigned to the oddest tasks; the courts are filled with the unlikeliest criminals. In what other country on earth would one see such items in the paper?

Eleven contractors, three householders and a petrol-kiosk proprietor, were fined a total of $6,035 yesterday for breeding mosquitoes.

Tan Teck Sen, 20, unemployed, was fined $20 for shouting in the lobby of the Cockpit Hotel yesterday.

Four people were fined $750 yesterday under the Destruction of Disease-Bearing Insects Act for allowing insects to breed.

Sulaimen Mohammed was fined $30 yesterday for throwing a piece of paper into a drain at the 15½ mile, Woodlands Road.

Seven or eight years is not an uncommon sentence for a political offence, and criminal offences usually include a whipping. An alien can be deported for having long hair, and anyone can be fined up to $500 for spitting or throwing paper on the ground. Essentially, these laws are passed so that foreign tourists will come to Singapore and, if the news gets out that Singapore is clean and well disciplined, then Americans will want to set up factories and employ the nonstriking Singaporeans. The government emphasizes control, but in such a small place control is not hard to achieve.

Here is a society where newspapers are censored and no

criticism of the government is tolerated; where television is a bland confection of quiz shows, American and British situation comedies, and patriotic programmes; where mail is tampered with and banks are forced to disclose the private accounts of their clients. It is a society where there is literally no privacy and where the government is in complete control. This is the Singaporeans' idea of technological advance:

How would you like to live in a futuristic Singapore where mail and newspapers arrive at your home electronically by facsimile 'print-out'? Sounds like science fiction, but to the Acting General Manager of the Singapore Telephone Board, Mr Frank Loh, they could 'become reality before long'.

He said, 'Developments in telecommunications have already done much to change the pattern of our lives. Concepts such as the "wired city" in which a single cable to each home or office would handle all communication needs could soon be put into practice.'

Mr Loh, who was speaking on 'Telephone Communication' at the convention of the Singapore-Malaysia Institutes of Engineers, gave more details of such exciting developments which the future holds.

'Imagine,' he said, 'at your home communication centre, both mail and newspapers might arrive electronically delivered by facsimile "print-out".'

(*Straits Times*, 20 November 1973)

It struck me as a kind of technology that reduced freedom, and in a society that was basically an assembly plant for Western business interests, depending on the goodwill of washerwomen and the cowardice of students, this technology was useful for all sorts of programmes and campaigns. In a 'wired city' you wouldn't need wall space for SINAGAPORE WANTS SMALL FAMILIES and PUT YOUR HEART INTO SPORTS and REPORT ANYTHING SUSPICIOUS: you would simply stuff it into the wire and send it into every home.

But that is not the whole of Singapore. There is a fringe,

latterly somewhat narrower than it was, where life continues aimlessly, unimpeded by the police or the Ministry of Technology. On this fringe, which is thick with bars, people celebrate Saturday with a curry lunch and drink beer all afternoon, saying, 'Singapore's a shambles – I'm going to Australia,' or 'You were lucky to get out when you did.' It is a place where nearly everyone talks of leaving, but no one goes, as if in leaving he would have to account for all those empty, wasted years playing the slot machines at the Swimming Club, signing chits at the Staff House, toying with a coffee, and waiting for the mail to arrive. On the fringe there are still a few brothels, massage parlours, coffee shops, and discounts for old friends; there are fans instead of air conditioners, and some of the bars have verandahs where in the evening a group of drinkers might find a half-hour's diversion in watching a fat gecko loudly gobble a sausage fly.

It was a gecko on the wall that provoked the reflection that sent me away. I was staying at The Mess, a tall airy house on a leafy hill, and I realized that I had been staring at a gecko on the wall for fifteen minutes or more. It was an old habit, begun in boredom. It seemed as if I had been in Singapore a long time ago, when I was young and didn't know anything, and being there this second time, after two years' absence, I had a glimpse of this other person. It is possible at a distance to maintain the fiction of former happiness – childhood or school days – and then you return to an early setting and the years fall away and you see how bitterly unhappy you were. I had felt trapped in Singapore; I felt as if I was being destroyed by the noise – the hammering, the traffic, the radios, the yelling – and I had discovered most Singaporeans to be rude, aggressive, cowardly, and inhospitable, full of vague racial fears and responsive to any bullying authority. I believed it to be a loathsome place: many of my students thought so too and they couldn't imagine why anyone would willingly stay there. At last I left, and on this return I could not imagine, watching this gecko, why I had stayed three years there; perhaps it was the deceived hesitation I had called patience, or maybe it was my lack of money. I was certain that I would not make the same mistake again, so after seeing a few friends – and everyone told me he was planning to leave soon – I flew out. The previous day I had spent at a club where I had once been a member. The secretary of this club was an overbearing man with a maniacal laugh, but he had been in Singapore since the thirties. He was a real old-timer, people said. I asked about him. 'You a friend of his?' said the man at the bar. I said I knew him. 'I'd keep that quiet if I were you. Last month he did a bunk with 180,000 dollars of the club's money.' Like me – like everyone I knew in Singapore – he had just been waiting for his chance to go.

## 24. The Saigon–Bien Hoa Passenger Train

I WENT to Vietnam to take the train; people have done stranger things in that country. The Trans-Vietnam Railway, which the French called the *Transindochinois*, took over thirty-three years to build, but in 1942, a short six years after it was finished, it was blown to bits and never repaired. A colonial confection, like one of those French dishes that take ages to prepare and are devoured swiftly: a brief delicacy that is mostly labour and memory. The line went along the beautiful coast few of our reluctant janizaries have praised, from Saigon to Hanoi; but now it is in pieces, like a worm chopped up for bait, a section here and there twitching with signs of life. It is mined by the Viet Cong – even more furiously since the cease-fire (which is, willy-nilly, a painful euphemism); it is also mined by local truckers, cash-driven terrorists who believe the continuance of these railway fragments (to Dalat, to Hué, to Tuy Hoa) will prevent them from earning the livelihood Americans have taught them to expect. Like much else in Vietnam, the railway is in ruins – in northern Binh Dinh Province the line has been turned into rice fields – but the amazing thing is that part of it is still running. The Deputy Director of Vietnam Railways, Tran Mong Chau, a short man with thick glasses, told me, 'We can't stop the railway. We keep it running and we lose money. Maybe we do some repairs. If we stop it everyone will know we've lost the war.'

Tran Mong Chau warned me against going from Nha Trang to Tuy Hoa, but said I might enjoy the run from Saigon to Bien Hoa – there were fourteen trips a day. He warned me that it was not like an American train. That particular warning (though how was he to know?) is like a recommendation.

Outside the office I asked Dial, my American translator, a
Marine turned cultural-affairs escort (he had – and smiled at the
lechery in the phrase – made a 'lateral entry'): 'Do you think it's
safe to take the train to Bien Hoa?'

'About a month ago the VC hit it,' Dial said. 'They got six
or seven of the passengers in an ambush. They stopped the train
with a pillar of salt – then they started shooting.'

'Maybe we should forget it.'

'No, it's secure now. Anyway, I've got a gun.'

At breakfast the next morning, Cobra One – this was the
code name of my American host in Saigon – told me that the
Vietnam Tourist Board wanted to see me before I took the train
to Bien Hoa. I said I'd be glad to pay them a visit. We were
eating on the roof of Cobra One's large house, enjoying the
coolness and the fragrance of the flowering trees. From time to
time a low-flying helicopter paddled past, weaving between the
housetops. Cobra One said there was going to be a big campaign
to attract tourists to Vietnam. I suggested that the idea might be
rather premature – after all, the war was still on.

'You'd never know it here,' said Cobra One's wife, Cobra
Two. She looked up from her newspaper. Below us in the
centre of the compound there was a swimming pool, set amidst
flower beds and rows of palms. A far wall held a coil of barbed
wire, but that only made it seem more like Singapore. There
was a hedge of red hibiscus along the driveway and clusters of
giant ferns, and a man in a yellow shirt raking the gravel paths
under the laburnum trees. Cobra Two, striking in her silk robe,
kicking a furry slipper up and down, and rattling *Stars and Stripes*,
said, 'Some of the best – hey, what hemisphere is this?'

'Eastern,' said Cobra One.

'Right. Some of the best lays in the eastern hemisphere are
right in this compound.'

The office of the Director of Planning of the Commission for
Vietnam Tourism was decorated in red velvet from floor to

ceiling, and there were ribbons on the margins of the walls. We seemed to be sitting in an empty box of expensive chocolates. I said I didn't have much time, since I was going to take the train to Bien Hoa. The Director of Planning and the Deputy Commissioner exchanged uneasy glances. Vo Doan Chau, the Director, said the train was in bad shape – what I should do, he said, was to take a car to Vung Tau and go swimming. 'Vietnam is famous for its beaches,' he said.

*Famous for its beaches!* 'And much else,' I was going to say, but Tran Luong Ngoc, the American-trained Deputy Commissioner, launched into the explanation of the campaign. They were going all-out for tourists, he said, and they had devised a publicity gimmick that could not fail, the *Follow Me!* scheme. Posters were being printed showing pretty Vietnamese girls in places like Danang, Hué, and Phu Quoc Island, and the slogan on the posters would be FOLLOW ME! These posters (PLEIKU – FOLLOW ME!, DALAT – FOLLOW ME!) would be sent all over the world, but most of the campaign money would be spent to encourage tourists in the United States and Japan. Mr Ngoc gave me a stack of brochures with titles like *Lovely Hué* and *Visit Viet-Nam*, and he asked me if I had any questions.

'About those beaches,' I said.

'*Very* nice beaches,' said Mr Ngoc. 'Also woods and greenery.'

'Vietnam has everything,' said Mr Chau.

'But the tourists might be a bit worried about getting shot,' I said.

'Noncombat areas!' said Mr Ngoc. 'What to worry about? You're travelling around the country yourself, no?'

'Yes, and I'm worried.'

'My advice to you,' said Mr Ngoc, 'is *don't worry*. We expect many tourists. We think they will be Americans, and maybe some Japanese. The Japanese like to travel.'

'They might prefer to go to Thailand or Malaysia,' I said. 'They have nice beaches, too.'

'They are so commercialized,' said Mr Chau. 'They have big

hotels and roads and crowds of people. They are not very interesting – I have seen them. In Vietnam the tourists can go back to nature!'

'And we have hotels,' said Mr Ngoc. 'Not five-star hotels, but sometimes air-conditioned or electric fan. Minimum comfort, you can say. And we have that bungalow, built for President Johnson when he visited. It could be turned into something. We don't have very much at the moment but we have plenty of scope.'

'*Plenty* of scope,' said Mr Chau. 'We will appeal to their curiosity – people in America. So many had friends or relatives in Vietnam. They have heard so much about this country.' Sounding distinctly ominous he said, 'Now they can find out what it is really like.'

Mr Ngoc said, 'Places like Bangkok and Singapore are just commercial. That's not interesting. We can offer spontaneity and hospitality, and since our hotels aren't very good we could also appeal to the more adventurous. There are many people who like to explore the unknown. Then these people can go back to the States and tell their friends they saw where this or that battle was fought –'

'They can say, "I slept in the bunker at Pleiku!"' said Mr Chau.

There were really two selling points, the beaches and the war. But the war was still on, in spite of the fact that nowhere in the forty-four-page booklet entitled *Visit Viet-Nam* was fighting mentioned, except the oblique statement, 'English [language] is making rapid progress under the pressure of contemporary events', which might have been a subtle reference to the American occupation and perhaps to the war. At that time – December 1973 – 70,000 people had been killed since the cease-fire, but the Commission for Vietnam Tourism was advertising Hué (a devastated city of muddy streets, occasionally shelled) as a place of 'scenic beauty ... where historic monuments, yards and porticoes bear the mark of its glorious past', and urging visitors to Danang to travel six miles south of the city to see 'brilliant stalactites and stalagmites', not mentioning the fact that there was still fierce fighting in that very area, where gunmen hid in the grottoes near Marble Mountain.

Before I left the office, Mr Chau took me aside. 'Don't go to Bien Hoa by train,' he said.

I asked him why.

'That is the worst train in the world,' he said. He was embarrassed that I should want to take it.

But I insisted, and, wishing him well with his campaign to attract tourists to the battlefields, I set off for the station. There is no sign on Saigon Station, and, though I was perhaps fifty feet away from it, no one in the area knew where it was. I found it purely by chance, cutting through an Air Vietnam ticket office, but even when I got on the platform I was not sure it was the railway station: there were no passengers and no trains at the platform. The train, it turned out, was a short distance up the line, but it was not due to leave for twenty minutes. The carriages were battered green boxes, some wooden (with protruding splinters) and some metal (with dents). The seating arrangements, a narrow bench running along the walls of the carriage, was neither comfortable nor convenient, and most of the passengers were standing. They smiled, clutching their very discouraged ducks and chickens and their cruelly sunburned half-American infants.

There was another even older train parked on the far side of the yard. Attracted by the wrought-iron railings on the porches – a French feature of the car – I sauntered over. I climbed into this semiderelict train and heard a sharp howl of complaint. A girl jumped up two cars away (I saw her figure framed by the broken doors) and pulled on a pair of jeans. Then I saw a boy fussing with his clothes. I started off in the opposite direction and ran into two sleeping heroin addicts, both pimply girls with tattoos and needle scars on their arms. One woke and shouted at me. I hurried away: there were other lovers on the train, and

254 The Great Railway Bazaar

children, and menacing-looking youths poking through the cars. But the train had no engine: it wasn't going anywhere.

The stationmaster, wearing a plastic-visored cap, crossed the track, waving to me. I hopped out of the derelict train and went over to shake his hand. Laughing sheepishly, he explained that it was not *this* train that was going to Bien Hoa but *that* one, and he pointed to the line of bulging boxcars. I headed for one of the cars and was about to swing myself up when the stationmaster called out, 'No! No!'

He motioned for me to follow him, and, still laughing, he led me to the tail end of the train, where there was quite a different sort of railway car. This wooden carriage, with a kitchen and three sleeping compartments and a large lounge, was obviously a relic from the *Transindochinois*, and, though it was not luxurious even by Indian standards, it was comfortable and spacious. It was, said the stationmaster, the director's: the director had requested that I ride in it. We got in; the stationmaster nodded to the signalman, and the train started up.

A free ride in the director's personal railway car, to confound the unreality of the place still further: it was not what I expected – not in Vietnam. But this emphasis on privilege is a version of American extravagance. It is a function of the war, which produced an obliging system for conditioning the sympathy of visitors, all of whom (for the risks they believed they were taking) wanted to be treated like VIPs. Every visitor was a potential publicist, the irony being that even the most furious dove was afforded the unlimited credit and comfort on which he could preen his sensibilities into outrage. This hospitality, heightened by the natural generosity of the Vietnamese, continues. It was almost shameful to accept it, for it had its origins in the same plan a company develops when it cynically mounts a campaign to popularize an unsuccessful product. It distorted the actual. But I reserved my scorn: the Vietnamese had inherited cumbersome and expensive habits of wastefulness.

We sat around the table in the lounge that took up a third of the director's carriage. The stationmaster put his cap away and smoothed his hair. He said that after the Second World War he had been offered a number of well-paying jobs, but he chose instead to go back to his old job on the railway. He liked trains and he believed Vietnam Railways had a great future. 'After we reopen the line to Loc Ninh,' he said, 'then we go to Turkey.'

I asked him how this was possible.

'We go up to Loc Ninh, then we build a line to Phnom Penh. That goes to Bangkok, no? Then somewhere, somewhere and somewhere — maybe India? — then Turkey. There is a railway in Turkey.'

He was certain Turkey was just over the hill, and the only difficulty he envisaged — indeed, it seemed a characteristic of the South Vietnamese grasp of political geography — was getting Loc Ninh out of the hands of the Viet Cong and laying track through the swamps of Cambodia. His transcontinental railway vision, taking in eight vast countries, had a single snag: evicting the enemy from this small local border town. For the Vietnamese citizen the rest of the world is simple and peaceful; he has the egoism of a sick man, who believes he is the only unlucky sufferer in a healthy world.

The stationmaster said, 'Sometimes we get ambushed here. A few weeks ago some four people were killed by rifle fire.'

I said, 'Perhaps we should close the windows then.'

'Ha! Very good!' he said, and translated the joke for his deputy, who was setting out glasses of Coca-Cola.

It was a single-line track, but squatters had moved their huts so close to it, I could look into their windows and across rooms where children sat playing on the floor; I could smell the cooking food — fish and blistering meat — and see people waking and dressing; at one window a man in a hammock swung inches from my nose. There was fruit on the window sills, and it stirred — an orange beginning to roll — as the train sped by. I have never had a stronger feeling of being *in* the houses I was passing, and I had a continuous sense of interrupting with my face some domestic routine. But I was imagining the intrusion: the people in those poor houses seemed not to notice the strangers at their windows.

From the back of the train I could see the market women and children reoccupying the track, and once – a swift sight of a leaping man – I thought I saw an American, in beard and flapping pyjamas, tall, light, round-shouldered, but with large revealing feet and a long stride. He disappeared between two tottering wooden buildings and was enclosed by lines of faded laundry. This was in one of the most crowded slums in the Saigon outskirts, and the glimpse of this man, who was the wrong size for the place – his ungainliness emphasizing his height over all the others – made me inquire about him later. Dial told me he was probably a deserter, one of about two hundred who remain in the country, mainly in the Saigon area. Some are heroin addicts, some work at legitimate jobs and have Vietnamese wives, and some are thugs – much of the breaking and entering in Saigon is attributable to the criminally versatile deserters: they know what to take at the PX; they can steal cars with greater anonymity than the Vietnamese. None of these men has identity papers, and Vietnam is a hard country to leave. Their only hope is to take a boat up the Mekong and cross into Thailand; or they could surrender. It was an odd community of practically nameless fugitives, and the idea of them – of that bearded man in pyjamas crossing the track on that very bright day, briefly exposed – filled me with curiosity and pity in the same degree. I saw in them a fictional possibility, a situation containing both a riddle and some clues for solving it. If one were to write about Vietnam in any coherent way one would have to begin with these outsiders.

I left the private car and moved through the train. It was filled with horribly mutilated people, amputees with rounded stumps, soldiers in wrinkled uniforms, and old men with stringy beards, leaning on walking sticks. A blind man wearing a straw Stetson was playing a guitar and singing tunelessly for a group of soldiers.

But it was not entirely a train of decrepit and abandoned people. The impression I had on the train to Bien Hoa, one that stayed with me throughout my time in Vietnam, was of the resourcefulness of the Vietnamese. It seemed incredible, but here were schoolgirls with book bags, and women with huge bundles of vegetables, and men with trussed fowl, and others, standing at the doors of what were essentially freight cars, off to work in Bien Hoa. After so many years one expected to see them defeated; the surprise was that they were more than survivors. From the cruel interruptions of war they had stubbornly salvaged a routine: school, market, factory. At least once a month the train was ambushed, and 'the offensive' was spoken about with the tone of inevitability people use about monsoons. But these passengers made their daily trip. It was a dangerous journey. They were resigned to danger. For them life would never change, and the menace of the enemy was as predictable and changeless as the weather.

A lady with a half-American baby followed me through the cars, and when I stopped at one coupling to make a cautious jump she tugged my arm and tried to hand him over. It was a child of about two, with fair skin, plump, round-eyed. I smiled and shrugged. She showed me his face, pinching his cheeks, and offered him. He began to cry and then the lady started to speak loudly, and a small group of people gathered to listen. She was pointing at me, gesturing with the child in accusation.

'We'd better move on,' said Dial.

He explained that the baby had been abandoned. The woman had found it and was caring for it. But it was not hers – it was an American child. She wanted to give the child to me, and she couldn't understand why I didn't want it. She was still shouting – I could hear her clearly as we moved through the next crowded car.

We made our way as far as the engine, a new diesel, and then into the engine itself and along the balcony to the front platform, facing the wind and squinting each time the whistle blew. But the view was not inspiring, and pointing to a hill on the right Dial said, 'That's where the VC launched a rocket attack a few weeks ago. But don't worry – they're not there now. They rush in, fire a few rockets, and then beat it.'

Hanging on the balcony rail at the front of the train, I could see the line stretching before us, and beyond that the yellow ruined landscape, bare of trees, at the horizon of which Bien Hoa lay, a jumble of grey roofs and chimneys. The wind stank of excrement, and all along the tracks there was a vile flood of shit, worse that anything I had seen in India, brimming right up to the line and still flowing from open drains that led down the bank from settlements of huts. They were not crudely built squatters' shacks: these were small houses, built by contractors, whose existence had some official sanction. The houses with no drains. They were appropriate in a country where great roads led nowhere, where planes flew to no purpose, and the government was just another self-serving tyranny. The conventional view was that the Americans had been imperialists; but that is an inaccurate jibe. The American mission was purely sententious and military; nowhere was there evidence of the usual municipal preoccupations of a colonizing power – road-mending, drainage, or permanent buildings. In Saigon, the embassy and the Abraham Lincoln Library exhausted the services of the one architect who was sent in nine years. These two buildings will survive an offensive because that architect learned to incorporate a rocket-screen into a decorative feature of the outside wall – but this is not much of an achievement compared to the French-built post office, cathedral, the several schools, the solid clubs like the Cercle Sportif Saigonnais, and all the grand residences, of which Cobra One's was a fairly modest example. And out here in the suburbs of Bien Hoa, created by the pressure of American occupation, the roads were falling to pieces and cholera streamed into the backyards. Planning and maintenance characterize even the briefest and most brutish empire; apart from the institution of a legal system there aren't many more imperial virtues. But

Americans weren't pledged to maintain. There is Bien Hoa Station, built fifty years ago. It is falling down, but that is not the point. There is no sign that it was ever mended by the Americans; even sagging under its corona of barbed wire it looks a good deal sturdier than the hangars at Bien Hoa airbase.

'If the VC had hit this train,' said Dial at Bien Hoa Station, hopping off the engine, 'we would have been the first to get snuffed.'

That afternoon I gave a lecture – my usual vapouring about the novel – at Van Hanh University in Saigon. It elicited a number of antagonistic questions about the position of blacks in America, which I replied to as honestly as I could. Afterwards the rector, the Venerable Thich Huyen-Vi, a Buddhist monk, gave me an inscribed copy of his doctoral thesis, 'A Critical Study of The Life and Works of Sariputta Thera', and I went off to the Cercle Sportif.

'Here we are in beleaguered Saigon,' said Cobra One. He took me around the ten acres where Chinese, Vietnamese, and perhaps a dozen languid Frenchmen were playing games (badminton, tennis, fencing, judo, ping-pong, bowling) under the lighted trees. We had a game of billiards and then went to a restaurant. There were lovers purring at some tables and '– opening a branch' drifted from a group of men. Cobra One said, 'Here we are in beleaguered Saigon.' We went to a night-club on Tu Do, Saigon's main street. It was very dark inside. We were served with ice cubes in our glasses of beer. Then a red light came on and a Vietnamese girl in a miniskirt sang a quick-tempo version of 'Where Have All the Flowers Gone?' The heads bobbing in the semidarkness were those of people dancing spiritedly to the song. I saw Cobra One gesturing at the end of the table and heard, just above the singer's twanging voice, '– beleaguered Saigon'.

The next day I flew – there was no train – to the delta town of Can Tho in a plane that had a wrinkled silver fuselage, like tinfoil from an old cigarette pack. Can Tho was once the home of thousands of GIs. With the brothels and bars closed, it had the abandoned look of an unused fairground after a busy summer. In all that decrepitude a wilfulness was revealed: we didn't want to stay in Vietnam, and so no vision of the country, except abstract notions of political and military order, were ever formed. The airport at Can Tho was almost destroyed and the main street was riddled with potholes; all the recent buildings had a tawdry temporary design – prefabs, huts, shelters of plywood. They will fall down soon – some already have been looted and pulled down for the lumber – and in a matter of time, very few years, there will be little evidence that the Americans were ever there. There are poisoned rice fields between the straggling fingers of the Mekong Delta and there are hundreds of blond and fuzzy-haired children, but in a generation even these unusual features will change.

# 25. The Hué–Danang Passenger Train

FROM the air, the grey unreflecting water of the South China Sea looked ice cold, there were round Buddhist graves all through the marshes, and the royal city of Hué lay half-buried in drifts of snow. But this was wet sand, not snow, and those circular graves were bomb craters. Hué had a bizarre appearance. There had been plenty of barbed wire on the barricades but little war damage in Saigon; in Bien Hoa there were bombed-out houses; in Can Tho stories of ambushes and a hospital full of casualties. But in Hué I could see and smell the war: it was muddy roads rutted by army trucks and people running through the rain with bundles, bandaged soldiers tramping through the monsoon slime of the wrecked town or peering across their rifle barrels from the backs of overloaded trucks. The movements of the people had a distressed simultaneity. Symmetrical coils of barbed wire obstructed most streets, and houses were sloppily sandbagged. The next day, in the train, Cobra One (who had come with Cobra Two and Dial for the ride) said, 'Look – every house has its own bullet hole!' It was true: few houses were without a violent gouge and most had a series of ragged plugs torn out of their walls. The whole town had a dark brown look of violation, the smirches of raids among swelling puddles. It held some traces of imperial design (Vietnamese, French) but this delicacy was little more than a broken promise.

And it was very cold, with the sudden chill from the low sky and the drizzle clinging in damp rooms. I paced up and down, hugging myself to keep warm, during my lecture at the University of Hué – a colonial building, in fact, not academic at all, but rather what was once a fancy shop called Morin Brothers, which outlying planters used as a guest house and provisioner. I lectured in one of the former bedrooms, and from the windy balcony I could see the neglected courtyard, the cracked fish-pond, the peeling shutters on the windows of the other rooms.

Later we drove to a bluff above the Royal Tombs, on the Perfume River. 'That's VC territory,' said Mr McTaggart, the local USIS official. He was a genial white-haired man, who cooked his own meals and sometimes rode his bicycle out here and practised his Vietnamese with the sentries on the bluff. Across the river, the Viet Cong territory was a number of scalped hills: it had been defoliated. But there was still shooting now and then. An ARVN boat would chug close to the enemy bank and spend an afternoon firing into the hills, not at a particular target, but more like the French man-of-war in *Heart of Darkness* that aimlessly – insanely, Conrad says – shells the African jungle. I must come during the hot season, one of the Vietnamese said. Then I could hire a boat and a girl and bring some food, and I could spend a night on the river like this, making love and eating where it was cool.

I promised I would. We went to the tombs next. The older the buildings were in Hué, the better their state of preservation: last year's Quonset huts were falling to bits, Mr McTaggart's forty-year-old house was seedy but comfortable, the hundred-year-old Royal Tombs were in very good shape, although these had been made with second-hand materials, in accordance with Vietnamese custom (to stress humility) – old lumber and stone, broken pottery, and cracked tiles. There were tangled gardens and carved gateways with panting dragons crouched over the arches; and in the interior rooms, the dusty mausoleums, ancient women hobbled from artifact to artifact, lighting tapers to show us the French clock (its hands missing), the crystal candelabra, the gilt altars and the cabinets inlaid with mother-of-pearl, the peacock fans with moulting feathers ('She says they're from the French king'). The hands of the old ladies trembled as they held the flames of the tapers close to the tinder-dry treasures, and I was afraid they'd set the place alight. When we left they blew out all the candles and remained in the dark tombs. It was a city people were constantly fleeing, but here in the tombs the old ladies — retainers to kings of the twenties and thirties — never left. They ate and slept in the precincts of the royal mausoleum.

It was cold that night; dogs barked in the muddy lane, and in spite of the chill my bedroom was filled with tormenting mosquitoes.

At Hué Station the next morning a tiny Vietnamese man in a grey gaberdine suit and porkpie hat rushed forward and took my arm. 'Welcome to Hué,' he said. 'Your carriage is ready.' This was the stationmaster. He had been notified of my arrival and had shunted on to the Danang passenger train one of the director's other private cars. Because Vietnam Railways has been blown to pieces, each separate section has a director's car on one of its sidings. Any other railway would have one such car, but Vietnam Railways is six separate lines, operating with laborious independence. As at Saigon, I boarded the private coach with some misgivings, knowing that my hand would tremble if I ever wrote anything ungenerous about these people. I felt loutish in my empty compartment, in my empty coach, watching Vietnamese lining up to buy tickets so that they could ride in overcrowded cars. The stationmaster had sped me away from the ticket window ('It is not necessary!'), but I had caught a glimpse of the fare: 143 piastres (twenty-five cents) to go to Danang, perhaps the cheapest seventy-five mile ride in the world.

Dial, the translator, and Cobras One and Two boarded and joined me in the compartment. We sat in silence, peering out the window. The blocky whitewashed station building, a version of the Alamo, was riddled with bullet holes that had broken off pieces of the stucco, revealing red brickwork beneath. But the station, the same vintage as McTaggart's bay-windowed villa and the Morin Brothers shop, had been built to last — a far cry from the patch of waste ground and cement foundations just outside Hué, where the First Marine Division's collapsed barracks and splintered obstacle course lay sinking in the mud. It was as if all the apparatus of war had been timed to self-destruct the day the Americans pulled out, leaving no trace of the brutal adventure behind. In the train yard, several armoured vans showed rips in their steel sides where mines had punched them apart. These vans were the homes of a number of sad-looking children. In most tropical countries adults stand, like those posed by William Blake, at the fringe of the echoing green, watching children at play. In Vietnam the children play alone, and the adults appear to have been swept away; you look for the parents among large groups of children, for the background figure of an adult. But (and this distorts the landscape) they are missing. That old woman carrying a child on her back, with the long muddy skirt and rain-drenched hair, is another child.

'Have you seen the sink in the w.c.?' asked Dial.

'No.'

'You turn on the tap and guess what comes out?'

'Rust,' I said.

'Nothing,' said Cobra Two.

Dial said, 'Water!'

'Right,' said Cobra One. 'Paul, take that down. The taps work. Running water available. What do you think of that?'

But this was the only sink in the train.

The stationmaster had said that the line to Danang had been open for four months, having been out of action for five years. So far there had been no recent disruptions. Why its reopening coincided with the American withdrawal no one could explain. My own theory was that there were now no American trucks plying back and forth along the only road that goes between Hué and Danang, Highway One, the poignantly named 'Street without Joy'; this shrinking of expensive road traffic had forced the Vietnamese into the more sensible course of opening the railway. The war had become not smaller, but less mechanized, less elaborate. Money and foreign troops had complicated it, but now the Vietnamese had reverted from the corporation-style hostilities of the Americans to the colonial superstructure, slower communications, a return to farming, housing in the old buildings, and a transport system based on the railway. The American design of the war had been abandoned – the empty firebases, the skeletons of barracks, and the torn-up roads showed this to be a fact, visible from the passenger train clanking towards Danang with its cargo of Hué-grown vegetables.

The bridges on that line speak of the war; they are recent and have new rust on their girders. Others, broken, simulating gestures without motion, lay beyond them where they had been twisted and pitched into ravines by volumes of explosives. Some rivers contained masses of broken bridges, black knots of steel bunched grotesquely at the level of the water. They were not all recent. In the gorges where there were two or three, I took the oldest ones to be relics of Japanese bombing, and others to be examples of demolition from the later terrorism of the fifties and sixties, each war leaving its own unique wreck. They were impressively mangled, like outrageous metal sculptures. The Vietnamese hung their washing on them.

It was at the rivers – at these bridges – that soldiers were most in evidence. These were strategic points: a bombed bridge could put the line out of action for as long as a year. So at each side of the bridge, just above it on outcrops of rock, there were igloos of sandbags, and pillboxes and bunkers, where sentries, most of them very young, waved to the train with carbines. On their shelters were slogans flying on red and yellow banners. Dial translated them for me. A typical one was, GREET THE PEACE HAPPILY BUT DON'T SLEEP AND FORGET THE WAR. The soldiers stood around in their undershirts; they could be seen swinging in hammocks; some swam in the rivers or were doing their washing. Some watched the train, with their rifles at their shoulders, in those oversize uniforms – a metaphor of mismatching that never failed to remind me that these men – these boys – had been dressed and armed by much larger Americans. With the Americans gone the war looked too big, an uncalled-for size, really, like those shirts whose cuffs reached to the soldiers' knuckles and the helmets that fell over their eyes.

'That's VC up there,' said Cobra One. He pointed to a series of ridges that grew, off in the distance, into hills. 'You could say 80 per cent of the country is controlled by the VC, but that doesn't mean anything because they only have 10 per cent of the population.'

'I was up there,' said Dial. I kept forgetting that Dial had been a Marine. 'We were on patrol for about three weeks. Christ, we were cold! But now and then we'd luck out and get to a village. The people would see us coming and run away, and we'd use their huts – sleep in their beds. I remember a couple of times – it really killed me – we had to burn all their furniture to keep warm. We couldn't find any firewood.'

The mountains had begun to rise, acquiring the shape of amphitheatres with a prospect of the China Sea; eerie and bare and blue, their summits smothered in mist, they trailed smoke from slash-and-burn fires. We were on the narrow coastal strip, moving south on the patchy shoreline that still belonged to the Saigon government, between the mountains and the sea. The weather had changed, or perhaps we had finally been dragged free of the drizzle that was constant in Hué. Now it was sunny and warm: the Vietnamese climbed up to the roofs of the coaches and sat with their legs hanging past the eaves. We were close enough to the beach to hear the pounding surf, and ahead in the curving inlets that doubled up the train, fishing smacks and canoes rode the frothy breakers to the shore, where men in parasol hats spun circular webbed nets over the crayfish.

'God, this is such a beautiful country,' said Cobra Two. She was snapping pictures out the window, but no picture could duplicate the complexity of the beauty: over there, the sun lighted a bomb scar in the forest, and next to it smoke filled the bowl of a valley; a column of rain from one fugitive cloud slanted on another slope, and the blue gave way to black green, to rice green on the flat fields of shoots, which became, after a strip of sand, an immensity of blue ocean. The distances were enormous and the landscape was so large it had to be studied in parts, like a mural seen by a child.

'I had no idea,' I said. Of all the places the railway had taken me since London, this was the loveliest.

'No one knows it,' said Cobra Two. 'No one in the States has the slightest idea how beautiful it is. Look at that – God, look at that!'

We were at the fringes of a bay that was green and sparkling in bright sunlight. Beyond the leaping jade plates of the sea was an overhang of cliffs and the sight of a valley so large it contained sun, smoke, rain, and cloud – all at once – independent quantities of colour. I had been unprepared for this beauty; it surprised and humbled me in the same degree the emptiness had in rural India. Who has mentioned the simple fact that the heights of Vietnam are places of unimaginable grandeur? Though we can hardly blame a frightened draftee for not noticing this magnificence, we should have known all along that the French would not have colonized it, nor would the Americans have fought so long, if such ripeness did not invite the eye to take it.

'That's the Ashau Valley,' said Cobra One, who until then had been doing an amusing imitation of Walter Brennan. The ridges mounted into the mist; below them, in the smoke and sun, were deep black gorges marked by waterfalls. Cobra One was shaking his head: 'A lot of good men died there.'

Dazzled by the scenery, I walked through the train and saw a blind man feeling his way to the door – I could hear his lungs working like a bellows; wrinkled old ladies with black teeth and black pyjamas clutched wicker bales of spring onions; and soldiers – one ashen-faced in a wheelchair, one on crutches, others with new bandages on their hands and heads, and all of them in the American uniforms that suggested travesty in its true sense. An official moved through the coaches checking the ID cards of civilian males, looking for draft evaders. This official got tangled in the piece of string held by a blind man and attached to the waist of a child leading him. There were many armed soldiers on the train, but none looked like escorts. The train was defended by concentrations of soldiers at those bridge emplacements, and this is perhaps why it is so easy to blow up the line with command-detonated mines. These mines are slipped under the rails at night; when the train goes over one of them, a hidden man – who might be a Viet Cong or a bomber hired by a trucker in Danang – explodes the charge.

Twice during that trip, at small station sidings, children were offered to me by old ladies; they were like the pale-skinned, light-haired children I had seen in Can Tho and Bien Hoa. But these were older, perhaps four or five, and it was strange to hear these American-looking children speaking Vietnamese. It was even stranger to see the small Vietnamese farmers in the vastness of a landscape whose beautiful trees and ravines and jade crags – these launched from cloud banks – hid their enemies. From the train I could turn my eyes to the mountains and almost forget the country's name, but the truth was closer and cruel: the Vietnamese had been damaged and then abandoned, almost as if, dressed in our clothes, they had been mistaken for us and shot at; as if, just when they had come to believe that we were identified with them, we had bolted. It was not that simple, but it was nearer to describing that sad history than the urgent opinions of anguished Americans who, stropping Occam's Razor, classified the war as a string of atrocities, a series of purely political errors, or a piece of interrupted heroism. The tragedy was that we had come, and, from the beginning, had not planned to stay: Danang was to be proof of that.

The train was under the gigantic Hai Van Pass ('The Pass of Clouds'), a natural division on the north side of Danang, like a Roman wall. If the Viet Cong got past it, the way would be clear to Danang, and already the Viet Cong were bivouacked on the far slopes, waiting. Like the other stretches between Hué and Danang, the most scenically dramatic mountains and valleys were – and are still – the most terrible battlefields. Beyond the Hai Van Pass we entered a long tunnel. By this time I had walked the length of the train and was standing on the front balcony of the diesel, under the bright headlights. Ahead, a large bat dislodged itself from the ceiling and flapped clumsily this way and that, winging against the walls, trying to keep ahead of the roaring engine. The bat swooped, grazing the track, then rose – more slowly now – as the end of the tunnel came into view, flying closer to the engine with every second. It was like a toy of wood and paper, its spring running down, and at last it was ten feet from my face, a brown panicky creature beating its bony wings. It tired, dropped a few feet, then in the light of the tunnel's exit – a light it could not see – its wings collapsed, it pitched forward, and quickly tumbled under the engine's wheels.

'The Street without Joy' was above us as we raced across a treeless promontory to the Nam Ho Bridge, five dark spans secured against underwater sappers by great rusting wreaths of barbed wire. These were the outer wastes of Danang, a grim district of supply bases that has been taken over by ARVN forces and squatters; shelters – huts and lean-tos – made exclusively with war materials, sandbags, plastic sheeting, corrugated iron stamped U.S. ARMY, and food wrappers marked with the initials of charitable agencies. Danang was pushed next to the sea and all the land around it had been stripped of trees. If ever a place looked poisoned, it was Danang.

Raiding and looting were skills the war had required the Vietnamese to learn. We got out at Danang Station and after lunch drove with an American official to the south side of the city, where GIs had been housed in several large camps. Once there had been thousands of American soldiers; now there were none. But the barracks were filled to bursting with refugees; because there had been no maintenance, the camps were in a sorry condition and looked as if they had been shelled. Laundry flew from the flagpoles; windows were broken or boarded-up;

there were cooking fires in the roads. The less lucky refugees had set up house in wheelless trucks and the sewage stink was terrible – the camps could be smelled two hundred yards away.

'The people were waiting at the gates and over by those fences when the Americans started packing,' said the American official. 'Like locusts or I-don't-know-what. As soon as the last soldier left they rushed in, looted the stores, and commandeered the houses.'

The refugees, using ingenuity, looted the barracks; the Vietnamese government officials, using their influence, looted the hospitals. I kept hearing stories in Danang (and, again, in the southern port of Nha Trang) of how, the day the Americans left, the hospitals were cleaned out – drugs, oxygen cylinders, blankets, beds, medical appliances, anything that could be carried. Chinese ships were anchored off shore to receive this loot, which was taken to Hong Kong and resold. But there is a just God in Heaven: a Swiss businessman told me that some of these pilfered medical supplies found their way, via Hong Kong, to Hanoi. No one knew what happened to the enriched government officials. Some of the looting stories sounded exaggerated; I believed the ones about the raided hospitals because no American official could tell me where there was a hospital receiving patients, and that's the sort of thing an American would know.

For several miles on the road south the ravaged camps swarmed with Vietnamese, whose hasty adaptations could be seen in doors knocked through barracks' walls and whole barracks torn down to make ten flimsy huts. The camps themselves had been temporary – they were all plywood panels, splitting in the dampness, and peeling metal sheets, and sagging fence posts – so none of these crude shelters would last. If one felt pity for the demoralized American soldiers who had lived in these horrible camps, one felt even sorrier for the inheritors of all this junk.

The bars, with flyblown signs advertising COLD BEER, MUSIC, GIRLS, were empty and most looked bankrupt, but it was in the late afternoon that I saw the real dereliction of Danang. We drove out to the beach where, fifty feet from the crashing waves, a fairly new bungalow stood. It was a cosy beach house, built for an American general who had recently decamped. Who was this general? No one knew his name. Whose beach house was it now? No one knew that either, but Cobra One ventured, 'Probably some ARVN honcho.' On the porch a Vietnamese soldier idled with a carbine, and behind him a table held a collection of bottles: vodka, whisky, ginger ale, soda water, a jug of orange juice, an ice bucket. Laughter, slightly drunken and mirthless, carried from inside the house.

'I think someone's moved in,' said Cobra One. 'Let's have a look.'

We walked past the sentry and up the stairs. The front door was open, and in the living room two Americans on sofas were tickling two busty Vietnamese girls. It was the absurd made symmetrical – both men were fat, both girls were laughing, and the sofas were side by side. If Conrad's dark re-enactment of colonialism, 'Outpost of Progress', were made into a comedy it would have looked something like that.

'Hey, we got company!' said one of the men. He banged the wall behind his head with his fist, then sat up and relit his cigar.

While we introduced ourselves, a side door opened from the wall the cigar smoker had punched and a muscular black man hurried out hitching up his trousers. Then a very tiny, batlike Vietnamese girl appeared from the room. The black said, 'Howdy' and made for the front door.

'We didn't mean to interrupt your picnic,' said Cobra One, but he showed no inclination to leave. He folded his arms and watched; he was a tall man with a severe gaze.

'You're not interrupting nothing,' said the man with the cigar, rolling off the sofa.

'This is the head of security,' said the American official who had driven us to the place. He was speaking of the fat man with the cigar.

As if in acknowledgement, the fat man set fire to his cigar

once again. Then he said, 'Yeah, I'm the head spook around
here. You just get here?' He was at that point of drunkenness
where, acutely conscious of it, he made an effort to hide it. He
walked outside, away from the spilled cushions, full ashtrays,
supine girls.

'You took the *what*?' asked the CIA man when we told him
we had come to Danang from Hué on the train. 'You're lucky
you made it! Two weeks ago the VC blew it up.'

'That's not what the stationmaster in Hué told us,' said Cobra
One.

'The stationmaster in Hué doesn't know whether to scratch
his watch or wind his ass,' said the CIA man. 'I'm telling you
they blew it up. Twelve people killed, I don't know how many
wounded.'

'With a mine?'

'Right. Command-detonated. It was horrible.'

The CIA man, who was head of security for the entire
province, was lying; but at the time I had no facts to refute the
story with. The stationmaster in Hué had said there hadn't been
a mining incident in months, and this was confirmed by the
railway officials in Danang. But the CIA man was anxious to
impress us that he had his finger on the country's pulse, the
more so since his girlfriend had joined us and was draped around
his neck. The other fat man was in the bungalow, talking in
frantic whispers to one of the girls, and the black man was a
little distance from the porch, doing chin-ups on a bar spliced
between two palms. The CIA man said, 'There's one thing you
gotta keep in mind. The VC don't have any support in the
villages – and neither do the government troops. See, that's why
everything's so quiet.'

The Vietnamese girl pinched his cheek and shouted to her
friend at the edge of the beach who was watching the black
man swing a heavy chain around his head. The man inside the
bungalow came out and poured himself a whisky. He drank it
worriedly, watching the CIA man rant.

'It's a funny situation,' the CIA man was saying. 'Like you say this village is clean and this village is all Charley, but there's one thing you gotta understand: most people aren't fighting. I don't care what you read in the papers – these journalists are more full of shit than a Christmas turkey. I'm telling you it's quiet.'

'What about the mine?'

'Yeah, the mine. You should stay off the train; that's all I can say.'

'It's different at night,' said the man with the whisky.

'Well, see, the country kinda changes hands after dark,' said the CIA man.

'I think we'd better go,' said Cobra One.

'What's the rush? Stick around,' said the CIA man. 'You're a writer,' he said to me. 'I'm a writer too – I mean, I do a little writing. I pound out articles now and then. *Boy's Life* – I do quite a bit for *Boy's Life*, and um –'

The girls, shouting in Vietnamese and giggling, were beginning to distract him.

'– anyway, where'd you say you're going? Marble Mountain? You wanna stay away from there about this time.' He looked at his watch. It was five-thirty. 'There might be Charley there. I don't know. I wouldn't want to be responsible.'

We left, and when we got to the car I looked back at the bungalow. The CIA man waved his cigar at us; he seemed to be unaware that a Vietnamese girl still clung to him. His friend stood on the porch with him, agitating in his hand a paper cup full of whisky and ginger ale. The black man had returned to the high-bar: he was doing chin-ups; the girls were counting. The sentry sat hugging his rifle. Beyond them was the sea. The CIA man called out, but the tide was coming in and the noisy surf drowned his words. The refugees in Danang had taken over the barracks; these three had the general's beach house. In a sense they were all that remained of the American stake in the war: degenerate sentiment, boozy fears, and simplifications. For them the war was over: they were just amusing themselves, raising a little Cain.

Four miles south of this, near Marble Mountain, our car stalled behind a slow ox cart. While we were waiting, a Vietnamese boy of about ten rushed over and screamed through the window.

'What did he say?' asked Cobra One.

'"Motherfucker",' said Dial.

'Let's get out of here.'

That evening I met Colonel Tuan who, under the name Duy Lam, writes novels. He was one of about ten writers in Vietnam who told me how severe censorship was under Thieu's regime – not simply political censorship, for *A Street-car Named Desire* is also banned. Afraid that their own books will be censored, Vietnam's novelists have chosen the safer course of translating inoffensive novels: Saigon's bookshops are full of Vietnamese versions of *Jane Eyre*, *Jonathan Livingston Seagull*, and the works of Washington Irving and Dorothy Parker. Colonel Tuan said he liked writing in Vietnamese, although he could write with equal ease in French or English.

'Vietnamese is a very beautiful language,' he said. 'But it is hard to translate. For example, if a man is addressing his wife there are so many ways he can do it. He might say "You" – but this is considered rude. Or he might call her "Little sister", and she will call him "Brother". The most beautiful is when a man calls his wife "Myself" – "How is myself?" he will say to her. And there are others. He might call her "Mother", and she will call him "Father" –'

'"Mother, Father",' said Cobra One. 'Why, Mister and Mrs Front-Porch America say *that*!'

Before he left I asked Colonel Tuan what the general feeling in Vietnam was towards Americans after so much war, disruption, and death, after all the years of occupation.

Colonel Tuan thought a long time before he replied, and when he did he chose his words carefully. 'We think the Americans,' he said, and stopped. 'We think they are well disciplined

. . . and they made many mistakes in the war. And of course we think they are generous. But we also believe they are people without culture – none at all, none that we have seen. I am not speaking for myself: I have read Faulkner and many other American writers. I am thinking of the average person – most of the people in Vietnam. That is what they think.'

I flew from Danang to Nha Trang to take a train to Thap Cham, but the day I arrived there was an attack by a squad of sappers on the oil depot outside Saigon, at Nha Be, and 50 per cent of Vietnam's fuel was wiped out in a morning. Fuel rationing started and I cancelled my trip. It was an unnecessary extravagance, since I would have to be driven a hundred miles back in a car. I got a bicycle and pedalled around the town of abandoned villas, then ate eels at a sea-front restaurant. The next day I waited hours at Nha Trang airport for a Saigon plane; and finally one came, a C-123 laden with Kleenex, Kotex, beans, toilet paper, grapefruit juice, a huge crate of Port of Call Extra Fancy Cal-Rose Rice (odd, since Nha Trang is in a rice-growing area), and a 1967 Dodge, belonging to one of the Americans there.

The flight back to Saigon in a thunderstorm scared the life out of me; I was strapped against the stomach wall of this pitching whale, and the three Chinese pilots gave me no reassurance. I recovered sufficiently to give two more lectures of which I remember little apart from what Auden described in 'On the Circuit' as

> A truly asinine remark,
> A soul-bewitching face.

And then I was off and waiting at Tan Son Nhut Airport to go to Japan. In better times I would have taken the train to Hanoi, changed for Peking, and gone via Shenyang and Seoul to Pusan for a boat linking to one of Japan's Kyushu expresses. Or I could have gone straight from Peking to Moscow via Ulan Bator in Mongolia, and then home. The way is clear, by rail, from Hanoi

Junction to Liverpool Street Station in London. Perhaps at some future date . . .[1]

[1] Now – April 1975 – most of the Vietnam towns I passed through by rail have been blown up, all have been captured, and many of their people killed. For the survivors the future is melancholy, and the little train no longer runs between Hué and Danang.

# 26. The Hatsukari ('Early Bird') Limited Express to Aomori

IN Japan I planned to outfit myself for Siberia. There were the trains, of course, and the lectures to pay for them; but clothing for my onward journey was my initial concern. I arrived in Tokyo with the clothes that had served me for three months in the tropics, my drip-dry wardrobe. These clothes, stained with curry juice, somewhat threadbare, the trouser seats worn shiny by my sedentary travelling, were inadequate for the freezing Japanese weather, which augured ill for what I had been fore-warned (Soviet railway timetables give average temperatures) would be thirty below in Khabarovsk. It was then December. Tokyo's winter was aggravated by wind-blown grit and exhaust fumes and those choking updrafts between buildings that characterize big-city winters. I spent two days searching for warm clothes. But Japanese clothes are not designed for the Siberian winter, and they are made only in small sizes, and they cost the earth.

It is with a kind of perverse pride that the Japanese point out how expensive their country has become. But this is as much a measure of wealth as of inflation, and I began to wonder if it was as crippling as people claimed. I asked about it, but this timid inquiry is the foreigner's first question and the knowing resident is prepared to shock you with joke prices. How much does a kimono cost? 'You can get a good one for a thousand dollars.' A meal? 'At most restaurants you can get away with paying about twenty dollars – for one person.' A bottle of gin? 'Imported stuff might set you back twenty dollars or more.' And when I laughed derisively, an American turned on me with what I thought was unwarranted savagery and said, 'Listen, you can't get a cup of coffee here for less than a dollar!' There was,

I learned later, a place in the Tokyo outskirts where a cup of coffee (including cream and sugar) was said to cost forty dollars. This information, offered so casually, is like a form of fagging at schools where the seniors' automatic response to the new boy is to exclude him by horrifying him. Americans in Thailand initiate you by saying, 'Never pat a Thai on the head – the head is sacred here. You could be killed for that.' The retailing of the Thai religious mystique, like the money mystique in Japan, is supposed to make you think twice about staying. No one says you can live cheaply in Japan – but it's possible, by staying in Japanese inns and developing a taste for the large bowls of noodle soup called *ra-men* (no charge for the tea) and using the train. Fruit is also inexpensive since Japan buys cut-price oranges, apples, and tangerines from the South Africans, who are so grateful to get radios in return, they have officially declared the Japanese to be white. And there is a McDonald's hamburger joint on the Ginza. Winter clothes were a different story. Most coats I saw were well over $100 and the one I settled for, a tight-fitting number with a rabbit-fur collar, cost me $150. Gloves, scarf, woollen hat, and so forth exhausted the fee I got for my first lecture, but I was prepared not only for Siberia but also for my speaking engagement in the December snows of Hokkaido, two train trips north.

The streets of Tokyo after dark were filled with glad groups of whooping Japanese. Less enthusiastic ones lay dead drunk in the doorways of Mori's Noddle House or the Pub Glasgow, or were slumped on the sidewalks of crooked back lanes – wherever they were overcome with alcoholic fatigue. These were casualties of the bonus. Twice a year Japanese employees are awarded a bonus: December is one of these months and it was my fate to arrive the day the money was dished out. Towards midnight I could see all the stages of Japanese drunkenness, from the early one, in which they raise their voices, to the last stage, where they simply flop down, collapsing on a restaurant floor or in a freezing street. Between the loudness and paralysis they throw up and sing. I thought of the casualties as 'bonuses', and I could see them being lugged by their friends, many of whom, at the singing stage, had enough boozy courage to howl in my direction. After twelve there were fewer of them; the streets were quiet enough for ladies in kimonos, shawls, and thick slippers to walk their dogs – invariably sleek well-bred hounds. Two ladies, chatting softly, advanced upon me. The dog paused, rocked back and shat; one lady flourished a paper she had held in readiness, and, still chatting to her friend, delicately scooped up the dog shit and deposited it in a near-by barrel.

I hadn't seen the barrel until she used it: Tokyo's order is apparent only up close – from a distance it is a jumble, but the jumble must be studied for the plan to emerge. Then you see the sliding doors, the neatly hidden lights in the wall and under the table connected to barely visible switches marked BRIGHT and DUSKY, the tables and waiters and spigots that materialize from the wall, the machines in the subway that sell you a ticket and then punch it, the disappearing chairs, and the silent trains you board with the help of the disembodied arm of a man who is hired to push people aboard. At seven o'clock in the evening when the stores close, two girls in uniform appear at the door; they bow, say 'Thank you' and 'Come again' to each customer, and they are back in the morning. At the enormous Isetan Department Store in Shinjuku, the groups of employees standing by display counters say, 'Good morning' to the first customers, making them feel like stock-holders. Everything works: the place spins with polite invention.

On a department-store wall there are forty-eight colour televisions, an impressive display of electronics, and, though even forty-eight images of a little Japanese politician giving a speech in living colour do not make him Winston Churchill, the array reveals the Japanese taste for gadgetry. There must be something in the Japanese character that saves them from the despair Americans feel in similar throes of consuming. The American, gorging himself on merchandise, develops a sense of guilty self-consciousness; if the Japanese have these doubts they do not show them. Perhaps hesitation is not part of the national character, or perhaps the ones who hesitate are trampled by the crowds of shoppers – that natural selection that capitalist society practises against the reflective. The strong impression I had was of a people who acted together because of a preconceived plan: a people programmed. You see them queuing automatically in the subway, naturally forming lines at ticket counters and machines, and it is difficult to avoid the conclusion that the people all have printed circuits. But my assessment changed with time and I began to see people struggling against order in these subway lines: as soon as the train drew in and the doors flashed open, many people who had waited silently for a long time in an orderly line broke ranks and began shoving and flailing their parcels and throwing themselves at the door.

So far on this trip (it is another bonus of the sleeping car) I had managed to avoid those so-called cultural evenings during which one was held captive in a hot room to applaud the degenerate spectacle of dancers and singers in feathers and beads performing numbers whose badness asked to be excused on the grounds it was traditional. But the night before I caught the Hatsukari to Aomori I had some time to spare and, for no particular reason that I can remember, decided to go to the Nichigeki Music Hall to see a two-hour show called *Red Flowers Fall on Fair Skin*. This was pedantically advertised as commemorating the two hundred and fiftieth anniversary of the birth of the Japanese playwright, Chikamatsu Monzaemon. Even the sadists in Japan, I was to discover, have a sense of history. There were only two or three *gaijins* in the audience. A cultural evening elsewhere would have been a tourist affair: I had a feeling this large local turnout would afford some insights in the Japanese use of leisure.

Just as the lights went down, two middle-aged women darted down the aisle and took their seats in the first row, giggling. The opening number was a kick line, ten Japanese girls in gold

Thai-style headdresses and little else, apart from tiny gold lamé bikini bottoms. The lead dancer ascended through the floor on a revolving pedestal and flourished gold snakes in front of the nimbly kicking troupe. I groaned. The music blared. After having searched the papers and rejected the *noh* and *kabuki* offerings I had come up with a tit-show. I wanted to leave, and I nearly did after the next number, a Japanese song, sung by a powdered androgynous wraith, which left me feeling as if I had just been subjected to the complete unstringing of a piano. I hung on, faintly attracted by the nakedness and finding a queer enjoyment in the dance routines, 'Cheerio! Charleston!' and 'Black Cry-Out' (a spirited episode, relating the death of Billie Holiday, with the Japanese in black–face – more a minstrel show than a comment on the race question). Up to that point most of the numbers mimicked Radio City Music Hall, but what followed owed absolutely nothing to the West.

'Aburagoroshi', which my Japanese neighbour gladly translated as 'oil-kill', began with a film of two women running into a room where, on the floor, oil lay in a wide pool. This film might have been shown at one of these university film societies that have an annual screening of *L'avventura*, *Pather Panchali*, and tedious East European cartoons: it had a pretentious chase, odd camera angles, and the kind of formal hysteria I had always associated with film-society offerings. Then one woman slipped in the oil and the other pounced on her and they began fighting. They screamed, tore at each other's hair, and gnashed their teeth, and each time the victim tried to escape she slipped in the oil and was pinned down by her pursuer. There were shots of dripping fingernails, oily hair, bums, breasts, and knees, as well as outrageous cinematic effects, like that of a mouth about to engorge the screen.

While this film – growing progressively sadistic – flickered at the back of the stage, two naked Japanese girls appeared from the well at the centre of the stage and performed a live stylized version of what was taking place on the screen – that is, aping the sadism, pretending to tear at each other. The women on the screen were now gleaming with oil, and you could see it was going to end badly when one sank her teeth into the other's bum, causing the victim to thrash. The biter straddled her. The simultaneous presentation continued, two writhing nudes on the stage, two thrashing nudes on the screen. The camera shifted to show wounds, blood mixed with oil, and blood and oil coursing down the breasts of a woman on all fours. This entertainment ended showing the two murderesses triumphant over the prostrate bodies of their victims, and there was much applause.

The next item, 'Ten No Amishima', began innocently enough with a film of a man fondling a woman. I asked my grinning neighbour what the title meant. He said it was simply the name of an island in the Sea of Japan where this quick feel was taking place, and I hoped, as it unfolded, that it was not on my itinerary. The man was behind the woman now and it took very little imagination to conclude that he was resolutely sodomizing her as he worked at her breast like a man squeezing lemons — lemons rather than grapefruits. Two girls came onstage as before and demonstrated in a way that might properly be called symbolic what the man and woman were doing in the film, and a full ten minutes of lubricious sex play passed before the final scene. This was an embrace, and as the girls onstage made the beast with two backs, the man in the film hopped into the missionary position and at the moment of orgasm — a wince its only warning — drew a glittering sword from beneath the mat and cut his lover's throat. There was a close shot of the fatal laceration, of blood running between the dead woman's breasts (this seemed a popular climax), and I moved to the lobby for a breath of fresh air.

I was not quite provoked to return for 'The Blood-Stained White Body', but I saw 'Japan Sinking'. This was a hilarious portrayal, by ten nude girls and ten epicene male dancers, of how Japan will finally go under. The last number was a solo entitled 'Onna Harakiri', which is fairly explicit once you know that Onna is the name of the girl stripping off her kimono and unsheathing a sword and holding it to her stomach. A man off-stage recited what sounded to be a mocking Japanese poem with the rhythm and metre of 'The Raven'. The tormented Onna, stark naked, pushed the blade in and pulled it sideways. Blood spurted from her belly, spraying the stage, and she tumbled over. But she was still alive. She knelt again and, as the poem proceeded, stabbed herself in the left thigh, the right thigh, and under each arm, releasing gouts of blood. So clever are the Japanese that it was not until her sixth attempt that I saw she was puncturing a small cellophane envelope of blood each time. Now she was covered in gore, her tatami mat was sticky with it, and the people in the front row wiped it from their faces with hankies. Finally, she succeeded: she exhibited her blood-stained body to the reverential audience and then pushed the dripping blade into her throat, impaling her head like a lollipop on a stick. Blood shot to her jaws, and, much perforated, she swooned and fell flat. The floor revolved, giving everyone a view of the carnage before the platform descended into the stage well, pausing briefly for Onna to raise a bloody floodlit hand: it was this hand the audience cheered as the lights went out.

Outside the Nichigeki Music Hall, the Japanese men who had watched with fastidious languor and then so enthusiastically applauded the savage eroticism that could enjoy no encore – baring their teeth as they did so – these men, as I say, bowed deeply to one another, murmured polite farewells to their friends, linked arms with their wives with the gentleness of old-fashioned lovers, and, in the harsh lights of the street, smiled, looking positively cherubic.

The bullet-nosed Hatsukari Limited Express (its name, 'Early Bird', refers to its arrival in Aomori, not its departure from Tokyo) leaves Ueno Station every afternoon on the dot of four. Ueno is crowded with people wearing fur hats, carrying skis and heavy coats for the snow at the end of the line: these are the vacationers. But there are returning residents, too, smaller, darker, Eskimo-faced people, on their way back to Hokkaido. The Japanese expression *nobori-san* ('rustics') describes them: it literally means 'the downers'; having taken the *nobori* 'down-train', these visitors, country-cousins spending a holiday in Tokyo, are considered yokels. On the train they stay in their seats, kick their heavy shoes off, and sleep. They look relieved to be going home and carry with them souvenirs from Tokyo: cookies wrapped in cellophane, flowers in paper cones, dried fruit bound with ribbon, dolls in tissue, stuffed toys in boxes. The Japanese are marvellous packagers of merchandise. These souvenirs are crammed in the plastic shopping bags that form the basis of the Japanese traveller's luggage. And there are other parcels, for the *nobori-san*, not trusting the food on Japanese National Railways, brings his own lunch pail. When he wakes, he rummages at his feet and discovers a sealed tin of rice and fish that, without stretching or rising from his padded armchair, he eats, blowing and smacking. The train itself is silent; my memory of Japanese train noises was this sound of eating, which is also the sound of a grown man inflating a balloon.

An amplified music box, ten plucking notes, and a recorded message preceded our stops. A warning is necessary because the stops are so brief: fifteen seconds at Minami-Urawa, a minute at Utsunomiya, and, two hours later, another one-minute halt at Fukushima. An unprepared passenger might be mangled by the door or might miss his stop altogether. Long before the music and the message, the experienced Japanese carry their shopping bags to the exit, and as soon as the train stops and a crack appears in the door, they begin pushing madly towards the platform. The platform, designed for laden, shoving people, is level with the threshold. The lights in the carriages are never off, making it impossible to sleep, but enabling a passenger to gather up his belongings at two in the morning when the train pulls in and pauses for fifteen seconds at his station.

Such efficiency! Such speed! But I longed for the sprawl of Indian Railways, the wide berths in the wooden compartments that smelled of curry and cheroots; the laundry chits with 'camisoles' and 'collars' marked on them; over the sink a jug of water; and out in the hall a man with a bottle of beer on his tray: trains that chugged to the rhythm of 'Alabammy Bound' or 'Chattanooga Choo-Choo', embodying what was best in the railway bazaar. On such a slow train it was almost impossible to get duffilled.

The odourless Japanese trains unnerved me and produced in me a sweaty tension I had always associated with plane travel. They brought back the symptoms of encapsulated terror I had felt in southern Thailand's International Express – a kind of leaden suspense that had stolen upon me after several months of travel. Travel – even in ideal conditions – had begun to make me anxious, and I saw that in various places the constant movement had separated me so completely from my surroundings that I might have been anywhere strange, nagged by the seamless guilt an unemployed person feels moving from failure to failure. This baffled trance overtook me on the way to Aomori, and I think it had a great deal to do with the fact that I was travelling in a fast, dry bullet-train, among silent people who, even if they spoke, would be incomprehensible. I was trapped by the double-glazing. I couldn't even open the window! The train swished past the bright empty platforms of rural stations at night, and for long moments, experiencing a heightened form of the alienation I'd felt before, briefly, in secluded pockets of time, I could not imagine where I was or why I had come.

The book I was reading on that train upset me further. It was *Japanese Tales of Mystery and Imagination* by Edogawa Rampo. Rampo's real name is Hirai Taro, and like his namesake – his pen name is a Japanese version of Edgar Allan Poe – he specializes in tales of terror. His fictional inventions were ungainly, and his shin-barking prose style was an irritation; and yet I was held, fascinated by the very ineptitude of the stories, for it was as impossible to dismiss these horrors as it had been the grisly rigadoon the Nichigeki audience had considered an entertainment. Here was another glimpse of the agonized Japanese spirit. But how to reconcile it with the silent figures in the overbright train, who moved as if at the command of transistors? Something was wrong; what I read contradicted the sight of these travellers. Here was the boy hero in 'A Hell of Mirrors', with his 'weird mania of optics', sealing himself in a globular mirror, masturbating at his monstrous reflection, and going mad with auto-voyeurism; and there, in the opposite seat in my train, was a boy the same age, peacefully transfixed by the head of the person in front of him. In another story, 'The Human Chair', a lecherous chairmaker, 'ugly beyond description', hides himself inside one of his own constructions, providing himself with food and water, and 'for another of nature's needs I also inserted a large rubber bag.' The chair in which he lies buried is sold to a lovely woman, who provides him with thrills each time she sits on him, not knowing she is sitting in the lap of a man who describes himself as 'a worm . . . a loathsome creature'. The human chair masturbates, then writes (somehow) the lovely woman a letter. A few seats up from me in the Hatsukari was a squat ugly man, whose fists were clenched on his knees: but he was smiling. Driven to distraction by Rampo, I finally decided to abandon him. I was sorry I knew so little of the Japanese, but even sorrier that there was no refuge on this speeding train.

There was a young girl seated beside me. Very early in the trip I had established that she did not speak English, and for nearly the whole time since we had left Ueno Station she had been reading a thick comic book. When we arrived at the far north of Honshu, at Noheji Station (fifteen seconds) on Mutsu Bay, I looked out the window and saw snow – it lay between the tracks and on blue moonlit fields. The girl rose, put her comic down, and walked the length of the car to the toilet. A green TOILET OCCUPIED light went on, and while that light burned I read the comic. I was instructed and cautioned. The comic strips showed decapitations, cannibalism, people bristling with arrows like Saint Sebastian, people in flames, shrieking armies of marauders dismembering villagers, limbless people with dripping stumps, and, in general, mayhem. The drawings were not good, but they were clear. Between the bloody stories there were short comic ones and three of these depended for their effects on farting: a trapped man or woman bending over, exposing a great moon of buttock and emitting a jet of stink (gusts of soot drawn in wiggly lines and clouds) in the captors' faces. The green light went off. I dropped the comic. The girl returned to her seat and, so help me God, serenely returned to this distressing comic.

The loudspeakers blared at Aomori, the ferry landing, giving instructions, and when the train pulled into the station the passengers, who crowded into the aisle as soon as the first syllable of the message was heard, sprinted through the doors and down the platform. The chicken farmers with their souvenirs, the old ladies hobbling on wooden clogs, the youths with skis, the girl with her comic: through the lobby of the station, up the stairs, down several ramps, gathering speed and bumping each other, and tripping in the sandals that splay their feet into two broad toes – women shuffling, men running. Then to the row of turnstiles where tickets were punched, and six conductors waved people up the gangway and into their sections: First-Class Green Ticket Room, Ordinary Room, Berths, Second-Class Uncarpeted, Second-Class Carpeted (here passengers sat cross-legged on the floor). Within ten minutes the twelve hundred passengers had transferred themselves from the train to the ferry, and fifteen minutes after the Hatsukari had arrived at Aomori, the *Towada Maru* hooted and drew away from the dock to cross the Tsugaru Straits. At the Indian port of Rameswaram, a similar operation involving a train and a ship had taken almost seven hours.

I was in the Green Ticket Room with about 150 other people, who were, like me, trying to adjust the barber chairs that had been assigned to them. These sloping chairs were tilted back, and before the lights dimmed many people were snoring. The four-hour crossing was very rough; the snow at Aomori had been deep, and we were now sailing in a blizzard. The ship twisted sharply, its fittings made low ominous groans, spray flew on to the deck, and snowflakes sifted past the portholes. I went out to the windy deck, but couldn't stand the cold and the sight of so much black water and snow. I settled into my chair and tried to sleep. Because of the snowstorm, every forty-five seconds the ship's horn blew a moan into the straits.

At four o'clock there was birdsong – twittering and warbling – over the loudspeaker: another recording. But it was still very dark. A few words from the loudspeaker and everyone rose and rushed to the cabin doors. The ferry slipped sideways, the gangway was secured, the doors flew open, and everyone made for the waiting train through the dry snow on the ramps at Hakodate Station. Now I was running, too: I was going at Japanese speed. I had learned at Aomori that I had less than fifteen minutes to board the northbound train to Sapporo, and I had no wish to be duffilled in such a desolate place.

# 27. The Ozora ('Big Sky') Limited Express to Sapporo

'THE train came out of the long tunnel into the snow country. The earth lay white under the night sky.' The opening lines of Kawabata's *Snow Country* (set elsewhere, on western Honshu) describe the Ozora, an hour after leaving Hakodate. It was still only five-thirty on that December morning; I had never seen such distances of snow, and after six when the sun came up and yellowed the drifts, giving the snow the harsh glare of desert sand, it was impossible to sleep. I walked up and down the train snapping pictures of everything in sight: it was something no Japanese could possibly object to.

In the dining car, a Japanese man told me, 'This train is called "Big Sky" because Hokkaido is the land of big sky.' I tried to engage him in further conversation, but he cried, 'Please!' and hurried away. There appeared to be no other English-speakers on the train, but while I was eating my breakfast, an American who introduced himself as Chester asked if he could join me. I said fine. I was glad to see him, to reassure myself that I was still capable of assessing strangers and appreciating travel. The mental motion-sickness I had experienced the day before had disturbed me; I had recognized it as fear, and it was an inconvenient state of mind in Japan. Chester was from Los Angeles. He had a handlebar moustache and wore lumberjack's clothes: checkered woollen shirt, twill pants, and lace-up boots. He taught English in Hakodate, where he had boarded the train. The people in Hakodate were real nice, but the weather was real bad, his rent was real high, and living was real expensive. He was on his way to Sapporo for the weekend to see a girl he knew. What was I doing?

I thought it would be unlucky to lie: a whiff of paranoia had made me superstitious. I told him exactly where I had been, naming the countries; I said that I had been taking notes and that, when I got back to England, I would write a book about the trip and call it *The Great Railway Bazaar*. And I went further: I said that as soon as he was out of sight I would write down what he said, that the people were real nice and the weather was real bad, and I would describe his moustache.

All this candour had a curious effect: Chester thought I was lying, and when I convinced him I was telling the truth he began speaking in a rather joshing conciliatory way, as if I were crazy and might shortly become violent. It turned out that he had an objection to travel books: he said he didn't want to hurt my feelings but that he thought travel books were useless. I asked him why.

'Because everyone travels,' said Chester. 'So who wants to read about it?'

'Everyone gets laid, too, but that doesn't eliminate screwing as a subject – I mean, people still write about it.'

'Sure, but you take travelling,' he said. 'Your average person in the States thinks nothing about going to Bally. I know lots of people – ordinary middle-class people – who go to really far-out places like Instantbull, Anchor, Taheedy, you name it – my folks are in Oh-sucker right this minute. So they've been there already: who wants to read about it?'

'I don't know, but the fact that they do travel might mean they'd be more interested in reading about it.'

'But they've *been* there already,' he said obstinately.

'By plane. That's like going in a submarine,' I said. 'A train's different. Look at us: we wouldn't be having this conversation if we were on a plane. Anyway, people don't always see the same things in foreign countries. I've got a theory that what you hear influences – maybe even determines – what you see. An ordinary street can be transformed by a scream. Or a smell might make a horrible place attractive. Or you might see a great Moghul tomb and while you're watching it you'll hear someone say "chickenzola" or "mousehole" and the whole tomb will seem as if it's made out of paste –'

What was this crackpot theory I was inventing for Chester? I couldn't rid myself of the notion that I had to prove to him I was sane. My urge to prove my sanity made me gabble, and my gabbling disproved my claim. Chester squinted at me, sizing me up in a pitying way that made me feel more than ever like Waugh's Pinfold.

'Maybe you're right,' he said. 'Look, I'd love to talk to you, but I've got piles of stuff to do.' He hurried away, and for the rest of the trip he avoided me.

The train had crossed a blunt peninsula, from Hakodate to Mori. We made a complete circuit of Uchiura Bay where the newly risen sun received intense magnification from the water and the snow on the shore. We continued along the coast, staying on the main line, which was straight and flat; inland there were mountain shelves and escarpments and the occasional volcano. Mount Tarumae rose on the left as the train began to turn sharply inland, towards Sapporo on the Chitose Line. People in hats with flapping earlaps and bulky coats worked beside the track, lashing poles together to make the skeleton of a snow fence. We left the shore of what was the western limit of the Pacific; within an hour we were near Sapporo, where, from the hills, one can see the blue Sea of Japan. This sea fills the cold Siberian winds with snow; the winds are constant, and the snow in Hokkaido is very deep in December.

But there were not more than three skiers on the train. Later, I asked for an explanation. It was not the skiing season: the skiers would come later, all together, crowding the slopes. The Japanese behaved in concert, giving a seasonal regularity to their pastimes and never jumping the gun. They ski in the skiing season, fly kites in the kite-flying season, sail boats and take walks in parks at other times custom specifies. The snow in Sapporo was perfect for skiing, but I never saw more than two people on a slope, and the ninety-metre ski jump, although covered in hard-packed snow and dusted with powder, was empty and would remain shut until the season opened.

Mr Watanabe, the consulate driver, met me at the station and offered me a guided tour of Sapporo. Sapporo has the look of a Wisconsin city in winter: it had been laid out with a T-square and in its grid of streets lined with dirty snow are used-car lots, department stores, neon signs, plastic hamburger joints, nightclubs, bars. After ten minutes I called off the tour, but it was a feeble gesture – we were stuck in traffic and not moving. Snow began to fall, a few large warning flakes, then gusts of smaller ones.

Mr Watanabe said, 'Snow!'

'Do you like to ski?' I asked.

'I like whisky.'

'Whisky?'

'Yes.' He looked stern. The car ahead moved a few feet; Mr Watanabe followed it and stopped.

I said, 'Mr Watanabe, is that a joke?'

'Yes.'

'You don't like to ski. You like whisky.'

'Yes,' he said. He continued to frown. 'You like ski?'

'Sometimes.'

'We go to ninety-metre ski jump.'

'Not today,' I said. It was darkening; the snowstorm in mid-morning had brought twilight to the city.

'This rejidential,' he said, indicating a row of cuboid houses, each on its own crowded plot and dwarfed by apartment complexes, hotels, and more bars, warming up their neon signs. Hokkaido was the last area in Japan to be developed: Sapporo's commercial centre was new and, with American proportions and the American chill, was not a place that invited a stranger to linger. Mr Watanabe guessed I was bored. He said, 'You want to see tzu?'

'What kind of tzu?'

'Wid enemas.'

'Enemas in cages?'

'Yes. Very big tzu.'

'No thanks.' The traffic had moved another five feet and stopped. The snow had increased, and among the shoppers on the sidewalk I saw three women in kimonos and shawls, their hair fixed into buns with wide combs. They carried parasols and held them against the driving snow as they minced along in three-inch clogs. Mr Watanabe said they were geishas.

'Now where would geishas be going at this hour?'

'Maybe to a crab.'

I thought a moment.

He said, 'You like crab?'

I said, 'Very much.'

'Go?'

I had to say no. What I wanted to see was the resort, Jozankei, twenty miles from Sapporo in the mountains, where there is a hot spring. It was the influence of Kawabata, that novel that seemed more and more to me like a version of Chekhov's 'The Lady With the Little Dog'. Shimamura, on holiday, makes a casual arrangement with a geisha at a hot-spring resort; and then he is possessed by her and goes back, love-struck against his will. He says, 'Why else would anyone come to such a place in December?'

Mr Watanabe agreed to take me, and he said, 'Buff?'

'Maybe buff or maybe look,' I said.

He understood, and the next day we went to Jozankei.

*Buff* is a good word for the Japanese bath, since it consists not of washing but of lying naked in a steamy communal pool and poaching yourself into a sense of well-being. But at 5,000 yen, nearly twenty dollars a bath, I realized I did not have the yen to be soaked that much. In any case, the snow at Jozankei had reached blizzard proportions: mattresses of snow clouds hung over the ugly little hamlet, which had the look, such was its heaped concentration, of having slipped from the walls of the beautiful mountain gorge. It snows throughout the winter in

Jozankei, and it gets so deep, the people tunnel under the immovable drifts. The roofs have wide Swiss eaves; the hydrant markers are fifteen feet high.

The falling snow muffled all sounds; it had stopped the cars and kept people indoors. It still fell, adding to the drifts of dry flakes already there, collecting on the floor of the gorge, reducing visibility, and making the low houses into a few dark shapes in that whiteness – a jutting eave, part of a wall, a smoking chimney pipe. Here was the top half of a sign, and, in the blur of whirling snow, a pine grove shattered into simple shapes by lumps of snow. I startled a flock of crows and only when they flew up did the trees they were hiding appear. There were more crows feeding on scraps at the back of a little inn; they took off and roosted in the white air, their black fretful feathers indicating the branches. I wanted to snap a picture of the crows taking flight in the snow. I clapped my hands and rushed at them. They didn't move. I tried again and fell over into a snowbank. As I got to my feet a Japanese woman with a basket went by; she spoke loudly in Japanese and tramped away. Mr Watanabe laughed and covered his face.

'What did she say?'

He hesitated.

'Tell me.'

'She say you are eccentric.'

I turned to the woman and cawed, *blawk! blawk! blawk!* She turned and yelled (according to Mr Watanabe), 'What did I tell you!'

We walked to the edge of the hamlet, to a slope where some snowbound skiers, three smudges in the blizzard, were waving their arms like stranded birds. No sound; only their blurred motion. Then we retraced out steps and found a restaurant. We ate while our shoes dried on the *kotatsu*. This charcoal brazier, the main source of warmth in most Japanese homes, is only one item in a lengthy charge sheet that proves the Japanese work in the twentieth century and live in an earlier one. We left towards the middle of the afternoon. Less than half a mile from Jozankei the snow let up: it turned sunny, and the mountains were large with light. I looked back to see Jozankei dark, grey, a storm still hanging over it like a curse.

Mr Watanabe said, 'You want to see Doctor Crack?'

One of the most respected figures in Sapporo's history is William S. Clark, a Massachusetts man. I had never heard of him, but learned he had been president of Massachusetts Agricultural College in Amherst. A stern fellow with an intelligent forehead and a saloon-keeper's moustache, Dr Clark was one of the founders of Sapporo's Agricultural College in 1876. His statue in bronze is one of the holy objects of the city. The story is that after eight months as Sapporo's dean he climbed on his horse and headed back to Massachusetts. His students followed him to the outskirts of Sapporo where, at Shimamatsu, he wheeled around and lectured them. His parting words were, 'Boys, be ambitious! Be ambitious not for money, not for selfish aggrand-izement, not for the evanescent thing which men call fame. Be ambitious for the attainment of all that a man ought to be.'

This ambiguous valediction excited the Japanese ('The phrase, "Boys, be ambitious!" has since embodied the life target of our young people.' – *Sapporo Handbook*), but the idea of a man from Mass. Aggie being remembered for telling the Japanese to be ambitious struck me as hilarious. Doctor Crack!

I gave my lecture. Over three months earlier, in Istanbul, I had spoken on the tradition of the American novel, implying that it was special and local. In India I contradicted most of this, and by the time I got to Japan I had come full circle, claiming that there was no real tradition in American writing that was not also European. The novel was of the West, and even the writers we considered most American, like Twain and Faulkner, were as affected by the British novel as by their native inspiration. It was as easy to define the American tradition as Borges did the Argentine one: all of Western culture. This thesis, which might be true, disconcerted the Japanese. They stood and bowed at the end of the lecture, saying, 'We have not read Mr Borges, but we have read Mr Leslie Fiedler. He has written as follows –'

'Why don't you stay and have a drink?' I said afterwards to the pretty Japanese girl in the hallway. It was the Shimamura in me talking. She hid her face in her fur collar and tossed her black hair.

'I can't,' she said.

'Why not?'

'Because,' she said, and started to make her getaway, 'because I am so shy!'

My offer was given impromptu, and it had to be turned down for that reason. It was the wrong time: the Japanese have a sense of occasion, which the following story may illustrate. That same night in Sapporo, an American woman, whose daughter was in a Japanese kindergarten, was invited to dinner by another mother, whose daughter was in her child's class. The dinner had two purposes – to introduce the American woman to Japanese culture, and to butter up the teacher, who had also been invited. This feeding of teachers – treating them at expensive restaurants – is a common feature of Japanese courtesy and presumably guarantees that your child will get the friendly attention he deserves. The dinner was served by two geishas; three more geishas played music, and the food came in such great quantities that after an hour the three diners abandoned the pretence of eating and spoke on subjects of mutual concern, the Japanese women revealing considerable interest in the age at which American ones begin menstruating.

The food stopped coming; more tea was brought, and the Japanese mother took out a parcel wrapped in cloth. She said it was a surprise and demurely she undid the ribbons and wrapping and took out a scroll. She said it was quite old, painted perhaps 150 years ago, and she laid it on the floor. The geishas put down their instruments and the eight women crouched on the tatami of this private restaurant cubicle while the owner of the scroll unrolled it eight inches. This was a panel showing a sturdy bald monk leering at a geisha. There was a poem beside it, which was read and translated before the next panel was shown. Here the monk was fumbling with the appalled geisha and tearing at the lower half of her kimono. The poem accompanying this picture was recited as ceremoniously as the one before, and the lady went on unrolling. This progressed, picture by picture; fully extended, the scroll showed a pornographic sequence of the lusty monk pictured in various stages of rape. Later on, I was able to examine it, and I can testify that the wounded vulva and the tumescent pistol-like penis were rendered in vivid detail, though I agree with the English critic William Empson, who (writing on Beardsley) said, '. . . the Japanese print-masters, too, lose their distinctive line when they turn aside and create Por-ners.' In the eighth panel the monk showed signs of fatigue, in contrast to the geisha who looked mightily aroused: she had redder eyes and she appeared in more predatory postures. Panel nine showed her seizing the fleeing monk's flaccid penis; panel ten had the agonized monk on his back and the geisha hunkered over him unsuccessfully stuffing his penis into her; and panel eleven, the clincher, depicted a much-aged monk being forced to fondle her: the geisha, wearing an ecstatic smile, had a firm grip on his hand, which she was directing against the bright bead of her clitoris. The Japanese mother clapped her hands and all the women laughed – the geishas loudest of all.

The sense of occasion, the formality of the dinner, the cost of the food, the presence of the geishas, the absence of men – all the rules observed – made the viewing of this antique piece of pornography possible. Any hint of the casual would have ruined it. The scroll, rolled up and wrapped, was gracefully presented to the American woman: she was told that she could show it to her husband, but she must not allow her little girl to see it. After a week it was to be returned to its owner. The American woman was baffled – and slightly embarrassed that the kindergarten teacher had witnessed it all. But the American woman (who told me the story) was flattered at being offered this glimpse of the Japanese cultural sorority, which was undoubtedly the whole intention.

'Little people in a big hurry,' said a man on the rapid train south, and he thought he'd nailed them down. But the more I thought about that ceremony in the Sapporo teahouse, the less Hokkaido looked like Wisconsin.

## 28. The Hikari ('Sunbeam') Super Express to Kyoto

BACK at Tokyo Central, on Platform 18, a hundred Japanese men in grey suits stood watching my train. There was a melancholy reverence in their faces. They had no luggage; they were not travellers. Grouped around one car in a respectful semicircle, they stared, their eyes fixed to one window. Inside the train, at that window, a man and woman stood next to their seats, their chins just showing below the window frame. The whistle was blown; the train started up, but before it moved an inch the man and woman began bowing at the window, again and again, and outside on the platform, the hundred men did the same – quickly, because the train was speeding. The bowing stopped: the hundred men burst into applause. The man and woman remained standing until we were out of the station and then they sat down and each opened a newspaper.

I asked the Japanese man next to me who they might be.

He shook his head. For a moment I thought he was going to say, 'No Engrish' – but he was thinking. He said, 'Offhand, I would say a company director. Or it could be a politician. I do not know him.'

'It's quite a send-off.'

'It is not unusual in Japan. The man is important. His employees must show some respect, even if' – he smiled – 'even if they do not feel it in their hearts.'

I wanted to pursue the matter, but I was framing a question when this man beside me reached into his briefcase and took out a well-thumbed copy of the Penguin edition of *The Golden Bowl*. He opened it in the middle, flexed the limp spine, and began reading. I did the same with *Silence*, by Shusaku Endo, feeling lucky beyond belief that I had Endo and not Henry James to cheer me up. The man clicked his ballpoint pen, scribbled three characters in an already scribbled margin, and turned the page. Watching someone read the later James can be very tiring. I read until the conductor came by, and when he had finished punching everyone's ticket he walked backwards up the aisle, bowing and saying, 'Thank you! Thank you! Thank you!' until he reached the door. The Japanese have perfected good manners and made them indistinguishable from rudeness.

I looked out the window, watching for the Tokyo suburbs to end, but they continued to appear, stretching as far as I could see along the flat biscuit-brown plain. The Hikari Super Express, the fastest passenger train in the world, which travels over 300 miles from Tokyo to Kyoto in less than three hours, never really leaves the pure horror of the megalopolis that joins these two cities. Under a sky, which tawny fumes have given the texture of wool, are pylons secured by cables, buildings shaped like jumbo rheostats, and an unzoned clutter of houses, none larger than two stories, whose picture windows front on to factories. Inside – I knew this from an evening visit in Tokyo – the houses are stark, austere, impeccable, impossible to date accurately; outside the faded wood retains the colour of soot that has sifted from the neighbourhood factory chimney, and no house is more than a foot from the one next door. To see this population density is to conclude that overcrowding requires good manners; any disturbance, anything less than perfect order, would send it sprawling.

A glimpse of two acres of farmland made me hopeful of more fields, but it was a novelty, no more than that: the tiny plough, the narrow furrows, the winter crops sown inches apart, the hay not stacked but collected in small swatches – a farm in miniature. In the distance, the pattern was repeated on several hills, but there the furrows were filled with snow, giving the landscape the look of seersucker. That was the image that occurred to me, but by the time I thought of it we were miles away. The train moved faster than my mind – so fast, everyone remained seated.

It was hard to ramble around a train moving at that speed – a single lurch would have you on the floor – and the only people who risked the aisles were the girls pushing trolleys with tea and cookies. Lacking the traditional features of the railway bazaar, the Japanese train relies on aircraft comforts: silence, leg room, a reading light – charging an extra ten dollars to sit two (instead of three) abreast, and discouraging passengers from standing and gabbing at the exits. Speed puts some people to sleep; others it makes breathless. It doesn't enliven conversation. I missed the slower trains with the lounge cars and the rackety wheels. Japanese train journeys were practical, uncongenial transitions from city to city: only the punctual arrival mattered. The frseeeeeeee-fronning trains of Asia were behind me. Still, I put my oar in.

'I see you're reading Henry James.'

The man laughed.

'I find the later James evasive,' I said.

'Hard to understand?'

'No, not hard to understand – just evasive.'

'You can take my course!'

'Do you give a course on James?'

'Well, I call the course simply "*The Golden Bowl*".'

'It sounds ambitious,' I said. 'How long does it take your average student to read *The Golden Bowl*?'

'The course lasts two years.'

'Which other book do they read?'

'Just that one.'

'Good God! How many lectures do you give?'

He did a little arithmetic, using his fingertips, then said, 'About twenty lectures a year. That would make forty lectures altogether.'

'I'm reading Shusaku Endo.'

'I noticed. He is one of our Christians.'

'Do you teach Japanese literature?'

'Oh, yes. But the students keep saying we're not modern enough. They want to read books written after the war.'

'Which war?'

'World War One – the ones written after the Meiji restoration.'

'So you concentrate on the classics?'

'Yes, eighth century, ninth century, also eleventh century.' He enumerated the works and put the James away. He was, he said, a university professor. His name was Professor Toyama and he taught at one of the universities in Kyoto. He said I would like Kyoto. Faulkner had liked it very much, and Saul Bellow – well, he had liked it too. 'Mr Saul Bellow was not enjoying himself. Then we took him to a strip show. He liked it quite a lot!'

'I bet.'

'Are you interested in strip shows?'

'Up to a point,' I said. 'But the one I saw wasn't a strip show. Sadists making love to masochists, nude suicides – I've never seen such blood! I really don't have the stomach for it. Have you ever been to Nichigeki Music Hall?'

'Yes,' said Professor Toyama. 'That's nothing.'

'Well, I don't find transfusions erotic, I'm sorry. I'd like to see the Japanese take sex out of the emergency ward.'

'In Kyoto,' he said, 'we have a very special strip show – three hours long. It is famous. Saul Bellow found it most interesting. Largely it is a lesbian show. For example, one girl will wear a mask – the special mask used in *kabuki* theatre. It is a fierce face with a very long nose. Quite obviously this is a phallic symbol. The girl does not wear it on her face – she wears it down here, under the waist. Her partner leans back and she inserts this nose and pretends to have intercourse. The high point of the evening is, excuse me, the showing of the cunt. When this is done, everyone claps. But it is a wonderful show. I think you should see it sometime.'

'Do you go very often?'

'When I was younger I used to go all the time, but recently I only go to accompany visitors. But we have many visitors!'

He spoke precisely, his hands clasped; he was diffident, but he could see I was interested, and I had told him I too had been a university lecturer. He knew my hosts in Kyoto: he said he might come to my lecture there. He asked me about my travelling and questioned me closely about my train journeys through Turkey and Iran.

'It is a long trip from London to Japan on the train.'

'It has its moments,' I said. I told him about Mark Twain's *Following the Equator*, and the wry traveller Harry De Windt who, at the turn of the century, had written *From Paris to New York by Land* and *From Pekin to Calais by Land*. Professor Toyama laughed when I quoted what I could of De Windt's advice in this last book:

I can only trust this book may deter others from following my example, and shall have satisfaction in knowing that its pages have not been written in vain. M. Victor Meignan concludes his amusing work *De Paris à Pekin par terre*, thus: – '*N'allez pas là! C'est la morale de ce livre!*' Let the reader benefit by our experience.

'Once,' said Professor Toyama, 'I sailed from London to Yokohama. It took forty days. It was a freighter – so not many passengers on board. There was only one woman on this ship. She was the girlfriend of a fellow – an architect. But they were as man and wife. That is the longest I have had to put up with lack of women. Of course, when we got to Hong Kong we went ashore and watched some pornographic films, but they weren't any good at all. It was a stuffy room and the projector kept breaking down. German films, I think. The prints were very bad. Then we went to Japan.'

'Was Hong Kong your only stop?'

'Penang was another.' The train came to a halt, the Sunbeam's only stop, forty-five seconds at Nagoya; then we were off.

'There are lots of girls in Penang!' I said.

'That is true. We went into a bar and found a pimp. We drank some beer and the pimp said, "We have girls upstairs." There were five of us – all Japanese students coming from England. We asked him if we could go up, but before he'd let us he insisted on saying all the prices. There was a language difficulty as well. He had a pencil and paper. He wrote down, "One intercourse" – so much; "two times" – so much again. Other things – well, you know what sort of thing. He told us to choose. This was very humiliating! We had to say how many times we would do it even before we went upstairs. So naturally we refused.

'I asked him if he had a lesbian show. But he was a clever pimp. He pretended not to understand! Then he understood – we explained it. He said, "The Chinese in Penang don't do those things. We have no lesbian show." We decided to go back to the ship. He was very interested for us to stay. He said, "We can have a show. I can find a girl and one of you can play the male part and the rest can watch." But of course this was out of the question.'

In reply I told him about the child brothel in Madras, the pimps in Lahore, and the sexual knacks in Vientiane and Bangkok. At this point in my trip my repertoire of anecdotes was very large, and Professor Toyama was so appreciative he gave me his calling card. For the remainder of the journey he read James, I read Endo, and the company director worked on what may have been a speech or report, covering a foolscap sheet he held on his briefcase with symmetrical columns of characters. Then the music box sounded, and we were warned in Japanese and English about the brevity of the stop in Kyoto.

'No need to hurry,' said Professor Toyama. 'The train will be here for a full minute.'

Travelling over a long distance becomes, after three months, like tasting wine or picking at a global buffet. A place is approached, sampled, and given a mark. A visit, pausing before the next train pulls out, forbids gourmandizing, but a return is possible. So from every lengthy itinerary a simpler one emerges, in which Iran is pencilled over, Afghanistan is deleted, Peshawar gets a yes, Simla a maybe, and so on. And it happens that after a while the very odour of a place or the sight of it from a corner seat in the Green Car is enough to influence the traveller to reject it and move on. I knew in Singapore that I would never return; Nagoya I had dismissed at the station in less than forty-five seconds; Kyoto I filed away for a return journey. Kyoto was like a wine bottle whose label you memorize to assure some future happiness.

It is the Heian Shrine, a comic red temple where in the winter-bare garden there is an antique trolley car amid the dwarf trees, on forty feet of track, upraised like a sacred object; it is the pleasant weather, the wooden teahouses, the surrounding mountains, the tram cars on the roads, the companionable atmosphere of drinking among learned men in tiny bars on the city's back lanes. No money changes hands in these bars; no chits are signed. The people who drink at these places are more than regular customers – they are members. The hostesses keep a record of what they eat, and the drinking is easily accounted for. Every man has in the bar's cupboard his own bottle of Very Rare Old Suntory Whisky, his name or number inked in white on the bottle.

By two o'clock in the morning, in one of these Kyoto bars, we had ranged in conversation from the varieties of Japanese humour to the subtle eroticism in Middleton's *Women Beware Women*. I brought up the subject of Yukio Mishima, whose suicide had appalled his Western readers but apparently had given relief to many Japanese, who saw in him dangerous imperial tendencies. They seemed to regard him the way an American would regard, say, Mary McCarthy, if she were a vocal Daughter of the American Revolution. I said I thought Mishima seemed to be basing his novels on Buddhist principles.

'His Buddhism is false – very superficial,' said Professor Kishi. 'He was just dabbling in it.'

Mr Shigahara said, 'It doesn't matter. The Japanese don't

know anything about Buddhism, and Mishima didn't feel it. We don't feel it as deeply as your Catholics feel Catholicism. It is our way of life, but not devotion or prayer. Your Catholics have a spiritual sense.'

'That's news to me,' I said. But I could see how a Japanese might reach that conclusion after reading Endo's *Silence*, which is about religious persecution and degrees of faith. I said that I had read Mishima's 'Sea of Fertility' novels. I had liked *Spring Snow* very much; *Runaway Horses* was rather more difficult; and *The Temple of Dawn* I found completely baffling on the subject of reincarnation.

'Well, that's what it's about,' said Professor Kishi.

'It sounded farfetched to me,' I said.

'And farfetched to me, too!' said Mr Iwayama.

'Yes,' said Mr Shigahara. 'But when you read those last novels you understand why he committed suicide.'

'I had that feeling,' I said. 'He believes in reincarnation, so presumably he expects to be back pretty soon.'

'I hope not!' said Professor Kishi.

'Really?'

'Yes, I really hope not. I hope he stays where he is.'

'Example of Japanese humour!' said Mr Iwayama.

'Brack humour!' said Professor Miyake.

A steamy white thing, the shape of a bar of soap, was set before me on the bar.

'That is a turnip. Kyoto is famous for them. Eat it – you will find it very tasty,' said Professor Kishi, who had assumed the role of host.

I took a bite: it was fibrous but fragrant. The bar hostess said something in Japanese to Professor Kishi.

'She says you look like Engelbert Humperdinck.'

'Tell her,' I said, 'I think she has beautiful knees.'

He told her. She laughed and spoke again.

'She likes your nose!'

The following day I took my hangover to the top of Mount

Hiei. I was guided by Professor Varley, a former teacher of mine, who saw in Kyoto a temporary refuge from the intensifying foolishness he had found in Amherst. Nearing retirement age, he had withdrawn in disgust and fled to Kyoto. We rode on the velvet seats of the Keifuku Electric Railway to Yase Park, where the maples still had some leaves, small orange twirling stars; then the cable car to the second summit – snow appearing on the ground as we rose; then to the ropeway, a dangling capsule that passes over the tops of snowbound cedars, to the top of the mountain. It was snowing here. We walked through the woods to various temples and at one remote spot met a group of twenty weather-beaten peasants, mainly old men and women and a few fat girls, taking their first holiday after the harvest and turning their red toughened faces towards these mountain shrines. Their leader had a flag, which he had draped on his head, like the Singhalese signalman in the monsoon, to keep dry. The group passed us, and shortly we heard them ringing the temple bell. The log clapper hit the colossal bronze, summoning and warning, and these booms carried through the snow-still forest and followed us all the way down.

## 29. The Kodama ('Echo') to Osaka

THE Kodama is brief: a fourteen-minute buzz, a sigh, and you've arrived. I had found my seat, dug out my notebook, and set it on my lap, but no sooner had I dated the page than the Echo was in Osaka and the passengers were scrambling out. Another echo reached me on the platform of Osaka Station, a thought the train had outstripped: *the suburbs of Kyoto are also the suburbs of Osaka.* Hardly worth writing down unless one also observes that the Osaka suburbs filled me with such a sense of desolation that, on arrival, I went to bed. I had planned to get tickets for the puppet theatre, *Bunraku* – it seemed the appropriate move for the travel writer to make in a strange city. If you see nothing you write nothing: you compel yourself to see. But I felt too gloomy to put myself into the greater gloom of the street. It was not only the grey buildings and the sight of a mob of people in surgical masks waiting on a sidewalk for the light to change (in itself worrying: a society without jaywalkers might indicate a society without artists); it was also the noxious Osaka air, said to be two fifth poisonous gas.

Witness, then, the aspirant to a travel book, with a pillow over his head at a hotel in Osaka, with no memory of his trip there except the sight of a notebook page, blank except for its date, and a horrid recollection of a city like a steel trap someone has forgotten to bait. I started drinking, assuming it was sundown, when it is no crime to drink or flirt with another man's wife; but the dim light had thrown me. It was mid-afternoon. I drank anyway, finished my half-bottle of gin, and started on the row of beer bottles the hotel proprietors had thoughtfully put in the room's refrigerator. I felt like a travelling salesman holed up in Baltimore with a full case of samples: what

was the point in getting out of bed? Like the paranoid salesman, I began to invent reasons for not leaving the hotel, excuses
I would deliver home instead of orders. Twenty-nine train
trips turn the most intrepid writer into Willy Loman. But: all
journeys were return journeys. The farther one travelled, the
nakeder one got, until, towards the end, ceasing to be animated
by any scene, one was most oneself, a man in a bed surrounded
by empty bottles. The man who says, 'I've got a wife and kids'
is far from home; at home he speaks of Japan. But he does not
know – how could he? – that the scenes changing in the train
window from Victoria Station to Tokyo Central are nothing
compared to the change in himself; and travel writing, which
cannot but be droll at the outset, moves from journalism to
fiction, arriving as promptly as the Kodama Echo at autobiography. From there any further travel makes a beeline to con-
fession, the embarrassed monologue in a deserted bazaar. The
anonymous hotel room in a strange city, I was thinking – the
pillow still over my head – drives one into the confessional
mode. But the moment I began to enumerate my sins, the
telephone rang.

'I'm in the lobby downstairs. It's about your lecture –'

It was a reprieve. At the Cultural Centre I breathed alcohol
into the microphone, and speaking about Nathanael West, said
patronizingly, 'A writer you may not be familiar with –'

'Professor Sato –' a Japanese girl began.

A man jumped up and ran out of the room.

'– has translated all his books.'

The running man was Professor Sato. Hearing his name, he
had panicked thoroughly, and afterwards, when I inquired about
him, the others apologized and said he had gone home. Had I
read Japanese novels? they wanted to know. I said yes, but that
I had a question. 'Ask Mister Gotoh!' one said and patted Mr
Gotoh on the shoulder. Mr Gotoh looked as if he were going
to cry. I said that the Japanese novelists I had read dealt with the
question of old age as few other writers did, with compassion

and insight, but that in at least four instances the high point of the novel came when the old man turned into a voyeur. Thinking of the Nichigeki Music Hall, Professor Toyama's lesbian show, and the girl's comic book on the Early Bird, I said that this voyeurism was always cleverly stage-managed by the protagonist: what was there about witnessing sexual shenanigans that so appealed to the Japanese?

'Maybe,' said Mr Gotoh, 'maybe it is because we are Buddhists.'

'I thought Buddhism taught conquering desire,' I said.

'Maybe watching is conquering,' said Mr Gotoh.

'I wonder.'

The question was unresolved, but I continued to think that the Japanese, who were tireless as factory workers, had arrived at some point of sexual exhaustion that had its refinement in watching an act they had no interest in performing themselves. In this, as in so many other things, was the Japanese combination of advanced technology and cultural decadence.

On my way back to the hotel alone, I stepped into a bookstore for a guidebook to the U.S.S.R. and not finding one settled for a copy of Gissing's *New Grub Street*. I walked until I found a bar. Through the window, decorated with Asahi and Kirin beer bottles, the bar looked cheerful, but it was not until I got inside that I saw the five Japanese drunks, the splashed floor, the broken chairs. The men's faces were pink, the flesh around their eyes swollen with alcohol, and they had lost their customary politeness. They staggered over and embraced me. One said, 'Wha yo fum!' Another thumped me on the back and said, 'Yo bey goo boy!' A man thrust his face into mine: 'Yo nose bey *beeg* one!' They demanded that I speak Japanese. I said I couldn't. The man who had called me a very good boy blew me a raspberry and said, 'Yo bey *bad* boy!'

I ordered a beer. The Japanese girl behind the counter poured it and took my money. A fat-faced man said, 'Japan goal! Yo lah Japan goal! She goo!' He tweaked my nose and laughed salaciously. He said I should take the girl home. I smiled at the girl. She winced.

A man sang.

> *Mitsubishi, mitsui, sanyo*
> *Honda yamasaki, ishikawa!*

Or words to that effect. He stopped, punched me on the arm and said, 'Yo sin a son!'

'I don't know any.'

'Bad boy!'

'Wha yo no lah me?' said the fat-faced man. He was a short beefy fellow. He began to shout accusingly in Japanese and when one of his friends tried to drag him away he put his hands behind my head, pulled my face towards his, and kissed me. There were delighted barks and shouts of pleasure; I managed a smile and then tipped myself through the door and ran.

It was, an American assured me, an untypical occurrence: 'What I mean is – no Japanese man ever tried to kiss *me*.' Something equally untypical happened on the Hikari back to Tokyo, a delay of twenty minutes. Outside Nagoya the Hikari came to a stop; the Japanese passengers grew restless and after fifteen minutes some were muttering. It was a rare moment of breakdown, and when we got to Tokyo I decided to go to the offices of Japanese National Railways to find out why the train had stopped. I went to the Kotetsue Building and put my question to a man in the Publicity Section. He bowed, led me to his desk, and made a phone call.

'A fire was reported on the line,' he said. 'Computer gets information. Computer corrects mistake. We hope it will not happen again.' He gave me a pamphlet explaining the computer that regulates the high-speed trains. 'It is all here.'

'May I ask you another question?'

'So.' He closed his eyes and smiled.

'Sometimes Japanese trains stop for thirty seconds at a

station. That's not very long. Do you ever have any accidents?'

'We do not keep a record of such accidents,' he said. 'I can say there are not many. Coffee?'

'Thank you.' A cup of coffee was placed at my elbow by a lady pushing a coffee trolley. She made a slight bow and wheeled to the next desk. We were in a large office, holding perhaps fifty desks, where men and women sat processing stacks of paper. 'But what about the passengers,' I said. 'Do they mind all this jumping on and off? They have to be so quick!'

'Japanese people are quick, I think,' he said.

'Yes, but they cooperate, too.'

'Passengers cooperate to make the trains normal. It is Japanese nature to cooperate.'

'In other countries passengers might want more than forty-five seconds at a major station.'

'Ah! Then the trains are slow!'

'Right, right, but why is it —'

As I spoke, orchestral music filled the large office. From my experience on Japanese railways I knew an announcement was coming. But there was no announcement immediately; the music played, loud and a bit off-key.

'You were saying?'

'I forgot my question,' I said. The music went on. I wondered how anyone could work in a place where this sound was so loud. I looked around. No one was working. Each clerk had put his pencil down and had risen. Now the voice came over the loudspeaker, first seeming to explain and then speaking in the familiar sing-song of the exercise leader. The office workers began to swing their arms, sighting along their forearms, doing semaphore; then they swayed, bending at the waist; then they did little balletic jumps. The female voice on the loudspeaker was naming the calisthenics, the patter that goes, 'Now here's one to make the blood flow in that aching neck. Twist *around* . . . two . . . three . . . four. And *again*, two . . . three . . . four . . .'

It was a few minutes past three. So every day this happened!

No shirking, either: the clerks were really going to town, doing deep knee-bends and jaunty arm-flutters. The effect was that of a scene in a musical in which an entire unembarrassed office gets to its feet and begins high-stepping among the filing cabinets.

'You're missing your exercises.'

'It is all right.'

The phone rang on the next desk. I wondered how they'd handle it. A head-wagging woman answered it, stopped wagging her head, muttered something, then hung up. She resumed her wagging.

'Any more questions?'

I said no. I thanked him and left. And now he joined the others in the office. He stretched out his arms and reached to the right, two-three-four; then to the left, two-three-four. All over the country, instruments were commanding the Japanese to act. The Japanese had made these instruments, given them voices, and put them in charge. Now, obeying the lights and the sound, the Japanese aspired to them, flexing their little muscles, kicking their little feet, wagging their little heads, like flawed clockwork toys performing for a powerful unforgiving machine that would one day wear them out.

# 30. The Trans-Siberian Express

## 1. *The M. V.* Khabarovsk

AT its eastern limit the Trans-Siberian Express is a stale-smelling Russian ship that sails two or three times a month out of the dust-storm smog of Yokohama, through the windy Tsugaru Straits and the Sea of Japan – in whose bucking currents whole blizzards vanish – to Nakhodka, in freezing Primorsk, a stone's throw from Vladivostok. It is the only way west to Nakhodka, the pneumonia route through gales to the rail head. Like the train, the ship follows Soviet custom: it is riddled with class distinctions so subtle, it takes a trained Marxist to appreciate them. I was in a four-berth cabin at the waterline, one of the subclassifications of 'Hard Class' (a truer description than the other class Intourist advertises as 'Soft'). Bruce and Jeff, the Australians in the upper bunks, were nervous about going to Siberia. Anders, a young Swede, carbuncular, with one of those unthawed Scandinavian faces that speaks of sexual smugness and a famished imagination, was in the bunk opposite. He listened to the Australians, and when he said, 'Hey, I hear it's cold in Siberia,' I knew it would be a rough crossing.

By late afternoon on the first day the coastline of Honshu was snowy and we were entering the straits. Already the bow and foredeck of the *Khabarovsk* were sealed in blue ice. Apart from the occasional lighthouse and a few rusty trawlers pitching wildly in the strong current, there were no signs of life. The shore and the mountains behind it were bleak. 'That is Osorayama,' said one of the Japanese students, motioning to a mountain. 'There are demons who live on the top. So people never go near here.' The Japanese stood at the rail, snapping pictures of this bewitched place. They took turns photographing each other, holding a little slate with the date, time, and place chalked on it: the poses were always the same, but the information on the slate altered rapidly. They were mostly students; some were tourists. There were a score of them, and they were going everywhere, but only one spoke English. The sociologist on his way to the Sorbonne did not speak French, nor did the man on his way to the Max Planck Institute speak German. They had phrase books. These they thumbed continually. But the phrase books weren't much help in conversation. They had been compiled by fastidious Japanese and contained such Japanese sentences as 'The room does not suit me!' in German, English, Italian, French, and Russian.

I took *New Grub Street* to the bar, but there were interruptions: Japanese students drew up chairs and sat in a circle, holding their phrase books like choristers with hymnals, inquiring about the price of a room in London; an American couple wanted to know what I was reading; and there was Jeff, the older Australian, on his way to Germany. Jeff had three days' growth of beard and he habitually wore a beret to cover his baldness. He hated the ship, but he was hopeful.

'Ever been on a ship like this?' he asked.

I said no.

'Listen, I had a friend who was on a ship like this. He was going from Sydney to Hong Kong, I think. He said everyone was very nice when they got on board, but as soon as they were at sea they started going crazy. You know what I mean? Doing things they didn't normally do.' He leered. 'Kind of losing their marbles.'

That night there was a film about Minsk in the lounge. Jeff went and later described it to me. It depicted Minsk as a sunny city of fashion shows and football games, and closed with detailed shots of a steel mill. Afterwards the Russian stewards got their instruments and organized a dance, but it was poorly attended. Two Yugoslav shipping officials danced with the librarians from

Adelaide; the American danced with his wife; the Japanese watched, clutching their phrase books.

'Anyone lose his marbles?' I asked.

'This is no voyage,' said Jeff. 'This is like a Sunday-school outing. If you ask me, I think it's because the Russians are in charge.'

The bartender, a muscular blonde lady in pink ankle socks, listened to Jeff's complaint. She said, 'You don't like?'

'I *like*,' said Jeff. 'It's just that I'm not used to it.'

Nikola, the Yugoslav, joined us. He said he'd had a wonderful time at the dance. He wanted to know the name of the shorter librarian. He said, 'I'm divorced – ha, ha!'

'Galina Petrovna,' I said to the bartender. 'Another beer, please.'

The blonde put down her knitting, and, mumbling to Nikola in Russian, filled my glass.

Nikola said, 'She wants you to call her Galya. It's more friendly.'

'I don't think I have anything to gain by calling her Galya.'

'You are right.' He winked. 'Nothing to gain.'

We talked about Yugoslavia. Nikola said, 'In Yugoslavia we have three things – freedom, women, and drinking!'

'But not all at the same time surely?' I said. The mention of freedom brought the conversation around to Djilas, the persecuted Yugoslav writer.

'This Djilas,' said Nikola. 'I tell you steury. I am in school. They make me rat Djilas. I have to rat all he has reet. About Staleen. He say, hum, Staleen same as Zayoosh. Zayoosh, the Greek gat. Not he *theenk* like Zayoosh, but *look* like Zayoosh – big face and great head. I call Djilas traitor of communeesh. This is why. He reet book – big book – call it, hum, *Conversation with Staleen*. But, hum! he says now Staleen is monstra. Monstra! First Zayoosh, then monstra. I ask you why. Why? Because Djilas is traitor –'

Nikola had been the captain of a Yugoslav ship. He was now

an official with a shipping company, on his way to Nakhodka to inspect a damaged freighter. He wished he was still a captain, and he reminisced about the time his ship had nearly sunk in a storm in these Tsugaru Straits. We were passing through dangerous currents, he said. 'Sometimes you have to pray, but don't let the men see you!'

Late at night the bar of the *Khabarovsk* held only the American couple, Nikola, a gloomy Pole whose name I never learned, and me. The American couple said they were 'into the occult'. I asked them for proof. They told me ghost stories. One was about a Japanese doll they had been given; it had a chipped nose. 'Get rid of it! It's alive!' a Japanese man told them. It had a soul. They went to a temple, sprinkled salt in a circle, and performed a purification ceremony. 'Or else something might have happened to our faces.' I said this was pure speculation. They told me another story. This happened in New Orleans. They were given a strange book. Dinner guests remarked on how depressing their house had become; the book was giving off emanations. They burned the book in an ash can, and a week later their house burned to the ground – no one knew why.

'I know a dealer in old prints,' I said, and began to tell them the most frightening story I know, 'The Mezzotint', by M. R. James.

'Yike!' said the woman when I finished. Her husband said, 'Hey, are you into the occult, too?'

The next morning we were out of the straits; I thought the Sea of Japan would be calmer, but it was much worse. Nikola explained that there were two currents in the Sea of Japan, the warm Kyushu current from the south, and the cold current from the Sea of Okhotsk: they met and made great turbulence. All day the ship rolled in a snow storm into the deepness of the swelling sea, at the far trough of each swell thumping an enormous wave that shook the windows. The dropping ship gave me a sensation of weightlessness, which the shuddering screws a moment later turned into nausea. The seasickness was half fear – that the ship would founder in that icy sea, that we would have to cope with the snow and those waves in frail lifeboats.

The Pole said I looked ill.

'I *feel* ill.'

'Get drunk.'

I tried, on Georgian wine, but felt worse afterwards, as if I had drunk turpentine. The ship was rocking tremendously; and it was loud with the explosions of waves on the hull, banging doors and loose cupboards and walls so shrill with vibrations it seemed they were about to burst apart. I went to my cabin. Anders was already in his bunk, looking ghastly. Jeff and Bruce were moaning. Now the ship seemed to be leaping clear of the sea, staying airborne for five noisy seconds, and then dropping sideways with a terrific wrenching of woodwork. I didn't take off my clothes. Lifeboat Seven was mine. In his sleep, Anders shrieked, '*No!*'

Just before dawn the sea was at its roughest. Again and again I was thrown upwards from my bunk, and once I hit my head on the bunk's frame. At dawn – the light showed through the ice on the porthole – the sea was calmer. I slept for an hour, before being awakened by another bump to hear the following exchange.

'Hey, Bruce.'

'Mm?'

'How's your little Ned Kelly?'

'Mawright.'

'Ya throw ya voice?'

'Naw.'

'Gee, it's rough! These beds make a hell of a racket.'

Jeff was silent for a while. Anders groaned. I tried to tune the radio I had bought in Yokohama.

'I wonder what's for brekkie?' Jeff said at last.

Breakfast (salami, olives, runny eggs, damp bread) was served to eight passengers. The rest, including all the Japanese, were seasick. I sat with the Pole and Nikola. The Pole and I were talking about Joseph Conrad. The Pole called him by his original family name, Korzeniowski. Nikola wondered at my interest and said, 'He writes about Staleen too, this Korzeniowski?'

That was our last day on the *Khabarovsk*. It was sunny, but the temperature was well below zero – much too cold to spend more than a few minutes on deck. I stayed in the bar reading Gissing. Around noon Nikola showed up with an old grizzled Russian in tow. They drank vodka, and, once primed, the Russian began telling stories about the war. The Russian (Nikola translated) had been a mate on a ship called the *Vanzetti* – its sister ship was the *Sacco* – a decrepit freighter captained by a notorious drunkard. In a convoy of fifty ships crossing the Atlantic the *Vanzetti* was so slow it dropped far behind, and one day, when the convoy was almost out of sight, a German submarine approached. The captain radioed for assistance, but the convoy sped away, leaving the *Vanzetti* to fend for herself. The *Vanzetti* somehow eluded two German torpedoes. The sub surfaced for a look, but the drunken captain had swung his rusty cannon around; he fired once, puncturing the sub and sinking it. The Germans came to believe that this hulk, manned by incompetents, was a secret weapon, and gave the convoy no further trouble. When the *Vanzetti* limped into Reykjavik, the British organized a special party for the Russians, who showed up two hours late, bellowing obscene songs, and the captain, paralytic with drink, was awarded a medal.

I saw seagulls in the afternoon, but it was five o'clock before the Soviet coast came into view. Surprisingly, it was bare of snow. It was brown, flat, and treeless, the grimmest landscape I had ever laid eyes on, like an immense beach of frozen dirt washed by an oily black sea. The Russian passengers, who until then had sloped around the ship in old clothes and felt slippers, put on wrinkled suits and fur hats for the arrival, and along the starboard deck I saw them pinning medals ('Exemplary Worker', 'Yakutsk Cooperative Society', 'Blagoveshchensk Youth League') to their breast pockets. The ship was a long time docking at Nakhodka. I found a sheltered spot on the deck, fiddled with my radio, and got gypsy music — violins scraping like a chorus of ripsaws. A deck hand in a mangy fur hat and ragged coat crouched by the davit. He asked me, in English (he had been to Seattle!), to turn the music louder. It was the Moldavian half-hour on Moscow Radio. He smiled sadly, showing me his metal dentures. He was from Moldavia, and far from home.

## 2. The Vostok

The Siberian port of Nakhodka in December gives the impression of being on the very edge of the world, in an atmosphere that does not quite support life. The slender trees are leafless; the ground is packed hard, and no grass grows on it; the streets have no traffic, the sidewalks no people. There are lights burning, but they are like lighthouse beacons positioned to warn people who stray near Nakhodka that it is a place of danger and there is only emptiness beyond it. The subzero weather makes it odourless and not a single sound wrinkles its silence. It is the sort of place that gives rise to the notion that the earth is flat.

At the station ('Proper name is Tikhookeanskaya Station' — Intourist brochure), a building with the stucco and proportions of the Kabul madhouse, I paid six rubles to change from Hard Class to Soft. The clerk said this was highly irregular, but I insisted. There were two berths in the Soft-Class compartments, four in Hard, and I had found the cabin in the *Khabarovsk* a salutary lesson in overcrowding. Russian travel had already made me class-conscious; I demanded luxury. And the demand, which would have got me nowhere in Japan, where not even the prime minister has his own railway compartment (though the emperor has eleven carriages), got me a plush berth in Car Five of the Vostok.

'Yes, you have question please?' said a lady in a fur hat. The platform was freezing, crisscrossed with the moulds of footprints in ice. The woman breathed clouds of vapour.

'I'm looking for Car Number Five.'

'Car Number Five is now Car Number Four. Please go to Car Number Four and show voucher. Thank you.' She strode away.

A chilly group of complaining people stood at the entrance to the car the lady had indicated. I asked if it was Car Number Four.

'This is it,' said the American occultist.

'But they won't let us in,' said his wife. 'The guy told us to wait.'

A workman came, dressed like a grizzly bear. He set up a ladder with the meaningless mechanical care of an actor in an experimental play whose purpose is to baffle a bored audience. My feet had turned to ice, my Japanese gloves admitted the wind, my nose burned with frostbite – even my knees were cold. The man's paws fumbled with metal plates.

'Jeepers, I'm cold!' said the woman. She let out a sob.

'Don't cry, honey,' said her husband. To me he said, 'Ever see anything like it?'

The man on the ladder had removed the 4 from the side of the car. He slipped 5 into the slot, pounded it with his fist, descended the ladder, and, clapping the uprights together, signalled for us to go inside.

I found my compartment and thought, How strange. But I was relieved, and almost delirious with the purest joy a traveller can know: the sight of the plushest, most comfortable room I had seen in thirty trains. Here, on the Vostok, parked on a platform in what seemed the most godforsaken town in the Soviet Far East, was a compartment that could only be described as High Victorian. It was certainly pre-revolution. The car itself had the look of a narrow lounge in a posh London pub. The passage floor was carpeted; there were mirrors everywhere; the polished brass fittings were reflected in varnished wood; poppies were etched on the glass globes of the pairs of lamps beside the mirrors, lighting the tasselled curtains of red velvet and the roman numerals on the compartment doors. Mine was VII. I had an easy chair on which crocheted antimacassars had been neatly pinned, a thick rug on the floor, and another one in the toilet, where a gleaming shower hose lay coiled next to the sink. I punched my pillow: it was full of warm goose feathers. And I was alone. I walked up and down the room, rubbing my hands, then set out pipes and tobacco, slippers, Gissing, my new Japanese bathrobe, and poured myself a large vodka. I threw myself on the bed, congratulating myself that 6,000 miles lay between Nakhodka and Moscow, the longest train journey in the world.

To get to the dining car that evening I had to pass through four carriages, and between them in the rubber booth over the coupling was a yard of Arctic. An icy wind blew through the rips in the rubber, there was snow on the floor, a thickness of heavy crystals on the car wall, and the door handles were coated with frost. I lost the skin from my fingertips on the door handles, and thereafter, whenever I moved between the cars of the Trans-Siberian Express, I wore my gloves. Two *babushkas* acknowledged me. In white smocks and turbans they stood with their red arms in a sink. More old ladies were sweeping the passage with brushwood brooms – a nation of stooping, labouring grannies. Dinner was sardines and stew, made palatable by two tots of vodka. I was joined halfway through by the American occultists. They ordered wine. The wife said, 'We're celebrating. Bernie's just finished his internship.'

'I had no idea occultists served internships,' I said.

Bernie frowned. He said, 'I'm an M.D.'

'Ah, a real doctor!' I said.

'We're celebrating by going around the world,' said the wife. 'We're on our way to Poland – I mean, after Irkutsk.'

'So you're really living it up.'

'Sort of.'

'Bernie,' I said, 'you're not going to go back and become

one of those quacks that charge the earth for curing halitosis, are you?'

'It costs a lot of money to go to medical school,' he muttered, which was a way of saying he was. He said he owed $20,000. He had spent years learning his job. Textbooks were expensive. His wife had had to work. It didn't sound much of an ordeal, I said. I owed more money than that. He said, 'I even had to sell my blood.'

'Why is it,' I said, 'that doctors are always telling people how they sold their blood as students? Don't you see that selling blood by the pint is just another example of your avarice?'

Bernie said, 'I don't have to take this from you.' He grabbed his wife by the arm and led her out of the dining car.

'The great occultist,' I said, and realized that I was drunk. I went back to Number VII, and just before I switched off the table lamp I looked out the window. There was snow on the ground, and in the distance, under a cold moon, those leafless sticklike trees.

It was pitch dark when I woke up, but my watch said it was past eight o'clock. There was a pale dawn breaking at the bleak horizon, a narrow semicircle of light, like the quick of a fingernail. An hour later this glowed, a winter fluorescence on the icy flatness of Primorsk, lighting the small wooden bungalows, like henhouses with smoking chimneys, surrounded by fields of stubble and snow drifts. Some people were already up, dressed for the cold in thick black coats and heavy felt boots that made them look clubfooted. They walked like roly-poly dolls, their heavily padded sleeves making their arms stick out. In the slow winter dawn I saw one especially agile man sliding down a slope, steering his feet like skis; he carried a yoke and two buckets. After breakfast I saw more of these scenes, bucket-carriers, a horse-drawn sleigh with a man in it who looked too cold to crack his whip, and another man pulling his children on a sled. But there were not many people out at that hour, nor were there many settlements, and there were no roads: the low smoking huts were set without any discernible pattern in trackless fields.

The sun broke through the band of haze and then shone in a cloudless sky, warming the curtains and rugs of the sleeping car. There were occasional stations, wood-framed, with gingerbread peaks, but we stopped long enough only to view the posters, portraits of Lenin, portraits of workers, and murals showing people of various colours looking courageous and linking arms. I looked for a reaction on the faces of the Japanese in the Vostok; they remained impassive. Perhaps the murals depicted Chinese and Russians? It was possible. This was a disputed area. All the way to Khabarovsk we travelled along the Chinese border, which is at that point the Ussuri River. But maps are misleading – this corner of China was no different from the Soviet Union: it lay frozen under deep snow and in the bright sunlight there were crooked forests of silver birch.

The city of Khabarovsk appeared in the snow at noon, and over the next week I grew accustomed to this deadly sight of a Soviet city approaching on the Trans-Siberian line, buried at the bottom of a heavy sky: first the acres of wooden bungalows on the outskirts; then, where the tracks divided, the work-gangs of women chipping ice from the switches; the huffing steam locomotives and the snow gradually blackening with fallen soot, and the buildings piling up, until the city itself surrounded the train with its dwellings, log cabins and cell blocks. But in the history of the Trans-Siberian Railway, Khabarovsk is an important place. The great railway, proposed in 1857 by the American Perry McDonough Collins and finally begun in 1891 under Tsarevich Nicholas, was completed here in 1916. The last link was the Khabarovsk Bridge over the Amur River; then the way was open by rail from Calais to Vladivostok (now off-limits to foreigners for military reasons).

Everyone got off the Vostok Express, most of them to catch a plane for the nine-hour flight to Moscow, some – including myself – to spend the night in Khabarovsk before taking the Rossiya Express. I jumped on to the platform, was seared by the cold, and ran back into the Vostok to put on another sweater.

'No,' said the Intourist lady. 'You will stay here on platform please.'

I said it seemed a little nippy out there.

'It is thirty-five below tzero,' she said. 'Ha, ha! But not Celsius!'

In the bus she asked whether there was anything special I'd like to do in Khabarovsk. I was stumped for a moment, then said, 'How about a concert or an opera?'

She smiled, as anyone in Bangor, Maine, might have if asked the same question. She said, 'There is musical comedy. You like musical comedy?'

I said no.

'Good, I do not recommend.'

After lunch I went in search of pipe tobacco. I was running low and faced six smokeless days to Moscow if I couldn't find any. I crossed Lenin Square, where a statue of the great man (who never visited the city) showed him posed with his arm thrust out in the gesture of a man hailing a taxi. On Karl Marx Street newspaper sellers in kiosks said they had no *tabak* but offered me *Pravda* with headlines of the 'Khabarovsk Heavy Industry Workers Applaud Smolensk Sugar Beet Workers on a Record Harvest' variety; then to a lunch counter. My glasses steamed up; I saw misty people in overcoats standing against a wall eating buns. No *tabak*. Outside, the steam turned to frost and blinded me. This I corrected in a grocery store, piled with butter and big cheeses and shelves of pickles and bread. I entered stores at random: the State Bank of the USSR, where a vast portrait of Marx glowered at depositors; the Youth League Head-quarters; a jewellery store, filled with hideous clocks and watches and people gaping as if in a museum. At the end of the street I found a small envelope of Bulgarian pipe tobacco. Coming out of the store I saw a familiar face.

'Hear about Bruce?' It was Jeff. His nose was red, his beret was pulled over his ears like a shower cap, his scarf was wound around his mouth, and he was dancing with the cold. He plucked at the scarf and said, 'He's butcher's hook.'

'What's that?'

'You don't know the lingo. Jesus, it's cold! That's rhyming slang.'

'Butcher's hook' in cockney rhyming slang means 'look'. He's *look*? It didn't make sense. I said, 'What's it rhyming slang for?'

'He's crook,' said Jeff, hopping, attracting the stares of passing Siberians. 'Crook – don't they say that in the States when someone's sick?'

'I don't think so.'

'He looked seedy this morning. Lips all cracked, glassy eyes, running a temperature. Intourist took him to a hospital. I think he got pneumonia in that fucking ship.'

We walked back to the hotel. Jeff said, 'It's not a bad place. It looks like it's coming up.'

'It doesn't look that way to me.'

We passed a shop where about 150 people were lined up. The ones at the end of the line stared at us, but in the front of the line, at the half-open door, they were quarrelling, and if you looked closely you could see them crashing through the narrow entrance, all elbows, one at a time. I wanted to see what they were queuing for – obviously something in short supply – but Jeff said, 'On your right,' and I turned to see an enormous policeman gesturing for me to move along.

There were some oriental-looking people in the crowd; Khabarovsk seemed to be full of them, plump Chinese with square dark faces. They are the aboriginal people of the region, distant cousins of the American Eskimos, and are called Goldis. 'A sartorially practical tribe,' writes Harmon Tupper in his history of the Trans-Siberian, remarking that they changed from wearing fish skins in summer to dog skins in winter. But in Khabarovsk that December day they were dressed the same as everyone else, in felt boots and mittens, overcoats and fur hats. Jeff wondered who they were. I told him.

He said, 'That's funny, they don't *look* like abos.'

In the hotel restaurant Jeff made a beeline for a table where two pretty Russian girls sat eating. They were sisters, they said. Zhenyia was studying English; Nastasya's subject was Russian literature ('I say *Russian* literature, not Soviet literature – this I do not like'). We talked about books: Nastasya's favourite author was Chekhov, Zhenyia's was J. D. Salinger – 'Kholden Khaulfield is best character in every literature.' I said I was an admirer of Zamyatin, but they had not heard of the author of *We* (a novel that inspired Orwell to write *1984*, which it much resembles), who died in Paris in the twenties trying to write a biography of Attila the Hun. I asked if there were any novelists in Khabarovsk.

'Chekhov was here,' said Nastasya.

In 1890, Anton Chekhov visited Sakhalin, an island of convicts, 700 miles from Khabarovsk. But in Siberia all distances are relative: Sakhalin was right next door.

'Who else do you like?' I asked.

Nastasya said, 'Now you want to ask me about Solzhenitsyn.'

'I wasn't going to,' I said. 'But since you mentioned him, what do you think?'

'I do not like.'

'Have you read him?'

'No.'

'Do you think there's any truth in the statement that socialist realism is anti-Marxist?' I asked.

'Ask my sister this question,' said Nastasya.

But Jeff was talking to Zhenyia and making her blush. Then he addressed both girls. 'Look, suppose you could go to any country you liked. Where would you go?'

Zhenyia thought a moment. Finally she said, 'Spam.'

'Yes, I think so,' said Nastasya. 'For me – Spam.'

'*Spam!*' shouted Jeff.

'Because it is always hot there, I think,' said Zhenyia. The sisters rose and paid their bill. They put on their coats and scarves and mittens and pulled their woollen pompom caps down to their eyes, and they set off into the driving wind and snow.

Later the Intourist lady took me on a tour of the city. I said I wanted to see the river. She said, 'First, factory!' There were five factories. They made, she said, 'Kebles, weenches, poolies, bults.' In front of each one were six-foot portraits of hard-faced men, 'Workers of the Month', but they might easily have been photographs of a Chicago bowling team. I said they looked tough. The Intourist lady said, 'They have an opera company.' This is meant to rebuke the visitor: these monkeys have an opera company! But opera is politically neutral and the Khabarovsk opera house was vacant most of the time. If there was an alley they'd have had a bowling team. There wasn't much to do in Khabarovsk – even the Intourist lady admitted that. After various obelisks and monuments and a tour of the museum, which was full of dusty tigers and seals, all facing extinction, we went to the east bank of the Amur River. The Intourist lady said she would wait in the car. She didn't like the cold (she wanted to go to Italy and work for Aeroflot).

The river at this point is half a mile wide. From where I was standing I could see dozens of men, huddled on the ice, each one near a cluster of holes. They were ice-fishermen, mainly aged men who spent the winter days like this, watching for a tug on their lines. I scrambled down the bank and, marching into a stiff wind, made my way across the ice to where an old man stood, watching me come near. I said hello and counted his lines; he had chopped fourteen holes in the two-foot-thick ice with a blunt axe. He had caught six fish, the largest about nine inches, the smallest about four inches, and all of them frozen solid. He made me understand that he had been fishing since eight o'clock that morning; it was then half-past four. I asked him if I could take his picture. '*Nyet!*' he said and showed me his ragged overcoat, his torn cap, the rips in his boots. He urged me to take a picture of one of his fish, but, as I was about to snap, something caught my eye. It was the comb of a fish spine, flecked with blood, the head and tail still attached.

'What happened to him?' I picked up the bones.

The old man laughed and made eating movements with his mittens, champing on his decayed teeth. So he had caught seven fish: the seventh was his lunch.

After ten minutes of this I was stiff with cold and wanted to go. I fumbled in my pockets and brought out a box of Japanese matches. Did he want them? Yes, very much! He took them, thanked me, and when I turned to go he hurried over to show them to a man fishing fifty yards away.

The ice-fishermen, the old ladies sweeping the gutters with twig brooms, the quarrelling line of people at the shop on Karl Marx Street; but there was another side to Khabarovsk. That night the restaurant of the hotel filled with army officers and some truly villainous-looking women. The tables were covered with empty vodka bottles, and many ate their Siberian dumplings (*pelmenye*) with champagne. I lingered, talking to a fierce captain about the declining Soviet birthrate.

'What about family planning?' I asked.

'We are trying to stop it!'

'Are you succeeding?'

'Not yet. But I think we can increase production.'

The band began to play, a saxophone, a piano, snare drums: 'Blue Moon'. And the army officers were dancing. The women, who wore sweaters under their low-cut dresses, hitched their clothes and staggered with their partners. Some men were singing. There were shouts. A waltzing couple bumped the arm of a man stuffing a dumpling into his mouth. A bottle crashed to the floor; there was a scuffle. The captain said to me, 'Now you must go.'

## 3. *The Rossiya*

Afterwards, whenever I thought of the Trans-Siberian Express, I saw stainless steel bowls of *borscht* spilling in the dining car of the Rossiya as it rounded a bend on its way to Moscow, and at the curve a clear sight from the window of our green and black steam locomotive – from Skovorodino onwards its eruptions of steamy smoke diffused the sunlight and drifted into the forest so that the birches smouldered and the magpies made for the sky. I saw the gold-tipped pines at sunset and the snow lying softly around clumps of brown grass like cream poured over the ground; the yachtlike snowploughs at Zima; the ochreous flare of the floodlit factory chimneys at Irkutsk; the sight of Marinsk in early morning, black cranes and black buildings and escaping figures casting long shadows on the tracks as they ran towards the lighted station – something terrible in that combination of cold, dark, and little people tripping over Siberian tracks; the ice-chest of frost between the cars; the protrusion of Lenin's white forehead at every stop; and the passengers imprisoned in Hard Class: fur hats, fur leggings, blue gym suits, crying children, and such a powerful smell of sardines, body odour, cabbage, and stale tobacco that even at the five-minute stops the Russians jumped on to the snowy platform to risk pneumonia for a breath of fresh air; the bad food; the stupid economies; and the men and women ('No distinction is made with regard to sex in assigning compartments' – Intourist brochure), strangers to each other, who shared the same compartment and sat on opposite bunks, moustached male mirroring moustached female from their grubby nightcaps and the blankets they wore as shawls, down to their hefty ankles stuck in crushed slippers. Most of all, I thought of it as an experience in which time had the trick distortions of a dream: the Rossiya ran on Moscow time, and after a lunch of cold yellow potatoes, a soup of fat lumps called *solyanka*, and a carafe of port that tasted like cough syrup,

I would ask the time and be told it was four o'clock in the morning.

The Rossiya was not like the Vostok; it was new. The sleeping cars of East German make were steel syringes, insulated in grey plastic and heated by coal-fired boilers attached to furnace and samovar that gave the front end of each carriage the look of a cartoon atom smasher. The *provodnik* often forgot to stoke the furnace, and then the carriage took on a chill that somehow induced nightmares in me while at the same time denying me sleep. The other passengers in Soft were either suspicious, drunk, or unpleasant: a Goldi and his white Russian wife and small leathery child rode in a nest of boots and blankets, two aggrieved Canadians who ranted to the two Australian librarians about the insolence of the *provodnik*, an elderly Russian lady who did the whole trip wearing the same frilly nightgown, a Georgian who looked as if he had problems at the other end, and several alcoholics who played noisy games of dominoes in their pyjamas. Conversation was hopeless, sleep was alarming, and the perversity of the clocks confounded my appetite. That first day I wrote in my diary, *Despair makes me hungry*.

The dining car was packed. Everyone had vegetable soup, then an omelette wrapped around a Wiener schnitzel, served by two waitresses – a very fat lady who bossed the diners incessantly, and a pretty black-haired girl who doubled as scullion and looked as if she might jump off the train at the next clear opportunity. I ate my lunch, and the three Russians at my table tried to bum cigarettes from me. As I had none we attempted a conversation: they were going to Omsk; I was an American. Then they left. I cursed myself for not buying a Russian phrase book in Tokyo.

A man sat down with me. His hands were shaking. He ordered. Twenty minutes later the fat lady gave him a carafe of yellow wine. He splashed it into his glass and drank it in two gulps. He had a wound on his thumb, which he gnawed as he looked worriedly around the car. The fat lady gave his shoulder a slap and he was off, moving tipsily in the direction of Hard. But the fat lady left me in peace. I stayed in the dining car, sipping the sticky wine, watching the scenery change from flat snow fields to hills – the first since Nakhodka. The drooping sun gilded them beautifully and I expected to see people in the shallow woods. I stared for an hour, but saw none.

Nor could I establish where we were. My Japanese map of the Soviet Union was not helpful, and it was only in the evening that I learned we had passed through Poshkovo, on the Chinese border. This added to my disorientation: I seldom knew where we were, I never knew the correct time, and I grew to hate the three freezers I had to pass through to get to the dining car.

The fat lady's name was Anna Feyodorovna and, though she screamed at her fellow countrymen, she was pleasant to me, and urged me to call her Annushka. I did and she rewarded me with a special dish, cold potatoes and chicken – dark sinewy meat that was like some dense textile. Annushka watched me eat. She winked over her glass of tea (she dipped bread into the tea and sucked it) and then cursed a cripple who sat down at my table. Eventually she banged a steel plate of potatoes and fatty meat in front of him.

The cripple ate slowly, lengthening the awful meal by sawing carefully at his meat. A waiter went by and there was a smash. The waiter had dropped an empty carafe on to our table, shattering the cripple's glass. The cripple went on eating with exquisite *sang-froid*, refusing to acknowledge the waiter, who was muttering apologies as he picked up pieces of broken glass from the table. Then the waiter plucked an enormous sliver of glass from the cripple's mashed potatoes. The cripple choked and pushed the plate away. The waiter got him a new meal.

'*Sprechen Sie Deutsch?*' asked the cripple.

'Yes, but very badly.'

'I speak a little,' he said in German. 'I learned it in Berlin. Where are you from?'

I told him. He said, 'What do you think of the food here?'

'Not bad, but not very good.'

'I think it's very bad,' he said. 'What's the food like in America?'

'Wonderful,' I said.

He said, 'Capitalist! You are a capitalist!'

'Perhaps.'

'Capitalism bad, communism good.'

'Bullshit,' I said in English, then in German, 'You think so?'

'In America people kill each other with pistols. *Pah! Pah! Pah!* Like that.'

'I don't have a pistol.'

'What about the Negroes? The black people?'

'What about them?'

'You kill them.'

'Who tells you these things?'

'Newspapers. I read it for myself. Also it's on the radio all the time.'

'Soviet radio,' I said.

'Soviet radio is good radio,' he said.

The radio in the dining car was playing jazzy organ music. It was on all day, and even in the compartments – each one had a loudspeaker – it continued to mutter because it could not be turned off completely. I jerked my thumb at the loudspeaker and said, 'Soviet radio is too loud.'

He guffawed. Then he said, 'I'm an invalid. Look here – no foot, just a leg. No foot, no foot!'

He raised his felt boot and squashed the toe with the ferrule of his cane. He said, 'I was in Kiev during the war, fighting the Germans. They were shooting – *Pah! Pah!* – like that. I jumped into the water and started swimming. It was winter – cold water – very cold water! They shot my foot off, but I didn't stop swimming. Then another time my captain said to me, "Look, more Germans –" and in the snow – very deep snow –'

That night I slept poorly on my bench-sized bunk, dreaming of goose-stepping Germans with pitchforks, wearing helmets like the Rossiya's soup bowls; they forced me into an icy river. I woke. My feet lay exposed in the draught of the cold window; the blanket had slipped off, and the blue night light of the compartment made me think of an operating theatre. I took an aspirin and slept until it was light enough in the corridor to find the toilet. That day, around noon, we stopped at Skovorodino. The *provodnik*, my jailer, showed a young bearded man into my compartment. This was Vladimir. He was going to Irkutsk, which was two days away. For the rest of the afternoon Vladimir said no more. He read Russian paperbacks with patriotic pictures on their covers, and I looked out the window. Once I had thought of a train window as allowing me freedom to gape at the world; now it seemed an imprisoning thing and at times took on the opacity of a cell wall.

At one bend outside Skovorodino I saw we were being pulled by a giant steam locomotive. I diverted myself by trying (although Vladimir sucked his teeth in disapproval) to snap a picture of it as it rounded curves, shooting plumes of smoke out its side. The smoke rolled beside the train and rose slowly through the forests of birch and the Siberian cedars, where there were footprints on the ground and signs of dead fires, but not a soul to be seen. The countryside then was so changeless it might have been a picture pasted against the window. It put me to sleep. I dreamed of a particular cellar in Medford High School, then woke and saw Siberia and almost cried. Vladimir had stopped reading. He sat against the wall sketching on a pad with coloured pencils, a picture of telephone poles. I crept into the corridor. One of the Canadians had his face turned to the miles of snow.

He said, 'Thank God we're getting off this pretty soon. How far are you going?'

'Moscow; then the train to London.'

'Tough shitsky.'

'So they say.'

He said, 'I don't even know what day it is. It's going to be

Christmas soon. Hey, did you see that house burning back there?'
'No.'

The previous day he had said, 'Did you see the truck that was crossing the river and crashed through the ice? Well, the back wheels anyway.' I wondered if he made it up. He was perpetually seeing disasters and events. I looked out the window and saw my anxious reflection.

I went back into the compartment and started to read *New Grub Street* again, but the combination of bad light and cold and drifting snow, and the decline of poor Edwin Reardon depressed me to the point of fatigue. I slept; I dreamed. I was in a mountain cabin with my wife and children. There was snow and a black mirror at the window. I was fretting: some people we knew, miles away, had to be told some tragic news. My feet were freezing, but I agreed to go and tell them this news. I kicked in a closet for a pair of boots and said, 'What about you, Anne? Aren't you coming?'

Anne said, 'It's so cold out! Anyway, I'm reading – I think I'll stay here.'

I addressed Annushka, the gorgon of the Rossiya dining car, who happened to be drinking tea in a corner of this cabin. 'You see? You *see*? She always says she wants to go with me, but when the time comes she never does!'

Anne, my wife, said, 'You're just delaying! Go, if you're going – otherwise, shut the door and stop talking about it.'

I held the cabin door open. Outside, it was all emptiness. The cold wind blew into the room, throwing up the skirts of the tablecloth and rattling the lampshades. Snow sifted on to the log floor.

I said, 'Well, I'm going if no one else will.'

'Can I come too, Daddy?' I looked into my little boy's white face. He was pleading. His shoulders were pathetic.

'No,' I said. 'I have to go alone.'

'*Shut the door!*'

I woke up. My feet were cold. The compartment window

was black and the carriage bounced (only the Trans-Siberian bounces, because the rails have square rather than staggered joints). The dream was an intimation of panic, guilty travelling, and a loneliness that made me lonelier still when I wrote it and examined it.

Vladimir had stopped sketching. He looked up and said, '*Chai?*'

I understood. The Swahili word for tea is also *chai*. He hollered for the *provodnik*. Over tea and cookies I had my first Russian lesson, copying the words down phonetically on a notebook page: a dreary occupation, but it passed the time and was preferable to dozing into nightmares.

The dining car that night was empty and very cold. There was frost on the windows and such a chill in the air that the breath of the arguing employees was visible in steamy clouds. Vassily Prokofyevich, the manager, was doing his accounts, snapping his abacus. I had now been in the dining car enough times to know that by late afternoon Vassily, a short scar-faced man, was drunk. He jumped up and showed me his breath – vodka-scented steam – then dragged out a case of beer and demonstrated how the beer had frozen inside the bottles. He rubbed one in his hands to thaw it for me and barked at Nina, the black-haired girl. Nina brought me a plate of smoked salmon and some sliced bread. Vassily pointed to the salmon and said, '*Kita!*'

I said, '*Eto karasho kita.*'

Vassily was pleased. He told Nina to get me some more.

I tapped on the frosty window and said, '*Eto okhnor.*'

'*Da, da.*' Vassily poured himself some more vodka. He guzzled it. He gave me an inch in a tumbler. I drank it and saw that Annushka was at her usual place, dipping bread into black tea and sucking the bread slice.

I motioned at her tea and said, '*Eto zhudki chai.*'

'*Da, da.*' Vassily laughed and refilled my glass.

I showed him my copy of Gissing and said, '*Eto ganyiga.*'

'*Da, da,*' said Vassily. Nina came near with the plate of salmon.

'*Eto Nina*,' said Vassily, seizing the pretty girl, 'and these' – I translated his gestures – 'are Nina's tits!'

The mornings now were darker, another trick of time on the railroad that seemed to be speeding me further into paranoia. After eight hours' sleep I woke up in pitch blackness. In the dim light of the December moon, a silver sickle, the landscape was bare – no trees, no snow. And there was no wind. It was weird, as dawn approached (at nine-thirty by my watch), to see the villages on the banks of the Shilka and the Ingoda rivers, the small collections of wooden huts aged a deep brown, with the smoke rising straight up, a puffing from each chimney that made me think of an early form of wood-burning vehicle stranded on these deserted steppes. After hours of this desolation we came to Chita, a satanic city of belching chimneys and great heaps of smoking ashes dumped beside the tracks. Outside Chita there was a frozen lake on which ice-fishermen crouched like the fat black crows with fluffed-out feathers that roosted in the larches at the verge of the lake.

I said, '*Vorona*.'

'*Nyet*,' said Vladimir and he explained they were fishermen.

'*Vorona*.' I insisted on the crow image until he saw what I was driving at. But it didn't take much insisting, for the sentimental fanaticism I had detected in the Russians I had met was a flight from their literal-mindedness. Vladimir was in the habit of reciting – reciting rather than saying – long sentences, and then muttering, 'Pushkin' or 'Mayakovsky'. This compulsive behaviour is taken for granted in the Soviet Union, but I think if I were on the old Boston and Maine and a man began to quote, 'This is the forest primeval –' I'd change my seat.

Vladimir bought a bottle of Hungarian wine and we played chess. He played aggressively, hovering over the board and moving his pieces as swiftly as checkers. Between moves he cracked his knuckles. I moved not to win – I knew that was beyond me – but to slow him down. He pushed at his chessmen;

the train pushed into wind. Outside, the snow had returned and I saw that now we were getting two landscapes a day. The low Mongolian hills on the edge of the Gobi Desert were covered by cedars as finely formed as tropical ferns, and by four o'clock, as we made our slow approach to the Central Siberian Plateau, snow was blowing past the windows, tiny flakes in the trailing smoke. At a distance the snowstorm created the effect of fog, a whiteness over the Gobi that blended with the birch trunks and made the cedars seem especially frail. Siberia was wood and snow – even the railway buildings matched the forest: throughout Chitinskaya the stations were wooden structures made of many carefully slanted bare planks plastered with frost.

My chess worsened, but as long as the wine held out we continued to play. Two more games saw the end of the vodka and then, without drink, there seemed no point in going on. But we had the whole evening ahead of us. My napping had divided the days into many parts, each part resembling a whole day, a lengthened distortion of time familiar to a person with a high fever in a seldom-visited sickroom. At times this feeling of experiencing a futile convalescence on the Trans-Siberian turned into a simpler occasion for boredom; simulating my bad dream, it was like being snowed-up in a mountain cabin. It was cold, the light was poor, and it was hard to move around the train since most of the passengers, assigned to overcrowded compartments, preferred to stand in the corridors. And, really, there was nowhere to go.

I took out a sheet of paper and taught Vladimir tick-tack-toe. He found this, as he said, very interesting – the Russian word is similar – and soon discovered the trick of beating me at that, too. He introduced me to an immensely complicated Russian game for killing time. This consisted of drawing on graph paper ten figures of slightly varying geometric size, made up of squares. The more irregular the figure, the higher the score – or perhaps one was shooting for a low score? I never got the hang of this game. Vladimir finally gave up trying to teach me and returned to his sketching. I persuaded him to show me his sketch pad, and, amazingly, it was filled with page after page of telephone poles, pylons, high-tension wires, pictures of girders with wires webbed to them, and skeletal-seeming apparatus. This was his hobby, sketching vertical monstrosities, though he might easily have been a spy. He showed me how to draw a telephone pole. I feigned an interest in this unappealing thing and the called to the *provodnik* for wine. Two more bottles of the Hungarian wine came – the *provodnik* wouldn't go until he got a glassful – and Vladimir drew a black cabin in a black and brown landscape, a low orangy red sun, and sky full of spiders. This he labelled 'Siberia'. Then he drew a picture of several spires, some large buildings, a blue sky, a sunny day.

'Leningrad?'

'*Nyet*,' he said. 'London.' He wrote 'London' on the picture. He did another picture of London – a harbour scene, a schooner, ships at anchor, a sunny day. He did one of New York – tall buildings, a sunny day. But they were fantasy pictures: Vladimir had never been out of the Soviet Union.

Because he had insisted on paying for the wine, I broke out my box of cigars. Vladimir smoked five of them, puffing them like cigarettes, and the wine and the cigars and the knowledge that we were now travelling along the shores of Lake Baikal, returned Vladimir to his own language. He strode up and down the compartment, waving away the smoke, telling me what a deep *ozero* Baikal was, and finally slipped his hand inside his coat and, blowing a great cloud of smoke, said, in the halting momentous voice Russians reserve for quotations, but coughing as he did so,

*'I dym otechestva nam sladok i pryaten!'*

and raised his eyes.

I said, 'Eh?'

'Pooshkin,' he said. '*Eugen Onegin!*'

(Months later, in London, I recited my phonetic transcription of this verse to a Russian-speaker, who assured me that it was indeed Pushkin and that it could be rendered in English as, 'Even the smoke of our motherland is sweet and pleasant to us.')

In the dark corridor early the next morning the Australian librarians and the Canadian couple sat on their suitcases. Irkutsk was two hours away, but they said that they were afraid of oversleeping and missing the place. I thought then, and I think now, that missing Irkutsk cannot be everyone's idea of a tragedy. It was still dark as Irkutsk's flaming chimneys appeared above a plain of shuttered bungalows with tarpaper roofs. It is not the steel fences or even the tall cell blocks where the workers live that give these Russian cities the look of concentration camps; it is the harsh light – searchlights and glaring lamps fixed to poles – that does it, diminishing the mittened figures and making them look like prisoners in an exercise yard. Vladimir shook my hand and said a sentimental farewell. I was moved and thought charitably about the poor fellow, stuck in Irkutsk for life, until I went back to the compartment and discovered that he had stolen my box of cigars.

The *provodnik* entered the compartment, gathered up Vladimir's blankets, and threw a new set of blankets on the berth. He was followed by a tall pale man who, although it was mid-morning, put on a pair of pyjamas and a bathrobe and sat down to solve complicated equations on a clipboard pad. The man did not speak until, at a small station, he said, 'Here – salt!'

That was the extent of his conversation, the news of a salt mine. But he had made his point: we were truly in Siberia. Until then we had been travelling in the Soviet Far East, two thousand miles of all but nameless territory on the borders of China and Mongolia. From now on, the Siberian forest, the *taiga*, thickened, blurring the distant hills with smudges of trees and hiding the settlements that had swallowed so many banished Russians. In places this dense forest disappeared for twenty miles; then there was tundra, a plain of flawless snow on which rows of light-poles trailed into the distance, getting smaller and smaller, like those diagramatic pictures that illustrate perspective, the last light-pole a dot. The hugeness of Russia overwhelmed me. I had been travelling for five days over these landscapes and still more than half the country remained to be crossed. I scanned the window for some new detail that would intimate we were getting closer to Moscow. But the differences from day to day were slight; the snow was endless, the stops were brief, and the sun, which shone so brightly on the *taiga*, was always eclipsed by the towns we passed through: an impenetrable cloud of smoky fog hung over every town, shutting out the sun. The small villages were different; they lay in sunlight, precariously, between the *taiga* and the tracks, their silence so great it was nearly visible.

I was now the only Westerner on the train. I felt like the last Mohican. Deprived of friendly conversation, denied rest by my bad dreams, irritated by the mute man in pyjamas and his pages of equations, doubled up with cramps from the greasy stews of the dining car – and, guiltily remembering my four months' absence, missing my family – I bribed Vassily for a bottle of vodka (he said they'd run out, but for two rubles he discovered some) and spent an entire day emptying it. The day I bought it I met a young man who told me in fractured German that he was taking his sick father to a hospital in Sverdlovsk.

I said, 'Serious?'

He said, '*Sehr schlim!*'

The young man bought a bottle of champagne and took it back to his compartment, which was in my sleeping car. He offered me a drink. We sat down; in the berth opposite the old man lay sleeping, the blankets drawn up to his chin. His face was grey, waxen with illness, and strained; he looked as if he were painfully swallowing the toad of death, and certainly the compartment had the dull underground smell of death about it, a clammy tomb here on the train. The young man clucked, poured himself more champagne, and drank it. He tried to give me more, but I found the whole affair appalling – the dying man in the narrow berth, his son beside him steadily drinking champagne, and at the window the snowy forests of Central Russia.

I went to my own compartment to drink my vodka and saw in my solitary activity something of the Russians' sense of desolation. In fact they did nothing else but drink. They drank all the time and they drank everything – cognac that tasted like hair tonic, sour watery beer, the red wine that was indistinguishable from cough syrup, the nine-dollar bottles of champagne, and the smooth vodka. Every day it was something new: first the vodka ran out, then the beer, then the cognac, and after Irkutsk one saw loutish men who had pooled their money for champagne, passing the bottle like bums in a doorway. Between drinking they slept, and I grew to recognize the confirmed alcoholics from the way they were dressed – they wore fur hats and fur leggings because their circulation was so poor; their hands and lips were always blue. Most of the arguments and all the fights I saw were the result of drunkenness. There was generally a fist fight in Hard Class after lunch, and Vassily provoked quarrels at every meal. If the man he quarrelled with happened to be sober, the man would call for the complaints' book and scribble angrily in it.

'*Tovarich!*' the customer would shout, requesting the complaints' book. I only heard the word used in sarcasm.

There was a nasty fight at Zima. Two boys – one in an army uniform – snarled at a conductor on the platform. The conductor was a rough-looking man dressed in black. He did not react immediately, but when the boys boarded he ran up the stairs behind them and leaped on them from behind, punching them both. A crowd gathered to watch. One of the boys yelled, 'I'm a soldier! I'm a soldier!' and the men in the crowd muttered, 'A fine soldier *he* is.' The conductor went on beating them up in the vestibule of the Hard-Class car. The interesting thing was not that the boys were drunk and the conductor sober, but that all three were drunk.

Another day, another night, a thousand miles; the snow deepened, and we were at Novosibirsk. Foreigners generally get off at Novosibirsk for an overnight stop, but I stayed on the train. I would not be home for Christmas, as I had promised – it was now 23 December and we were more than two days from Moscow – but if I made good connections I might be home before New Year's. The tall pale man changed from pyjamas into furs, put his equations away, and got off the train. I cleared his berth and decided that what I needed was a routine. I would start shaving regularly, taking fruit salts in the morning, and doing push-ups before breakfast; no naps; I would finish *New Grub Street*, start Borges' *Labyrinths*, and begin a short story, writing in the afternoon and not taking a drink until seven, or six at the earliest, or five if the light was too poor to write by. I was glad for the privacy: my mind needed tidying.

That morning I spent putting my thoughts into order, sorting out my anxieties and deciding to start my short story immediately. A woman of forty falls in love with a boy of nineteen. The boy wants to marry her. The woman agrees to meet the boy's mother. They meet – they're the same age – and hit it off, discussing their divorces, their affairs, ignoring the boy who, callow, inexperienced, only embarrasses them both by his surly insistence on marriage. So:

The Strangs had one of those marriages that goes on happily for years, filling friends with envious generosity, and then falls to pieces in an afternoon of astonishing abuse that threatens every other marriage for miles around. Friends were relieved when, instead of lingering in New York and persuading them to support her in her bitter quarrel with Ralph, Milly chose to go to . . .

The door flew open with a bang and a man entered carrying a cloth bundle and several paper parcels. He smiled. He was about fifty, baldness revealing irregular contours on his head, with large red hands. He had the rodent's eyes of someone very nearsighted. He threw the cloth bundle on his berth and placed a loaf of brown bread and a quart jar of maroon jam on my story.

I put my pen down and left the compartment. When I returned he had changed into a blue track suit (a little hero-medal pinned to his chest), and, staring through the eye-enlarging lenses of a pair of glasses askew on his nose, he was slapping jam on a slice of bread with a jack-knife. I put my story away. He munched his jam sandwich and, between bites, belched. He finished his sandwich, undid a newspaper parcel, and took out a chunk of grey meat. He cut a plug from it, put it in his mouth, wrapped the meat, and took off his glasses. He sniffed at the table, picked up my yellow sleeve of pipe cleaners, put on his glasses, and studied the writing. Then he looked at his watch and sighed. He monkeyed with my pipe, my matches, tobacco, pen, radio, timetable, Borges' *Labyrinths*, checking his watch between each item and sniffing, as if his nose would reveal what his eyes could not.

This went on for the rest of the day, defeating what plans I had for establishing a routine and eliminating any possibility of my writing a story. His prying motions made me hate him almost immediately and I imagined him thinking, as he tapped his watch crystal between sniffs of my belongings, 'Well, there's thirty seconds gone.' He had a little book of Russian railway maps. At each station he put on his glasses and found its name on the map. There were about fifteen stations on each map, so he dirtied the pages in sequence with his thumbs before the train moved to a new page, and I grew to recognize from the jam smears and thumbprints on his maps how far the Rossiya had gone. He read nothing else for the rest of the trip. He didn't speak; he didn't sleep. How did he pass the time? Well, he yawned: he could sustain a yawn for five seconds, sampling it with his tongue, working it around his jaws, and finally biting it with a loud growl. He sighed, he groaned, he sucked his teeth, he grunted, and he made each into a separate activity that he timed, always looking at his watch when he had completed a yawn or a sigh. He also coughed and choked in the same deliberate way, studying his eructations, belching with disgusting thoroughness as he exhausted himself of wind in three keys. In between times he looked out the window or stared at me, smiling when our eyes met. His teeth were stainless steel.

I find it very difficult to read and impossible to write with another person near by. If the person is staring at me over a quart of jam and a crumbling loaf of bread, I am driven to distraction. So I did nothing but watch him because there was nothing but that to do. He was odd in another way: if I glanced out the window, so did he; if I went into the corridor, he followed; if I talked to the boy next door, whose father lay dying among empty champagne bottles, the zombie was at my heels and then peering over my shoulder. I couldn't rid myself of him – and I tried.

Fearing that I would be left behind, I had not gotten off the train at any of the brief stops. But when this haunting creature parked himself in my compartment and shadowed me everywhere, I conceived a plan for ditching him in Omsk. It would be a simple duffilling: I would get off the train and lead him some distance away, and then, just as the train started up, I'd spring over and leap aboard, pausing on the stairs to block him from gaining a foothold. I tried this in Barabinsk. He followed me to the door, but no further. Omsk, three hours later, was a better opportunity. I encouraged him to follow me, led him to a kiosk doing a brisk trade in buns, and then lost him. I entered the train at the last minute, believing he was duffilled, but found him back in the compartment sniffing over his maps. After that he never left the compartment. Perhaps he suspected I was trying to ditch him.

He had his own food, this simpleton, so he had no need of the dining car. His meals were extraordinary. He surrounded himself with the food he had brought: a fist of butter in greasy paper, the bread loaf, the hunk of meat and another newspaper parcel of pickles, the jar of jam. He tore off a segment of bread and slathered it with a jack-knife blade of butter. Then he set out a pickle and a plug of meat and took a bite of each in turn, pickle, bread, meat, then a spoonful of jam; then another bite of the pickle, and so forth, filling his mouth before he began to chew. I could no longer bear to watch him. I spent more and more time in the dining car.

When the drunken soldiers had been turned out of the dining car, and the others, either very gaunt or very fat, lifted their faces from their metal bowls and left, scuffling their boots, the dining-car doors were locked and the kitchen employees cleaned the place up. They allowed me to stay, because, under the terms of our agreement, Vassily continued to supply me with bottles of Hungarian white wine as long as I bribed him for it and shared it with him. Vassily turned the accounts over to his assistant, Volodya, who had his own abacus; Sergei, the cook, ogled Nina from the kitchen door; Annushka wiped the tables; and Viktor, a waiter – who later told me that he paid Anna to do his work (he said she would do anything for five rubles) – Viktor sat with Vassily and me and pumped me for information about hockey teams: 'Bostabroons, Doront Mupplekhleef, Moon-droolkanadeens, and Cheegago Blekaks.' Viktor often stood behind Vassily and scratched his right cheek, meaning that Vassily was a drunkard.

There was a young black-haired man who swept the floor and rarely spoke to anyone. Viktor pointed him out to me and said, 'Gitler! Gitler!'

The man ignored him, but to make his point Viktor stamped on the floor and ground his boot as if killing a cockroach. Vassily put his forefinger under his nose to make a moustache and said, '*Heil Gitler!*' So the young man might have been an anti-Semite or, since Russian mockery is not very subtle, he might have been a Jew.

One afternoon the young man came over to me and said, 'Angela Davis!'

'Gitler!' said Viktor, grinning.

'Angela Davis *karasho*,' said Gitler and began to rant in Russian about the way Angela Davis had been persecuted in America. He shook his broom at me, his hair falling over his eyes, and he continued quite loudly until Vassily banged on the table.

'Politics!' said Vassily. 'We don't want politics here. This is a restaurant, not a university.' He spoke in Russian, but his message was plain and he was obviously very angry with Gitler.

The rest were embarrassed. They sent Gitler to the kitchen and brought another bottle of wine. Vassily said, 'Gitler – *ni karasho!*' But it was Viktor who was the most conciliatory. He stood up and folded his arms, and, shushing the kitchen staff, he said in a little voice:

> Zee fearst of My,
> Zee 'art of spreeng!
> Oh, leetle seeng,
> En everyseeng we do,
> Remember always to say 'pliz'
> En dun forget 'sank you'!

Later, Viktor took me to his compartment to show me his new fur hat. He was very proud of it since it cost him nearly a week's pay. Nina was also in the compartment, which was shared by Vassily and Anna – quite a crowd for a space no bigger than an average-sized clothes closet. Nina showed me her passport and the picture of her mother and, while this was going on, Viktor disappeared. I put my arm around Nina and with my free hand took off her white scullion's cap. Her black hair fell to her shoulders. I held her tightly and kissed her, tasting the kitchen. The train was racing. But the compartment door was open, and Nina pulled away and said softly, '*Nyet, nyet, nyet.*'

On the day before Christmas, in the afternoon, we arrived at Sverdlovsk. The sky was leaden and it was very cold. I hopped out the door and watched the old man being taken down the stairs to the platform. While he was being moved, the blankets had slipped down to his chest, where his hands lay rigid, two grey claws, their colour matching his face. The son went over and pulled the blankets high to cover his mouth. He knelt in the ice and packed a towel around the old man's head.

Seeing me standing near by, the son said in German, 'Sverdlovsk. This is where Europe begins and Asia ends. Here are the Urals.' He pointed towards the back of the train and said, 'Asia,' and then towards the engine, 'Europe.'

'How is your father?' I asked, when the stretcher-bearers arrived and put on their harnesses. The stretcher was a hammock, slung between them.

'I think he's dead,' he said. '*Das vedanya.*'

My depression increased as we sped towards Perm in a whirling snowstorm. The logging camps and villages lay half-buried and behind them were birches a foot thick, the ice on their branches giving them the appearance of silver filigree. I could see children crossing a frozen river in the storm, moving so slowly in the direction of some huts, they broke my heart. I lay back on my berth and took my radio, its plastic cold from standing by the window, and tried to find a station. I put up the antenna – the zombie watched me from behind his clutter of uncovered food. A lot of static, then a French station, then 'Jingle Bells'. The zombie smiled. I switched it off.

Late on Christmas Eve I knocked on the door of the dining car and was admitted by Vassily. He told me, with gestures of shrugging, that the place was closed. I said, 'It's Christmas Eve.' He shrugged. I gave him five rubles. He let me in and got a bottle of champagne, and, as he shot off the cork, I looked around at the deserted car. In the best of times it was cold, but without the trickle of warmth from the stove and buffeted by the snowy wind, it was colder than usual – lighted by a single flourescent tube and holding only the two of us. I could not imagine anything worse for watching Christmas approach. In the funereal chill Vassily drew up a chair and poured us both a drink. He tossed his back, as if the champagne were rotgut, screwing up his face and saying, '*Yagh!*'

We sat facing each other, drinking, not speaking, until Vassily lifted his glass and said, 'U.S.A.!'

By then I was drunk enough to remember one of the Russian lessons Vladimir had given me. I touched Vassily's glass with mine and said, '*Soyuz Sovietski Sosialistichiski Respublik.*'

'*Steppe!*' hollered Vassily. He was singing. '*Steppe! Steppe!*'

We finished the bottle, got another, and Vassily continued to sing. Around midnight he broke into a military song that I recognized – the tune at least. I hummed along with him, and he said, '*Da, da!*' urging me to sing. I sang the only words I knew, Italian obscenities to his patriotic Russian verses:

> *Compagna Polacca,*
> *Hai fatto una cacca?*
> *Si, Vassili!*
> *Ho fatto venti kili!*
> *Io ho fatto nelle grande steppe . . .*

Vassily applauded and joined with me in Russian. We stood in the dining car, singing our duet, drinking between verses.

> *Compagna Tatyana,*
> *Hai fatto un' putana?*
> *Si, Bonanno!*
> *Ho fatto per un' anno,*
> *Io ho fatto nelle grande steppe . . .*

'Merry Christmas,' I said when the fourth bottle appeared. Vassily was smiling and nodding and chuckling hoarsely. He showed me a sheaf of restaurant bills he had been adding up. He shook them and then threw them into the air: '*Whee!*' We sat down again, and Vassily, too drunk to remember that I couldn't speak Russian, harangued me for fifteen minutes. I suppose he was saying, 'Look at me. Fifty-five years old and I'm running this crummy dining car. Urp. Back and forth, every two weeks, from Moscow to Vladivostok, sleeping in Hard Class, too busy to take a piss, everyone giving me lip. Urp. You call that a life?' Towards the end of his harangue his head grew heavy, his eyelids drooped, and his speech became thick. He put his head down on the table, and, still holding tight to the bottle, he went to sleep.

'Merry Christmas.'

I finished my drink and went back to my compartment through the bouncing train.

The next morning, Christmas, I woke and looked over at the zombie sleeping with his arms folded on his chest like a mummy's. The *provodnik* told me it was six o'clock Moscow time. My watch said eight. I put it back two hours and waited for dawn, surprised that so many people in the car had decided to do the same thing. In darkness we stood at the windows, watching our reflections. Shortly afterwards I saw why they were there. We entered the outskirts of Yaroslavl and I heard the others whispering to themselves. The old lady in the frilly nightgown, the Goldi man and his wife and child, the domino-playing drunks, even the zombie who had been monkeying with my radio: they pressed their faces against the windows as we began rattling across a long bridge. Beneath us, half-frozen, very black, and in places reflecting the flames of Yaroslavl's chimneys, was the Volga.

> . . . Royal David's city,
> Stood a lowly cattle shed . . .

What was that? Sweet voices, as clear as organ tones, drifted from my compartment. I froze and listened. The Russians, awe-struck by the sight of the Volga, had fallen silent; they were hunched, staring down at the water. But the holy music, fragrant and slight, moved through the air, warming it like an aroma.

Where a mother laid her baby
In a manger, for his bed . . .

The hymn wavered, but the silent reverence of the Russians and the slowness of the train allowed the soft children's voices to perfume the corridor. My listening became a meditation of almost unbearable sadness, as if joy's highest refinement was borne on a needlepoint of pain.

Mary was that mother mild,
Jesus Christ, her little child . . .

I went into the compartment and held the radio to my ear until the broadcast ended, a programme of Christmas music from the BBC. Dawn never came that day. We travelled in thick fog and through whorls of brown blowing mist, which made the woods ghostly. It was not cold outside: some snow had melted, and the roads – more frequent now – were rutted and muddy. All morning the tree trunks, black with dampness, were silhouettes in the fog, and the pine groves at the very limit of visibility in the mist took on the appearance of cathedrals with dark spires. In places the trees were so dim, they were like an afterimage on the eye. I had never felt close to the country, but the fog distanced me even more, and I felt, after 6,000 miles and all those days in the train, only a great remoteness; every reminder of Russia – the women in orange canvas jackets working on the line with shovels, the sight of a Lenin statue, the station signboards stuck in yellow ice, and the startled magpies croaking in Russian at the gliding train – all this annoyed me. I resented Russia's size; I wanted to be home.

The dining car was locked at nine. I tried again at ten and found it empty. Vassily explained that, as we would be in Moscow soon, the dining car was closed. I swore at him, surprising myself with my own anger. Under protest he made me an omelette; he handed it to me with a slice of bread and a glass of tea. While I was eating, a woman came in. She wore a black coat and had a Soviet Railway badge pinned to her black hat. She spoke to Vassily: '*Kleb*' (bread). Vassily waved her away: '*Nyet kleb!*' She pointed at my meal and repeated her request for bread. Vassily shouted at her. She stood her ground and got an almighty shove from Vassily, who smiled at me apologetically as he delivered the blow. The woman came back and put out her hand and screamed loudly at him. This infuriated Vassily. His eyes became small, and he threw himself on her, beating her with his fists. He twisted her arm behind her back and kicked her hard. The woman howled and was gone.

Vassily said to me, '*Ni karasho!*' The fight had left him breathless. He smiled his idiotic smile. I was ashamed of myself for not helping the woman. I pushed my food away.

'Pavel?' Vassily blinked at me.

'You are a fucking monkey.'

'*Pozhal'sta*,' said Vassily, in glad welcome.

The train was going at half-speed for the approach to Moscow. I walked down the corridors of Hard Class to my compartment, to pack my belongings. The other passengers were already packed. They stood in their arrival suits, smoking by the windows. I passed each one, seeing criminality and fraud in their faces, brutishness in their little eyes, fists protruding from unusually long sleeves.

'Monkey,' I said, squeezing through a group of soldiers.

A man stroking his fur hat blocked my way. I went up to him. He agitated his enormous jaw with a yawn.

'Monkey!' He moved aside.

Monkey to the *provodnik*, monkey to the man at the samovar, monkey to the army officer in Soft Class; and, still muttering, I found the zombie sitting by the window in an overcoat, his jam-flecked thumb on *Mockba*. 'Monkey!' I wished him a Merry Christmas and gave him two pipe cleaners, a can of Japanese sardines, and a ballpoint pen that would run out of ink as soon as he wrote his name.

*

That was the end of my trip, but it was not the end of my journey. I still had a ticket to London, and, hoping to catch the next train west, I cancelled my hotel reservation and spent the afternoon arranging for a de luxe berth on the train to the Hook of Holland, via Warsaw and Berlin. I was packed and ready, and I arrived at the station on Christmas night with an hour to spare. The Intourist guide brought me to the barrier and said good-bye. I stood for forty-five minutes on the platform, waiting to be shown to my compartment.

It was not a porter who inquired about my destination, but an immigration official. He leafed through my passport, rattling the pages. He shook his head.

'Polish visa?'

'I'm not stopping in Poland,' I said. 'I'm just passing through.'

'*Transit* visa,' he said.

'What do you mean?' I said. 'Hey, this train's going to leave!'

'You must have Polish transit visa.'

'I'll get it at the border.'

'Impossible. They will send you back.'

'Look' – the whistle blew – 'I've *got* to get on this train. *Please* – it's going to leave without me!' I picked up my suitcase. The man held me by the arm. A signalman passed by, motioning with his green flag. The train began to move.

'I can't stay here!' But I let the man hold on to my sleeve and watched the Holland-bound express tooting its way out of the station: *frseeeeeeeefronnng*. There were travellers' faces at the windows. They were happy, safely leaving. *It's Christmas, darling*, they were saying, *and we're off*. It was the end, I thought, as I saw the train receding, taking my heart with it. It's the end: duffilled!

Two days later I was able to leave Moscow, but the trip to London was not outwardly remarkable. I tried to collect my wits for the arrival; I slept through Warsaw, glared at Berlin, and entered Holland with a stone in my stomach. I felt flayed by the four months of train travel: it was as if I had undergone some harrowing cure, sickening myself on my addiction in order to be free of it. To invert the cliché, I had had a bellyful of travelling hopefully – I wanted to arrive. The whistle blew at level crossings – a long moronic hoot – and I was mocked by it, not bewitched. I had been right: anything was possible on a train, even the urge to get off. I drank to deafen myself, but still I heard the racket of the wheels.

All travel is circular. I had been jerked through Asia, making a parabola on one of the planet's hemispheres. After all, the grand tour is just the inspired man's way of heading home.

And I had learned what I had always secretly believed, that the difference between travel writing and fiction is the difference between recording what the eye sees and discovering what the imagination knows. Fiction is pure joy – how sad that I could not reinvent the trip as fiction. It would have had (now we were boarding a blue ferry at the Hook) such a pleasing shape if I had artfully distributed light and shadow and played with the grammar of delay. I would have plotted myself into danger: Sadik would have had a switchblade and gold teeth, the Hué track an erupting mine, the Orient Express a lavish dining car, and Nina – imploring me – would have rapped softly on my compartment door and flung off her uniform as we crossed the Volga. It did not happen that way, and in any case I might have been too busy for that gusto. I had worked every day, bent over my rocking notebook like Trollope scribbling between postal assignments remembering to put it all in the past tense.

Gladly, made nimble by sanity's seamless glee, I boarded the train for London – correction: I am now leaving Harwich (there were often twenty miles between clauses and a hundred more before I finished a sentence) and setting my face at the hairless January fields. On my lap I have four thick notebooks. One has a Madras water stain on it, another has been slopped with *borscht*, the blue one (lettered, in gold, *Punjab Stationery Mart*) has the ring from a damp glass on its front, and the red one's colour has been diluted to pink by the Turkish sun. These stains are like notations. The trip is finished and so is the book, and in a moment I will turn to the first page, and to amuse myself on the way to London will read with some satisfaction the trip that begins, *Ever since childhood, when I lived within earshot of the Boston and Maine, I have seldom heard a train go by and not wished I was on it.*

Now read the first chapter of *Ghost Train to the Eastern Star*, in which the author retraces the steps of *The Great Railway Bazaar* thirty years on . . .

# 1. The Eurostar

You think of travellers as bold, but our guilty secret is that travel is one of the laziest ways on earth of passing the time. Travel is not merely the business of being bone-idle, but also an elaborate bumming evasion, allowing us to call attention to ourselves with our conspicuous absence while we intrude upon other people's privacy – being actively offensive as fugitive freeloaders. The traveller is the greediest kind of romantic voyeur, and in some well-hidden part of the traveller's personality is an unpickable knot of vanity, presumption and mythomania bordering on the pathological. This is why a traveller's worst nightmare is not the secret police or the witch doctors or malaria, but rather the prospect of meeting another traveller.

Most writing about travel takes the form of jumping to conclusions, and so most travel books are superfluous, the thinnest, most transparent monologuing. Little better than a licence to bore, travel writing is the lowest form of literary self-indulgence: dishonest complaining, creative mendacity, pointless heroics and chronic posturing, much of it distorted with Munchausen syndrome.

Of course, it's much harder to stay at home and be polite to people and face things, but where's the book in that? Better the boastful charade of pretending to be an adventurer:

> Yes, swagger the nut-strewn roads,
> Crouch in the fo'c'sle
> Stubbly with goodness,

in a lusty 'Look-at-me!' in exotic landscapes.

This was more or less my mood as I was packing to leave home. I also thought: *But there is curiosity*. Even the most timid fantasists need the satisfaction of now and then enacting their fantasies. And sometimes you just have to clear out. Trespassing is a pleasure for some of us. As for idleness, 'An aimless joy is a pure joy.'

*And there are dreams:* one, the dream of a foreign land that I enjoy at home, staring east into space at imagined temples, crowded bazaars and what V. S. Pritchett called 'human architecture', lovely women in gauzy clothes, old trains clattering on mountainsides, the mirage of happiness; two, the dream state of travel itself. Often on a trip, I seem to be alive in a hallucinatory vision of difference, the highly coloured unreality of foreignness, where I am vividly aware (as in most dreams) that I don't belong; yet I am floating, an idle anonymous visitor among busy people, an utter stranger. When you're strange, as the song goes, no one remembers your name.

Travel can induce such a distinct and nameless feeling of strangeness and disconnection in me that I feel insubstantial, like a puff of smoke, merely a ghost, a creepy revenant from the underworld, unobserved and watchful among real people, wandering, listening while remaining unseen. Being invisible – the usual condition of the older traveller – is much more useful than being obvious. You see more, you are not interrupted, you are ignored. Such a traveller isn't in a hurry, which is why you might mistake him for a bum. Hating schedules, depending on chance encounters, I am attracted by travel's slow tempo.

Ghosts have all the time in the world, another pleasure of long-distance aimlessness – travelling at half speed on slow trains and procrastinating. And this ghostliness, I was to find, was also an effect of the journey I had chosen, returning to places I had known many years ago. It is almost impossible to return to an early scene in your travelling life and not feel like a spectre. And many places I saw were themselves sad and spectral, others big and hectic, while I was the haunting presence, the eavesdropping shadow on the ghost train.

Long after I took the trip I wrote about in *The Great Railway Bazaar* I went on thinking how I'd gone overland, changing trains across Asia, improvising my trip, rubbing against the world. And reflecting on what I'd seen – the way the unrevisited past is always looping in your dreams. Memory is a ghost train too. Ages later, you still ponder the beautiful face you once glimpsed in a distant country. Or the sight of a noble tree, or a country road, or a happy table in a café, or some angry boys armed with rusty spears shrieking, 'Run you life, *dim-dim*!' – or the sound of a train at night, striking that precise musical note of train whistles, a diminished third, into the darkness, as you lie in the train, moving through the world as travellers do, 'inside the whale'.

Thirty-three years went by. I was then twice as old as the person who had ridden those trains, most of them pulled by steam locomotives, boiling across the hinterland of Turkey and India. I loved the symmetry in the time difference. Time passing had become something serious to me, embodied in the process of my growing old. As a young man I regarded the earth as a fixed and trustworthy thing that would see me into my old age; but older, I began to understand transformation as a natural law, something emotional in an undependable world that was visibly spoiled. It is only with age that you acquire the gift to evaluate decay, the epiphany of Wordsworth, the wisdom of *wabi-sabi*: nothing is perfect, nothing is complete, nothing lasts.

'Without change there can be no nostalgia,' a friend once said to me, and I realized that what I began to witness was not just change and decay, but imminent extinction. Had my long-ago itinerary changed as much as me? I had the idea of taking the same trip again, travelling in my own footsteps – a serious enterprise, but the sort of trip that younger, opportunistic punks often take to make a book and get famous.*

The best of travel seems to exist outside of time, as though the years of travel are not deducted from your life. Travel also holds the magical possibility of reinvention: that you might find a place you love, to begin a new life and never go home. In a distant place no one knows you – nearly always a plus. And you can pretend, in travel, to be different from the person you are, unattached, enigmatic, younger, richer or poorer, anyone you choose to be, the rebirth that many travellers experience if they go far enough.

The decision to return to any early scene in your life is dangerous but irresistible, not as a search for lost time but for the grotesquerie of what happened since. In most cases it is like meeting an old lover years later and hardly recognizing the object of desire in this pinched and bruised old fruit. We all live with fantasies of transformation. Live long enough and you see them enacted – the young made old, the road improved, houses where there were once fields; and their opposites, a good school turned into a ruin, a river poisoned, a pond shrunk and filled with

---

* The list is very long and includes travellers' books in the footsteps of Graham Greene, George Orwell, Robert Louis Stevenson, Leonard Woolf, Joseph Conrad, Mr Kurtz, H. M. Stanley, Leopold Bloom, Saint Paul, Basho, Jesus and Buddha.

rubbish, and dismal reports: 'He's dead,' 'She's huge,' 'She committed suicide,' 'He's now prime minister,' 'He's in jail,' 'You can't go there any more.'

A great satisfaction in growing old – one of many – is assuming the role of a witness to the wobbling of the world and seeing irreversible changes. The downside, besides the tedium of listening to the delusions of the young, is hearing the same hackneyed opinions over and over, not just those of callow youth but, much worse and seemingly criminal, the opinions of even callower people who ought to know better, all the lies about war and fear and progress and the enemy – the world as a wheel of repetition. They – I should say 'we' – are bored by things we've heard a million times before, books we've dismissed, the discoveries that are not new, the proposed solutions that will solve nothing. 'I can tell that I am growing old,' says the narrator in Borges's story 'The Congress'. 'One unmistakable sign is the fact that I find novelty neither interesting nor surprising, perhaps because I see nothing essentially new in it – it's little more than timid variations on what's already been.'

Older people are perceived as cynics and misanthropes – but no, they are simply people who have at last heard the still, sad music of humanity played by an inferior rock band howling for fame. Going back and retracing my footsteps – a glib, debunking effort for a shallower, younger, impressionable writer – would be for me a way of seeing who I was, where I went, and what subsequently happened to the places I had seen.

Since I will never write the autobiography I once envisioned – volume one, *Who I Was*; volume two, *I Told You So* – writing about travel has become a way of making sense of my life, the nearest I will come to autobiography – as the novel is, the short story, and the essay. As Pedro Almodóvar once remarked, 'Anything that is not autobiography is plagiarism.'

The thing to avoid while in my own footsteps would be the tedious reminiscences of better days, the twittering of the nostalgia bore, whose message is usually *I was there and you weren't*. 'I remember when you could get four of those for a dollar.' 'There was a big tree in a field where that building is now.' 'In my day . . .'

Oh, shut up!

What traveller backtracked to take the great trip again? None of the good ones that I know. Greene never returned to the Liberian bush, nor to Mexico, nor to Vietnam. In his late fifties, Waugh dismissed modern travel altogether as mere tourism and a waste of time. After 1948, Thesiger did not return to Rub' al Khali, the Empty Quarter of Arabia. Burton did not mount another expedition to Utah, or to substantiate the source of the Nile – at my age he was living in Trieste, immersed in erotica. Darwin never went to sea again. Neither did Joseph Conrad, who ended up hating the prospect of seafaring. Eric Newby went down the Ganges once, Jonathan Raban down the Mississippi once, and Jan Morris climbed Everest once. Robert Byron did not take the road to Oxiana again, Cherry-Garrard made only one trip to Antarctica, Chatwin never returned to Patagonia, nor did Doughty go back to Arabia Deserta, nor Wallace to the Malay Archipelago, nor Waterton to the Amazon, nor Trollope to the West Indies, nor Edward Lear to Corsica, nor Stevenson to the Cévennes, nor Chekhov to Sakhalin, nor Gide to the Congo, nor Canetti to Marrakesh, nor Jack London to the Solomon Islands, nor Mark Twain to Hawaii. So much for some of my favourite authors.

You could ask, 'Why should they bother?' but the fact is that each of these travellers, grown older, would have discovered what the heroic traveller Henry Morton Stanley found when he recrossed Africa from west to east ten years after his first successful crossing from east to west from 1874 to 1877 – a different place, with ominous changes, and a new book. Richard Henry Dana added a chastened epilogue to *Two Years Before the Mast* when, twenty-four years after its publication in 1840, he returned to San Francisco (but no longer travelling in the forecastle) and found that it had changed from a gloomy Spanish mission station with a few shacks to an American boom town that had been transformed by the Gold Rush. Dana was scrupulous about reacquainting himself with people he'd met on his first visit and sizing up the altered landscape, completing, as he put it, 'acts of pious remembrance'.

Certain poets, notably Wordsworth and Yeats, enlarged their vision and found enlightenment in returning to an earlier landscape of their lives. They set the standard in the literature of revisitation. If it is a writer's lot to repeat the past, writing it in his or her own way, this return journey might be my own prosaic version of 'The Wild Swans at Coole' or 'Tintern Abbey'.

My proposed trip to retrace the itinerary of *The Great Railway Bazaar* was mainly curiosity on my part, and the usual idleness, with a hankering to be away; but this had been the case thirty-three years before, and it had yielded results. All writing is launching yourself into the darkness, and hoping for light and a soft landing.

'I'm going to do a lot of knitting while you're away,' my wife said. That was welcome news. I needed Penelope this time.

Though I had pretended to be jolly in the published narrative, the first trip had not gone as planned.

'I don't want you to go,' my first wife had said in 1973 – not in a sentimental way, but as an angry demand.

Yet I had just finished a book and was out of ideas. I had no income, no idea for a new novel, and – though I didn't know what I was in for – I hoped that this trip might be a way of finding a subject. I had to go. Sailors went to sea, soldiers went to war, fishermen went fishing, I told her. Writers sometimes had to leave home. 'I'll be back as soon as I can.'

She resented my leaving. And though I did not write about it, I was miserable when I set off from London, saying goodbye to this demoralized woman and our two small children.

It was the age of aerograms and postcards and big black unreliable telephones. I wrote home often. But I succeeded in making only two phone calls, one from New Delhi and another from Tokyo, both of them futile. And why did my endearments sound unwelcome? I was homesick the whole way – four and a half months of it – and wondered if I was being missed. That was my first melancholy experience of the traveller's long lonely evenings. I was at my wits' end on the trip. I felt insane when I got home. I had not been missed. I had been replaced.

My wife had taken a lover. It was hypocritical of me to object: I had been unfaithful to her. It wasn't her sexual exploit that upset me, but the cosy domesticity. He spent many days and nights in my house, in our bed, romancing her and playing with the children.

I did not recognize my own voice when I howled, 'How could you do this?'

She said, 'I pretended you were dead.'

I wanted to kill this woman, not because I hated her, but (as homicidal spouses often say) because I loved her. I threatened to kill the man who, even after I was home, sent her love letters. I became an angry brute, and by chance I discovered a wickedly helpful thing: threatening to kill someone is an effective way of getting a person's attention.

Instead of killing anyone, or threatening it any more, I sat in my room and wrote in a fury, abusing my typewriter, trying to lose myself in the book's humour and strangeness. I had a low opinion of most travel writing. I wanted to put in everything that I found lacking in the other books – dialogue, characters, discomfort – and to leave out museums, churches and sightseeing generally. Though it would have added a dimension, I concealed everything about my domestic turmoil. I made the book jolly, and like many jolly books it was written in an agony of suffering, with the regret that in taking the trip I had lost what I valued most: my children, my wife, my happy household.

The book succeeded. I was cured of my misery by more work – an idea I had on the trip for a new novel. Yet something had been destroyed: faith, love, trust and a belief in the future. After my travel, on my return, I became an outsider, a ghostly presence, with my nose pressed against the window. I understood what it was like to be dead: people might miss you, but their lives go on without you. New people take your place. They sit in your favourite chair and dandle your children on their knees, giving them advice, chucking them under the chin; they sleep in your bed, look at your paintings, read your books, flirt with the Danish nanny; and as they belittle you for having been an over-industrious drudge, they spend your money. Most of the time, your death is forgotten. 'Maybe it was for the best,' people say, trying not to be morbid.

Some betrayals are forgivable, but others you never quite recover from. Years later, when my children were out of the house, I left that life, that marriage, that country. I began a new life elsewhere.

Now, thirty-three years older, I had returned to London. To my sorrow, about to take the same trip again, I relived much of the pain that I thought I'd forgotten.

Nothing is more suitable to a significant departure than bad weather. It matched my mood, too, the rain that morning in London, the low brown sky leaking drizzle, darkening the porous city of old stone, and because of it – the rain descending like a burden – everyone was hunched, their wet heads cast down, eyes averted, thinking, Filfy wevva. Traffic was louder, the heavy tyres swishing in the wet streets. At Waterloo Station I found the right platform for the Eurostar, the 12.09 to Paris.

Even at Waterloo, the reminders of my old London were almost immediate. The indifference of Londoners, their brisk way of walking, their fixed expressions, no one wearing a hat in the rain yet some carrying brollies – all of us, including honking public school hearties, striding past a gaunt young woman swaddled in dirty quilts, sitting on the wet floor at the foot of some metal steps at the railway station, begging.

And then the simplest international departure imaginable: a cursory security check, French immigration formalities, up the escalator to the waiting train, half empty on a wet weekday in early March. In 1973 I had left from Victoria Station in the morning, got off at the coast at Folkestone, caught the ferry, thrashed across the English Channel, boarded another train at Calais, and did not arrive in Paris until midnight.

That was before the tunnel had been dug under the channel. It had cost $20 billion and taken fifteen years and everyone complained that it was a money loser. Though the train had been running for twelve years, I had never taken it. Never mind the expense – the train through the tunnel was a marvel. I savoured the traveller's lazy reassurance that I could walk to the station and sit down in London, read a book, and a few hours later stand up and stroll into Paris without ever leaving the ground. And I intended to go to central Asia the same way, overland to India, just sitting and gaping out of the window.

This time, I had been refused a visa to enter Iran, and civilians were being abducted and shot in Afghanistan, but studying a map, I found other routes and railway lines – through Turkey to Georgia and on to the Islamic republics. First Azerbaijan, then a ferry across the Caspian, and then trains through Turkmenistan, past the ancient city of Merv, where there was a railway station, to the banks of the Amu Darya River – Oxiana indeed – and more tracks to Bukhara, Samarkand and Tashkent, in Uzbekistan, within spitting distance of the Punjab railways.

After that, I could follow my old itinerary through India to Sri Lanka and on to Burma. But it was a mistake to anticipate too much so early in the trip, and anyway, here I was a few minutes out of Waterloo, clattering across the shiny rain-drenched rails of Clapham Junction, thinking: I have been here before. On the line through south London, my haunted face at the window, my former life as a Londoner began to pass before my eyes.

Scenes of the seventies, along this very line, through Vauxhall, and making the turn at Queenstown Road, past Clapham High Street and Brixton and across Coldharbour Lane, a name that sent chills through me. Across the common, in 1978, there had been race riots on Battersea Rise, near Chiesman's department store ('Est. 1895'), where clerks sidled up and asked, 'Are you being served?' I bought my first colour TV set there, near the street on Lavender Hill where Sarah Ferguson, later the Duchess of York, lived; on the day her marriage to Prince Andrew was announced, my charlady, carrying a mop and bucket, sneered, saying, 'She's from the gutter.'

We were travelling in a deep railway gully, veering away from Clapham Junction, and from the train I got a glimpse of a cinema I had gone to until it became a bingo hall, the church that was turned into a daycare centre, and beyond the common the Alfarthing Primary School, where my kids, all pale faces and skinny legs, were taught to sing by Mrs Quarmby. These were streets I knew well: one where my bike was stolen, another where my car was broken into; greengrocers and butcher shops where I'd shopped; the chippie, the florist, the Chinese grocer; the newsagent, an Indian from Mwanza who liked speaking Swahili with me because he missed the shores of Lake Victoria; the Fishmonger's Arms – known as the Fish – an Irish pub where refugees from Ulster swore obscenely at the TV whenever they saw Prince Charles on it, and laughed like morons the day Lord Mountbatten was blown up by the IRA, and where, every evening, I drank a pint of Guinness and read the *Evening Standard*; this very place.

From scenes like these I had made my London life. In those days I prayed for rain, because it kept me indoors – writing weather. So much of what I saw today was familiar and yet not the same – the usual formula for a dream. I looked closer. The trees were bare under the grey tattered clouds, and most of the buildings were unchanged, but London was younger, more prosperous. This district that had been semi-derelict when I moved here – empty houses, squatters, a few ageing residents still holding on – had become gentrified. The Chinese grocer's was now a wine shop, and one of the pubs a bistro, and the fish-and-chip shop was a sushi bar.

But the wonderful thing was that I was whisked through south London with such efficiency, I was spared the deeper pain of looking closely at the past. I was snaking through tunnels and across viaducts and railway cuttings, looking left and right at the landscapes of my personal history and, happily, moving on, to other places that held no ambiguous memories. *Don't dwell on it*, the English say with their hatred of complaint. *Mustn't grumble. Stop brooding. It may never happen.*

I loved the speed of this train and the knowledge that it wasn't stopping anywhere but just making a beeline to the coast, past Penge, Beckenham,

Bromley – the edge of the London map and the old grumpy-looking bungalows I associated with novels of the outer suburbs, the fiction of twitching curtains, low spirits and anxious families, especially *Kipps* and *Mr Beluncle*, by the Bromleyites H. G. Wells and V. S. Pritchett, who escaped and lived to write about it.

In the satisfying shelf of English literature concerned with what we see from trains, the poems with the lines 'O fat white woman whom nobody loves' and 'Yes, I remember Adlestrop' stand out, and so do the trains that run up and down the pages of P. G. Wodehouse and Agatha Christie. But the description that best captures the English railway experience for me is Ford Madox Ford's in his evocation of the city, his first successful book, *The Soul of London*, published a hundred years ago. Looking out of the train window, Ford speaks of how the relative silence of sitting on a train and looking into the busy muted world outside invites melancholy. 'One is behind glass as if one were gazing into the hush of a museum; one hears no street cries, no children's calls.' And his keenest observation, which was to hold true for me from London to Tokyo: 'One sees, too, so many little bits of uncompleted life.'

He noted a bus near a church, a ragged child, a blue policeman. I saw a man on a bike, a woman alighting from a bus, schoolchildren kicking a ball, a young mother pushing a pram. And, as this was a panorama of London back gardens, a man digging, a woman hanging laundry, a workman – or was he a burglar? – setting a ladder against a window. And 'the constant succession of much smaller happenings that one sees, and that one never sees completed, gives to looking out of train windows a touch of pathos and of dissatisfaction. It is akin to the sentiment ingrained in humanity of liking a story to have an end.'

'Little bits of uncompleted life' – what the traveller habitually sees – inspire pathos and poetry, as well as the maddening sense of being an outsider, jumping to conclusions and generalizing, inventing or re-creating places from vagrant glimpses.

It was only twenty minutes from soot-crusted Waterloo to its opposite, the open farmland of Kent, many of the fields already raked by a harrow, ploughed and awaiting planting in this first week of March.

'Will you be having wine with your lunch?'

A woman in a blue uniform brought me a bottle of Les Jamelles Chardonnay Vin de Pays d'Oc 2004, praised on the menu for its 'subtle vanilla from the oak and a buttery finish'.

And then the lunch tray: *terrine de poulet et de brocoli, chutney de tomates,* the main course a fillet of lightly peppered salmon, with *coupe de chocolat* for dessert. This was, superficially at least, a different world from the one I had seen on the Railway Bazaar, that long-ago trip to Folkestone, and then standing at the rail of the ferry, feeling guilty and confused, eating a cold pork pie.

The tunnel was a twenty-two-minute miracle, the ultimate rabbit hole, delivering me from my English memories, speeding me beneath the channel to France, where I had only superficial and spotty recollections, of pleasures and misunderstandings, of eating and drinking, of looking at pictures, or hearing oddities, like that of the young pretty French woman who said to me, 'I am seeing tonight my fiancé's mistress. I seenk we will have sex. I love stupid women.' And then she said, 'You are smiling. You Americans!'

After the tunnel, rain falling from the French sky on the tiled roofs and the tiny cars driving on the right, but apart from that it could have been Kent: the same smooth hills and chalky plateau, and the same blight, the same warehouses, the low industrial outbuildings and workshops, the rows of bare poplars in the misty mid afternoon.

It was such a swift train trip, and so near was France to England, that it was hard to think of it as a separate country, with its own food and its peculiar scandals and language and religion and dilemmas. Enraged Muslim youths setting cars on fire was one of the current problems; only one death but lots of blazing Renaults.

Why is the motorway culture drearier in Europe than anywhere in America? Perhaps because it is imitative and looks hackneyed and unstylish and ill fitting, the way no European looks quite right in a baseball cap. While the petrol stations and industrial parks matched the disposable dreariness of American architecture, set against a French landscape they looked perverse, with Gothic spires and haywains and medieval chalets in the distance, like a violation of an old trust, the compact villages and ploughed fields and meadows set off by ugly roads and crash barriers.

Because of what Freud called 'the narcissism of minor differences', all these open fields, battlegrounds since ancient times, were the landscapes of contending armies, a gory example of civilization and its discontents. And so whatever else one could say, it was a fact that the route of this railway, once soaked in blood and thick with the graves of dead soldiers

– millions of them – had been serene for the past half century, perhaps its longest period of peace.

We crossed a river with a tragic name. One day in July ninety years ago, where the soft rain fell on the lovely meadows and low hills, in sight of the distant spires of Amiens on one side of the train and the small town of Péronne on the other, the valley of this river, the Somme, had been an amphitheatre of pure horror. On that first day of battle, 60,000 British soldiers were killed, plodding slowly because of the 66-pound packs on their backs. They advanced into German machine-gun fire, the largest number of soldiers killed on one day in British history. In the four months of this bloodbath, the first battle of the Somme, which ended in November 1916, more than one million soldiers were killed – British 420,000; French 194,000; German 440,000. And to no purpose. Nothing was gained, neither land nor any military advantage, nor even a lesson in the futility of war, for twenty-five years later – in my own lifetime – the same armies were at it again, warring in these same fields. All of them were colonial powers, which had annexed vast parts of Africa and Asia, to take their gold and diamonds, and lecture them on civilization.

The colours and clothes of the pedestrians on the streets nearer Paris reflected French colonial history – Africans, West Indians, Algerians, Vietnamese. They were kicking footballs in the rain. They were shoppers in the street markets, residents of the dreary tower blocks and tenements, the public housing at the edge of Paris that the Eurostar was passing and penetrating. We entered the city of mellow cheese-like stone and pitted façades and boulevards. London is largely a low city of single-family homes – terraces, cottages, townhouses, mews houses, bungalows, semi-detached villas. Paris is a city of rococo apartment buildings, bosomy with balconies, not a house to be seen.

With my small bag and a briefcase I looked such a lightweight that the porters at the Gare du Nord ignored me. I passed through the station to the front entrance, in the floodlit glow of the lovely façade with its classical-looking statues representing the cities and larger towns of France. They were sculpted in the early 1860s by (so a sign said) 'the greatest names in the Second Empire'.

The streets were thick with unmoving cars and loud honking and angry voices. I asked a smiling man what the problem was.

'*Une manifestation,*' he said.

'Why today?'

He shrugged. 'Because it's Tuesday.'

Every Tuesday there was a large, riotous demonstration in Paris. But for its size and its disruption this one was to be known as Black Tuesday.

# PAUL THEROUX

## GHOST TRAIN TO THE EASTERN STAR

'Long after the trip I wrote about in *The Great Railway Bazaar* I went on thinking about how I'd gone overland, changing trains across Asia, improvising my trip, rubbing against the world. And reflecting on what I'd seen – the way the unrevisited past is always looping in your dreams . . . Thirty-two years went by. I was then twice as old as the person who had ridden those trains, most of them pulled by steam locomotives, boiling across the hinterland of Turkey and India. I loved the symmetry in the time difference . . . Had my long-ago itinerary changed as much as me? I had the idea of taking the same trip again, travelling in my own footsteps . . .'

Starting off on the Eurostar from London, Paul Theroux once again sets out on a railway journey through the East, travelling overland through Eastern Europe, and eventually reaching India and Asia. Infused with the changes that have shaped the exterior landscape and enriched with developments to his own perceptions and psychology, *Ghost Train to the Eastern Star* is an absorbing and beautifully written follow-up to *The Great Railway Bazaar*.

'Theroux needs no more than three or four brush strokes of his pen to complete the most vivid of pictures' *The Times*

'The world's most perceptive travel writer' *Daily Mail*

'Theroux's work remains the standard by which other travel writing must be judged' *Observer*

# He just wanted a decent book to read ...

Not too much to ask, is it? It was in 1935 when Allen Lane, Managing Director of Bodley Head Publishers, stood on a platform at Exeter railway station looking for something good to read on his journey back to London. His choice was limited to popular magazines and poor-quality paperbacks – the same choice faced every day by the vast majority of readers, few of whom could afford hardbacks. Lane's disappointment and subsequent anger at the range of books generally available led him to found a company – and change the world.

*'We believed in the existence in this country of a vast reading public for intelligent books at a low price, and staked everything on it'*
**Sir Allen Lane, 1902–1970, founder of Penguin Books**

The quality paperback had arrived – and not just in bookshops. Lane was adamant that his Penguins should appear in chain stores and tobacconists, and should cost no more than a packet of cigarettes.

Reading habits (and cigarette prices) have changed since 1935, but Penguin still believes in publishing the best books for everybody to enjoy. We still believe that good design costs no more than bad design, and we still believe that quality books published passionately and responsibly make the world a better place.

So wherever you see the little bird – whether it's on a piece of prize-winning literary fiction or a celebrity autobiography, political tour de force or historical masterpiece, a serial-killer thriller, reference book, world classic or a piece of pure escapism – you can bet that it represents the very best that the genre has to offer.

## Whatever you like to read – trust Penguin.